上海市浦东新区统计局·编
SHANGHAI PUDONG NEW AREA STATISTICAL BUREAU

上海浦东新区统计年鉴
SHANGHAI PUDONG NEW AREA STATISTICAL YEARBOOK

2009

(总第16期 No.16)

中国统计出版社
China Statistics Press

感受浦东
Experiencing Pudong

环球金融中心与金茂大厦
World Financial Center and Jinmao Tower

东方艺术中心
Shanghai Oriental Art Center

世纪广场
Century Plaza

陆家嘴夜景
Night Scenes in Lujiazui

璀璨浦江夜
Amazing Night over Huangpu River

东方明珠电视塔
Oriental Pearl TV Tower

越江观光隧道
Cross-Huangpu River Sightseeing Tunnel

感受浦东 Experiencing Pudong

浦东国际机场
Pudong International Airport

磁悬浮列车
Maglev Train

上海国际会议中心
Shanghai International Convention Center

浦东新区办公中心
Pudong New Area Office Center

世纪大道
Pudong Century Avenue

世纪公园
Century Park

上海科技馆
Shanghai Science and Technology Museum

大型国际车展
Auto Show

上海证券交易所
Shanghai Stock Exchange

上海贝尔阿尔卡特股份有限公司
Alcatel Shanghai Bell Co., Ltd.

联想电脑生产线
Production Line of Lenovo Laptops

陆家嘴金融贸易区
Lujiazui Finance & Trade Zone

金桥出口加工区
Jinqiao Export Processing Zone

外高桥保税区码头
Waigaoqiao Free Trade Zone

张江高科技园区
Zhangjiang Hi-tech Park

新区生产总值(亿元)
Gross Output Value of Pudong New Area (100 million yuan)

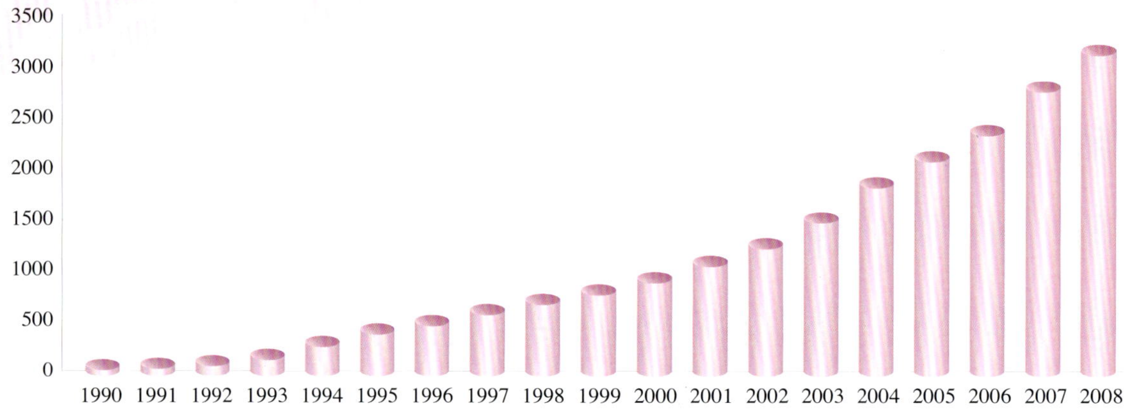

2008年第三产业增加值构成(%)
Composition of Value Added of Tertiary Industry in 2008 (%)

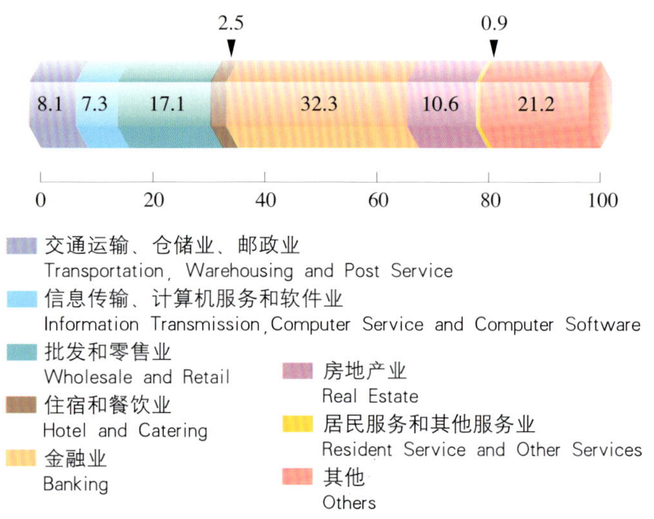

新区生产总值构成(%)
Composition of GDP of PNA (%)

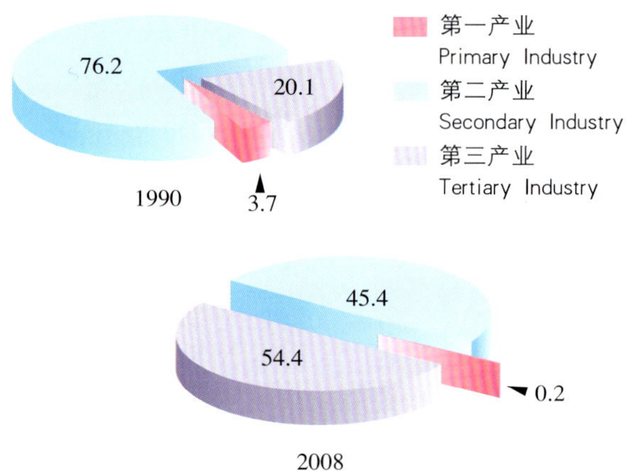

新区生产总值指数(以1990年为100)
Gross Output Value Indexes of PNA (1990 as 100)

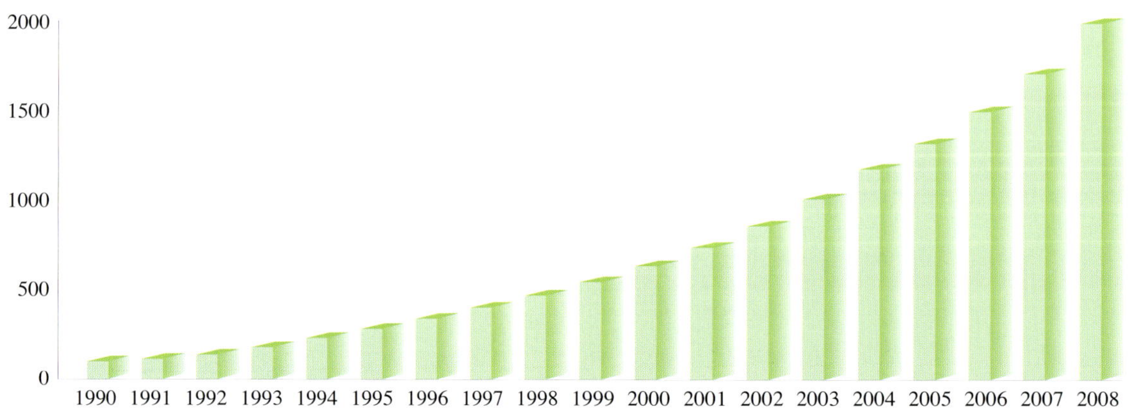

财政收入(亿元)
Financial Revenue (100 million yuan)

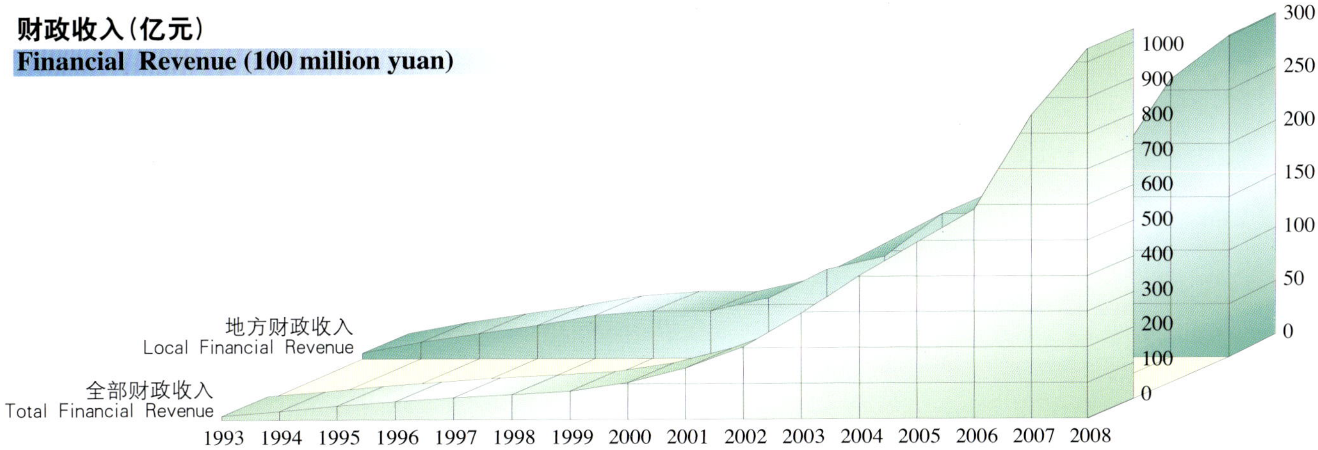

农业总产值(亿元)
Gross Output Value of Agriculture (100 million yuan)

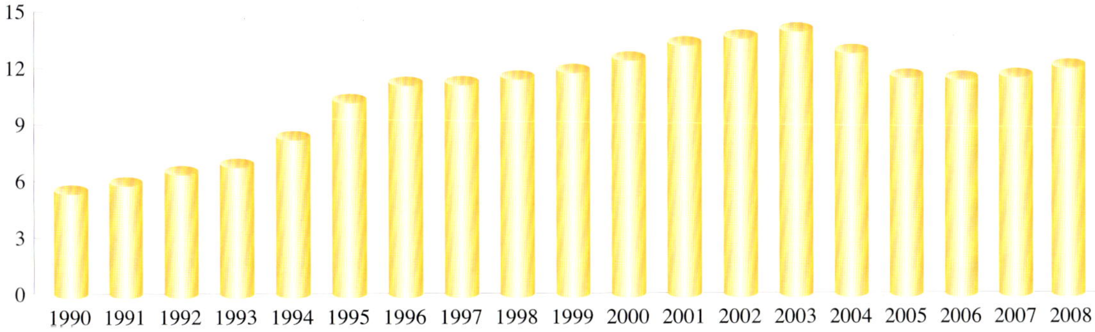

工业总产值指数(以1990年为100)
Indices of Gross Output Value of Industry (1990 as 100)

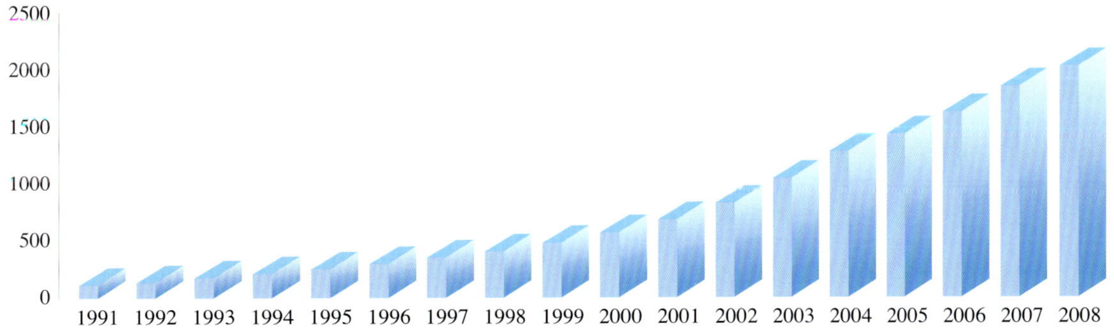

2008年六个工业重点发展行业产值构成(%)
Composition of Gross Output Value of Six Key Industries in 2008 (%)

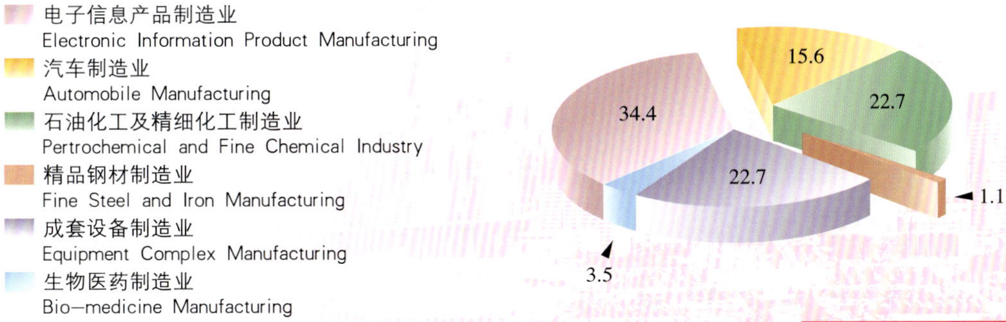

固定资产投资和城市基础设施投资(亿元)
Total Investment in Fixed Assets and Urban Infrastructure Investment (100 million yuan)

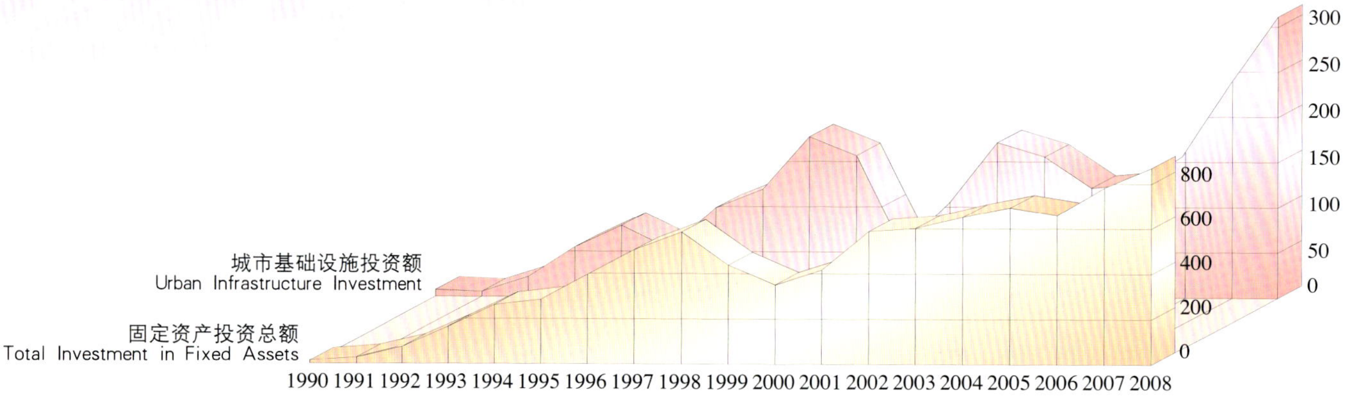

城市基础设施投资额构成(%)
Composition of Urban Infrastructure Investment (%)

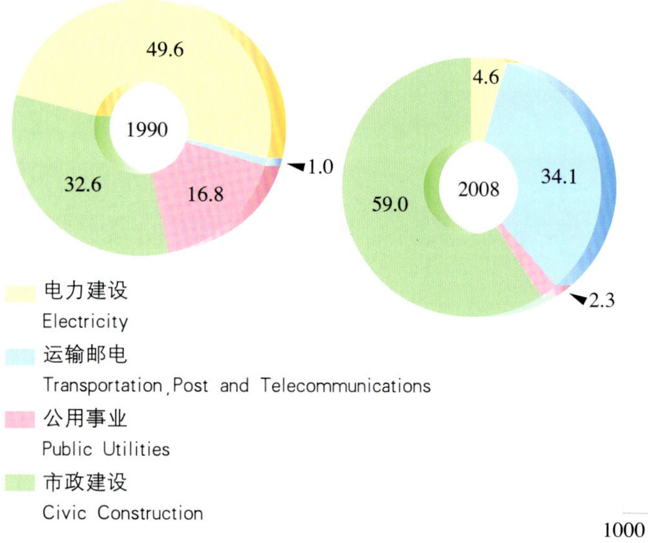

进出口货物总值(亿美元)
Total Value of Imports and Exports (USD 100 million)

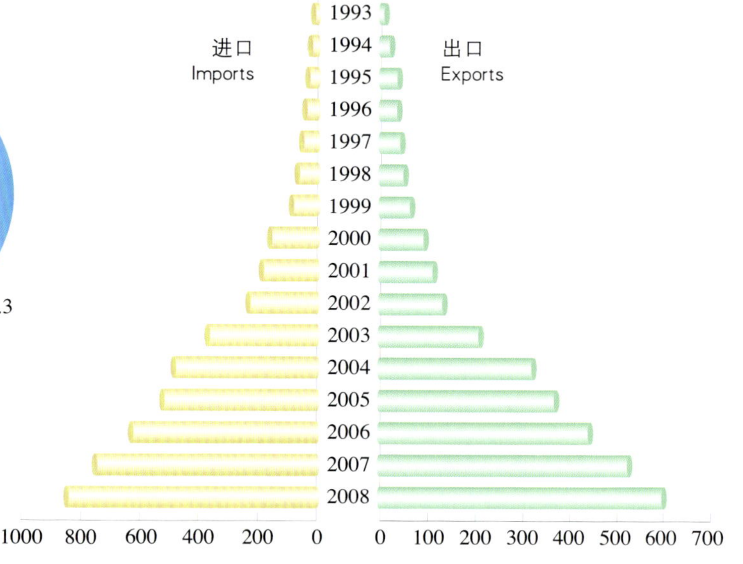

开发小区固定资产投资额(亿元)
Investment in Key Development Zones (100 mllion yuan)

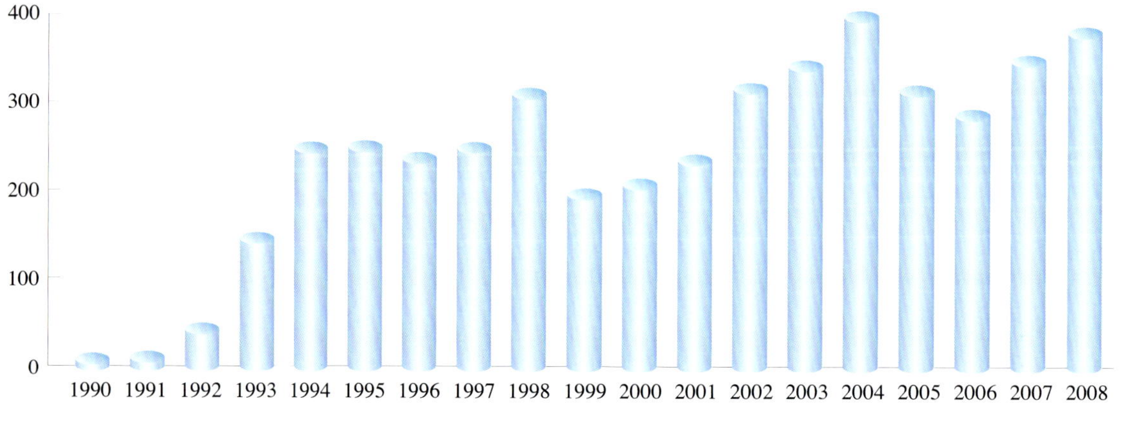

社会消费品零售总额(亿元)
Total Retail Sales of Consumer Goods (100 million yuan)

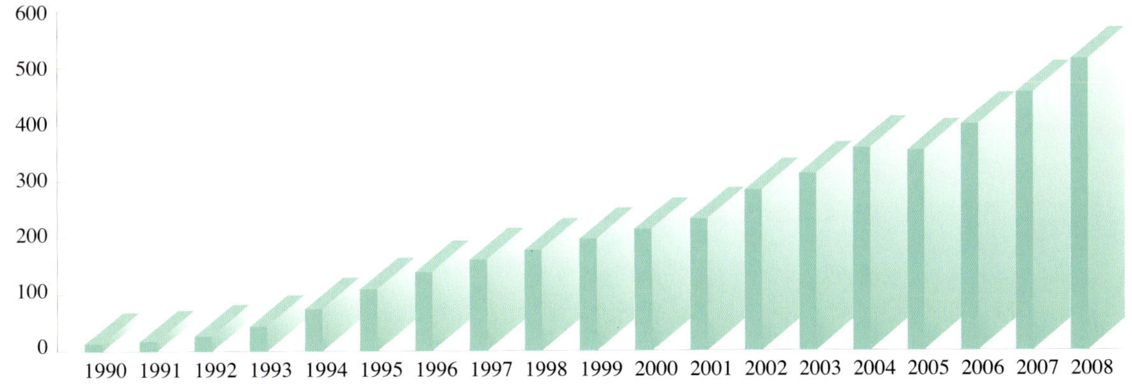

社会消费品零售总额构成(%)
Composition of Retail Sales of Consumer Goods (%)

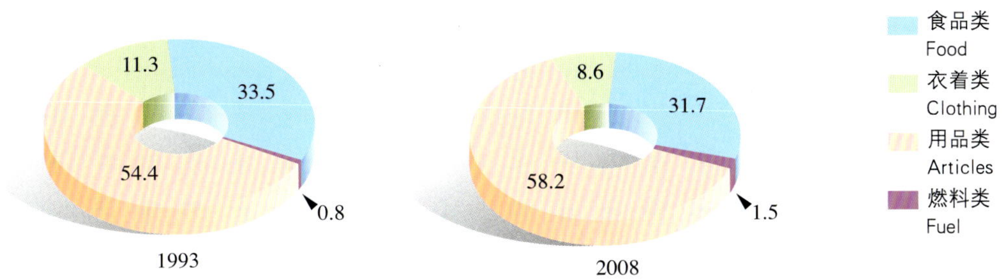

至2008年末外商直接投资的国家(地区)构成(%)
Composition of Countries (Regions) Invested Directly in PNA at the Year-end of 2008 (%)

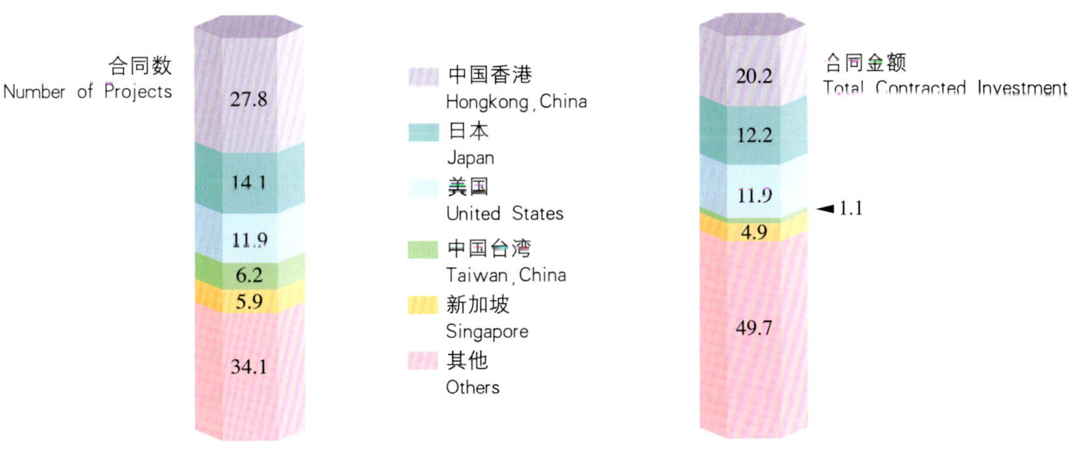

外商合同投资额的投资方式构成(%)
Composition of Contract Value of Foreign Investment by Ways of Investment (%)

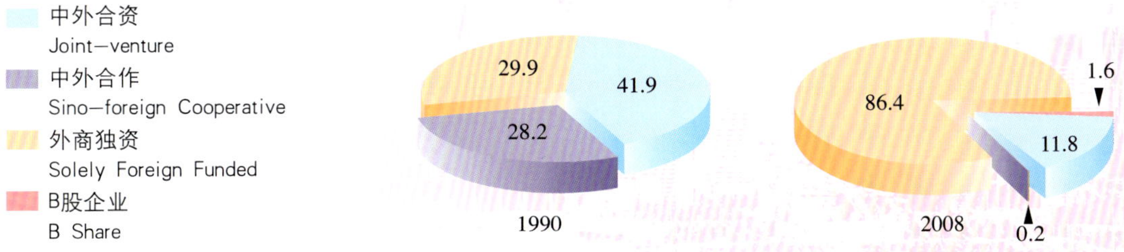

中外资银行本外币存贷款年末余额(亿元)
Balance of RMB and Foreign Currencies Deposits and Loans in Chinese and Foreign Banks (100 million yuan)

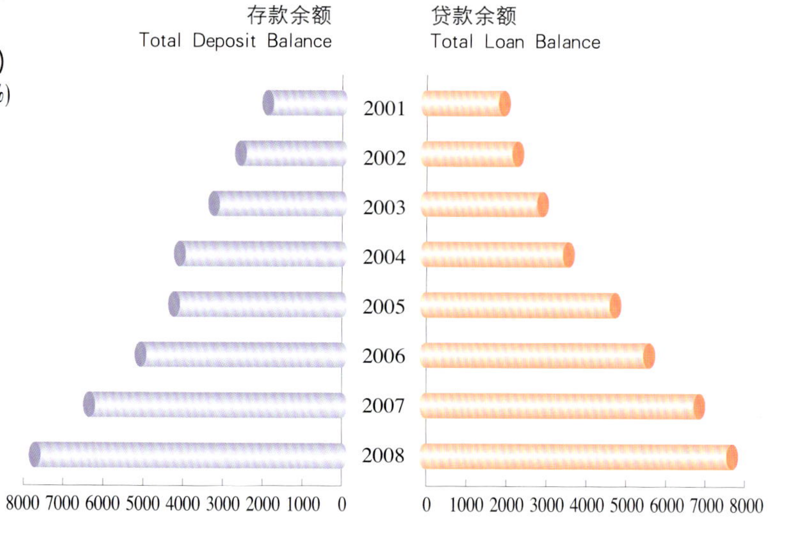

2008年房地产投资本年完成投资按工程用途分(%)
Completed Investment in Real Estate Development by Project Use in 2008 (%)

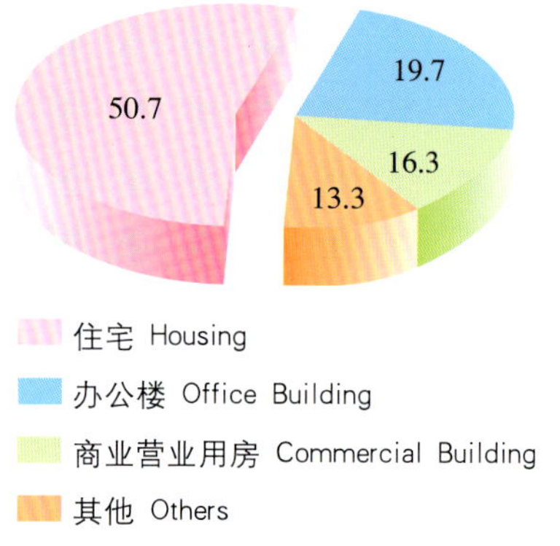

居民储蓄存款年末余额(亿元)
Resident Savings Deposit (100 million yuan)

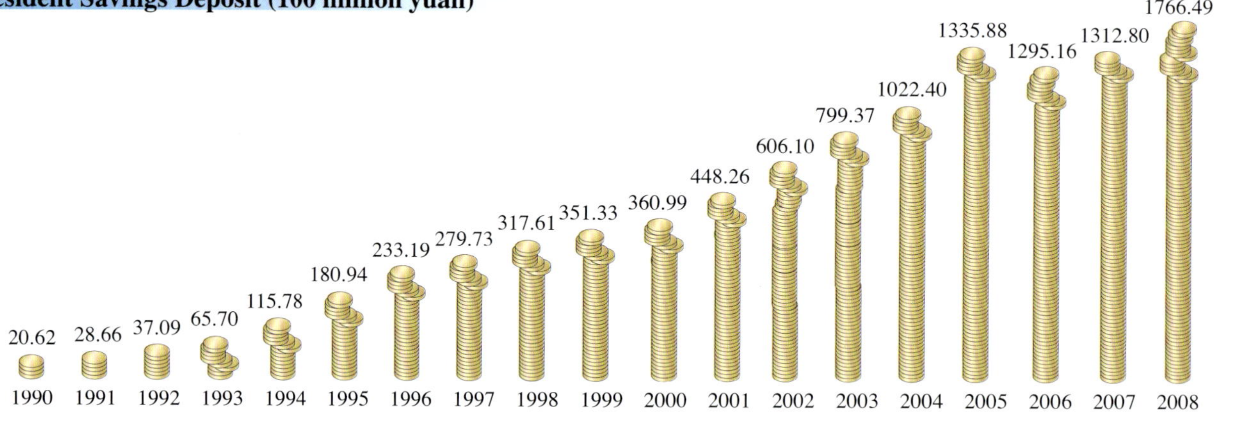

上海证券交易所市价总值(亿元)
Market Value of Shanghai Stock Exchange (100 million yuan)

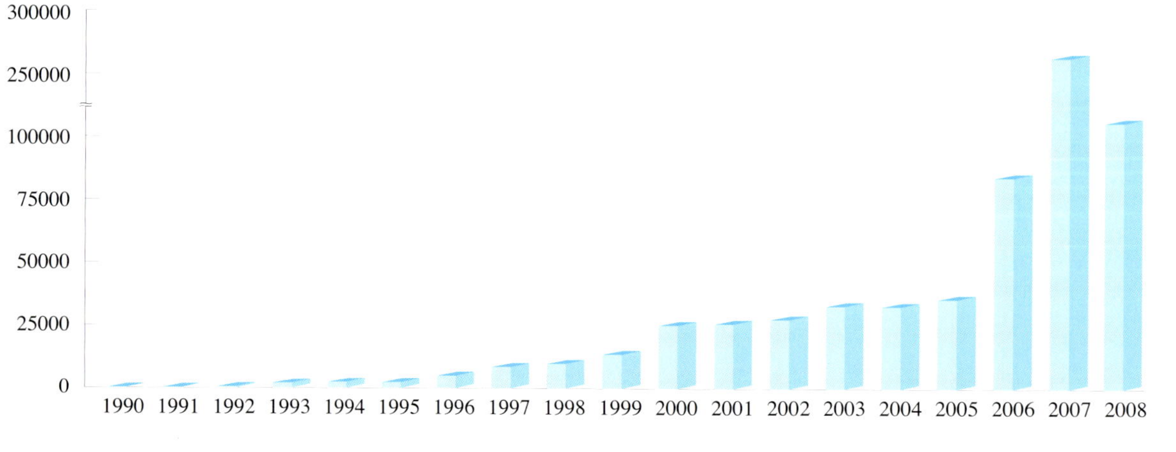

人口自然增长率和净迁移率(‰)
Natural Growth Rate and Net Migration Rate of Population (‰)

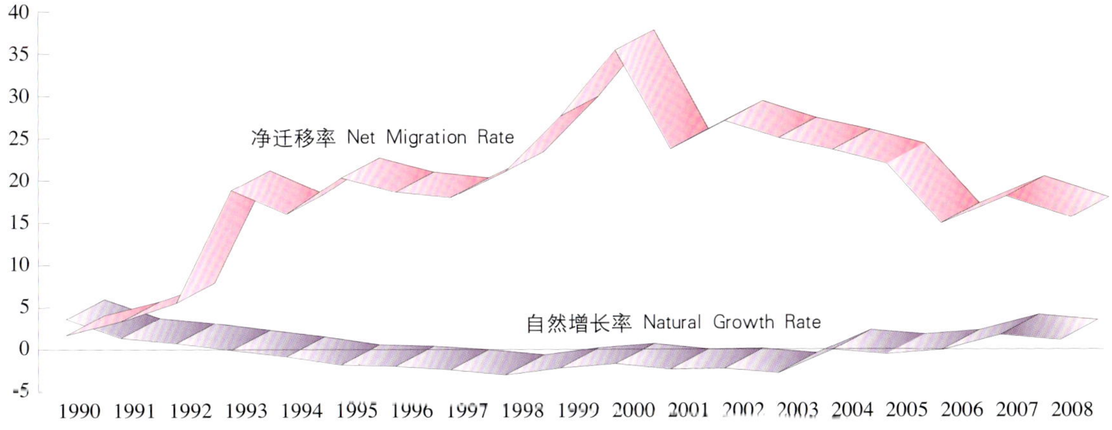

2008年城镇居民家庭消费支出构成(%)
Composition of Consumption Expenditure of Urban Families in 2008 (%)

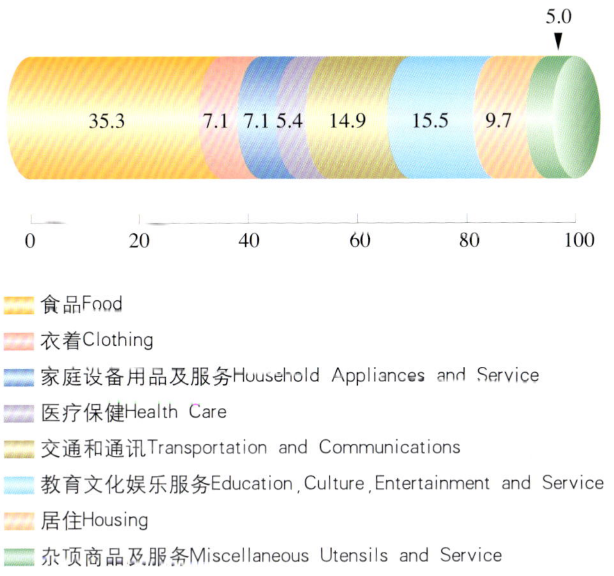

从业人员三次产业构成(%)
Employed Persons by Industry (%)

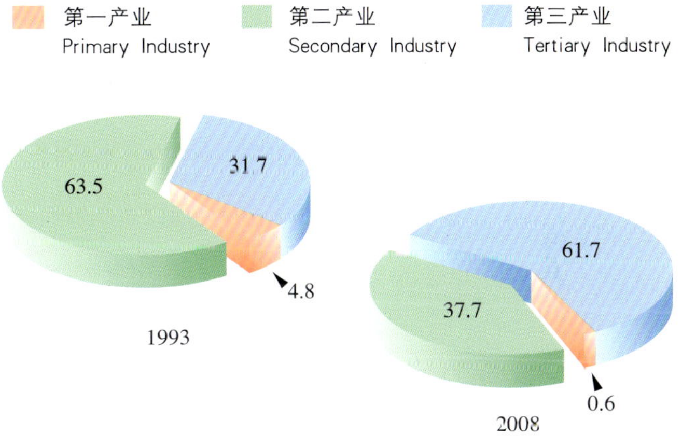

职工平均工资指数(以1990年为100)
Average Wage Index of Staff and Workers (1990 as 100)

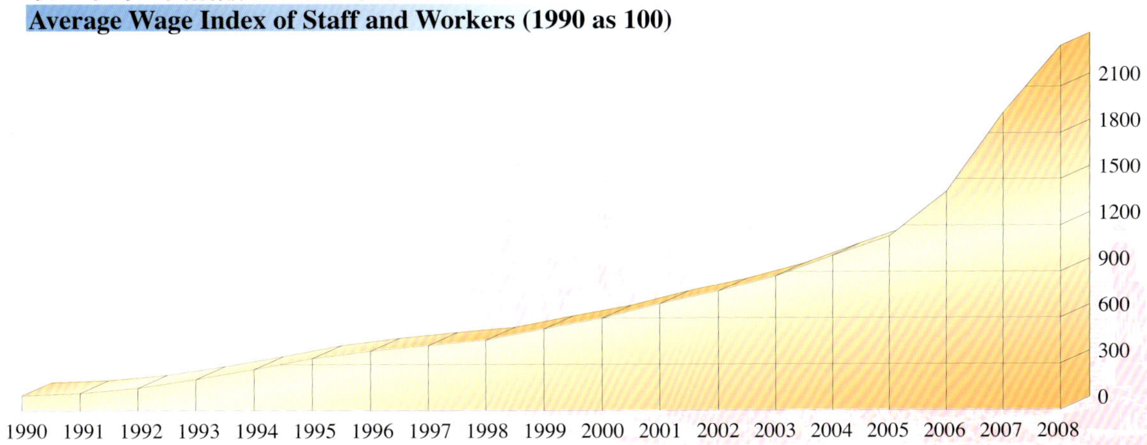

2008年郊区居民家庭收入构成(%)
Income Composition of Suburban Residents in 2008(%)

人均公共绿地面积(平方米)
Public Green Space Per Capita (sq.m)

集装箱吞吐量(10000万吨)
Volume of Cargo Handled at Port (10000TEUs)

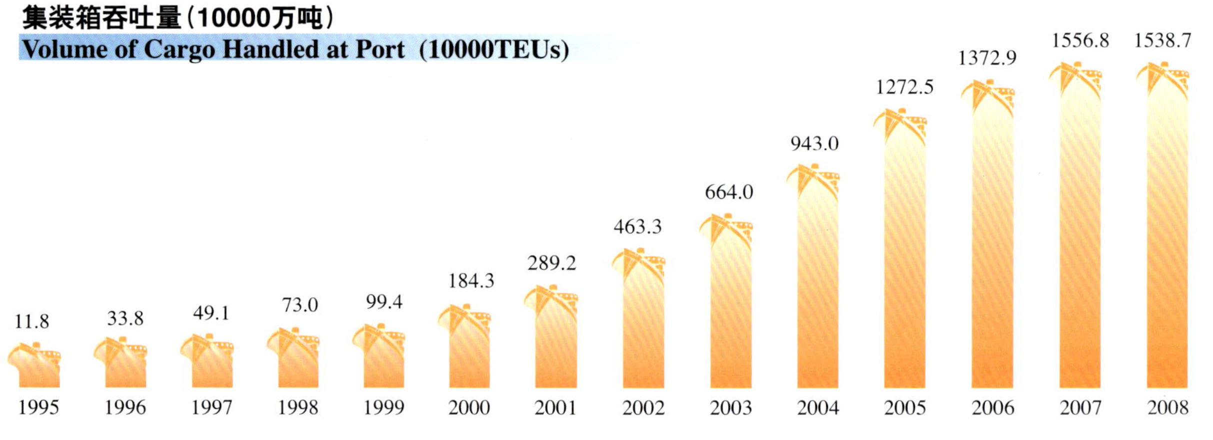

水电消耗情况
Consumption of Tap Water and Electricity

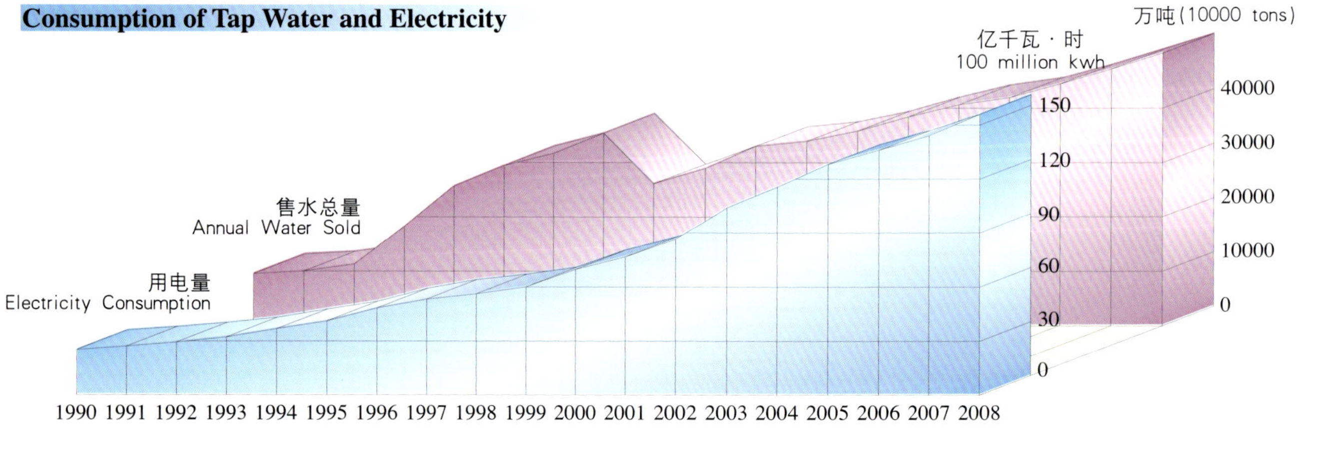

2008年区属企业、事业单位各类专业人员职务构成(%)
Composition of Professional Personnel Working in Enterprises and Institutions in PNA in 2008 (%)

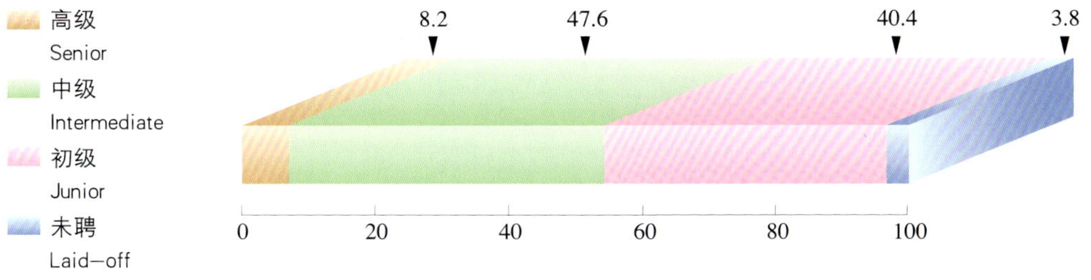

2008年前十位疾病死亡原因构成(%)
Composition of Top 10 Death-Causing Diseases in 2008 (%)

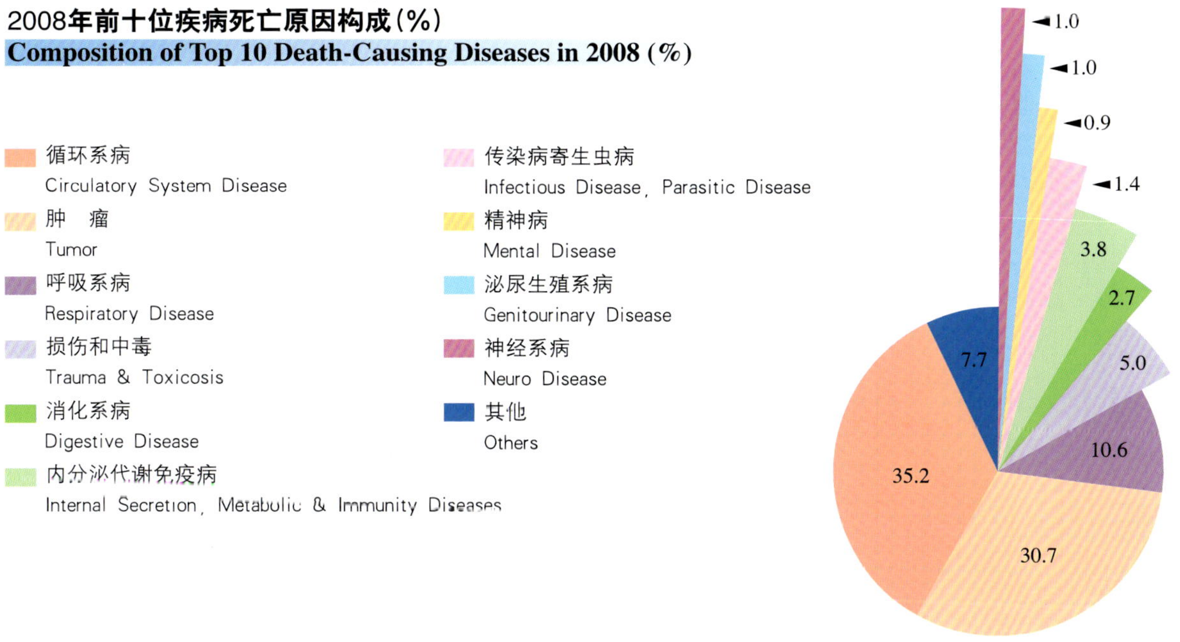

各级学校在校学生数构成(%)
Composition of Students Enrollment by Various Schools (%)

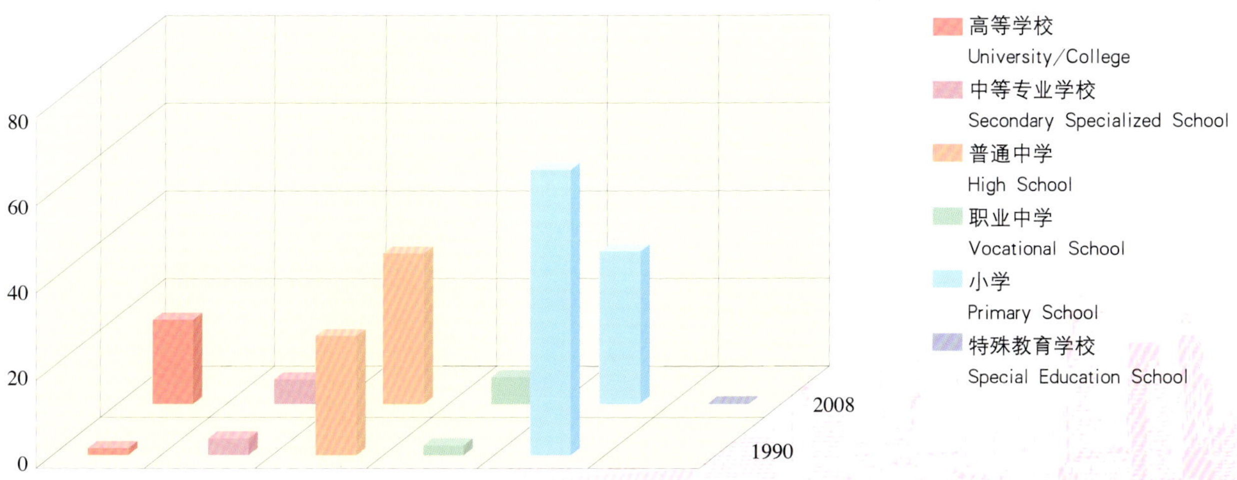

编 者 说 明

一、《上海浦东新区统计年鉴—2009》是一部集浦东新区资料于一体的大型工具书。全书通过大量的统计数据,以中英文对照的形式记录了浦东新区开发开放以来社会经济发展的历程,全面展示了2008年浦东新区在基础开发和功能开发并举的新阶段中,经济、社会、科技和功能区域各方面的发展变化。年鉴为各级领导、理论研究和实际工作者,以及国内外各界关心上海浦东开发开放的人士了解浦东、研究浦东、参与浦东开发建设提供了案头工具。

二、全书内容分为十八个篇目。内含:1. 综合; 2. 人口; 3. 固定资产投资; 4. 招商引资; 5. 农业; 6. 建筑业、工业; 7. 金融业及要素市场; 8. 房地产; 9. 国内外贸易; 10. 旅游和住宿业; 11. 科学技术; 12. 人民生活; 13. 就业与社会保障; 14. 教育、文化、体育、卫生; 15. 法律、社会治安及其他; 16. 城市建设; 17. 功能区域和重点开发小区; 18. 上海市统计资料。

三、资料中使用的度量衡单位均采用国际统一标准计量单位。

四、本年鉴部分数据总计数或相对数由于单位取舍不同产生的计算误差均未作机械调整。

五、浦东新区在行政管理体制上于1995年11月撤乡建镇,实行镇管村体制。因此,本年鉴中有关"镇"和"镇及镇以上工业"等指标含义与全国的"乡"和"乡及乡以上工业"等指标的含义相同。

六、本年鉴中的符号使用说明:"#"表示某一指标的其中主要项;"…"表示数据不足本表最小计量单位数;"空格"表示该项统计指标数据不详或无该项数据。

七、根据国务院和国家统计局有关我国GDP核算和数据发布制度的规定,浦东新区国内生产总值自2004年起更名为"浦东新区生产总值",简称"新区生产总值"。

八、本年鉴中各项增加值和总产值绝对数均按当年价格计算,增长速度按可比价格计算。

九、读者在使用统计资料时,凡与本年鉴有出入的,均以本年鉴为准。

十、《上海浦东新区统计年鉴》公开出版以来,受到国内外广大读者的爱护和支持,对此我们深表谢意,竭诚欢迎读者继续对本年鉴的不足之处给予批评和指正。

此外,本年鉴的编制还得到上海市统计局、外高桥管委会、浦东新区各委、办、局及各功能区域管委会等有关单位的大力支持,在此一并表示谢意。

EDITOR'S NOTE

Ⅰ. Statistical Yearbook of Shanghai Pudong New Area (PNA) — 2009 is a large, comprehensive reference book. With great amount of data and in both Chinese and English versions, it records recent years' social, economic development in PNA. It describes the changes in economy, science and technology, functional zones in PNA's new stage of growth both in infrastructure and functional developments in 2008. It is a desktop tool-book meant for leaders at all levels, theorists, practitioners, and people at home and abroad who are interested in PNA, want to do research work on Pudong and intend to participate in its development and its construction.

II. The book falls into eighteen chapters: 1. General Survey; 2. Population; 3. Investment in Fixed Assets; 4. Business Promotion and Foreign-fund Attraction; 5. Agriculture; 6. Construction and Industry; 7. Finance and Banking, and Factor Markets; 8. Real Estate; 9. Domestic and Foreign Trades; 10. Tourism and Hotels; 11. Science and Technology; 12. People's Livelihood; 13. Employment and Social Security; 14. Education, Culture, Sports and Public Health; 15. Laws, Public Order and Others; 16. Urban Construction; 17. Functional Zones and Key Development Zones; 18. Statistics of Shanghai Municipality.

III. The units of measurement in this book are consistent with international standards.

IV. No adjustment has been made to correct the deviations of some of the figures in the Yearbook caused by different methods used in rounding.

V. In November 1995, PNA rescinded township system and adopted town system. Villages are supervised by towns in the town system. Therefore, in this book, the meanings of "town" and "town and town-above industry" are the same as "township" and "township and township-above industry" in other Chinese statistical books.

VI. Notations used in the Yearbook: "#" indicates the major item; "…" indicates the figure which is too small to be measured by the smallest unit in the table; "blank" indicates the data unavailable.

VII. According to relevant stipulations by the State Council and National Bureau of Statistics, GDP of Pudong New Area is to be renamed as Gross Output Value of Pudong New Area, shortened as PNA Gross Output Value starting from 2004.

VIII. All added values and gross output vales in the Yearbook are listed in terms of current prices while growth rates listed in terms of comparable prices.

IX. If any statistics data from other sources conflict with the data in the present Yearbook, data in the present Yearbook shall apply.

X. The publication of Pudong New Area Statistical Yearbook has received great attention. Our gratitude and appreciation go to all the readers who have offered their comments. We welcome and are open to more comments and suggestions from our readers when presenting this new edition.

In particular, we thank Shanghai Statistics Bureau, Waigaoqiao Administration Commission, all the commissions, officees and bureaus in PNA, and six Functional Zones for their great support in the compilation of the present Yearbook.

目　　录
CONTENTS

综　述
ABSTRACT

第一篇　综　合
CHAPTER 1 GENERAL SURVEY

第二篇　人　口

CHAPTER 2　POPULATION

第三篇　固定资产投资

CHAPTER 3　INVESTMENT IN FIXED ASSETS

第四篇　招商引资
CHAPTER 4 BUSINESS PROMOTION AND FOREIGN-FUND ATTRACTION

第五篇　农　业
CHAPTER 5 AGRICULTURE

第六篇　建筑业、工业
CHAPTER 6 CONSTRUCTION AND INDUSTRY

第七篇　金融业及要素市场
CHAPTER 7 FINANCE AND BANKING, AND FACTOR MARKETS

第八篇　房地产
CHAPTER 8 REAL ESTATE

第九篇　国内外贸易
CHAPTER　9　DOMESTIC AND FOREIGN TRADES

第十篇　旅游和住宿业
CHAPTER　10　Tourism and Hotels

第十一篇 科学技术
CHAPTER 11 SCIENCE AND TECHNOLOGY

第十二篇 人民生活
CHAPTER 12 PEOPLE'S LIVELIHOOD

第十三篇　就业与社会保障
CHAPTER 13　EMPLOYMENT AND SOCIAL SECURITY

第十四篇　教育、文化、体育、卫生
CHAPTER 14　EDUCATION, CULTURE, SPORTS AND PUBLIC HEALTH

第十五篇 法律、社会治安及其他

CHAPTER 15 LAWS, PUBLIC ORDER AND OTHERS

第十六篇 城市建设

CHAPTER 16 URBAN CONSTRUCTION

第十七篇 功能区域和重点开发小区

CHAPTER 17 FUNCTIONAL ZONES AND KEY DEVELOPMENT ZONES

第十八篇　上海市统计资料

CHAPTER 18　STATISTICS OF SHANGHAI MUNICIPALITY

2008 年浦东新区经济和社会发展情况

2008 年是很不平凡的一年。浦东新区在市委、市政府的领导下，积极应对国内外宏观经济形势剧烈变动产生的不利影响，一手抓经济建设、推进产业结构优化升级，一手抓社会民生、促进浦东的和谐稳定，努力克服困难，保持了经济社会总体平稳发展的态势。

一、产业结构优化取得新突破，经济效益不断提高

1. 经济总量稳步增长。新区积极应对复杂多变的形势，采取有效措施，保持经济较快增长，全年实现生产总值 3150.99 亿元，同比增长 11.6%，高于全市 1.9 个百分点。其中，第一产业实现增加值 5.88 亿元，下降 5.8%；第二产业实现增加值 1430.25 亿元，增长 9.1%；第三产业实现增加值 1714.86 亿元，增长 14%。

2. 产业结构优化取得新突破。第三产业占生产总值的比重进一步提高，达到 54.4%，比上年提高 1.4 个百分点。受证券和房产市场的影响，现代服务业发展速度明显回落，但以商务服务为主的其他服务业发展迅速，全年实现增加值 364.07 亿元，增长 22.3%，占第三产业增加值比重从上年的 20% 提高至 21.2%。在汽车制造业负增长的影响下，新区工业增长速度有所放缓，全年实现增加值 1351.44 亿元，增长 9%；实现工业总产值 5649.22 亿元，增长 9.4%，其中高技术产业增长较快，增速达 14.9%。

3. 综合经济效益不断提高。新区财政收入总体保持平稳增长态势，地方财力继续增强。全年实现财政收入突破千亿元，达到 1042.44 亿元，增长 22%；地方财政收入 302.61 亿元，增长 16%。节能减排稳步推进。新区分解落实各项目标和任务，加大产业结构调整力度，实施“腾笼换鸟”，推进宾馆、民用建筑、公交等重点领域节能工作，区属企业万元生产总值能耗同比下降 4.01%。

二、综合功能开发不断深化，“两个聚焦”战略日益凸现

1. 金融服务功能深入拓展。全年金融业增加值增长 15.1%，占新区生产总值 17.6%。中外资银行本外币存贷款余额分别为 7704.87 亿元和 7708.85 亿元，增长 22.2% 和 12%。以陆家嘴金融城为核心，金融机构加快集聚，全年净增各类金融机构 51 家，金融机构数累计达 544 家，其中外资法人银行 14 家；成长型中小企业创业基金正式设立；个人本外币兑换特许业务获准率先试点；陆家嘴金融法庭正式设立；张江小额贷款公司和金浦小额贷款公司成为上海首批小额贷款公司试点。

2. “聚焦张江”战略进一步深化。科技创新优势更趋明显，张江高科技园区已集聚研发机构 297 家，R&D 投入占生产总值比重达到 3.34%；创新成果大量涌现，新区专利申请量和发明专利申请量分别达到 8980 件和 3065 件，居全市各区县前列。在企业不断创新的带动下，新区高技术产业产值达到 1471.18 亿元，增长 14.9%，占工业总产值比重从上年的 25.6% 提高至 26%。

3. 物流口岸、总部等功能继续强化。商业、物流、贸易稳步发展，商品销售总额和社会消费品零售总额分别增长 28.6% 和 15.5%。外高桥港区集装箱吞吐量达到 1539 万标箱；浦东国际机场货邮吞吐量达到 263 万吨，增长 4.8%。总部功能继续强化，集聚跨国公司地区总部 115 家，占全市一半以上。会展旅游功能不断提升，全年实现展出面积 392 万平方米，增长 18%；游客人数达到 1960.6 万人次。

三、对内对外开放水平不断提升

1. 投资促进保持增长格局。新区以扩大对内对外开放为先导，着力抓好招商引资，全年吸引合同外资 49.92 亿美元，增长 0.9%，占全市的 29.2%；实际到位金额 34.35 亿美元，增长 3.9%，其中千万以上大项目 201 个，占实到外资总量的 83.7%，第三产业吸引实到外资 27.04 亿美元，占总量的 78.8%。全年吸引市外在沪投资企业 1360 户，涉及注册资本 108.86 亿元。

2. 对外贸易总体发展平稳。在国际贸易环境日益严峻的情况下，新区外贸进出口总体发展平稳，全年进出口总额首次超过 1400 亿美元，达到 1449.59 亿美元，增长 13.2%。其中出口总额 604.23 亿美元，增长

14.4%；机电产品出口继续领先，全年出口363.56亿美元，增长16.6%，高于出口平均水平2.2个百分点；对新兴市场出口保持较快增长，全年对东盟、非洲、南美洲的出口增幅分别达到28%、30.4%和37%。进口总额845.36亿美元，增长12.4%；自欧美发达国家进口出现回升，其中自欧盟进口增长19.7%，增幅同比提高4.2个百分点；自美国进口增长11.4%，增幅同比提高5个百分点。

四、"和谐浦东"建设大力推进，社会民生不断改善

1. 就业保障体系不断完善，城乡居民收入稳步增长。鼓励创业带动就业，提升培训促进就业，全区新增就业岗位14.27万个，职业技能培训6.3万人。城镇登记失业人数3.91万人，控制在市下达指标内。社会保障覆盖面进一步扩大，4132名农民纳入本市养老保障体系，59.66万来沪务工人员参加综合保险，征地养老人员、农保养老人员和城镇无保老职工三类人群养老待遇进一步提高。新增养老床位1650张，2.78万名老人享受居家养老服务。城乡居民收入保持较快增长，城镇和农村居民可支配收入达到27797元和13778元，分别增长14.5%和12.5%。积极做好支援四川灾区抗震救灾工作。

2. 教育整体水平进一步提升。继续加大教育投入，全年财政教育事业经费达到30.18亿元，增长18.4%。推动城郊教育均衡发展，加强郊区师资队伍建设，加大城郊教师交流力度。积极促进民办教育发展，8所农民工子女学校被批准为民办学校。进一步扩大义务教育对非户籍人口的覆盖面，农民工子女进入公办学校就读人数比上年净增两千余人。深化"管办评"联动机制改革，引进同济大学合办陆行中学、海事大学共建高桥职校，与上师大合作共建上海实验学校。探索构建学校、家庭、社区合作协商制度。新区被教育部确定为首批"全国社区教育示范区"。

3. 医疗服务水平不断提高。完成第二轮公共卫生体系三年行动计划和第二轮健康城区建设三年行动计划，公共卫生服务体系不断完善。医疗卫生投入力度不断加大，财政医疗卫生支出增长48.5%。组织专家对口支援郊区社区卫生服务中心，提高郊区医疗卫生水平。推进医疗卫生管理体制和运行机制改革，川沙医疗联合体正式运行。进一步推动中医药事业发展，成立新区中医药协会，积极创建全国中医药特色社区卫生服务示范区。

4. 文化体育事业进一步推进。公共文化设施建设加快推进，完成张闻天故居保护用房建设，积极推进浦东图书馆(新馆)、内史第恢复重建工程。成功举办庆祝浦东开发开放18周年系列活动、张江科技文化节、三林龙狮文化节等大型文化活动。文化产业发展亮点频显，张江国家数字出版基地和张江"动漫谷"揭牌，外高桥文化服务贸易平台投入运营。积极开展市民文明礼仪培训和实践活动。体育事业呈现良好发展态势，圆满完成奥运会火炬接力传递活动和足球训练场地保障工作，成功举办中国乒乓球大奖赛、中国羽毛球公开赛等赛事；完成7片社区公共运动场的建设和38片农村体育健身家园工程。

5. 实事工程全面完成。以解决与人民群众密切相关的问题为重点，着力解决居民在就业、出行、就医、安居等方面的困难，为民办实事。新区11大类实事项目全面完成。

6. 切实加强新农村建设。落实各项支农政策，提高农业设施化、标准化水平，稳步推进现代农业发展。加大农村基础设施建设和经费投入。积极推进川沙新镇、合庆镇和曹路镇等首批15个行政村的村庄改造。全面实施新农村污水纳管工程，开工建设合庆、曹路、川沙等镇的污水纳管工程。创建40个整洁村。

五、围绕"世博推动"战略，城市建设与管理不断加强

1. 基础设施建设顺利推进。围绕"世博推动"战略，大力推进城市基础设施建设。全社会固定资产投资完成872.68亿元，其中基础设施投资311.3亿元。由新区负责实施的"两环两道"等25项世博配套道路项目进展顺利，其中1项竣工、23项在建、1项正在作前期准备。协助推进的市重大项目正在加快前期动迁，进展顺利。

2. 生态环境质量不断优化。新区第三轮环保三年行动计划确定的市区共108项任务基本完成。全年SO_2和COD排放量下降2%左右，环境空气质量进一步提高，可吸入颗粒物和二氧化氮浓度分别下降3.8%和6.5%，环境空气质量优良率达到93.1%。完成杨思港、三林塘港等541条(段)河道整治，整治黑臭河道187条。城市污水纳管率达到76%。生态绿化建设进一步推进，公共绿地总量达到4452公顷，绿化覆盖率达到

37.3%。

六、综合配套改革试点进入新阶段，制度环境进一步优化

按照全市《2008～2010年浦东综合配套改革试点三年行动计划框架》，新区形成了《浦东新区综合配套改革2008年重点工作实施要点》，围绕转变政府职能、促进金融发展、推动自主创新"三个重点"，明确了30项改革任务和50个改革子项，并明确改革内容、时间节点、责任单位、考核机制等，形成行政审改领域重点推进的四项专项改革方案和人才、金融、自主创新、服务业发展等四项政策的"4+4"格局。明确的50项具体改革任务，除OTC等少数事项因宏观经济形势变化需要延后或调整外，其他改革事项均已全部完成，同时还新增了个人本外币兑换试点、"海关十条"和新华"08"等3项改革事项。综合配套改革的社会知晓度、认同度不断增加。

ECONOMIC AND SOCIAL DEVELOPMENT OF SHANGHAI PUDONG NEW AREA IN 2008

The year of 2008 is an uncommon year. Under the wise leadership of Shanghai Municipal Committee and Government, the People's Government of Pudong New Area (PNA) has actively responded to the adverse effects due to the drastic changes of the macro economic situations both home and abroad. We have succeeded in overcoming many difficulties and kept the economic society with the favorable trend of steady development, by means of both advancing the optimization and upgrading of the industrial structure with emphasis on the economic construction, and promoting harmony and stability in PNA with emphasis on the people's livelihood.

I. New breakthroughs in optimizing industrial structure, with economic benefits constantly increased

1. Total economic power steadily increased. The government of PNA has actively responded to the complicated and ever-changing situations and taken effective measures to keep a rapid economic growth. The total output value achieved RMB 315.099 billion yuan in the whole year, an increase of 11.6% over the previous year, which is 1.9 % higher than that of the municipality. The primary industry realized an added value of RMB 588 million yuan, a decrease of 5.8% over the previous year, the secondary industry realized an added value of RMB 143.025 billion yuan, an increase of 9.1%, and the tertiary industry realized an added value of RMB 171.486 billion yuan, increased by 14%.

2. The optimization of industrial structure achieved new breakthroughs. The proportion of the output value of the tertiary industry in the total output value has further increased to 54.4%, an increase of 1.4% over the previous year. Under the influence of the recession of securities and the real estate market, the rate of modern service development has obviously fallen back. However, other services, such as the commercial service, have rapidly developed, realizing an added value of RMB 36.407 billion yuan, an increase of 22.3%, which made the ratio of it in the added value of the tertiary industry increase to 21.2% from the number of 20% of the previous year. Under the influence of the negative growth in the automobile industry, the industry increase in PNA has slightly slowed down its pace, realizing an added value of RMB 135.144 billion yuan, an increase of 9%, and realizing a gross industrial output value of RMB 564.922 billion yuan, increased by 9.4%, in which the high-tech industry achieved a rapid growth with the rate up to 14.9%.

3. Comprehensive economic results constantly increased. As a whole, the financial revenue in PNA has kept its trends of stead growth, and the local fiscal capacity has kept on increasing. The financial revenue achieved RMB 104.244 billion yuan, an increase of 22%, and the local fiscal revenue, RMB 30.261 billion yuan in the whole year, increased by 16%. The policy of energy saving and emission reduction has been steadily advancing. We have implemented all kinds of targets and tasks, strengthened the readjustment of the industrial structure, carried out the policy of "Displacing Traditional Manufacturing Industry with Advanced Productivity", boosted the energy saving work in major fields such as hotels, civil construction and public transportation, in which it is estimated that the energy consumption per 10,000 yuan of the total output value will decrease by about 4.01% in enterprises belonging to the government of PNA.

II. Development of comprehensive functions constantly deepened, with strategy of "Two Highlights" obviously emerged

1. The function of financial service deeply expanded. The added value of financial sector has increased by

15. 1% in the whole year, occupying 17. 6% of the total output value in PNA. The balances of deposits and loans for both RMB and foreign currencies in Chinese banks and foreign banks have reached RMB 770. 487 billion yuan and RMB 770. 885 billion yuan, an increase of 22. 2% and of 12%, respectively. Taking Lujiazui, the Financial City, as its core, financial institutions hastened to gather together. Fifty-one financial institutions of different kinds have been registered in the whole year, which the number of financial institutions has added up to 544, among which 14 are foreign corporate banks. We have formally established the start-up fund for the growing middle and small businesses and taken the lead to try the chartered service of exchanging foreign currencies with RMB for individuals. Lujiazui Financial Court has been formally established. Zhangjiang Micro Credit Loan Company and Jinpu Micro Credit Load Company became the first experiments of micro credit loan companies in Shanghai.

2. Strategy of "Focus on Zhangjiang" further deepened. As the advantage for scientific innovations has been more obvious, Zhangjiang High-tech Park has gathered 297 R&D institutions, and it is estimated that the amount of investment in research and development will account for 3. 34% of the total output value. A great deal of innovative achievements has emerged. The number of patent applications and that of applications for patents of invention in PNA reached 8980 and 3065, respectively, which are listed the first among those of districts and counties in the whole municipality. Driven by the continuous innovations made by the enterprises, we achieved the production value of high-tech industries amounting to RMB 147. 118 billion yuan, an increase of 14. 9% over that of the previous year. And the ratio of that value in the gross industrial output value is 26%, while that number is 25. 6% in the previous year.

3. Functions such as logistics and headquarters continued to be consolidated. As the commerce, logistics and trade steadily develop, the gross sales of commodities and the total volume of retail sales for social consumer goods increased by 28. 6% and 15. 5%, respectively. The throughputs of containers in Waigaoqiao Port Area reached 15. 39 million TEUs, and the throughput of cargoes and mails in Pudong International Airport reached 2. 63 million tons, an increase of 4. 8%. As the function of headquarters continued to be strengthened, we have gathered 115 regional headquarters of multinational corporations, more than half of those in the whole city. The function of exhibition and tourism constantly increased. We have realized an exhibition area of 3. 92 million square meters, an increase of 18%, with the number of tourists amounting to 19. 606 million person-times.

III. Opening up to both home and abroad constantly increased

1. Investment and promotion kept growing. Guided by the expansion of the policy of opening to both home and abroad, the government of PNA has managed to carry out business promotion and foreign fund attraction. We attracted contracted foreign capital amounting to USD 4. 992 billion in the whole year, an increase of 0. 9%, which is 29. 2% of that in the whole municipality. And the actual paid amount of capital reached USD 3. 435 billion, increased by 3. 9%, in which there are 201 projects with an investment of over USD 10 million, 83. 7% of that of the total actual paid amount of foreign capital. The tertiary industry has attracted actual paid capital worthy of USD 2. 704 billion, 78. 8% of that of the total amount. We attracted a total of 1360 enterprises registered out of Shanghai in the whole year, and the registered capital of all these enterprises reached RMB 10. 886 billion yuan.

2. Foreign trade generally made stead progress. Under the circumstances of increasingly austere environment for international trades, the import and export business in PNA has made stead progress. The total volume of foreign trade exceeded USD 140 billion for the first time in 2008, which amounted to USD 144. 959 billion, increased by 13. 2%. The total export value reached USD 60. 423 billion, an increase of 14. 4% over the previous year. The export of machinery and electrical equipment continued to take the lead among other exports, with the value of exports amounting to USD 36. 356 billion, an increase of 16. 6%, which is 2. 2% higher than that of the averaged export level. The export to emerging markets has kept a rapid growth. Our exports to the ASEAN, Africa and South America have increased by 28%, 30. 4% and 37%, respectively. The total import value in PNA reached USD 84. 536 billion in 2008, increased by 12. 4%. The amount of imported goods from developed countries in Europe and the United States began to rise again, in which the amount of imports from EU increased by 19. 7% in 2008, with a rise

of 4.2% over the previous year, and that the amount of imports from the United States increased by 11.4%, with a rise of 5% over the previous year.

IV. Construction of "Harmonious Pudong" vigorously promoted, with people's livelihood constantly improving

1. The system of employment security continued to improve and the incomes of both urban and suburban residents steadily increased. Young people are encouraged to set up their own business, which drives the employment. Trainings are promoted, which boosts the employment. We created new jobs for 142,700 employees and trained 63,000 persons with professional skills in the whole year. We have also made registration for 39,100 unemployed persons, which is under the target made by the municipality. The coverage for social security further enlarged. We have provided 4132 farmers with the municipal endowment insurance and brought 596,600 migrant workers into the comprehensive insurance coverage. We have further increased pensions for three kinds of persons which are persons of land-for-security, with agricultural medical insurance for pensions, and old urban workers without social guarantees. We have increased 1650 beds for old-aged persons and provided 27,800 old persons with the service of living in their own families. The incomes of both urban and suburban residents have kept its pace of fast growth. The disposable incomes of urban and suburban residents have reached RMB 27,797 yuan and RMB 13,778 yuan, increased by 14.5% and 12.5%, respectively. We have also made great efforts to support the relief work for Sichuan earthquake disaster.

2. The whole educational level further advanced. We have continued to put more investment in education, and the educational appropriations amounted to RMB 3.018 billion yuan in the whole year, an increase of 18.4%. We have pushed on the balanced development of education between urban and suburban areas, strengthened the construction of suburban teachers' team, and paid more attention on the exchanging between urban teachers and their suburban counterparts. We have actively promoted the development of non-government education and eight schools for the children of migrant workers have been approved as non-government schools. We have further enlarged the coverage of compulsory education for the non-residents and the number of children of migrant workers who were enrolled in public schools increased by more than 2000 over the previous year. We have deepened the reforms of the interaction mechanism of "Management, Conduct and Evaluation", which we introduced Tongji University to jointly establish Luhang Middle School, introduced Shanghai Maritime University to jointly establish Gaoqiao Vocational School, and cooperated with Shanghai Normal University to jointly establish Shanghai Experimental School. We have explored to design the cooperation and negotiation systems among schools, families and communities. PNA has been authorized as one of the first batch of "National Community Education Demonstration Districts" by the Ministry of Education.

3. Medical service level constantly increased. We have fulfilled the second round of "Three-Year Action Program" in the public health system and the second round of "Three-Year Action Program" of the healthy urban area construction, which have made the public health and service system more perfect. We have also put more investment on the medical service, and the fiscal expenditure for medical service increased by 48.5% over the previous year. And we have organized medical experts to support community health service centers in suburban areas in order to improve the medical service level there. We have advanced the reform for the managerial system and operational mechanism of medical services. Chuansha Medical Association has formally put into operation. We have further promoted the development of the Chinese Traditional Medicine cause, established the Chinese Traditional Medical Association in PNA, and actively created national community health service demonstration district specialized with Chinese Traditional Medicine.

4. Cultural and sports causes further boosted. We have fastened the promotion of the construction of public cultural facilities, finished the construction of protective buildings for the former residence of Mr. Zhang Wentian, a famous Marxist in Chinese Communist Party, and actively advanced the construction of Pudong Library (New Hall) and the reconstruction of Shineidi, a famous residence built in Qing Dynasty. We have also successfully hosted some

large-scaled cultural activities, such as a series of activities celebrating the 18th anniversary of the development and opening-up of PNA, Zhangjiang Science and Technology Festival, and Sanlin Dragon and Lion Cultural Festival. The development highlight of cultural industry has been very obvious. National and municipal leaders have declared the establishment of Zhangjiang National Digital Publishing Base and Zhangjiang Cartoon Valley, and the trading platform of Waigaoqiao cultural service has put into operation. We have actively conducted the training of citizens for etiquettes and practical activities. The sports cause has been developed with a favorable trend, in which we have successfully finished the activity of torch relay for the 2008 Olympic Games and the guarantee work for the training field of soccer, and successfully held some important match events such as China Table Tennis Tournament and China Badminton Open. We have also completed the construction of seven community public playgrounds and thirty-eight rural sports and fitness courts.

5. Practical projects completely finished. Focusing on the resolution of problems closely related to the people, we have emphasized to resolve the practical difficulties of the residents on employment, transportation, medical treatment and residence. We have completely achieved the practical projects of 11 categories in PNA.

6. Construction of new villages practically strengthened. We have implemented all kinds of agriculture-supporting policies, improved the agricultural facilities and standards, steadily promoted the development of modern agriculture. We have also put more investment on the construction of rural infrastructure, actively boosted to rebuild fifteen administrative villages that are among the first related villages, such as Chuansha New Town, Heqing Town and Caolu Town. We have completely carried out the project of sewage piping for new villages, and we have commenced the projects of sewage piping for towns such as Heqing, Caolu and Chuansha. A total of 40 clean villages have been founded.

V. Strategy of "Expo Promotion" encircled, with urban construction and management constantly strengthened

1. Infrastructure construction smoothly proceeded. We have encircled the strategy of "Expo Promotion" and strongly promoted the construction of urban infrastructure. The total social investment on fixed assets has achieved RMB 87.268 billion yuan, in which the investment on infrastructure has amounted to RMB 31.13 billion yuan. Twenty-five supporting road projects for the 2010 World Exposition, such as "Two Rings and Two Roads" carried out by PNA, have smoothly proceeded, in which one project has completed, twenty-three have been under construction, and one is conducting its preliminary work. Some municipal important projects have been assisted to hasten the preliminary work of resettlement by PNA, which have smoothly proceeded.

2. Quality of ecologic environment constantly optimized. One hundred and eight tasks determined by the third round of three-year environmental protection action plan in PNA have been elementally completed. The discharge amount of sulfur dioxide and that of chemical oxygen demand decreased by about 2%, which the quality of environmental air has been further improved. The number of inhalable particulate matter and the concentration of nitrogen dioxide decreased by 3.8% and 6.5%, respectively, the high quality rate of environmental air has reached 93.1%. We have regularized 541 (sections of) rivers such as Yangsi Port and Sanlintang Port and regularized 187 rivers with blackening and stinking water. The rate of urban sewage piping has reached 76%. We have further promoted the construction of biological green space, in which the total area of public green land has reached 4,452 hectares and the coverage of green space has reached 37.3%.

VI. Comprehensive supporting reform package in PNA entering new phase, with the system environment further optimized

According to the Three-Year Action Plan Frame of the Experiments on Pudong Comprehensive Supporting Reform Package from 2008 to 2010 in the whole municipality, we have formed the Implement Outline of Key Jobs in 2008 for Comprehensive Supporting Reform Package of PNA. Encircled with "Three Emphases", which are to change the functions of the government, to promote the development of financial industry, and to advance the independent innovations, we have determined 30 items of reforming tasks and 50 sub-items of reforming tasks, and made clear the contents of reforms, time limits, responsible units and assess mechanism, and formed the pattern of "Four plus Four", which means four special reforming plans that are significantly boosted in the field of administrative examination and approval, and four policies on talented persons, finance, independent innovations and the development of service industry. We have finished all of the 50 specific reforming tasks except that some items need to be delayed or readjusted because of the change of macro economic situations such as OTC. On the other hand, we have increased three reforming items that are experiments on exchange of RMB and foreign currencies for individuals, "Ten Clauses of Customs" and "08" of Xinhua. The social understanding and recognition for the comprehensive supporting reforms have been constantly improved by the mass.

第一篇 Chapter 1

综　合
GENERAL SURVEY

SHANGHAI PUDONG NEW AREA STATISTICAL YEARBOOK

2009 / 上海浦东新区统计年鉴

表 1-1 气象概况
Climate
(2008)

月 份 Month		气 温(℃) Temperature(℃) 平均气温 Average Temperature	平均最高气温 Average Highest Temperature	平均最低气温 Average Lowest Temperature	35℃以上高温日数(天) >35℃(day)	0℃以下低温日数(天) <0℃(day)
年平均	**Annual Average**	**17.0**	**21.1**	**13.7**	**16**	**28**
1 月	January	4.2	7.2	2.0		6
2 月	February	3.8	8.5	0.0		16
3 月	March	11.0	15.8	6.7		
4 月	April	15.5	19.6	12.0		
5 月	May	21.0	26.1	16.9		
6 月	June	23.8	27.1	21.3	1	
7 月	July	29.8	34.0	26.6	9	
8 月	August	28.0	32.1	25.0	6	
9 月	September	25.7	29.4	23.1		
10 月	October	20.5	24.2	17.3		
11 月	November	12.9	16.9	9.5		
12 月	December	7.4	12.6	3.4		6

表 1-1 续表 Continued

月 份 Month		日 照(小时) Sunshine(hour)	降 水 Rainfall 雨 量(毫米) Rainfall(mm)	雨 日(天) Rainy Day(day)	蒸发量(毫米) Evaporation(mm)	相对湿度(%) Relative Humidity(%)
全年总计	**Annual Total**	**1 824.6**	**1 517.0**	**154**	**1 362.6**	**75**
1 月	January	57.7	94.9	16	34.8	78
2 月	February	161.2	31.1	4	58.8	69
3 月	March	179.9	29.0	9	102.7	69
4 月	April	128.3	61.3	15	104.4	73
5 月	May	222.0	108.0	11	161.4	71
6 月	June	83.2	400.5	22	100.1	85
7 月	July	250.7	119.4	11	241.3	75
8 月	August	193.1	419.5	18	173.2	81
9 月	September	168.1	69.9	15	138.3	79
10 月	October	117.8	60.0	14	116.0	78
11 月	November	104.7	93.0	12	68.1	76
12 月	December	157.9	30.4	7	63.5	70

注：2008 年极端最高气温 38.1℃，出现在 7 月 24 日；极端最低气温 -4.4℃，出现在 2 月 14 日；初霜日 11 月 20 日，终霜日 3 月 20 日，无霜期 244 天。
Note: The utmost highest temperature amounted to 38.1℃ on July 24 in 2008. The utmost lowest temperature came to-4.4℃ on February 14 in 2008. The frost season started on November 20, 2008 and ended on March 20. There were 244 frost-free days in total.

表1-2　行政区划
Administrative Regions
(2008)

单位:个　　　　(unit)

地　区 Subdistrict/Town		居民委员会 Neighborhood Committee	村民委员会 Village Committee	地　区 Subdistrict/Town		居民委员会 Neighborhood Committee	村民委员会 Village Committee
街镇总计(23个)	**Total**	**618**	**226**				
街　道(12个)	**Subdistrict**	**391**	**3**	**镇(11个)**	**Town**	**227**	**223**
潍坊新村街道	Weifangxincun Subdistrict	27		川沙新镇	Chuansha New Town	48	59
陆家嘴街道	Lujiazui Subdistrict	31		高桥镇	Gaoqiao Town	24	15
周家渡街道	Zhoujiadu Subdistrict	33		北蔡镇	Beicai Town	42	12
塘桥街道	Tangqiao Subdistrict	23		合庆镇	Heqing Town	5	29
上钢新村街道	Shanggangxincun Subdistrict	23		唐　镇	Tangzhen Town	8	17
南码头路街道	Nanmatou Road Subdistrict	27		曹路镇	Caolu Town	9	34
沪东新村街道	Hudongxincun Subdistrict	32		金桥镇	Jinqiao Town	7	6
金杨新村街道	Jinyangxincun Subdistrict	47		高行镇	Gaohang Town	19	7
洋泾街道	Yangjing Subdistrict	34		高东镇	Gaodong Town	11	15
浦兴路街道	Puxing Road Subdistrict	39		张江镇	Zhangjiang Town	22	11
东明路街道	Dongming Road Subdistrict	34		三林镇	Sanlin Town	32	18
花木街道	Huamu Subdistrict	41	3				

注：本表由浦东新区劳动保障局提供。
Note: This table is provided by Pudong Labor & Social Security Bureau.

表1-3 主要年份经济发展主要指标
Major Indicators of Economic Development in Main Years

指 标	Indicators	1993	2000	2005	2007	2008
新区生产总值(亿元)	**Gross Domestic Product of PNA(100 million yuan)**	**164.00**	**923.51**	**2 108.79**	**2 793.39**	**3 150.99**
第一产业	Primary Industry	2.12	5.72	6.09	6.06	5.88
第二产业	Secondary Industry	114.45	488.60	1 070.96	1 306.49	1 430.25
第三产业	Tertiary Industry	47.43	429.19	1 031.74	1 480.84	1 714.86
财 政	**Finance**					
财政收入(亿元)	Financial Revenue(100 million yuan)	11.15	103.21	494.94	854.49	1 042.44
#地方财政收入	Local Financial Revenue	5.53	56.40	155.31	260.80	302.61
地方财政支出(亿元)	Local Financial Expenditure(100 million yuan)	9.53	69.60	198.79	287.24	370.30
固定资产投资总额(亿元)	**Total Investment in Fixed Assets(100 million yuan)**	**164.56**	**351.06**	**693.61**	**784.10**	**872.68**
#房地产开发投资	Investment in Real Estate Development		110.74	287.92	247.46	279.97
#城市基础设施投资额	Investment in Urban Infrastructure	54.73	54.51	125.95	234.54	311.30
招商引资	**Business Promotion and Foreign-Fund Attraction**					
外商直接投资合同项目(项)	Number of Contracts(unit)	924	693	1 734	1 254	803
外商直接投资合同金额(亿美元)	Direct Foreign Investment (USD 100 million)	17.57	28.84	56.54	49.49	49.92
期末内资企业注册数(个)	Number of Registered Domestically-Funded Enterprises at End of Term(unit)				12 703	12 423
科技创新	**Technological Innovations**					
研发机构数(个)	Number of R&D Institutions(unit)			161	220	297
申请专利数(项)	Patent Claiming(item)		718	3 141	8 435	8 980
授权专利数(项)	Number of Authorized Patents(Piece)			1 204	4 086	3 677
R&D占全社会GDP比重(%)	Ratio of R&D in Social GDP(%)				2.83	3.34

注：1. 2005年起“港口货物吞吐量”和“集装箱吞吐量”为外高桥港区数据。
2. 表中研发机构数由浦东新区科委提供。
3. “中外资保险机构原保费收入”与历年年鉴中的“保费收入”统计口径相同，下同。

Note: 1. The items of “Volume of Cargo Handled at Port” and “Container Handling Capacity” are the data at Waigaoqiao Port since 2005.
2. The number of research and development institutions in this table is provided by Science and Technology Commission of Pudong New Area.
3. The item of “Former premium income of insurances by Chinese and foreign insurance institution” of insurance institutions has the same statistical approach with that of “Premium income” of previous years. The below are the same.

表 1-3 续表 Continued

指 标	Indicators	1993	2000	2005	2007	2008
工业总产值(亿元)	**Gross Output Value of Industry(100 million yuan)**	**604.40**	**1 625.77**	**4 242.47**	**5 188.12**	**5 649.22**
#高技术工业	Industrial Output of High Technologies			1 190.72	1 329.37	1 471.18
国内外贸易	**Domestic and Foreign Trades**					
商品销售总额(亿元)	Aggregate Sales of Commodities (100 million yuan)		752.94	2 807.47	3 613.46	4 646.70
社会消费品零售总额(亿元)	Total Retail Sales of Consumer Goods (100 million yuan)	41.92	215.17	353.69	456.04	526.89
外贸进出口总额(亿美元)	Total Import and Export(USD 100 million)	25.92	254.86	894.75	1 280.52	1 449.59
出口总额	Total Export	12.02	95.80	372.12	528.10	604.23
进口总额	Total Import	13.90	159.06	522.63	752.42	845.36
功能开发	**Functional Development**					
中外资金融机构数(个)	Number of Chinese and Foreign Financial Institutions (unit)			369	493	544
中外资银行本外币存款余额(亿元)	Balance of RMB and Foreign Currencies Deposits in Chinese and Foreign Banks (100 million yuan)			4 244.07	6 304.06	7 704.87
中外资银行本外币贷款余额(亿元)	Balance of RMB and Foreign Currencies Loans in Chinese and Foreign Banks (100 million yuan)			4 667.88	6 882.05	7 708.85
期末认定跨国公司地区总部入驻数(户)	Settled Headquarters of Transnational Companies at End of Term (in number)			64	96	115
举办展览(博览)(次)	Number of Exhibitions Hosted(time)			114	99	117
举办国际性会议(次)	Number of International Conferences Hosted(time)			199	21	21
接待国内外游客总数(万人次)	Foreign and Domestic Tourists Received (10 000 person-times)		1 133	1 660	2 018	1 961
浦东国际机场旅客吞吐量(万人次)	Passenger Capacity at Pudong International Airport (10 000 person-times)			2 358	2 895	2 815
浦东国际机场货邮吞吐量(万吨)	Volume of Cargo Handled at Pudong International Airport(10 000 tons)			185	251	263
港口货物吞吐量(万吨)	Volume of Cargo Handled at Port(10 000 tons)	9 017	4 990	10 646	13 077	13 123
集装箱吞吐量(万标箱)	Container Handling Capacity(10 000 TEU)		184.3	1 272.5	1 556.8	1 538.7

表 1-4 主要年份社会发展主要指标
Major Indicators of Social Development in Main Years

指 标	Indicators	1993	2000	2005	2007	2008
人 口	**Population**					
年末常住人口(万人)	Permanent Population at Year-end (10 000 persons)		240.23	279.19	305.35	305.70
年末户籍总人口(万人)	Registered Population at Year-end (10 000 persons)	143.73	164.87	184.81	191.16	194.29
年末总户数(户)	Total Households at Year-end (household)	486 325	605 186	689 529	713 474	722 946
自然增长率(‰)	Natural Growth rate(‰)	-0.08	-1.71	-0.58	1.58	0.90
劳动就业	**Labor and New Jobs**					
从业人员(万人)	Employed Person(10 000 persons)	104.40	104.04	144.08	149.08	150.76
第一产业	Primary Industry	4.98	4.25	1.99	1.27	0.93
第二产业	Secondary Industry	66.37	48.06	57.07	60.06	56.83
第三产业	Tertiary Industry	33.05	51.73	85.02	87.75	93.00
职工人数(万人)	Staff and Workers(10 000 persons)	78.88	67.75	70.16	63.17	66.79
新增就业岗位(万人)	Number of New Jobs(10 000 Persons)			11.50	12.94	14.27
期末城镇登记失业人数(万人)	Number of Registered Unemployed Persons in Towns at End of Term (10 000 Persons)			4.29	4.00	3.91
人民生活	**People's Livelihood**					
城镇居民人均年可支配收入(元)	Annual Disposable Income Per Capita of Urban Residents (yuan)			19 089	24 273	27 797
郊区居民人均年可支配收入(元)	Annual Disposable Income Per Capita of Rural Residents(yuan)			9 779	12 246	13 778
职工工资总额(亿元)	Total Wages of Staff and Workers (100 million yuan)	47.26	120.59	235.03	354.32	480.33
职工年平均工资(元)	Average Wages of Staff and Workers(yuan)	5 999	17 607	33 186	56 878	69 872
城镇居民人均住宅建筑面积(平方米)	Floor Space of Urban Residents Per Capita(sq · m)			32.73	33.61	35.39
平均期望寿命(岁)	Life Expectancy (year)	76.10	78.01	80.85	81.61	81.78

表1-4 续表 Continued

指 标 Indicators		1993	2000	2005	2007	2008
教 育	**Education**					
高等学校在校学生数(人)	Student Enrollment of Higher Education(person)	3 776	11 940	41 034	46 991	55 917
中等学校在校学生数(人)	Student Enrollment at High Schools(person)	79 751	138 941	149 407	137 969	133 895
小学在校学生数(人)	Student Enrollment at Primary Schools(person)	131 204	110 573	92 062	98 391	101 449
高考上线率(%)	Pass Rate of Entrance Examination for Colleges(%)				87.2	87.3
市实验性、示范性高中和区重点高中就读学生比例(%)	Rate of Students Enrolled in Municipal Experimental and Demonstration High Schools and District-Key High Schools(%)				48.2	52.1
学龄儿童入学率(%)	Rate of School-age Child Enrollment (%)	99.2	99.5	100.0	100.0	100.0
幼儿园幼儿数(人)	Young Child Enrollment at Kindergartens(person)	42 378	34 030	44 554	51 042	53 844
卫 生	**Health**					
医疗机构数(个)	Healthcare Institutions(unit)	378	586	630	693	707
#医 院	Hospitals	47	48	57	67	68
医院病床(张)	Hospital Bed (bed)	4 840	6 947	6 520	8 078	8 297
卫生技术人员(人)	Healthcare Professionals (person)	7 717	8 810	9 794	12 467	13 778
#执业医生	Medical Practitioners	4 102	4 552	4 726	5 265	5 773
注册护士	Registered Nurses	2 179	2 739	3 390	4 725	5 120
城市建设、环境保护	**Urban Construction and Environmental Protection**					
建成区绿化覆盖率(%)	Coverage of Urban Green Areas (%) in PNA		30.2	37.8	37.3	37.3
城镇污水纳管率(%)	Rate of Sewage Pipe in Towns(%)			70.4	74.0	76.0
空气质量优良率(%)	Rate of Fine Air Quality (%)			89.3	91.2	93.1
人均公共绿地(平方米)	Public Green Space Per Capita(sq·m)	3.40	11.00	24.42	24.29	24.25

表1-5 历年社会经济主要指标增长率(以上年为基期)

单位:%

指 标	Indicators	1993	1994	1995	1996
年末总户数	Total Households at Year-end		2.6	3.1	3.1
年末户籍总人口	Registered Population at Year-end	2.2	1.7	1.7	1.7
男	Male	2.3	1.9	1.8	1.8
女	Female	2.0	1.6	1.5	1.6
年末常住人口	Permanet Population at Year-end				
从业人员	Employed Persons		0.6	2.8	-3.7
第一产业	Primary Industry		-6.6	2.4	-5.3
第二产业	Secondary Industry		-6.7	2.1	-0.4
第三产业	Tertiary Industry		16.2	4.1	-8.7
职工人数	Staff and Workers	46.5	-2.8	4.1	-9.9
新区生产总值	Gross Output Value of PNA	30.2	28.6	22.0	20.2
第一产业	Primary Industry	-8.5	5.1	14.2	1.9
第二产业	Secondary Industry	22.0	21.6	21.9	17.4
第三产业	Tertiary Industry	46.6	42.8	22.6	30.0
工业总产值	Gross Domestic Product of Industry	28.7	20.1	19.3	18.2
财政收入	Financial Revenue		1.2倍 (times)	62.9	30.5
#地方财政收入	Local Financial Revenue		1.8倍 (times)	51.6	32.1
地方财政支出	Local Financial Expenditure		1.1倍 (times)	93.9	10.1
固定资产投资总额	Total Investment in Fixed Assets	1.2倍 (times)	58.7	9.2	38.6
#房地产开发投资	Investment in Real Estate Development				
#城市基础设施投资额	Investment in Urban Infrastructure	1.5倍 (times)	43.9	-32.2	84.7
商品销售总额	Aggregate Sales of Commodities			16.7	21.2
社会消费品零售总额	Total Retail Sales of Consumer Goods	48.5	97.4	32.9	27.5
外贸进出口总额	Total Import and Export		82.7	52.0	12.2
出口总额	Total Export		93.1	70.8	-2.2
进口总额	Total Import		73.7	33.9	30.0
浦东国际机场旅客吞吐量	Passenger Capacity in Pudong International Airport				
浦东国际机场货邮吞吐量	Volume of Cargo Handled at Pudong International Airport				
港口货物吞吐量	Volume of Cargo Handled at Port	21.8	-7.8	-27.6	19.7
集装箱吞吐量	Container Handling Capacity				1.9倍 (times)

注：凡财政指标均为2004年财税体制改革后的同口径对比数,后续相关指标口径相同。
Note: Every financial indicator is the comparative number with the same approach after reforms of finance and taxation system in 2004. Hereinafter are the same.

Growth Rate of Major Indicators of Social Economy in Main Years (the Previous Year as Base)

(%)

1997	1998	1999	2000	2001	2002	2003	2004	2005	2006	2007	2008
2.8	3.4	3.1	4.1	2.3	2.4	2.6	2.3	3.3	1.7	1.8	1.3
1.5	1.8	2.5	3.0	2.2	2.6	2.2	2.4	2.2	1.5	1.9	1.6
1.5	2.0	2.6	3.2	2.3	2.7	2.4	2.4	2.1	1.4	1.8	1.4
1.5	1.7	2.4	2.8	2.0	2.5	2.1	2.3	2.2	1.5	2.1	1.9
				3.1	3.0	3.0	3.1	3.1	2.2	7.0	0.1
-0.6	-1.9	2.1	5.8	7.1	7.7	5.7	2.7	10.6	1.8	1.6	1.1
-10.6	35.0	-21.1	-0.9	-4.7	9.9	-29.7	-24.3	-16.0	-32.7	-5.2	-26.8
-10.4	-0.2	-11.2	-4.0	4.2	7.6	-3.4	4.5	4.9	6.6	-1.3	-5.4
3.4	-8.3	27.3	17.5	10.8	7.6	16.3	2.5	15.7	-0.6	3.8	6.0
-7.8	-0.3	2.4	…	1.5	2.1	-4.4	-8.5	14.3	-5.1	-5.1	5.7
18.3	16.8	16.1	16.5	16.1	16.7	17.5	16.4	12.1	13.4	15.2	11.6
5.3	5.9	3.8	4.9	6.1	4.9	1.6	-7.3	-4.0	-5.1	-5.4	-5.8
16.3	14.0	13.5	15.2	16.3	16.4	19.3	17.2	10.5	12.1	10.1	9.1
24.3	24.2	22.5	19.6	16.1	17.1	15.8	15.7	14.0	15.0	20.4	14.0
18.4	15.1	17.3	18.9	20.1	21.0	26.4	22.4	11.8	13.3	14.3	9.4
21.4	13.0	13.2	30.1	39.1	41.2	46.1	25.7	10.5	18.7	45.4	22.0
30.0	10.2	-0.5	27.6	47.2	14.6	41.6	20.9	13.0	14.8	46.3	16.0
18.2	10.8	4.8	19.1	26.9	36.9	32.6	20.7	2.7	12.0	29.1	28.9
27.7	15.6	-24.9	-19.9	18.5	41.1	2.5	8.3	6.4	-4.8	18.8	11.3
			6.6	6.5	93.6	13.9	13.7	3.0	-10.5	-4.0	13.1
20.9	48.5	-11.7	-65.2	93.3	62.6	-9.2	-22.1	3.9	23.9	50.3	32.7
28.3	-1.6	93.8	26.9	33.5	77.9	35.5	21.0	-4.3	4.9	22.7	28.6
15.7	10.3	10.8	8.5	8.3	22.0	10.2	14.4	13.2	13.1	14.0	15.5
22.6	21.0	28.2	65.9	16.9	21.9	57.5	39.0	10.7	19.9	19.3	13.2
18.3	15.1	26.3	43.7	15.0	18.2	55.8	52.8	14.9	19.5	18.8	14.4
26.5	26.1	29.8	82.9	17.9	24.2	58.6	31.1	7.9	20.2	19.7	12.4
					64.9	36.3	39.7	12.1	13.1	8.6	-2.8
					79.5	81.8	38.5	-1.1	16.8	16.2	4.8
2.9	-5.8	-1.3	10.1	20.9	36.9	16.5	36.0	33.2	6.6	15.3	0.4
45.3	48.7	36.2	85.4	56.9	60.2	43.3	42.0	34.9	7.9	13.4	-1.2

表1-5　续表　Continued

指　标	Indicators	1993	1994	1995	1996
外商直接投资合同项目	Projects of Foreign Direct Investment	63.0	12.0	-19.0	-4.3
外商直接投资合同金额	Actual Paid Amount of Foreign Direct Investment	29.9	47.6	25.6	-44.4
举办展览(博览)	Number of Exhibitions Hosted				
举办国际性会议	Number of International Conferences Hosted				
接待国内外游客总数	Foreign and Domestic Tourists Received				
中外资银行本外币存款余额	Balance of RMB and Foreign Currencies Deposits in Chinese and Foreign Banks				
中外资银行本外币贷款余额	Balance of RMB and Foreign Currencies Loans in Chinese and Foreign Banks				
城镇居民人均年可支配收入	Annual Disposable Income Per Capita of Urban Residents				
郊区居民人均年可支配收入	Annual Disposable Income Per Capita of Rural Residents				
职工工资总额	Total Wages of Staff and Workers	1.0倍(times)	28.5	32.2	3.8
职工平均工资	Average Wages of Staff and Workers	37.9	31.8	26.4	13.6
居民储蓄存款年末余额	Residents'Savings Deposit Balance (Year End)	77.1	76.2	56.3	28.9
高等学校在校学生数	Student Enrollment of Higher Education	26.4	11.3	13.0	6.6
中等学校在校学生数	Student Enrollment at High Scools	9.6	17.1	15.6	8.2
小学在校学生数	Student Enrollment at Primary Schools	7.7	0.2	-1.8	-0.1
幼儿园幼儿数	Young Child Enrollment at Kindergartens		-12.0	-3.5	-9.0
医院病床	Hospital Beds	3.1	3.7	4.8	2.8
卫生技术人员	Healthcare Professionals	3.4	4.0	2.3	4.4
#执业医生	Medical Practitioners	6.6	5.1	3.0	6.4
注册护士	Registered Nurses	3.7	4.9	2.6	3.7
公共交通全年客运量	Annual Volume of Public Transport	-16.8	-2.0	4.6	-36.8
期末认定跨国公司地区总部入驻数	Settled Headquarters of Transnational Companies at End of Term				

(%)

1997	1998	1999	2000	2001	2002	2003	2004	2005	2006	2007	2008
-23.2	-9.9	-15.2	47.4	27.0	9.5	73.4	1.0	2.7	-16.6	-13.3	-36.0
-0.5	55.0	-61.5	1.7倍 (times)	-30.6	33.3	7.8	12.1	75.4	-14.4	2.2	0.9
					2.8倍 (times)	32.1	54.3	5.6	-21.1	10.0	18.2
					20.0	26.7	-6.8	12.4	-76.9	-54.4	持平 (same as)
	17.6	56.5	52.7	-8.6	47.5	-29.3	43.5	7.0	10.8	9.7	-2.8
								25.3	18.8	25.0	22.2
								21.4	20.2	23.8	12.0
								12.4	12.4	13.2	14.5
								11.4	11.6	12.2	12.5
1.0	6.6	18.9	13.1	16.4	14.3	6.6	7.6	27.7	18.7	27.0	35.6
9.5	8.0	16.0	13.1	15.6	11.7	12.7	15.2	12.4	25.7	36.3	22.8
20.0	13.5	10.6	2.7	24.2	35.2	31.9	27.9	30.7	17.1	1.4	34.6
11.9	29.0	21.7	34.4	28.0	86.2	21.3	9.6	8.5	5.9	8.2	19.0
5.0	5.9	6.2	0.8	-1.0	0.2	-1.5	12.3	-2.0	-4.1	-3.8	-3.0
1.3	-2.7	-6.7	-6.7	-6.3	-2.3	-0.6	-11.4	3.3	3.5	3.3	3.1
0.5	-0.5	1.0	3.0	-1.9	11.0	6.4	7.3	5.4	4.2	9.9	5.5
-1.2	3.4	9.8	2.2	5.3	6.0	4.6	-0.6	-5.4	17.4	5.6	2.7
5.2	3.1	1.2	1.4	0.9	-1.3	-0.1	12.3	0.1	6.5	19.6	10.5
4.5	2.6	1.6	1.5	0.5	-8.4	-0.2	3.7	-0.1	1.4	9.9	9.6
7.6	5.1	2.7	2.6	3.9	9.9	0.6	7.4	1.6	18.0	18.2	8.4
16.9	13.0	0.7	22.8	3.3	7.7	1.2	9.0	3.2	0.6	-1.2	25.3
									29.7	15.7	19.8

表1-6　社会经济主要指标年均增长速度
Average Annual Growth Rate of Main Social Economic Indicators

单位:%　　　　(%)

指　标	Indicators	平均每年增长 Annual Growth Rate 1991~2008	1991~1995	1996~2000	2001~2005	2006~2008
年末户籍总人口	Registered Population at Year-end	2.1	2.1	2.1	2.3	1.7
新区生产总值	Gross Domestic Product	17.8	23.0	17.6	15.7	13.4
第一产业	Primary Industry	0.9	2.4	4.4	0.1	-5.4
第二产业	Secondary Industry	15.9	20.0	15.3	15.9	10.4
第三产业	Tertiary Industry	21.9	29.8	24.1	15.7	16.4
工业总产值	Gross Output Value of Industry	18.2	20.3	17.6	20.3	12.3
*财政收入	Financial Revenue	35.0		21.4	36.8	28.2
# *地方财政收入	Local Financial Revenue	30.6		19.2	22.5	24.9
*地方财政支出	Local Financial Expenditure	27.6		12.5	23.4	23.0
全社会固定资产投资总额	Total Investment in Fixed Assets	31.8	96.5	16.1	17.8	5.5
城市基础设施投资额	Investment in Urban Infrastructure	25.6	66.5	28.8	32.2	34.3
社会消费品零售总额	Total Retail Sales of Consumer Goods	22.2	50.4	14.4	14.0	14.2
*外贸进出口总额	Total Import and Export	30.8		28.8	28.6	17.4
*出口总额	Total Export	29.8		19.3	31.2	17.5
*进口总额	Total Import	31.5		37.5	26.9	17.4
外商直接投资合同项目	Projects of Foreign Direct Investment	32.0	1.4倍 (times)	-3.7	20.1	…
外商直接投资合同金额	Actual Paid Amount of Foreign Direct Investment	40.0	1.8倍 (times)	-10.4	4.4	…
职工平均工资	Average Wages of Staff and Workers	19.2	27.7	12.0	13.5	28.2
中外资银行本外币存款余额	Balance of RMB and Foreign Currencies Deposits in Chinese and Foreign Banks					22.0
中外资银行本外币贷款余额	Balance of RMB and Foreign Currencies Loans in Chinese and Foreign Banks					18.2
*国内保险费收入	Domestic Insurance Premium	35.2		36.0	17.3	18.0
居民储蓄存款年末余额	Residents' Savings Deposit Balance at Year-end	28.0	54.4	14.8	29.9	16.9

注：1. 带"*"指标宾栏第一栏年均增长速度的年份为"1994~2008"。
2. 带"*"指标宾栏第二栏因仅有二年增长速度,故不再计算该指标的年均增长速度。
3."固定资产投资额"、"城市基础设施投资额"和"外商合同投资"的增长速度均采用累计法计算。

Note: 1. The year with the annual growth rate in the first horizontal column that is indicated with the symbol of "*" is from 1994 to 2008.
2. Because the second column in the field of indicators with the sign of "*" only have the growth rate of the recent two years, we will not calculate the annual growth rate of this indicator.
3. The increase rates of "the amount of fixed capital investment", "the amount of urban infrastructure investment" and "foreign contract investment" are processed by the cumulative method.

表1-7 社会经济结构主要指标
Main Indicators of Economic and Social Structures

单位:% (%)

指标	Indicators	2005	2007	2008
第三产业增加值占GDP比重	Ratio of added value of the tertiary industry in GDP	48.9	53.0	54.4
新区财政收入相当于GDP比例	Ratio of PNA financial revenue in GDP	23.5	30.6	33.1
地方财政收入相当于GDP比例	Ratio of local financial revenue in GDP	7.4	9.3	9.6
固定资产投资相当于GDP比例	Ratio of fixed capital investment in GDP	32.9	28.1	27.7
外贸进出口总额相当于GDP比例	Ratio of total volume of foreign trade in GDP	342.4	334.9	314.4
外贸出口总额相当于GDP比例	Ratio of total export of foreign trade in GDP	142.4	138.1	147.8
社会消费品零售总额相当于GDP比例	Ratio of total volume of retail sales for social consumer goods in GDP	16.8	16.3	16.7
R&D占全社会GDP比重	Ratio of R&D in Social GDP		2.83	3.34
六个重点发展行业总产值占工业总产值比重	Ratio of total output value of six key industries in total value of industrial output	68.1	68.6	68.0
高技术产业工业总产值占工业总产值比重	Ratio of total output value of hi-tech industries in total value of industrial output		25.6	26.0
城市基础设施投资占固定资产投资总额比重	Ratio of investment for urban infrastructure in gross investment in fixed assets	18.2	29.9	35.7
房地产开发投资占固定资产投资总额比重	Ratio of investment for real estate development in gross investment in fixed assets	41.5	31.6	32.1
机电产品出口占外贸出口商品总额比重	Ratio of export of machinery and electrical equipment in total export of foreign trade	61.0	59.0	60.2
高技术产品出口占外贸出口商品总额比重	Ratio of export of hi-tech products in total export of foreign trade	33.4	29.4	28.3
第三产业实到外资占新区实到外资金额比重	Ratio of foreign investment in place for the tertiary industry in total of foreign investment in place in PNA	71.8	88.3	78.7
发明专利申请量占专利申请量比重	Ratio of the number of applications for invention patents in the volume of patent applications	57.1	36.2	34.1
城镇居民家庭人均食品支出占人均消费支出比重	Ratio of expenses for food per capita of urban families in consumption expenditure per capita	36.2	35.2	35.3
城镇居民家庭人均服务性消费支出占人均消费支出比重	Ratio of expenses for service consumptions per capita of urban families in consumption expenditure per capita	32.7	32.2	33.8

表1-8 主要年份社会经济部分指标平均每天水平
Daily Average Level of Major Economic and Social Indicators in Main Years

指 标	Indicators	单 位 Unit	2000	2005	2007	2008
新区生产总值	Gross Output Value of PNA	万元 10 000 yuan	25 223	57 775	76 531	86 328
工业总产值	Gross Output Value of Industry	万元 10 000 yuan	44 542	116 232	142 140	154 773
财政收入	Financial Revenue	万元 10 000 yuan	2 828	13 560	23 411	28 560
#地方财政收入	Local Financial Revenue	万元 10 000 yuan	1 545	4 255	7 145	8 291
固定资产投资额	Total Investment in Fixed Assets	万元 10 000 yuan	9 618	19 003	21 482	23 909
新增固定资产	Newly Acquired Fixed Assets	万元 10 000 yuan	10 400	10 409	10 437	17 499
商品销售总额	Total Sales of Commodities	万元 10 000 yuan	20 628	76 917	98 999	127 307
社会消费品零售额	Retail Sales of Consumer Goods	万元 10 000 yuan	5 895	11 370	12 494	14 435
外贸出口货物总额	Total Export Value of Commodities in Foreign Trade	万美元 USD 10000	2 625	10 195	14 468	16 554
外商直接投资合同项目	Projects of Foreign Direct Investment	个 unit	1.90	4.75	3.44	2.20
外商直接投资合同金额	Actual Paid Amount of Foreign Direct Investment	万美元 USD 10000	790	1 549	1 356	1 368
港口货物吞吐量	Volume of Cargo Handled at Port	万吨 10 000 tons	13.67	29.17	35.83	35.95
函 件	Mail	万份 10 000 pieces	12.37	14.82	36.07	48.90
自来水售水量	Sales of Tap Water	万吨 10 000 tons	90.45	114.87	128.44	136.48
售电量	Electricity Sales	万千瓦·时 10 000 kwh	1 911	3 512	3 957	4 294
管道燃气售气量	Sales of Pipelined Gas	万立方米 10 000 cu·m	30.43	121.37	130.14	140.00
公交车辆乘客人数	Passengers Carried by Public Vehicles	万人次 10 000 person-times	136.70	173.12	172.19	215.74
隧道、大桥过江车辆数	Vehicle Across the Huangpu River through Tunnels and Bridges	万车次 10 000 vehicle-times	35.07	53.02	82.92	83.31
医院诊疗人数	Outpatient Treated	万人次 10 000 person-times	2.53	3.49	4.57	5.26
出生人数	Birth	人 person	23	34	46	44
死亡人数	Death	人 person	30	37	38	39

表1-9 主要年份社会经济人均指标
Annual Average Level of Major Social and Economical Indicators Per Capita in Main Years

指 标	Indicators	单 位 Unit	2000	2005	2007	2008
工业总产值	Gross Output Value of Industry	元 yuan	68 598	154 244	175 672	184 902
财政收入	Financial Revenue	元 yuan	4 355	17 995	28 933	34 120
#地方财政收入	Local Financial Revence	元 yuan	2 380	5 647	8 831	9 905
固定资产投资额	Total Investment in Fixed Assets	元 yuan	14 813	25 218	26 550	28 563
新增固定资产	Newly Acquired Fixed Assets	元 yuan	16 017	13 813	12 899	20 905
社会消费品零售额	Total Retail Sales of Consumer Goods	元 yuan	9 079	12 859	15 442	17 245
外贸出口总额	Total Exports Value of Foreign Trade	美元 USD	4 042	13 529	17 882	19 777
外贸进口总额	Total Imports Value of Foreign Trade	美元 USD	6 711	19 001	25 477	27 669
居民年末储蓄存款余额	Savings Deposit Balance(Year End)	元 yuan	15 232	40 209	44 452	57 818
职工年平均工资	Annual Average Wage of Staff and Workers	元 yuan	17 607	33 186	56 878	69 872
城镇居民年人均可支配收入	Annual Disposable Income Per Capita of Urban Residents	元 yuan		19 089	24 273	27 797
郊区居民年人均可支配收入	Annual Disposable Income Per Capita of Suburban Residents	元 yuan		9 779	12 246	13 778
公共绿地占有面积	Green Area	平方米 sq · m	11.00	24.42	24.29	24.25
邮政订销报刊数	Total Circulation of Newspapers and Magazines	份 in number	53	43	44	49
城镇居民人均住房建筑面积	Building Area of Housing Per Capita	平方米 sq · m		32.73	33.61	35.39
每万人拥有病床数	Number of Sickbeds per 10 000 Persons	张 bed		23.35	26.45	27.14
每万名中小学生拥有教职员工数	Number of Teaching Staff per 10 000 Primary and Middle School Students	人 person		882	853	829
实有人口万人发案率	Ratio of Criminal Cases per 10 000 Persons	起/万人 in number /10 000persons		61.76	59.24	57.75
每万人拥有律师数	Number of Lawyers per 10 000 Persons	人 person		5.4	5.9	6.3

注：1. 上述指标除特别注明外，人均水平均采用常住人口计算。
2. 居民年人均可支配收入为住户调查资料。

Note：1. The average level per capita has been calculated in the permanent population except the above-mentioned indicators are otherwise specified.
2. The data of annual disposable income per capita are surveyed from household residents.

表 1-10 历年新区生产总值
Gross Domestic Product of Pudong New Area in Main Years
(1990～2008)

单位:亿元 (100 million yuan)

年 份 Year	新区生产总值 Gross Domestic Product of PNA	第一产业 Primary Industry	第二产业 Secondary Industry	#工 业 Industry	第三产业 Tertiary Industry	#金 融 Banking	房 产 Real Estate
1990	60.24	2.22	45.89	43.13	12.13	3.07	
1991	71.54	2.41	53.45	50.46	15.68	4.46	
1992	101.49	1.89	73.72	70.25	25.88	6.96	
1993	164.00	2.12	114.45	108.16	47.43	16.40	
1994	291.20	3.19	197.13	177.45	90.88	23.73	
1995	414.65	4.22	283.92	260.07	126.51	28.59	36.52
1996	496.47	4.57	320.31	286.32	171.59	39.08	40.61
1997	608.22	4.95	376.87	325.38	226.40	69.10	46.20
1998	704.27	5.30	412.82	349.97	286.15	101.31	52.68
1999	801.36	5.47	435.66	388.88	360.23	138.35	47.26
2000	923.51	5.72	488.60	445.43	429.19	159.88	55.36
2001	1 087.53	6.06	560.29	508.62	521.18	170.12	70.39
2002	1 244.00	6.38	635.54	579.86	602.08	166.04	100.51
2003	1 510.32	6.67	767.53	708.98	736.12	183.48	129.12
2004	1 850.13	6.00	952.25	894.13	891.88	218.13	168.25
2005	2 108.79	6.09	1 070.96	1 009.47	1 031.74	249.69	174.48
2006	2 365.33	5.88	1 194.47	1 133.76	1 164.98	313.98	169.24
2007	2 793.39	6.06	1 306.49	1 237.36	1 480.84	474.83	185.38
2008	3 150.99	5.88	1 430.25	1 351.44	1 714.86	553.46	181.49

表1-11 历年新区生产总值结构
Structure of Total Gross Domestic Product in PNA in Main Years (1990～2008)

单位:% (%)

年 份 Year	新区生产总值 Gross Domestic Product of PNA	第一产业 Primary Industry	第二产业 Secondary Industry	#工 业 Industry	第三产业 Tertiary Industry	#金 融 Banking	房地产 Real Estate
1990	100.0	3.7	76.2	71.6	20.1	5.1	
1991	100.0	3.4	74.7	70.5	21.9	6.2	
1992	100.0	1.9	72.6	69.2	25.5	6.9	
1993	100.0	1.3	69.8	66.0	28.9	10.0	
1994	100.0	1.1	67.7	60.9	31.2	8.1	
1995	100.0	1.0	68.5	62.7	30.5	6.9	8.8
1996	100.0	0.9	64.5	57.7	34.6	7.9	8.2
1997	100.0	0.8	62.0	53.5	37.2	11.4	7.6
1998	100.0	0.7	58.6	49.7	40.7	14.4	7.5
1999	100.0	0.7	54.4	48.6	44.9	17.3	5.9
2000	100.0	0.6	52.9	48.2	46.5	17.3	6.0
2001	100.0	0.6	51.5	46.8	47.9	15.6	6.5
2002	100.0	0.5	51.1	46.6	48.4	13.4	8.1
2003	100.0	0.5	50.8	46.9	48.7	12.1	8.6
2004	100.0	0.3	51.5	48.3	48.2	11.8	9.1
2005	100.0	0.3	50.8	47.9	48.9	11.8	8.3
2006	100.0	0.2	50.5	47.9	49.3	13.3	7.2
2007	100.0	0.2	46.8	44.3	53.0	17.0	6.6
2008	100.0	0.2	45.4	42.9	54.4	17.6	5.7

表 1-12 主要年份新区生产总值(新行业分类)
Gross Domestic Product in Main Years (Grouped by New Sectors)

单位:亿元 (100 million yuan)

指 标	Indicators	2000	2005	2007	2008
新区生产总值	**Gross Domestic Product of PNA**	**923.51**	**2 108.79**	**2 793.39**	**3 150.99**
第一产业	Primary Industry	5.72	6.09	6.06	5.88
第二产业	Secondary Industry	488.60	1 070.96	1 306.49	1 430.25
工 业	Industry	445.43	1 009.47	1 237.36	1 351.44
建筑业	Construction	43.17	61.49	69.13	78.81
第三产业	Tertiary Industry	429.19	1 031.74	1 480.84	1 714.86
交通运输、仓储业、邮政业	Transportation, Warehousing and Post Service	23.38	88.88	121.19	138.16
信息传输、计算机服务和软件业	Information Transmission, Computer Service and Computer Software	15.60	73.34	104.42	125.85
批发和零售业	Wholesale and Retail	109.61	212.05	246.50	293.09
住宿和餐饮业	Hotel and Catering	10.39	28.13	39.47	43.13
金融业	Banking	159.88	249.69	474.83	553.46
房地产业	Real Estate	55.36	174.48	185.38	181.49
居民服务和其他服务业	Resident Service and Other Services	8.33	9.48	13.06	15.61
其 他	Others	46.64	195.69	295.99	364.07
构 成(%)	**Composition (%)**	**100.0**	**100.0**	**100.0**	**100.0**
第一产业	Primary Industry	0.6	0.3	0.2	0.2
第二产业	Secondary Industry	52.9	50.8	46.8	45.4
工 业	Industry	48.2	47.9	44.3	42.9
建筑业	Construction	4.7	2.9	2.5	2.5
第三产业	Tertiary Industry	46.5	48.9	53.0	54.4
交通运输、仓储业、邮政业	Transportation, Warehousing and Post Service	2.5	4.2	4.3	4.4
信息传输、计算机服务和软件业	Information Transmission, Computer Service and Computer Software	1.7	3.5	3.7	4.0
批发和零售业	Wholesale and Retail	11.9	10.1	8.8	9.3
住宿和餐饮业	Hotel and Catering	1.1	1.3	1.4	1.4
金融业	Banking	17.3	11.8	17.0	17.6
房地产业	Real Estate	6.0	8.3	6.6	5.7
居民服务和其他服务业	Resident Service and Other Services	0.9	0.4	0.5	0.5
其 他	Others	5.1	9.3	10.6	11.5

表 1-13 历年新区生产总值指数

Gross Domestic Product Indexes of PNA in Main Years (1991 ~ 2008)

（以 1990 年为 100） (1990 as 100)

年 份 Year	新区生产总 值 Gross Domestic Product of PNA	第一产业 Primary Industry	第二产业 Secondary Industry	#工 业 Industry	第三产业 Tertiary Industry	#金 融 Banking	房地产 Real Estate
1991	113.9	101.2	113.1		119.5	141.0	
1992	138.0	102.3	137.6		143.8	179.1	
1993	179.7	93.6	167.9	121.9	210.7	332.7	
1994	231.1	98.4	204.2	148.0	301.0	408.5	
1995	282.0	112.4	248.9	172.1	369.0	440.0	105.2
1996	339.0	114.5	292.2	199.8	479.7	576.9	111.6
1997	401.0	120.6	339.9	227.4	596.2	856.7	120.8
1998	468.3	127.7	387.4	256.7	740.5	1 210.5	132.1
1999	543.8	132.6	439.7	301.4	907.1	1 571.2	105.4
2000	633.5	139.1	506.5	352.9	1 084.9	1 850.9	127.7
2001	735.5	147.6	589.1	406.2	1 259.6	1 937.9	157.4
2002	858.3	154.8	685.7	473.3	1 475.0	1 941.7	214.3
2003	1 008.5	157.3	818.0	570.3	1 708.1	2 145.6	250.3
2004	1 173.9	145.8	958.7	678.1	1 976.3	2 488.9	276.5
2005	1 315.9	140.0	1 059.4	752.0	2 253.0	2 854.8	273.5
2006	1 492.2	132.9	1 187.6	849.0	2 591.0	3 565.6	261.7
2007	1 719.0	125.7	1 307.5	935.6	3 119.5	4 963.3	267.7
2008	1 918.5	118.3	1 426.7	1 019.8	3 555.9	5 712.8	257.0

注：工业增加值以 1992 年为 100，房地产增加值以 1994 年为 100。
Note: The added industrial value takes the data of 1992 as 100, and the added real estate value takes the data of 1994 as 100.

表1-14　历年新区生产总值指数

Gross Domestic Product Indexes of PNA in Main Years

(1991～2008)

(以上年为环比基期)　　(Previous Year as Chain Base)

年　份 Year	新区生产总　值 Gross Domestic Product of PNA	第一产业 Primary Industry	第二产业 Secondary Industry	#工　业 Industry	第三产业 Tertiary Industry	#金　融 Banking	房地产 Real Estate
1991	113.9	101.2	113.1	113.8	119.5	141.0	
1992	121.2	101.1	121.7	120.1	120.3	127.0	
1993	130.2	91.5	122.0	121.9	146.6	185.8	
1994	128.6	105.1	121.6	121.4	142.8	122.8	
1995	122.0	114.2	121.9	116.3	122.6	107.7	105.2
1996	120.2	101.9	117.4	116.1	130.0	131.1	106.1
1997	118.3	105.3	116.3	113.8	124.3	148.5	108.2
1998	116.8	105.9	114.0	112.9	124.2	141.3	109.4
1999	116.1	103.8	113.5	117.4	122.5	129.8	79.8
2000	116.5	104.9	115.2	117.1	119.6	117.8	121.1
2001	116.1	106.1	116.3	115.1	116.1	104.7	123.3
2002	116.7	104.9	116.4	116.5	117.1	100.2	136.1
2003	117.5	101.6	119.3	120.5	115.8	110.5	116.8
2004	116.4	92.7	117.2	118.9	115.7	116.0	110.5
2005	112.1	96.0	110.5	110.9	114.0	114.7	98.9
2006	113.4	94.9	112.1	112.9	115.0	124.9	95.7
2007	115.2	94.6	110.1	110.2	120.4	139.2	102.3
2008	111.6	94.2	109.1	109.0	114.0	115.1	96.0

表1-15 历年第三产业增加值指数(旧行业分类)
Indexes of Value Added in Tertiary Industry in Main Years (Grouped By Old Sectors) (1991~2000)

(以上年为环比基期) (Previous Year as Chain Base)

年 份 Year	第三产业增加值 Value Added in Tertiary Industry	#交通、运输、仓储、邮电通讯业 Transportation, Warehousing, Post and Telecommunications	批发和零售贸易、餐饮业 Wholesale, Retail and Catering	金融保险 Banking and Insurance	房地产 Real Estate
1991	119.5	108.8	108.1	141.0	
1992	120.3			127.0	
1993	146.6	137.3	124.8	185.8	
1994	142.8	105.4	154.1	122.8	
1995	122.6	115.2	172.8	107.7	105.2
1996	130.0	128.4	158.9	131.1	106.1
1997	124.3	112.2	118.5	148.5	108.2
1998	124.2	117.0	118.3	141.3	109.4
1999	122.5	122.1	129.1	129.8	79.8
2000	119.6	117.9	119.1	117.8	121.1

表1-16 历年第三产业增加值指数(新行业分类)
Index of Value Added in Tertiary Industry in Main Years(Grouped by New Sectors) (2001~2008)

(以上年为环比基期) (Previous Year as Chain Base)

年 份 Year	第三产业增加值 Value Added in Tertiary Industry	#交通运输、仓储业、邮政业 Transportation, Warehousing and Post Service	信息传输、计算机服务和软件业 Information Transmission, Computer Service and Computer Software	批发和零售业 Wholesale and Retail	金融业 Banking	房地产业 Real Estate
2001	116.1	127.5	109.4	121.6	104.7	123.3
2002	117.1	127.1	109.7	116.9	100.2	136.1
2003	115.8	115.8	164.3	113.6	110.5	116.8
2004	115.7	122.2	121.4	112.6	116.0	110.5
2005	114.0	118.6	118.3	114.8	114.7	98.9
2006	115.0	115.2	119.1	112.9	124.9	95.7
2007	120.4	115.7	116.4	114.7	139.2	102.3
2008	114.0	110.9	120.3	115.4	115.1	96.0

表1-17 社会经济主要指标占全市比重
The Proportion of Major Economic and Social Indicators in Shanghai

指 标 Indicators		2007			2008		
		浦东新区 PNA	全市 Shanghai	浦东新区占全市比重(%) Proportion of PNA in Shanghai(%)	浦东新区 PNA	全市 Shanghai	浦东新区占全市比重(%) Proportion of PNA in Shanghai(%)
土地面积(平方公里)	Land Area (sq. km)	569.57	6 340.50	9.0	569.57	6 340.50	9.0
年末常住人口(万人)	Permanet Population at Year-end (10 000 persons)	305.35	1 858.08	16.4	305.70	1 888.46	16.2
年末户籍总人口(万人)	Registered Population at Year-end (10 000 persons)	191.16	1 378.86	13.9	194.29	1 391.04	14.0
从业人员(万人)	Employment (10 000 persons)	149.08	909.08	16.4	150.76	1 053.24	14.3
职工人数(万人)	Staff and Workers (10 000 persons)	63.17	522.67	12.1	66.79	554.39	12.0
生产总值(亿元)	Gross Domestic Product (100 million yuan)	2 793.39	12 188.85	22.9	3 150.99	13 698.15	23.0
第一产业	Primary Industry	6.06	101.84	6.0	5.88	111.80	5.3
第二产业	Secondary Industry	1 306.49	5 678.51	23.0	1 430.25	6 235.92	22.9
#工 业	Industry	1 237.36	5 298.08	23.3	1 351.44	5 784.99	23.4
第三产业	Tertiary Industry	1 480.84	6 408.50	23.1	1 714.86	7 350.43	23.3
#金 融	Banking	474.83	1 209.08	39.3	553.46	1 442.60	38.4
房地产	Real Estate	185.38	806.79	23.0	181.49	747.00	24.3
工业总产值(亿元)	Gross Output Value of Industry (100 million yuan)	5 188.12	23 108.63	22.5	5 649.22	25 638.97	22.0
固定资产投资总额(亿元)	Total Investment in Fixed Assets (100 million yuan)	784.10	4 458.61	17.6	872.68	4 829.45	18.1
城市基础设施投资额(亿元)	Investment in Urban Infrastructure (100 million yuan)	234.54	1 466.33	16.0	311.30	1 733.18	18.0
财政收入(亿元)	Financial Revenue (100 million yuan)	854.49	7 310.26	11.7	1 042.44	7 532.91	13.8
地方财政收入(亿元)	Local Government Revenue (100 million yuan)	260.80	2 102.63	12.4	302.61	2 382.34	12.7
地方财政支出(亿元)	Local Government Expenditure (100 million yuan)	287.24	2 201.92	13.0	370.30	2 617.68	14.1

表 1-17　续表　Continued

指　标　Indicators		2007 浦东新区 PNA	2007 全市 Shanghai	2007 浦东新区占全市比重(%) Proportion of PNA in Shanghai(%)	2008 浦东新区 PNA	2008 全市 Shanghai	2008 浦东新区占全市比重(%) Proportion of PNA in Shanghai(%)
商品销售总额(亿元)	Aggregate Sales of Commodities (100 million yuan)	3 613.46	20 400.79	17.7	4 646.70	26 798.45	17.3
社会消费品零售总额(亿元)	Retail Sales of Consumer Goods (100 million yuan)	456.04	3 847.79	11.9	526.89	4 537.14	11.6
年末居民储蓄存款余额(亿元)	Savings Deposit Balance of Rural and Urban Residents (100 million yuan)	1 312.80	9 326.45	14.1	1 766.49	12 083.66	14.6
外贸进出口商品总额(亿美元)	Total Value of Import and Export (USD 100 million)	1 280.52	2 829.73	45.3	1 449.59	3 221.38	45.0
# 出口总额	Value of Export	528.10	1 439.28	36.7	604.23	1 693.50	35.7
外商直接投资合同项目(个)	Projects of Foreign Direct Investment(unit)	1 254	4 206	29.8	803	3 748	21.4
外商直接投资合同金额(亿美元)	Contracted Amount of Foreign Direct Investment(USD 100 million)	49.49	148.69	33.3	49.92	171.12	29.2
外商直接投资实际到位金额(亿美元)	Foreign Direct Investment Actually Absorbed (USD 100 million)	33.06	79.20	41.7	34.35	100.84	34.1
国际机场旅客吞吐量(万人次)	Passenger Capacity in Pudong International Airport (10 000 person-times)	2 895.15	5 156.64	56.1	2 815.48	5 111.31	55.1
港口货物吞吐量(万吨)	Volume of Cargo Handled at Port (10 000 tons)	13 077	56 145	23.3	13 123	58 170	22.6
集装箱吞吐量(万标箱)	Container Handling Capacity (10 000 TEUs)	1 556.8	2 615.2	59.5	1 538.7	2 800.6	54.9
各级各类学校在校学生数(万人)	Student Enrollment by Level and Type of Schools (10 000 persons)	28.40	187.45	15.2	29.18	171.6	17.0
医院病床(张)	Number of Hospital Beds (bed)	8 078	95 900	8.4	8 297	97 780	8.5
专业卫生技术人员(万人)	Medical Technical Personnel (10 000 persons)	1.25	12.24	10.2	1.38	12.77	10.8
# 执业医生	Medical Practitioners	0.53	4.88	10.8	0.58	5.12	11.3
申请专利(项)	Patent Claiming (item)	8 435	47 205	17.9	8 980	52 835	17.0
跨国公司地区总部(家)	Settled Headquarters of Transnational Companies at End of Term (in number)	96	184	52.2	115	224	51.3

表 1-18 财政收支
Financial Revenue and Expenditure

单位:万元 (10 000 yuan)

	指 标 Indicators	2000	2005	2007	2008
全部财政收入	**Total Financial Revenue**	**1 032 077**	**4 949 366**	**8 544 910**	**10 424 372**
地方财政收入	**PNA Government Revenue**	**564 020**	**1 553 141**	**2 607 957**	**3 026 053**
区级财政收入	**PNA Financial Revenue**	**355 863**	**1 553 141**	**2 870 589**	**3 407 453**
#增值税	Value Added Tax	44 293	275 873	402 357	449 284
营业税	Business Income Tax	122 200	528 808	914 203	923 824
企业所得税	Enterprise Tax	72 712	251 733	514 825	736 436
个人所得税	Individual Income Tax	77 662	199 439	320 501	406 999
城市维护建设税	Tax on Urban Construction and Maintenance	11 603	24 329	37 326	38 364
房产税	Tax on Real Estate	13 418	35 192	73 411	74 247
印花税	Stamp Tax	3 588	22 007	62 039	79 746
契 税	Contract Tax	7 107	202 445	227 761	196 854
地方财政支出	**PNA Government Expenditure**	**695 999**	**1 987 939**	**2 872 367**	**3 702 959**
#一般公共服务	Ordinary community services			156 000	172 868
公共安全	Public security			117 044	128 632
教 育	Education			269 374	309 056
科学技术	Technology			160 457	192 243
文化体育与传媒	Culture, Sports and Media			51 724	84 097
社会保障和就业	Social security and employment			306 151	254 316
医疗卫生	Health care			82 030	121 792
环境保护	Environmental protection			10 699	36 962
城乡社区事务	Urban and suburban community affairs			1 111 379	1 456 266
农林水事务	Agricultural, forest and water affairs			107 428	192 048
交通运输	Traffic and transportation			10 342	17 314
工业商业金融等事务	Industrial, commercial and financial affairs			445 927	701 904

注：本表由浦东新区财政局提供,2007 年财政部进行财税体制改革,起用新科目,2000 及 2005 年口径数据无法提供。
Note: This table is provided by PNA Financial Bureau. The Financial Department has started the reform of the finance and taxation system since 2007, which began to use the new subject. Data approached in 2000 and in 2005 are not available.

主要统计指标解释

气　温

气温是指空气的温度，一般以摄氏度（℃）为单位表示。气象观测的温度表是放在离地面约1.5米处通风良好的百叶箱里测量的，因此，通常说的气温指的是离地面1.5米处百叶箱中的温度。其统计计算方法为：

月平均气温是将全月各日的平均气温相加，除以该月的天数而得。

年平均气温是将12个月的月平均气温累加后除以12而得。

降水量

降水量是指从天空降落到地面的液态或固态（经融化后）水，未经蒸发、渗透、流失而在地面上积聚的深度。其统计计算方法为：

月降水量是将全月各日的降水量累加而得。

年降水量是将12个月的月降水量累加而得。

日照时数

日照时数是指太阳实际照射地面的时间。其统计方法与降水量相同。

生产总值（原国内生产总值）

国内生产总值是指按市场价格计算的一个地区所有常住（驻）单位在一定时期内生产活动的最终成果。生产总值有三种表现形态，即价值形态、收入形态和产品形态。从价值形态看，它是所有常驻单位在一定时期内所生产的全部货物和服务价值超过同期投入的全部非固定资产货物和服务价值的差额，即所有常住（驻）单位的增加值之和；从收入形态看，它是所有常住（驻）单位在一定时期内所创造并分配给常住（驻）单位和非常住（驻）单位的初次（分配）收入之和；从产品形态看，它是所有常住单位在一定时期内最终使用的货物和服务减去进口货物和服务。在实际核算中，生产总值有三种计算方法，（其三种表现形态体现为三种计算方法，）即生产法、收入法和支出法。三种方法分别从不同的方面反映生产总值及其构成。根据国务院和国家统计局有关我国GDP核算和数据发布制度的规定，浦东新区国内生产总值自2004年起更名为“浦东新区生产总值”，简称“浦东新区GDP”。

三次产业

根据社会生产活动历史发展的顺序对产业结构的划分，产品直接取自自然界的部门称为第一产业，对初级产品进行再加工的部门称为第二产业，为生产和消费提供各种服务的部门称为第三产业。

第一产业：农林牧渔业（包括农业、林业、畜牧业、渔业和农林牧渔服务业）。

第二产业：包括采矿业、制造业、电力、燃气及水的生产和供应业与建筑业。

第三产业：除第一、第二产业以外的其他各业。

指　数

指数是一种表明社会经济现象动态的相对数。运用指数可以测定不能直接相加和直接对比的社会经济现象的总动态；可以分析社会经济现象总变动中各因素变动的影响程度；可以研究总平均指标变动中各组标志水平和总体结构变动的作用。它是在把各个年份的产值换算成可比价格的基础上，根据定基数等于相应各个环比指数的连乘积这个换算关系计算出来的。

平均每年增长速度

在我国计算平均增长速度有两种方法，一种是习惯上经常使用的“水平法”，又称几何平均法，是各以间隔期最后一年的水平同基期水平对比来计算平均每年增长（或下降）速度。另一种是“累计法”，又称代数平均法或方程法，是以间隔期内各年水平的总和同基期水平对比来计算平均每年增长（或下降）速度。

在一般正常情况下，两种方法计算的平均每年增长速度比较接近，但在经济发展不平衡，出现大起大落时，两种方法计算的结果差别较大。

本年鉴内所列的平均每年增长速度，除固定资产投资、直接吸收外资是用“累计法”计算以外，其余均用“水平法”计算。

财政收入

指国家财政参与社会产品分配所取得的收入，是实现国家职能的财力保证。财政收入所包括的内容几经变化，目前主要包括：

（1）各项税收：包括增值税、营业税、消费税、土地增值税、城市维护建设税、资源税、城市土地使用税、企业所得税、个人所得税、关税、证券交易印花税、车辆购置税、农牧业税和耕地占用税等。

（2）专项收入：包括排污费收入、城市水资源费收入、矿产资源补偿费收入、教育费附加收入等。

（3）其他收入：包括利息收入、基本建设贷款归还收入、基本建设收入、捐赠收入等。

（4）国有企业亏损补贴：此项为负收入，冲减财政收入。

主要包括对工业企业、商业企业、粮食企业的补贴。

中央财政收入和地方财政收入

指按现行分税制财政体制划分的中央本级收入和地方本级收入。1994 年实行分税制财政体制以后，属于中央财政的收入包括关税、海关代征消费税和增值税，消费税，中央企业所得税，地方银行和外资银行及非银行金融企业所得税，铁道部门、各银行总行、各保险总公司等集中缴纳的营业税、利润和城市维护建设税，车辆购置税，船舶吨税，增值税的 75% 部分，证券交易税（印花税）94% 部分，个人所得税中的利息所得税，利息所得税之外的个人所得税中央分享的部分，海洋石油资源税。属于地方财政的收入包括营业税，地方企业所得税，利息所得税之外的个人所得税地方分享的部分，城镇土地使用税，固定资产投资方向调节税，城镇维护建设税，房产税，车船使用税，印花税，屠宰税，农牧业税，农业特产税，耕地占用税，契税，土地增值税、国有土地有偿使用收入，增值税 25% 部分，证券交易税（印花税）6% 部分和除海洋石油资源税以外的其他资源税。

地方财政支出

地方财政支出指根据政府在经济和社会活动中，按照政府的责权划分确定的支出。地方财政支出主要包括地方行政管理和各项事业费，地方统筹的基本建设、技术改造支出，支援农村生产支出，城市维护和建设经费，价格补贴支出等。

EXPLANATORY NOTES ON MAJOR STATISTICAL INDICATORS

Temperature

Temperature refers to the air temperature. It often uses centigrade as the unit. The thermometry used for weather observation is put in a breezy shutter, which is 1.5 meters high from the ground. Therefore, the commonly used temperature refers to the temperature in the breezy shutter 1.5 meters away from the ground. The calculation method is as follows:

Monthly average temperature is the summation of average daily temperature of one month divided by the actual days of that particular month. Annual average temperature is the summation of monthly average of a year divided by 12 months.

Volume of Precipitation

Volume of Precipitation refers to the deepness of liquid state or solid state (thawed) water falling from the sky to the ground that has not been evaporated, infiltrated or run off. The calculation method is as follows:

Monthly precipitation is the summation of daily precipitation of a month.

Annual precipitation is the summation of 12 months precipitation of a year.

Sunshine Hours

Sunshine Hours refer to the actual hours of sun irradiating the earth. The calculation method is the same as that of the precipitation.

Gross Product

Gross Product refers to the final products at market prices by (of) all resident units of a region during a certain period of time. Gross product is expressed in three different forms, i. e value, income, and products respectively. The form of value added refers to the total value of all products and services produced by all resident units during a certain period of time minus the total value of inputs of non-fixed-assets products and services or the summation of the value added of all resident units; the form of income includes all the income items produced by all resident units and distributed primarily to all resident and non-resident units; the form of product refers to all final goods and services minus imports of goods and services. In the practice of national accounting, it is calculated by three approaches, i. e. product approach, income approach, and expenditure approach, respectively, to reflect Gross Product and its composition of different aspects. According to the regulations of GDP national accounting and data release issued by the State Council and National Bureau of Statistics, since 2004 Pudong New Area Gross Domestic Product has been renamed as Pudong New Area Gross Product Value, for short PNA GDP.

Three Industries

Three Industries have been classified according to the historical sequence of development. Primary industry refers to extraction of natural resources; secondary industry involves processing of primary products; and tertiary industry provides services of various kinds for production and consumption.

Primary industry: Agriculture, forestry, animal husbandry and fishery. (including farming, forestry, animal husbandry, fishery industry and service industry for farming, forestry, animal husbandry and fishery).

Secondary industry: Mining, manufacturing, power, steam and water production and supply and construction.

Tertiary industry: All other industries not included in primary or secondary industries.

Index

Index refers to the relative figures indicating social and economic phenomena and developments. Index is used to evaluate the overall development of social and economic phenomena which can not be determined by simple addition or direct comparison. It is also used to analyze the outcome of various changes in the general phenomenon movement of social and economic development, and to study the level of each sub-index in the changes of general average index and the role of the changes of the overall structure. It is calculated at the comparable prices conversed from the output value of each year, using the formula of index number with fixed base period equal to the continuous product of its relative chain index.

Average Annual Growth Rate

Two methods for calculating Average Annual Growth Rate are applied in China, one is often called "level approach" or geometry average, which is derived by comparing the growth rate for the last year of the interval with that of the beginning year; the other is called "accumulating approach" or algebraic average or equation method, which is calculated by comparing the total growth rate of each year for the interval with that of base year.

Usually the results calculated by the two methods are fairly close, but they differ sharply when imbalance occurred in economic development with striking fluctuations in growth.

The Average Annual Growth Rates listed in this statistical yearbook are calculated by "level approach" except for the growth rate of investment in fixed assets and foreign capital absorbed.

Government Revenue

Government Revenue refers to the revenue of the government finance by means of participating in the distribution of the social products, which is the financial resources for ensuring the government to function. The contents of government revenue have been changed several times. Now it includes the following main items:

(1) Various tax revenues, including value added tax, business tax, consumption tax, land value added tax, tax on city maintenance and construction, resources tax, tax on use of urban land, enterprise income tax, personal income tax, tariff, stamp tax on security transactions, tax on purchase of motor vehicles, tax on agriculture and animal husbandry and tax on occupancy of cultivated land, etc.

(2) Special revenues, including revenues from the fee on sewage treatment, fee on urban water resources, fee for the compensation of mineral resources and extra-charges for education, etc.

(3) Other revenues, including revenue from interest, revenue from the repayment of capital construction loan, revenue from capital construction projects, and donations and grants.

(4) Subsidies for the losses of the state-owned enterprises. This is an item of negative revenue, consisting of subsidies to industrial, commercial and grain purchasing and supply enterprises.

Revenue of the Central Government and Revenue of the Local GoVernment

Revenue of the central government and revenue of the local governments: refers to the revenue of the central government and that of the local governments as defined by the decentralized taxation system starting from 1994. In accordance with this system, the revenue of the central government includes tariff, consumption tax and value added tax levied by the customs, consumption tax, income tax of the enterprises subordinate to the central government, income taxes of the local banks, foreign-funded banks and non-bank financial institutions, business tax and profits of railways, head offices of banks, head office of insurance company , which are handed over to the government in a centralized way, tax on city maintenance and construction, tax on purchasing motor vehicles, tonnage tax of ships, 75% of the value added tax, 94% of the tax on stock dealing (stamp tax), interest income tax in the personal income tax, proportion of the personal income tax (other that interest income tax) to be shared by the central government, and tax on ocean petroleum resources,. The revenue of the local governments includes business tax, income tax of the enterprises subordinate to the local government, proportion of the personal income tax (other that interest income tax) to be shared by the central government, tax on the use of urban land, tax on the adjustment of the investment in fixed assets, tax on town maintenance and construction, tax on real estates, tax on the use of vehicles and ships, stamp tax, slaughter tax, tax on agriculture and animal husbandry, tax on special agricultural products, tax on the occupancy of cultivated land, contract tax, value-added tax on land, income from charges on use of state-owned land, 25% of the value added tax, 6% of the tax on stock dealing (stamp tax) and tax on resources other than the ocean petroleum resources.

Expenditure of the Local Government

Expenditure of the local government includes mainly the administrative expenses and various operating expenses at the level of local governments, the expenditure for capital construction and technological innovation with the funds raised by the local government, expenditure for supporting rural production, expenditure for city maintenance and construction and expenditure for price subsidies, etc.

第二篇 Chapter 2

人口

POPULATION

表2-1　历年常住人口、户籍人口、流动人口情况

单位:万人

年　份 Year	常住人口 Permanent Population	常住人口密度 (人/平方公里) Density of Permanent Population (Persons/sq. km)	年末户籍人口 Year-end Population	按户籍 Grouped by Types of
				非农业 Non-agriculture
1990			133.94	81.67
1991			137.34	85.45
1992			140.67	89.65
1993			143.73	97.78
1994			146.20	104.63
1995			148.63	109.73
1996			151.11	113.84
1997			153.40	119.20
1998			156.18	123.70
1999			160.08	128.51
2000	240.23	4 503	164.87	134.57
2001	247.56	4 641	168.45	139.85
2002	255.11	4 782	172.82	146.25
2003	262.89	4 616	176.69	153.46
2004	270.91	4 756	180.90	160.13
2005	279.19	4 902	184.81	170.17
2006	285.30	5 009	187.56	175.24
2007	305.35	5 361	191.16	179.90
2008	305.70	5 367	194.29	183.62

Permanent Population, Household Registered Population and Migrating Population in Main Years

(10 000 Persons)

性质分 Residence Registration	按性别分 Grouped by Sex		户籍人口密度（人/平方公里） Population Density (persons/sq. km)	期末登记流动人口数 Number of Registered Migrating Population
农 业 Agriculture	男 Male	女 Female		
52.27	66.41	67.53	2 584	
51.89	68.22	69.12	2 650	
51.02	69.96	70.71	2 714	
45.95	71.59	72.14	2 749	
41.57	72.92	73.28	2 797	
38.90	74.23	74.40	2 843	
37.27	75.53	75.58	2 891	
34.20	76.70	76.70	2 934	
32.48	78.21	77.97	2 988	
31.57	80.22	79.86	3 001	
30.30	82.75	82.12	3 091	
28.60	84.66	83.79	3 158	
26.57	86.97	85.85	3 240	67.94
23.23	89.03	87.66	3 102	80.16
20.77	91.20	89.70	3 176	82.58
14.64	93.12	91.69	3 245	93.73
12.32	94.45	93.11	3 293	119.75
11.26	96.13	95.03	3 356	130.97
10.67	97.48	96.81	3 411	127.30

表2-2　土地面积、户数、人口、人口密度及人口迁移情况
（2008年底）

单位:人

地　区 Subdistrict/Town		土地面积（平方公里）Land Area (sq. km)	户　数（户）Household (household)	年末人口 Year-end Population	按户籍性质分 Grouped by Types of Residence Registration	
					非农业 Non-agriculture	农　业 Agriculture
总　计	**Total**	**569.57**	**722 946**	**1 942 889**	**1 836 196**	**106 693**
街道小计	**Subdistrict Tot**	**84.64**	**424 712**	**1 129 383**	**1 129 304**	**79**
潍坊新村街道	Weifangxincun Subdistrict	3.74	32 443	93 423	93 423	
陆家嘴街道	Lujiazui Subdistrict	6.89	38 554	119 577	119 577	
周家渡街道	Zhoujiadu Subdistrict	5.52	44 157	116 049	116 049	
塘桥街道	Tangqiao Subdistrict	3.86	21 927	59 536	59 530	6
上钢新村街道	Shanggangxincun Subdistrict	7.54	38 141	106 234	106 232	2
南码头路街道	Nanmatou Road Subdistrict	4.25	29 951	81 785	81 784	1
沪东新村街道	Hudongxincun Subdistrict	5.39	28 245	70 685	70 685	
金杨新村街道	Jinyangxincun Subdistrict	8.02	51 833	129 604	129 603	1
洋泾街道	Yangjing Subdistrict	7.38	37 332	105 064	105 064	
浦兴路街道	Puxing Road Subdistrict	6.25	38 750	92 528	92 528	
东明路街道	Dongming Road Subdistrict	4.90	24 040	57 878	57 823	55
花木街道	Huamu Subdistrict	20.90	39 339	97 020	97 006	14
镇小计	**Town Tot**	**484.93**	**298 234**	**813 506**	**706 892**	**106 614**
川沙新镇	Chuansha New Town	139.73	58 732	167 419	128 939	38 480
高 桥 镇	Gaoqiao Town	39.07	32 432	84 203	76 432	7 771
北 蔡 镇	Beicai Town	23.71	45 364	116 625	112 029	4 596
合 庆 镇	Heqing Town	41.97	20 733	54 307	31 374	22 933
唐　　镇	Tangzhen Town	32.32	14 063	38 579	35 155	3 424
曹 路 镇	Caolu Town	45.58	22 023	65 731	50 856	14 875
金 桥 镇	Jinqiao Town	25.28	10 088	28 868	27 418	1 450
高 行 镇	Gaohang Town	22.85	16 946	45 331	45 258	73
高 东 镇	Gaodong Town	35.21	12 776	35 967	30 987	4 980
张 江 镇	Zhangjiang Town	45.02	22 487	67 735	67 714	21
三 林 镇	Sanlin Town	34.19	42 590	108 741	100 730	8 011

注：1.本表至表2-4数据由浦东新区公安分局提供的资料加工整理而成。
2.本表中各街镇的土地面积系行政区域调整后的量估面积仅供参考。凡未调整行政区域的街镇,仍为全国第二次土地普查面积。

Note: 1. Some data in this table to Table 2-4 are processed from the materials provided by Pudong Public Security Bureau.
2. The land area of PNA subdistricts/towns is the approximate area after the re-adjustment of administrative division, and is only for reference. How-ever, the 2nd nation-wide census of land area is still applicable to those without going through any re-adjustment.

Land Area, Households, Population, Density of Population and Migration of Population
(End of 2008)

(person)

按性别分 Grouped by Sex		平均每户人口 Average Persons Per Household	人口密度（人/平方公里） Population Density (persons/sq·km)	人口迁移情况 Population Mobility		
男 Male	女 Female			迁入 Population Moved-in	迁出 Population Moved-out	净迁入 Net Mobility
974 777	**968 112**	**2.69**	**3 411**	**89 605**	**60 001**	**29 604**
569 136	**560 247**	**2.66**	**13 343**	**53 788**	**40 583**	**13 205**
46 557	46 866	2.88	24 979	3 043	2 768	275
59 742	59 835	3.10	17 355	5 232	4 339	893
58 023	58 026	2.63	21 023	4 051	4 538	-487
29 701	29 835	2.72	15 424	2 538	2 360	178
53 486	52 748	2.79	14 089	3 610	3 483	127
40 660	41 125	2.73	19 244	2 986	2 195	791
36 313	34 372	2.50	13 114	3 798	2 327	1 471
65 162	64 442	2.50	16 160	5 241	4 667	574
53 829	51 235	2.81	14 236	7 400	6 484	916
47 755	44 773	2.39	14 804	4 835	2 916	1 919
29 522	28 356	2.41	11 812	4 887	1 743	3 144
48 386	48 634	2.47	4 642	6 167	2 763	3 404
405 641	**407 865**	**2.73**	**1 678**	**35 817**	**19 418**	**16 399**
82 710	84 709	2.85	1 198	4 771	3 079	1 692
42 124	42 079	2.60	2 155	2 531	1 241	1 290
58 748	57 877	2.57	4 919	6 370	3 112	3 258
26 796	27 511	2.62	1 294	1 157	627	530
18 886	19 693	2.74	1 194	1 135	756	379
32 635	33 096	2.98	1 442	3 197	2 204	993
14 690	14 178	2.86	1 142	1 503	1 080	423
22 917	22 414	2.68	1 984	2 581	1 465	1 116
17 851	18 116	2.82	1 021	1 118	691	427
34 176	33 559	3.01	1 505	4 691	2 330	2 361
54 108	54 633	2.55	3 180	6 763	2 833	3 930

表2-3 各街镇人口自然变动
Natural Changes in Population in Sub-districts and Towns
(2008)

单位:人 (person)

地 区	Subdistrict /Town	出生人口 Birth Population			死亡人口 Death Population			自然增加人口 Natural Growth		
		合计 Total	男 Man	女 Female	合计 Total	男 Man	女 Female	合计 Total	男 Man	女 Female
总 计	**Total**	**15 962**	**8 215**	**7 747**	**14 227**	**7 393**	**6 834**	**1 735**	**822**	**913**
街道小计	**Subdistrict Tot**	**8 969**	**4 645**	**4 324**	**8 593**	**4 496**	**4 097**	**376**	**149**	**227**
潍坊新村街道	Weifangxincun Subdistrict	634	317	317	757	397	360	-123	-80	-43
陆家嘴街道	Lujiazui Subdistrict	856	439	417	917	472	445	-61	-33	-28
周家渡街道	Zhoujiadu Subdistrict	701	377	324	1 012	542	470	-311	-165	-146
塘桥街道	Tangqiao Subdistrict	472	239	233	429	223	206	43	16	27
上钢新村街道	Shanggangxincun Subdistrict	618	333	285	972	504	468	-354	-171	-183
南码头路街道	Nanmatou Road Subdistrict	571	303	268	647	361	286	-76	-58	-18
沪东新村街道	Hudongxincun Subdistrict	572	279	293	569	294	275	3	-15	18
金杨新村街道	Jinyangxincun Subdistrict	1 011	530	481	896	488	408	115	42	73
洋泾街道	Yangjing Subdistrict	873	461	412	613	315	298	260	146	114
浦兴路街道	Puxing Road Subdistrict	1 065	555	510	679	356	323	386	199	187
东明路街道	Dongming Road Subdistrict	421	219	202	536	273	263	-115	-54	-61
花木街道	Huamu Subdistrict	1 175	593	582	566	271	295	609	322	287
镇小计	**Town Tot**	**6 993**	**3 570**	**3 423**	**5 634**	**2 897**	**2 737**	**1 359**	**673**	**686**
川沙新镇	Chuansha New Town	1 264	636	628	1 098	578	520	166	58	108
高 桥 镇	Gaoqiao Town	697	350	347	598	300	298	99	50	49
北 蔡 镇	Beicai Town	1 055	558	497	970	486	484	85	72	13
合 庆 镇	Heqing Town	381	209	172	394	186	208	-13	23	-36
唐 镇	Tangzhen Town	296	141	155	265	144	121	31	-3	34
曹 路 镇	Caolu Town	573	277	296	436	223	213	137	54	83
金 桥 镇	Jinqiao Town	305	169	136	157	78	79	148	91	57
高 行 镇	Gaohang Town	452	222	230	296	147	149	156	75	81
高 东 镇	Gaodong Town	280	137	143	282	153	129	-2	-16	14
张 江 镇	Zhangjiang Town	694	357	337	374	200	174	320	157	163
三 林 镇	Sanlin Town	996	514	482	764	402	362	232	112	120

表2-4 主要年份人口变动
Population Change/Mobility in Main Years

单位:人 (person)

指 标	Indicators	1990	1993	1995	2000	2005	2007	2008
人口自然变动	**Natural Changes in Population**							
出生人口	Birth Population	13 459	9 785	7 877	8 229	12 363	16 710	15 962
出生率(‰)	Birth Rate (‰)	10.20	6.88	5.34	5.07	6.76	8.82	8.28
死亡人口	Death Population	8 711	9 899	10 538	11 007	13 423	13 718	14 227
死亡率(‰)	Death Rate (‰)	6.60	6.96	7.15	6.78	7.34	7.24	7.38
自然增长人口	Natural Growth	4 748	-114	-2 661	-2 778	-1 060	2 992	1 735
自然增长率(‰)	Natural Growth Rate (‰)	3.60	-0.08	-1.81	-1.71	-0.58	1.58	0.90
人口迁移变动	**Population Mobility**							
迁入人口	Population Moved in	18 079	59 214	54 560	160 975	128 476	101 619	89 605
#市外迁入	Non-Shanghai Population Moved in	8 102	10 469	10 419	18 522	18 346	23 101	24 404
迁入率(‰)	Rate of Population Moved-in (‰)	13.50	41.20	37.01	99.10	70.26	53.66	46.49
迁出人口	Population Moved-out	15 820	32 457	24 600	103 486	88 315	68 683	60 001
#迁出市外	Population Moved Out of Shanghai	5 843	3 356	3 836	5 734	2 612	4 812	5 315
迁出率(‰)	Rate of Population Moved-out (‰)	11.81	22.58	16.69	63.70	48.30	36.27	31.13
迁移增长人口	Growth of Population Mobility	2 259	26 757	29 960	57 489	40 161	32 936	29 604
#市外迁移增长	Growth of Inward Mobility	2 259	7 113	6 583	12 788	15 734	18 289	19 089
净迁移率(‰)	Rate of Net Mobility (‰)	1.69	18.62	20.32	35.40	21.96	17.39	15.36

表2-5　年末流动人口登记情况
Registered Migrating Population at Year End

单位:人　　(person)

指　标	Indicators	2005	2006	2007	2008
总　计	**Total**	**937 331**	**1 197 479**	**1 309 730**	**1 272 983**
潍坊新村街道	Weifangxincun Subdistrict	10 975	14 289	14 932	17 525
陆家嘴街道	Lujiazui Subdistrict	17 538	20 244	23 071	23 476
周家渡街道	Zhoujiadu Subdistrict	13 614	15 010	16 285	16 705
塘桥街道	Tangqiao Subdistrict	7 319	10 451	11 175	11 458
上钢新村街道	Shanggangxincun Subdistrict	9 998	11 809	12 715	13 356
南码头路街道	Nanmantou Road Subdistrict	9 295	9 015	12 031	16 395
沪东新村街道	Hudongxincun Subdistrict	11 559	13 465	15 938	17 102
金杨新村街道	Jinyangxincun Subdistrict	27 016	37 799	32 246	35 981
洋泾街道	Yangjing Subdistrict	19 041	26 084	20 924	25 734
浦兴路街道	Puxing Road Subdistrict	15 898	20 621	29 936	27 283
东明路街道	Dongming Road Subdistrict	14 981	15 919	19 851	17 520
花木街道	Huamu Subdistrict	36 626	41 845	40 445	37 006
川沙新镇	Chuansha New Town	123 566	149 025	161 907	150 520
高 桥 镇	Gaoqiao Town	51 477	65 060	63 318	69 671
北 蔡 镇	Beicai Town	75 586	117 972	139 198	126 057
合 庆 镇	Heqing Town	40 144	52 866	44 951	54 109
唐　　镇	Tangzhen Town	49 296	64 422	49 180	61 186
曹 路 镇	Caolu Town	55 245	66 471	70 253	72 600
金 桥 镇	Jinqiao Town	69 312	90 194	92 974	76 449
高 行 镇	Gaohang Town	45 035	60 998	49 177	50 390
高 东 镇	Gaodong Town	59 380	67 598	63 557	67 661
张 江 镇	Zhangjiang Town	51 157	56 273	83 950	75 670
三 林 镇	Sanlin Town	119 904	168 060	239 503	203 025
水上派出所	Boat Police Station	333	435		270
世博治安派出所	Shibo Public Security and Police Station				5 332
外高桥保税区	Waigaoqiao Free Trade Zone	3 036	1 554	2 213	502

表2-6 主要年份婚姻登记和计划生育情况
Marriage Registration and Family Planning in Main Years

单位:人 (person)

指标	Indicators	1993	1995	2000	2005	2007	2008
婚姻登记	**Marriage Registration**						
准予登记结婚(对)	Registered Marriage (couple)	7 362	8 968	11 083	14 602	17 399	20 491
离婚登记(对)	Registered Divorce (couple)	489	1 049	2 102	4 402	5 332	5 408
计划生育	**Planned Birth**						
出 生	**Birth**						
出生人数	Birth Population	9 785	7 877	9 958	12 363	16 710	15 962
第一孩	First Child	9 309	7 560	9 669	11 928	16 047	15 304
第二孩	Second Child	471	157	285	424	654	644
多 孩	≥ Third Child	5		4	11	9	14
符合计划生育人数	Planned Parenthood	9 760	7 519	9 903	12 323	16 663	15 871
计划生育率(%)	Planned Birth Rate (%)	99.74	95.46	99.45	99.68	99.72	99.43
节 育	**Birth Control**						
已婚育龄妇女人数(万人)	Married Women at Child-bearing Age (10 000 persons)	31.69	31.73	32.34	29.33	28.73	29.37
已领独生子女证人数(万人)	Persons Who Have Applied for One-child Certificate (10 000 persons)	22.66	22.95	15.48	10.84	10.06	10.32
独生子女领证率(%)	Rate of One-child Certificate (%)	71.50	72.34	47.86	36.98	35.00	35.13
晚 婚	**Late Marriage**						
女性初婚人数	Number of First Marriage of Female	5 712	7 736	7 564	11 594	13 477	9 811
#23岁以上	≥ 23 Years Old	2 115	3 833	4 217	8 941	11 407	8 814
晚婚率(%)	Rate of Belated Marriage (%)	37.03	49.55	55.75	77.12	84.60	89.84

注：本表由浦东新区劳动保障局和社会发展局提供。
Note: This table is jointly provided by Pudong Labor & Social Security Bureau and Social Development Bureau.

主要统计指标解释

人口数

为每年12月31日的年末总人口。根据统计口径的不同,分为户籍人口和常住人口。户籍人口是指在公安部门办理了户籍登记的人口。常住人口是指实际上经常居住在一个地方(住所)的人口,一般都以在其住所居住半年以上者为常住人口。年鉴中除特别注明是常住人口、实有人口等统计口径外,其他均为户籍人口数。

农业人口、非农业人口

是人口按经济特征分组的主要指标。农业人口指依靠从事农业(包括种植业、林业、牧业、渔业)维持生活的全部人口,即包括从事农、林、牧、渔业生产的人口以及由他们抚养的人口。非农业人口指依靠从事农业以外职业的人口以及由他们抚养的人口。但长期来在户籍管理上,往往把在农村中就业并按工资形式获得劳动报酬及由其抚养的人口统计为非农业人口;在农村劳动并参加农村合作经济收益分配的人,及由其抚养的人口作为农业人口统计。

出生率(又称粗出生率)

指在一定时期内(通常为一年)一定地区的出生人数与同期平均人数(或期中人数)之比,一般用千分率表示。计算公式:

$$出生率 = \frac{年出生人数}{年平均人数} \times 1000‰$$

出生人数是指活产婴儿,即胎儿脱离母体时(不管怀孕月数),有过呼吸或其他生命现象。年平均人数是年初、年底人口数的平均数,也可用年中人口数代替。

死亡率(又称粗死亡率)

指在一定时期内(通常为一年)一定地区的死亡人数与同期平均人数(或期中人数)之比,一般用千分率表示。计算公式:

$$死亡率 = \frac{年死亡人数}{年平均人数} \times 1000‰$$

人口自然增长率

指在一定时期内(通常为一年)人口自然增加数(出生人数减死亡人数)与该时期内平均人数(或期中人数)之比,一般用千分率表示。计算公式:

$$人口自然增长率 = \frac{本年出生人数 - 本年死亡人数}{年平均人数} \times 1000‰$$

人口自然增长率 = 人口出生率 - 人口死亡率

EXPLANATORY NOTES TO MAJOR STATISTICAL INDICATORS

Population

Population refers to the total population by December 31 every year. According to different statistical approaches, there are two definitions of population named as population with registered residence and population with permanent residence. The former refers to the population with registration in the police while the latter refers to the population that actually reside in a place (residence) permanently ,usually longer than half a year. Unless the statistical approaches are specified as permanent population and present population, the others are the number of registered population in this Yearbook.

Agricultural Population, Non-agricultural Population

Agricultural Population, Non-agricultural Population are main indicators of population grouped by economic features. Agricultural Population refers to the total number of people who live on agriculture, including farming, forestry, husbandry and fishery, and their dependents. Non-agricultural Population refers to the number of people who live on non-agricultural jobs and their dependents. According to the resident registering control system, however, the people who are employed in rural area, receive income, and their dependents are actually registered as non-agricultural population. The people who work in rural area and receive their income from agricultural collective units and their dependents are statistically defined as agricultural population.

Birth Rate

Birth Rate (or gross birth rate) means the ratio of the number of births in a certain period (usually a year) to the average population in the same period (or mid-year figure). It is usually calculated in terms of permillage and its calculating formula is:

$$\text{Birth Rate} = \frac{\text{Number of Births}}{\text{Average Number of Popualtion}} \times 1000‰$$

Number of Births refers to live births, when babies have showed any vital phenomena regardless of the length of pregnancy.

Average Number of Population is the average of the number of population at the beginning of the year and, at the end of the year and sometimes is substituted for with mid-year population.

Death Rate

Death Rate (or Gross Death Rate) refers to the ratio of number of deaths to the average population (or mid-year population) during a certain period of time (usually a year), which is often presented as permillage. Its calculating formula is :

$$\text{Death Rate} = \frac{\text{Number of Deaths}}{\text{Average Number of Population}} \times 1000‰$$

Natural Growth Rate of Population

Natural Growth Rate of Population refers to the ratio of natural increase in population (number of births minus number of deaths) in a certain period of time (usually a year) to the average population (or mid-year population) of the same period, which is often presented as permillage. The following formula are applied:

$$\text{Natural Growth Rate of Population} = \frac{\text{Number of Births} - \text{Number of Deaths}}{\text{Average Number of Population}} \times 1000‰$$

Natural Growth Rate of Population = Birth Rate - Death Rate

第三篇

Chapter 3

固定资产投资

INVESTMENT IN FIXED ASSETS

表3-1　固定资产投资主要指标
(2008)

单位:万元

指　标	Indicators	合　计 Total	内　资 Domestic Investment	国　有 State-owned	集　体 Collective-owned
投资总额	**Total Investment**	**8 726 848**	**6 920 360**	**3 600 849**	**17 500**
按构成分	**By Use of Funds**				
建筑安装工程	Construction and Installation	4 416 814	3 654 664	1 329 600	17 500
设备工具器具购置	Purchase of Equipment and Instrument	1 670 376	848 014	646 752	
其他费用	Others	2 639 658	2 417 682	1 624 497	
按建设性质分	**By Type of Construction**				
#新　建	New Construction	4 444 232	4 030 410	3 134 447	
改　建	Reconstruction	975 782	725 461	355 823	
扩　建	Expansion	180 784	142 285	38 603	
按三次产业分	**By Industry**				
第一产业	Primary Industry				
第二产业	Secondary Industry	1 585 860	743 179	529 553	
第三产业	Tertiary Industry	7 140 988	6 177 181	3 071 296	17 500
按主要行业分	**By Main Sector**				
#工　业	Industry	1 585 860	743 179	529 553	
交通运输、仓储和邮政业	Transportation, Warehousing and Post Service	1 100 725	1 017 655	985 284	
信息传输、计算机服务和软件业	Information Transmission, Computer Service and Computer Software	60 890	54 838	12 364	
批发和零售业	Wholesale and Retail	1 101	1 101	428	
住宿和餐饮业	Hotel and Catering	27 090	27 090	9 197	
金融业	Banking	179 367	179 367	53 396	
新增固定资产	**Investment in Newly Increased Fixed Assets**	**6 386 996**	**3 690 975**	**1 235 468**	
固定资产交付使用率(%)	Rate of Fixed Assets Put into Use (%)	73.2	53.3	34.3	
房屋建筑面积(万平方米)	**Floor Area of Buildings (10 000 sq·m)**				
施工面积	Floor Area Under Construction	2 259.51	1 786.89	154.95	34.93
#住　宅	Residential Housing	1 062.63	928.66	33.09	31.61
竣工面积	Floor Area Completed	545.55	443.43	12.08	
#住　宅	Residential Housing	259.42	236.34		

Major Indicators of Investment in Fixed Assets

(10 000 yuan)

联 营 Jointly Operated	有限责任公司 Companies with Limited Liability	股份有限公司 Companies Limited by Shares	私营及个体 Private/ Individual	其 他 Others	港澳台商投资 Hong Kong/ Macao/Taiwan Funded	#独资企业 Solely Foreigner Funded Enterprises	外商投资 FIE	#独资企业 Solely Foreigner Funded Enterprises
558 141	**1 588 286**	**378 545**	**774 902**	**2 137**	**455 202**	**266 049**	**1 351 286**	**721 612**
489 461	1 098 450	201 321	516 327	2 005	314 420	209 006	447 730	340 705
7 903	138 547	19 202	35 610		96 906	40 488	725 456	233 122
60 777	351 289	158 022	222 965	132	43 876	16 555	178 100	147 785
8 235	673 242	201 014	13 472		64 518	38 620	349 304	56 140
354 588	9 418		3 495	2 137	12 134	9 428	238 187	77 082
	100 717	2 965					38 499	37 910
9 705	164 543	25 779	11 462	2 137	94 002	51 713	748 679	237 903
548 436	1 423 743	352 766	763 440		361 200	214 336	602 607	483 709
9 705	164 543	25 779	11 462	2 137	94 002	51 713	748 679	237 903
	23 728	8 643			23 078		59 992	3 770
	42 274		200				6 052	6 052
		673						
8 235	9 658							
	14 851	111 120						
	1 528 133	**149 595**	**777 052**	**727**	**402 020**	**199 236**	**2 294 001**	**1 167 871**
	96.2	39.5	100.3	34.0	88.3	74.9	169.8	161.8
74.80	696.71	183.93	641.57		234.33	109.25	238.29	168.38
57.73	316.83	81.19	408.21		54.77	3.63	79.20	78.80
	189.41	43.94	198.00		27.01	8.22	75.12	55.92
	108.82	16.31	111.21		14.6		8.48	8.48

表3-2　历年固定资产投资总额
Total Investment in Fixed Assets in Main Years
(1990～2008)

单位:亿元　　(100 million yuan)

年　份 Year	投资总额 Total Investment	建设改造 Construction and Renovation	房地产开发 Real Estate Development	农村集体 Rural Collective	其他投资 Other Investment
1990	14.15	12.58		1.01	0.56
1991	28.95	25.78		2.07	1.10
1992	75.00	58.98		14.17	1.85
1993	164.56	150.80		11.46	2.30
1994	261.13	238.37		20.01	2.75
1995	285.07	244.86	18.26	18.07	3.88
1996	395.04	269.70	95.45	22.11	7.78
1997	504.36	345.79	125.00	20.25	13.32
1998	583.22	419.42	134.87	21.70	7.23
1999	438.20	310.50	103.88	18.46	5.36
2000	351.06	216.69	110.74	22.74	0.89
2001	416.18	285.23	111.66	17.52	1.77
2002	587.20	371.36	215.80		0.04
2003	602.16	356.29	245.81		0.06
2004	651.94	372.45	279.49		
2005	693.61	405.69	287.92		
2006	659.97	402.16	257.81		
2007	784.10	536.64	247.46		
2008	872.68	592.71	279.97		
1990～2008年累计 Accumulated from 1990 to 2008	8 368.58	5 616.00	2 514.12	189.57	48.89

注：根据上海市统计局要求，从2002年起，浦东不再单独划分农村集体投资。
Note: Based on the requirement of Shanghai Statistics Bureau, collective-owned investment in rural area in Pudong is not to be listed in the table since 2002.

表3-3 各行业固定资产投资额
Investment in Fixed Assets by Sector
(2008)

指 标	Indicators	施工项目(个) Projects Under Construction (unit)	竣工项目(个) Projects Completed (unit)	投资额(万元) Investment (10 000 yuan)	新增固定资产(万元) Newly Increased Fixed Assets (10 000 yuan)
总 计	**Total**	**347**	**79**	**8 726 848**	**6 386 996**
制造业	Manufacturing	87	32	1 372 751	2 020 176
电力、燃气及水的生产和供应业	Production and Supply of Electricity, Gas and Water	7	4	213 109	845 032
交通运输、仓储和邮政业	Transportation, Warehousing and Post sevice	36	9	1 100 725	95 971
信息传输、计算机服务和软件业	Information Transmission, Computer Service and Computer Softwar	4	1	60 890	163 900
批发和零售业	Wholesale and Retail	2	1	1 101	851
住宿和餐饮业	Hotel and Catering	3		27 090	
金融业	Banking	7	2	179 367	180 036
房地产业	Real Estate	46	5	3 069 340	2 902 341
租赁和商务服务业	Leasing and Business Service	11		553 085	
科学研究、技术服务和地质勘查业	Scientific Research, Technical Service and Geological Prospecting	8	1	80 566	70 200
水利、环境和公共设施管理业	Water Conservancy, Environment and Public Facilities Administration	86	13	1 907 981	90 823
居民服务和其他服务业	Resident Service and Other Service	3	3	1 222	1 222
教 育	Education	25	1	33 115	13 914
卫生、社会保障和社会福利业	Healthcare, Social Security and Social Welfare	10		38 434	
文化、体育和娱乐业	Culture, Sports and Entertainment	5		84 648	
公共管理和社会组织	Public Administration and Social Organizations	7	7	3 424	2 530

表3-4　固定资产投资房屋建筑面积
Floor Space of Housing and Buildings in Fixed Assets Investment

单位:万平方米　　(10 000 sq · m)

指　标	Indicators	2005	2007	2008	1990～2008年累计 Totally Completed Investment (1990～2008)
房屋施工面积	**Floor Area Under Construction**				
合　计	**Total**	**2 483.56**	**2 269.61**	**2 259.51**	
住　宅	Residential Housing	1 510.04	1 267.03	1 062.63	
厂房仓库	Factory Building and Warehouse	120.52	122.14	171.60	
商业营业用房	Commerce	276.76	198.54	256.81	
办公室	Office	196.68	297.23	324.69	
教育用房	Education	20.35	20.62	25.28	
医疗用房	Healthcare	7.39	7.50	8.47	
其　他	Others	351.82	356.55	410.03	
房屋竣工面积	**Floor Area Completed**				
合　计	**Total**	**615.37**	**567.70**	**545.56**	**9 650.83**
住　宅	Residential Housing	408.44	379.00	259.42	6 138.58
厂房仓库	Factory Building and Warehouse	43.89	31.67	46.80	1 134.22
商业营业用房	Commerce	85.64	33.42	52.14	568.41
办公室	Office	54.08	43.39	79.11	708.03
教育用房	Education	8.37	3.62	8.48	189.32
医疗用房	Healthcare		1.93	3.85	54.93
其　他	Others	14.95	74.67	95.76	857.34

表3-5 历年新增固定资产
Newly Increased Fixed Assets In Main Years

指 标	Indicators	1994	1995	1996	1997	1998	1999	2000
新增固定资产（亿元）	Newly Increased Fixed Assets (100 million yuan)	141.03	150.76	260.75	329.84	331.79	396.22	379.60
固定资产交付使用率(%)	Rate of Fixed Assets Transferred and in Use (%)	54.0	52.9	66.8	65.4	56.9	90.4	108.1

表3-5 续表 Continued

指 标	Indicators	2001	2002	2003	2004	2005	2006	2007	2008
新增固定资产（亿元）	Newly Increased Fixed Assets (100 million yuan)	261.82	279.79	407.66	633.37	379.92	522.56	380.96	638.70
固定资产交付使用率(%)	Rate of Fixed Assets Transferred and in Use(%)	62.9	47.6	67.7	97.2	54.8	79.2	48.6	73.2

表3-6 主要年份固定资产投资资金来源
Capital Resources of Investment in Fixed Assets in Main Years

单位:亿元 (100 million yuan)

指 标	Indicators	2005	2007	2008
资金来源合计	**Total Capital Resources**	**1 057.43**	**1 098.90**	**1 196.27**
上年末结余资金	Balance at End of Previous Year	170.99	163.55	213.59
本年资金来源小计	Sub-total Capital Resources of this Year	886.44	935.35	982.68
国家预算内资金	State Budgetary Funds	16.05	6.27	5.96
国内贷款	Domestic Loans	166.05	318.43	253.31
债 券	Bonds		18.79	26.02
利用外资	Foreign Investment	61.96	41.79	50.66
#外商直接投资	Foreign Direct Investment	40.36	11.73	40.07
自筹资金	Self-Financed Capital	395.39	285.69	497.14
#市自筹	Self-Financed by Municipal Government	36.95	11.73	44.14
企事业自有资金	Self-Financed by Enterprises and Institutions	311.07	253.23	361.01
其他资金	Other Capital	246.99	264.38	149.59
#集 资	Raised Funds	0.42		
本年各项应付投资款	Investment Due to Pay this Year	108.32	143.92	167.21
#工程款	Project Funds	57.76	70.51	60.24

表 3-7　城市基础设施投资额
Investment in Urban Infrastructure

指　标	Indicators	2005	2007	2008	1990～2008 年累计 Totally Completed Investment (1990～2008)
投资额总计(万元)	**Total (10 000 yuan)**	**1 259 548**	**2 345 407**	**3 113 016**	**22 093 616**
电力建设	Electricity	75 089	586 967	141 954	2 955 575
运输邮电	Transportation, Post and Telecommunications	800 236	1 488 125	1 061 327	10 643 633
#市内公共交通	Urban Public Transportation	188 595	476 113	435 539	3 212 938
公用设施	Public Facilities	384 223	270 315	1 909 735	8 494 408
公用事业	Public Utilities	42 376	35 967	71 155	981 292
自来水	Tap Water	30 627	19 692		422 725
燃　气	Gas	11 749	16 275	71 155	558 567
市政建设	Civic Construction	341 847	234 348	1 838 580	7 513 116
市政工程	Civic Projects	323 614	173 275	1 690 680	6 977 272
园林绿化	Garden/Park	18 046	57 974	53 081	355 622
环境卫生	Environmental Sanitation	187	3 099	94 819	173 280
其　他	Others				6 942
构　成(%)	**Composition(%)**				
投资额总计	**Total**	**100.0**	**100.0**	**100.0**	**100.0**
电力建设	Electricity	6.0	25.0	4.6	13.4
运输邮电	Transportation, Post and Telecommunications	63.5	63.5	34.1	48.2
#市内公共交通	Urban Public Transportation	15.0	20.3	14.0	14.5
公用设施	Public Facilities	30.5	11.5	61.3	38.4
公用事业	Public Utilities	3.4	1.5	2.3	4.4
自来水	Tap Water	2.5	0.8	0.0	1.9
燃　气	Gas	0.9	0.7	2.3	2.5
市政建设	Civic Construction	27.1	10.0	59.0	34.0
市政工程	Civic Projects	25.7	7.4	54.3	31.6
园林绿化	Garden/Park	1.4	2.5	1.7	1.6
环境卫生	Environmental Sanitation		0.1	3.0	0.8
其　他	Others				…

表3-8 工业各行业投资主要指标
Main Indicators of Investment By Industrial Sectors
(2008)

指 标	Indicators	施工项目（个） Projects Under Construction (unit)	全部建成投产项目（个） Projects Completed and Put into Production (unit)	建成投产率（%） Rate of Projects Completed and Put into Use(%)	工业投资额（万元） Amount of Investment in Industry (10 000 yuan)
总 计	**Total**	**94**	**36**	**38.3**	**1 585 860**
#制造业	**#Manufacturing**	**87**	**32**	**36.8**	**1 372 751**
#食品制造业	Food Manufacturing	2			21 078
烟草制品业	Tobacco Manufacturing	7	4	57.1	1 087
印刷业和记录媒介的复制	Printing and Record Duplicating	2	1	50.0	12 896
石油加工、炼焦及核燃料加工业	Oil Processing, Coking and Nuclear Fuel Processing	4	2	50.0	24 468
化学原料及化学制品制造业	Raw Chemical Materials and Chemical Products Manufacturing	10	7	70.0	67 551
医药制造业	Medicine Manufacturing	8	4	50.0	17 276
塑料制品业	Plastic Products Manufacturing	2	1	50.0	5 941
黑色金属冶炼及压延加工业	Smelting and Pressing of Ferrous Metal				135
金属制品业	Metal Products Manufacturing	1			180
通用设备制造业	General Equipment Manufacturing	2	1	50.0	11 551
专用设备制造业	Special Purpose Equipment Manufacturing				14 495
交通运输设备制造业	Transportation Equipment Manufacturing	25	4	16.0	485 822
电气机械及器材制造业	Electric Machinery and Equipments Manufacturing	4	2	50.0	14 633
通信设备、计算机及其他电子设备制造业	Communications Equipment, Computer and Other Electronic Equipment Manufacturing	18	6	33.3	617 097
工艺品及其他制造业	Artworks and Other Manufacturing	2			78 541
电力、燃气及水的生产和供应业	**Power, Gas and Water Production and Supply**	**7**	**4**	**57.1**	**213 109**
电力、热力的生产和供应业	Power and Heat Production and Supply	2	1	50.0	141 954
燃气生产和供应业	Gas Production and Supply	5	3	60.0	71 155

表3-9　建设改造投资主要指标
Major Indicators of Construction Transformation

指　标　Indicators		单　位　Unit	2007	2008
投资总额	**Total Investment**	**万元 10 000 yuan**	**5 366 412**	**5 927 131**
按建设性质分	**Grouped by Type of Construction**			
#新　建	New Construction	万元 10 000 yuan	3 478 148	4 444 232
改　建	Reconstruction	万元 10 000 yuan	959 053	975 782
扩　建	Expansion	万元 10 000 yuan	714 489	180 784
按产业分	**Grouped by Type of Industry**			
第一产业	Primary Industry			
第二产业	Secondary Industry	万元 10 000 yuan	2 245 936	1 585 860
第三产业	Tertiary Industry	万元 10 000 yuan	3 120 476	4 341 271
按行业分	**Grouped by Economic Sectors**			
工　业	Industry	万元 10 000 yuan	2 245 936	1 585 860
交通运输、仓储和邮政业	Transportation, Storage and Post Industries	万元 10 000 yuan	1 579 321	1 100 725
信息传输、计算机服务和软件业	Information Transmission, Computer Servcie and Software Industries	万元 10 000 yuan	105 930	60 890
批发和零售业	Retail and Wholesale	万元 10 000 yuan	668	1 101
住宿和餐饮业	Hotel and Eateries	万元 10 000 yuan	26 369	27 090
金融业	Financial Industry	万元 10 000 yuan	52 057	179 367
房地产业	Real Estate Industry	万元 10 000 yuan	710 767	269 623
租赁和商务服务业	Leasing and Business Service	万元 10 000 yuan	74 187	553 085
科学研究、技术服务和地质勘查业	Scientific Research, Technology Service and Geological Prospecting	万元 10 000 yuan	81 280	80 566
水利、环境和公共设施管理业	Water Conservancy, Environment and Public Facility Management	万元 10 000 yuan	291 853	1 907 981
居民服务和其他服务业	Resident Service and Other Service	万元 10 000 yuan		1 222
教　育	Education	万元 10 000 yuan	39 789	33 115
卫生、社会保障和社会福利业	Health, Social Security and Welfare	万元 10 000 yuan	22 990	38 434
文化、体育和娱乐业	Culture, Sports and Entertainment	万元 10 000 yuan	127 787	84 648
公共管理和社会组织	Public Administration and Social Organizations	万元 10 000 yuan	7 478	3 424
新增固定资产	**Newly Increased Fixed Assets**			
固定资产交付使用率	Rate of Fixed Assets Transfered and in Use	%	38.2	59.4
房屋建筑面积	**Floor Space of Buildings**			
施工面积	Floor Space Under Construction	万平方米 10 000 sq·m	285.75	292.01
#住　宅	Residential Housing	万平方米 10 000 sq·m	11.72	3.65
竣工面积	Floor Space Completed	万平方米 10 000 sq·m	99.44	66.59
#住　宅	Residential Housing	万平方米 10 000 sq·m	8.07	3.65

表3-10　主要年份住宅投资按经济类型分
Investment in Residential Housing by Ownership in Main Years

单位:万元　　　　　　(10 000 yuan)

指　标	Indicators	2005	2007	2008
住宅投资额总计	**Total Investment in Residential Housing**	**2 013 328**	**1 349 569**	**1 421 002**
占固定资产投资额比重(%)	As Percentage of Investment in Fixed Assets(%)	29.0	17.2	16.3
内　资	Domestic Investment	1 625 348	1 039 649	1 187 424
国　有	State-owned	364 095	81 461	38 378
集　体	Collective-owned	35 100	35 720	15 810
股份合作	Share-holding	11 010	51 170	
联　营	Jointly-operated	43 162	33 232	164 137
有限责任公司	Companies with Limited Liability	547 107	395 672	392 993
股份有限公司	Companies Limited by Shares	10 823	50 654	100 860
私　营	Private	612 798	391 740	475 246
其　他	Others	1 253		
港澳台商投资	Hong Kong/Macao/Taiwan Invested	122 652	157 319	61 172
#港澳台商独资	Solely Hong Kong/Macao/Taiwan Funded	60 196	43 408	19 184
外商投资	FIE	265 328	152 601	172 406
#外商独资	Solely Foreigner Funded	129 903	141 478	167 072

表3-11 主要重大项目(浦东部分)投资完成额

Amount of Completed Investment in Key Civic Projects in PNA (2008)

单位:亿元 (100 million yuan)

序号 No.	项目名称	Projects	计划总投资 Total Planned Investment	累计完成投资 Accumulated Investment	#2008年完成投资 Investment Completed in 2008
	合 计	**Total**	**1 307.32**	**1 306.45**	**321.13**
1	中芯国际集成电路厂房	IC Workshops of SMIC	123.00	356.38	23.37
2	上海通用汽车浦东轿车项目	Sedan Project in Pudong of GM Shanghai	113.44	123.30	1.10
3	宏力半导体厂房	Workshops of GSMC	135.00	121.74	1.62
4	轨道交通6号线	M6	116.16	105.93	17.09
5	外高桥电厂三期工程	Phase III Project of Waigaoqiao Power Plant	93.20	82.91	13.22
6	中海发展股份有限公司船舶购置	Ship Purchasing Project of China Shipping Development Co., Ltd.	85.96	61.02	25.23
7	机场北通道	North Passage Project of Pudong International Airport	71.46	48.94	40.84
8	中环线	Mid-Ring Route	70.43	44.26	34.38
9	中海集装箱船舶购建	Purchase and Construction of Ships Project of China Shipping Containers Company	40.43	35.18	21.04
10	东西通道	East-West Passage	71.95	34.89	26.53
11	上海天马微电子第4.5代TFT—LCD生产线	The 4.5 Generation TFT-LCD Product Line Project of Tianma (Shanghai) Microelectronics Co. Ltd.	31.72	31.68	7.83
12	轨道交通二号线东延伸工程	East Extension Project of L2	95.50	29.61	17.61
13	日月光半导体一期厂房工程及增资项目	Phase I Workshop Project and Capital Increase Project of ASE Shanghai Co., Ltd.	29.80	27.95	2.93
14	通用汽车增资生产新一代中高级轿	New Generation Medium-High Level Automobile Project of GM	18.38	26.82	8.51
15	上海索广映像有限公司工厂建设项目	Factory Construction Project of Shanghai Sony Vision Co., Ltd.	31.19	23.39	12.42
16	中海工业更新改造	Innovation and Reconstruction Project of China Shipping Industries	10.00	21.69	12.49
17	软件园软件出口基地三期工程	Phase III Project of Software Export Base of Pudong Software Park	23.14	20.39	3.90
18	世博园区世博轴北段及地下空间	North Section of Exposition Axis and Underground Space Project of World Exposition Park	34.67	20.03	12.98
19	银行卡二期土地开发	Phase II Land Development Project of Bank Card Industrial Park	16.00	17.52	1.49
20	机场北通道绿带	Green Belt Project of North Passage of Pudong International Airport	19.62	16.95	15.33
21	高桥石化原油适应性改造工程	Adaptability Alteration Project for Crude Oil of Gaoqiao Petroleum Chemical Co., Ltd.	15.59	15.00	1.00
22	外高桥粮食储备库及码头设施项目	Waigaoqiao Grain Reserve Depot and Wharf Facilities Project	15.47	14.29	2.82
23	中国2010年上海世博会公共活动中心	Public Activity Center for Shanghai World Exposition 2010 in China	22.03	13.50	7.70
24	世博园区世博村工程	Expo Village Project of World Exposition Park	23.18	13.08	9.70

表 3-12 当年建成部分大项目一览表
Major Projects Completed in Current Year
(2008)

单位:万元 (10 000 yuan)

序号 No.	项目名称	Projects	计划总投资 Total Planned Investment	累计完成投资 Accumulated Investment	#2008 年完成投资 Investment Completed in 2008
1	上海环球金融中心	Shanghai World Financial Center	870 700	803 713	207 435
2	天马微电子第4.5代TFT—LCD生产线	The 4.5 Generation TFT-LCD Product Line Project of Tianma (Shanghai) Microelectronics Co. Ltd.	317 150	316 750	78 310
3	银行卡产业园二期土地开发	Phase II Land Development Project of Bank Card Industrial Park	160 000	175 236	14 851
4	由由国际广场	Youyou International Plaza	170 000	162 514	14 126
5	高桥石化原油适应性改造工程	Adaptability Alteration Project for Crude Oil of Gaoqiao Petroleum Chemical Co., Ltd.	155 852	150 000	10 000
6	时代金融中心	Times Financial Center	147 660	147 660	36 481
7	云间绿大地	Willowbrook (Greenhills)	145 930	136 280	8 187
8	财富海景花园	Fortune Seaside Garden	132 494	132 494	3 808
9	中融碧玉蓝天商务综合楼	Zhongrong Jade and Sky Commercial Complex Building	130 000	130 000	41 897
10	未来资产大厦(原合生国际大厦)	Future Capital Mansion (the former Hesheng International Mansion)	102 957	102 957	37 433
11	中国石化三井化工12万吨/年双酚A工程	Annual Yield of 120,000 Tons of Bisphenol A Project of SSMC	100 744	100 742	30 064
12	证大五道口大厦	Zhengda Fifth Crossing Mansion	80 940	71 629	7 485
13	张江新园区研发中心(二期)	R&D Center of New Park in Zhangjiang (Phase II)	70 000	70 200	28 200
14	蓝山小城	Blue Hills	67 607	67 607	9 660
15	昌邑路(荣城路-罗山路)	Changyi Road (Rongcheng Road-Ruoshan Road)	51 000	44 192	20 123
16	日月光封装测试技改设备及安装增资项目	Technical Innovation Equipment for Assembly and Test and Capital Increase Project of ASE Shanghai Co., Ltd.	9 923	29 826	29 826
17	赛科利汽车模具新增模具生产能力增资项目	Capital Increase Project for Production Capacity of New Mold	27 129	27 107	7 865
18	日月光封装测试厂房项目技术改造	Technical Innovation for Work Shop Project of ASE Shanghai Co., Ltd.	7 683	20 929	20 929
19	沪东中华造船液化天然气船(LNG)建造配套	Construction and Supporting Project for LNG Ships of Hudong-Zhonghua Shipping Company	19 841	20 351	964
20	张江生物医药基地研发C区	C Section for R&D Center in Zhangjiang Biological Medicine Base	17 886	18 008	11 843
21	浦明路(浦电路-龙阳路)	Puming Road (Pudian Road-Longyang Road)	28 000	15 485	13 124
22	半岛科技园	Peninsula Science and Technology Park	14 690	14 981	2 734
23	上海高桥石油化工烟气脱硫工程	Project of Sulfur Dioxide and Nitrous Oxide Removal for Flue Gas in Shanghai Gaoqiao	12 768	12 768	9 768

主要统计指标解释

全社会固定资产投资

固定资产投资是国民经济再生产活动的一个重要部分。固定资产投资额是以货币形式表现的在一定时期内建造和购置固定资产的工作量以及与此有关的费用总称。它是反映固定资产投资规模、结构和发展速度的综合性指标。按照现行国家统计制度，全社会固定资产投资包括建设改造、房地产开发、城乡集体经济单位、城乡私人建房和其他经济单位投资。

从1997年起，固定资产投资统计起点为50万元（含50万元）以上项目。

房地产开发投资

指各种登记注册类型的房地产开发公司、商品房建设公司及其他房地产开发法人单位和附属于其他法人单位实际从事房地产开发或经营活动的单位统一开发的包括统代建、拆迁还建的住宅、厂房、仓库、饭店、宾馆、度假村、写字楼、办公楼等房屋建筑物和配套的服务设施，土地开发工程（如道路、给水、排水、供电、供热、通讯、平整场地等基础设施工程）的投资；不包括单纯的土地交易活动。

固定资产投资按国民经济行业分

固定资产投资按国民经济行业分是根据建设项目建成投产后的主要产品或主要用途及社会经济活动性质来确定国民经济行业。一般情况下，一个建设项目或一个企业、事业单位只能属于一种国民经济行业。

固定资产投资按构成分

固定资产投资按构成分是按其工作内容和实现方式来划分的，主要分为建筑安装工程，设备、工具、器具购置，其他费用三个部分。

（1）建筑安装工程（建筑安装工作量）：指各种房屋、建筑物的建造工程和各种设备、装置的安装工程。包括各种房屋建造工程；各种用途设备基础和各种工业窑炉的砌筑工程及金属结构工程；为施工而进行的各种准备工作和临时工程以及完工后的清理工作等；铁路、道路的铺设，矿井的开凿及石油管道的架设等；水利工程；防空地下建筑等特殊工程；列入房屋工程预算内的暖气、卫生、通风、照明、煤气等设备的价值及装设油饰工程；列入建筑工程预算内的各种管道（蒸汽、压缩空气、石油、给排水等管道）、电力、电讯电缆导线等的敷设工程；以及各种机械设备的安装工程；为测定安装工程质量，对设备进行的试运工作；房地产开发单位进行的商品房屋开发建设工程、土地开发工程。

在安装工程中，不包括被安装设备本身的价值。

（2）设备、工具、器具购置：指建设单位或企、事业单位购置或自制的，达到固定资产标准的设备、工具、器具的价值。新建单位及扩建单位的新建车间，按照设计或计划要求购置或自制的全部设备、工具、器具，不论是否达到固定资产标准均计入“设备、工具、器具购置”中。

（3）其他费用：指在固定资产建造和购置过程中发生的，除上述几项内容以外的各种应分摊计入固定资产的费用。

固定资产投资按建设性质分

建设项目的性质一般分为新建、扩建、改建、迁建、恢复。房地产开发单位、农村投资、城镇工矿区私人建房投资不划分建设性质。基本建设按建设项目划分建设性质，更新改造、国有经济中其他固定资产投资及城镇集体投资等按整个企业、事业单位的建设情况确定建设性质。

（1）新建：一般指从无到有“平地起家”开始建设的企业、事业和行政单位或独立的工程。现有企业、事业、行政单位一般不属于新建。但如有的单位原有基础很小，经过建设后新增的固定资产价值超过该企、事业、行政单位原有固定资产价值（原值）三倍以上的也应作为新建。

（2）扩建：指在厂内或其他地点，为扩大原有产品的生产能力（或效益）或增加新的产品生产能力，而增建主要的生产车间（或主要工程）、分厂、独立的生产线。行政、事业单位在原单位增建业务用房（如学校增建教学用房、医院增建门诊部、病房等）也作为扩建。

现有企、事业单位为扩大原有主要产品生产能力或增加新的产品生产能力，增建一个或几个主要生产车间（或主要工程）、分厂，同时进行一些更新改造工程的，也应作为扩建。

（3）改建：指对原有设施进行技术改造或更新（包括相应配套的辅助性生产、生活福利设施），没有增建主要生产车间、分厂等。现有企、事业单位为适应市场变化的需要，而改变企业的主要产品种类（如军工企业转产民品等），或原有产品生产作业线由于各工序（车间）之间能力不平衡，为填平补齐充分发挥原有生产能力而增建不增加本企业主要产品设计能力的车间，也应作为改建。

新增固定资产

新增固定资产又称交付使用的固定资产，是指已经完成建造和购置过程，并已交付生产或使用单位的固定资产价值。新增固定资产是表示固定资产投资成果的价值量指标，也是反映建设进度、计算固定资产投资效果的必要数据。

固定资产交付使用率

固定资产交付使用率又称固定资产运用系数，是指一定时期新增固定资产与同期完成投资额的比率。它反映各个时期固定资产动用速度，衡量建设过程中宏观投资效果的综合性指标。

施工项目

施工项目指报告期内进行过建筑或安装施工活动的项目。凡是报告期内施过工的建设项目，不论施工时间长短，均作为施工项目统计。施工项目个数可以反映一定时期固定资产投资的实际规模，与同期建成投产的建设项目个数相比，可以从建设速度的角度反映固定资产投资的效果。根据建设项目施工活动的不同性质，施工项目又分为：本年正式施工项目、本年收尾项目和以前年度全部停缓建项目。

全部建成投产项目

工业项目指设计文件规定形成生产能力的主体工程及其相应配套的辅助设施全部建成，经负荷试运转，证明具备生产设计规定合格产品的条件，并经过验收鉴定合格或达到竣工验收标准，与生产性工程配套的生活福利设施可以满足近期正常生产的需要，正式移交生产的建设项目。非工业项目指设计文件规定的主体工程和相应的配套工程全部建成，能够发挥设计规定的全部效益，经验收鉴定合格或达到竣工验收标准，正式移交使用的建设项目。

建成投产率

指一定时期内全部建成投产项目个数与同期施工项目个数的比率。该指标是从建设单位建设速度的角度反映投资效果的指标。

EXPLANATORY NOTES TO MAJOR STATISTICAL INDICATORS

Total Investment in Fixed Assets

Investment in Fixed Assets constitutes an important portion of the national economic reproduction. Fixed assets investment is a general term for both the work volume of production and purchase of fixed assets and relevant expenditure, in the form of currency, during a certain period. It is a comprehensive indicator of scale, structure and development speed of fixed assets investment. As stipulated in the current national statistics regulations, the social fixed assets investment includes the investment into infrastructure and reformation, real estate development, urban and rural collective economic bodies, private house construction in urban and rural areas and other economic bodies.

From 1997 on, the fixed assets items only include those with investment of 0.5 million yuan and above.

Investment in Real Estate Development

Investment in Real Estate Development refers to the investment by the real estate development companies, commercial buildings construction companies and other real estate development units of various types of ownership in the construction of house buildings, such as residential buildings, factory buildings, warehouses, hotels, guesthouses, holiday villages, office buildings, and the complementary service facilities and land development projects, such as roads, water supply, water drainage, power supply, heating, telecommunications, land leveling and other projects of infrastructure. It excludes the activities in pure land transactions.

Investment in Fixed Assets by Sector

Investment in Fixed Assets by Sector refers to determining the classification of construction projects by the major products or the purpose of the projects when they are put into production or use, and by the nature of their social economic activities. In general, one project or one enterprise or institution can only be classified into one sector.

Investment in Fixed Assets by Structure

Investment in Fixed Assets by Structure is classified by their contents. It is mainly classified into 3 categories, i. e. construction and installation, purchase of equipment and instrument, and other expenses.

(1) Construction and installation (work volume of construction and installation) refers to the construction of various houses and buildings and installation of various kinds of equipment and instruments. They include construction of various houses; equipment foundations, industrial kilns and stoves, and metal structure work; preparation works for project construction, and clearing up works post project construction; pavement of railways and roads, drilling of mines and putting up of oil pipes; construction of projects of water conservancy; construction of underground air-raid shelters and construction of other special projects; value of equipment for heating, sanitation, ventilation, lighting, gas, painting, etc. that are covered by the budget of housing projects; laying out of various pipelines (for steam, compressed air, petroleum, tap water and sewage) and lines for electric power and for communications; installation of various machinery equipment, testing operation for pre-testing the quality of installation projects, and land and other development work conducted by real estate developers for commercial housing. The value of equipment installed is not included in the value of installation projects.

(2) Purchase of equipment and instruments refers to the total value of equipment, tools, and instruments purchased or self-produced which come up to standards for fixed assets by the construction units or investing enterprises or institutions. Equipment, tools and instruments purchased or self-produced for new workshops by newly established or expanded units are categorized as "purchase of equipment and instruments" no matter whether they come up to the standards for fixed assets.

(3) Other expenses refer to expenses occurring during the construction or purchase of fixed assets other than those mentioned above.

Investment in Fixed Assets by Type of Construction

The construction projects in general can be classified, by the type of construction, into new construction, expansion, reconstruction and construction of living facilities.

(1) New construction in general refers to newly constructed enterprises, institutions, administrative agencies or independent projects from scratch. Construction in the existing enterprises, institutions or agencies is not considered as new construction. In case the assets of the existing unit is quite small, and the value of newly added fixed assets exceeds the original value of assets by three times, the expansion will be considered as new construction.

(2) Reconstruction refers to construction projects by existing enterprises or institutions in innovation or technical transformation of the old facilities (including auxiliary production equipment and welfare facilities). Also considered as reconstruction is the construction of new workshops by the existing enterprises or institutions to change the variety of products to meet the market demand (such as the production of civil products by defence industries), or to bring the designed production capacity into full play through a more balanced production process on production lines.

(3) Expansion refers to construction of new major production workshop, branch factory or independent production line within a factory or in other locations, for the purpose of increasing the production capacity (or improving efficiency) of the original products. Newly constructed houses for the operation of institutions and administrative organizations (such as the newly constructed buildings for teaching in schools, buildings for clinics or wards in hospitals, etc.) are also classified as expansion.

Also included in the expansion are investments by existing enterprises or institutions in building major production line (s) or branch factory (ies) along with some work on innovation, for the purpose of expending the production capacity of original products or producing new products.

Newly Increased Fixed Assets

Newly Increased Fixed Assets, also called fixed assets put into operation, refers to the value of fixed assets that has been put into production or handed over to the production units after the completion of the process of construction and purchase. The newly increased fixed asset is an value indicator of the result of investment. It is also the necessary data for reflecting the construction process and the result of investment in fixed assets.

Rate of Fixed Assets Completed and Put into Operation

Rate of Fixed Assets Completed and Put into Operation, also called the fixed assets-operation ratio, refers to ratio of newly increased fixed assets to total investment completed in the same period, which is a comprehensive indicator, reflecting the development of fixed assets investment and investment efficiency.

Projects under Construction

Projects under Construction refer to projects with construction and installation activities undertaken in the reference period. All projects that have construction activities undertaken during the reference period are reported as projects under construction irrespective of the length of construction work. The number of projects under construction can reflect the actual size of investment in fixed assets during a given period, and when compared with the number of projects completed and put into use during the same period, it demonstrates the results of investment in fixed assets. Depending on the nature of construction activities, projects under construction can also be classified into projects under construction in current year, winding-up projects in current year and stopped or suspended projects in previous years (with preservation work in current year).

Projects Completed and Put into Use

Industrial projects refer to the major projects and accessory facilities completed which result in forming production capacity and have been checked and accepted while the living and welfare facilities have been completed and can ensure normal production and formally put into production. Non-industrial projects refer to the major projects and accessory facilities completed which possess the designed capacity and have been checked, accepted and formally put into production.

Rate of Construction Projects Completed and Put into Use

Rate of Construction Projects Completed and Put into Use refers to the ratio of the number of construction projects completed and put into use in certain period of time to the number of projects under construction in the same period. This reflects the investment efficiency from the perspective of the speed of projects construction.

第四篇 Chapter 4

招商引资

BUSINESS PROMOTION AND FOREIGN-FUND ATTRACTION

表 4-1　历年外商直接投资情况

单位:亿美元

年　份 Year	外商直接投资合同项目 Contracted Projects of Foreign Direct Investment	项 (unit)		
		# 中外合资 Joint-venture	中外合作 Sino-foreign Cooperative	外商独资 Solely Foreigner Funded
1990	28	22	2	4
1991	92	79	4	9
1992	567	467	38	56
1993	924	610	38	275
1994	1 035	547	51	432
1995	838	340	41	455
1996	802	285	38	479
1997	615	132	36	447
1998	554	88	30	435
1999	470	71	18	380
2000	693	109	21	563
2001	880	110	10	758
2002	964	119	14	829
2003	1 563	175	15	1 370
2004	1 688	188	9	1 489
2005	1 734	149	8	1 574
2006	1 446	143	7	1 292
2007	1 254	112	3	1 138
2008	803	90	3	710

注：从 2004 年起,外商直接投资实际到位金额中不包含间接吸收外资。
Note: The actual paid amount of foreign direct investment will not include the indirectly-attracted foreign capital after the year of 2004.

Foreign Direct Investment in Main Years

(USD 100 million)

外商直接投资合同金额 Contracted Value of Foreign Direct Investment	#中外合资 Joint-venture	中外合作 Sino-foreign Cooperative	外商独资 Solely Foreigner Funded	外商直接投资实际到位金额 Capital in Place of Foreign Direct Investment
0.34	0.29	0.01	0.05	0.13
1.01	0.92	0.03	0.06	0.68
13.53	7.28	0.82	2.77	2.49
17.57	13.08	1.53	2.78	4.29
25.93	14.14	4.10	7.32	6.85
32.56	10.47	2.56	17.43	12.81
18.09	5.04	5.84	7.21	14.25
18.00	13.39	0.82	3.79	10.13
27.90	13.77	0.63	2.90	15.37
10.73	2.95	0.55	6.91	5.92
28.84	2.73	0.47	25.63	8.85
20.02	4.51	1.12	14.16	23.04
26.68	5.72	1.36	17.22	18.47
28.75	6.47	0.12	21.19	18.01
32.24	5.05	0.56	26.08	23.78
56.54	7.84	0.38	42.20	31.11
48.42	7.67	0.32	39.46	32.20
49.49	5.08	0.39	41.30	33.06
49.92	5.87	0.12	43.12	34.35

表4-2 外商直接投资合同项目
Number of Contracted Projects of Foreign Direct Investment

单位:个 (unit)

指 标	Indicators	2000	2005	2007	2008	至2008年末累计 Accumulated by the End of 2008
总 计	**Total**	**693**	**1 734**	**1 254**	**803**	**16 967**
按投资方式分	**By Way of Investment**					
中外合资	Joint-venture	109	149	112	90	3 887
中外合作	Sino-foreign Cooperative	21	8	3	3	393
外商独资	Solely Foreigner Funded	563	1 574	1 138	710	12 654
B股企业	B Share		3	1		33
按投资行业分	**By Sector**					
#第二产业	Secondary Industry	168	209	134	78	3 849
#工 业	Industry	167	188	126	75	3 255
第三产业	Tertiary Industry	522	1 524	1 119	725	13 093
#批发零售业	Wholesale and Retail	2	672	605	373	7 185
交通运输、仓储和邮政业	Transportation, Warehousing, Post and Telecommunications	3	18	55	33	657
房地产业	Real Estate	3	25	15	9	313
租赁和商务服务业	Leasing and Business Service		295	258	176	2 378
按总投资规模分	**By Investment Scale**					
1000万美元以上	>USD 10 million	34	59	62	51	989
500~1000万美元	USD 5~10 million	15	51	33	34	466
300~500万美元	USD 3~5 million	14	29	25	15	389
100~300万美元	USD 1~3 million	101	150	144	97	2 108
50~100万美元	USD 0.5~1.0 million	150	153	133	89	2 489
30~50万美元	USD 0.3~0.5 million	70	97	104	62	1 597
30万美元以下	<USD 0.3 million	309	1195	753	455	8 929
按投资国别、地区分	**By Country/Region**					
#中国香港	Hong Kong, China	174	307	299	276	4 707
中国澳门	Macao, China	1	2		2	58
中国台湾	Taiwan, China	40	82	62	32	1 058
日 本	Japan	80	270	130	72	2 385
新加坡	Singapore	41	107	76	51	1 007
韩 国	Republic of Korea	14	80	63	24	499
英 国	United Kingdom	12	35	29	15	313
德 国	Germany	25	52	46	29	437
法 国	France	5	26	9	8	154
荷 兰	the Netherlands	14	24	21	7	202
瑞 士	Switzerland	7	14	9	15	155
美 国	the United States of America	104	146	137	71	2 026
加拿大	Canada	6	19	17	12	264
澳大利亚	Australia	12	22	18	7	257
海外中资集团	Overseas Chinese Group Companies	1				72

注:1. 本表至表12-2由浦东新区经济贸易委员会提供。
2. 当年增资部分不计算项目个数。

Note: 1. The data in from this table to Table 12-2 are provided by Pudong Economic & Trade Commission.
2. The increase of investment in the current year is not listed as new project.

表4-3 外商直接投资合同金额

Contract Value Capital of Foreign Direct Investment

单位:万美元 (USD 10 000)

指标	Indicators	2000	2005	2007	2008	至2008年末累计 Accumulated by the End of 2008
总计	**Total**	**288 376**	**565 369**	**494 930**	**499 237**	**4 565 341**
按投资方式分	**By Way of Investment**					
中外合资	Joint-venture	27 318	78 437	50 755	58 695	1 103 513
中外合作	Sino-foreign Cooperative	4 714	3 771	3 880	1 180	135 450
外商独资	Solely Foreigner Funded	256 295	421 985	412 957	431 216	3 056 776
B股企业	B Share	49	61 176	27 338	8 146	269 602
按投资行业分	**By Sector**					
#第二产业	Secondary Industry	235 421	172 056	108 988	72 418	1 751 118
#工　业	Industry		162 312	108 158	72 220	1 281 753
第三产业	Tertiary Industry	52 896	393 242	385 916	426 841	2 812 241
#批发零售业	Wholesale and Retail		61 919	74 337	76 599	
交通运输、仓储和邮政业	Transportation, Warehousing, Post and Telecommunications		114 776	49 516	52 562	262 273
房地产业	Real Estate		49 390	52 430	50 535	
租赁和商务服务业	Leasing and Business Service		114 149	103 725	127 683	
按总投资规模分	**By Investment Scale**					
1000万美元以上	> USD 10 million	240 825	162 738	112 991	79 875	2 300 275
500~1000万美元	USD 5~10 million	7 311	16 141	4 310	6 366	108 332
300~500万美元	USD 3~5 million	4 561	5 620	3 192	2 694	47 887
100~300万美元	USD 1~3 million	14 252	16 233	11 519	5 393	174 522
50~100万美元	USD 0.5~1.0 million	8 702	6 972	3 844	2 024	78 933
30~50万美元	USD 0.3~0.5 million	2 996	2 464	2 715	1 605	34 269
30万美元以下	< USD 0.3 million	9 729	15 817	3 187	1 753	134 383
当年增资	Capital Increase in Current Year		339 384	353 172	399 527	1 686 740
按投资国别、地区分	**By Country/Region**					
#中国香港	Hong Kong, China	15 543	68 253	107 076	161 362	923 869
中国澳门	Macao, China	20	68		13	6 518
中国台湾	Taiwan, China	1 775	2 795	2 985	1 446	48 173
日　本	Japan	15 513	69 789	30 973	44 166	558 157
新加坡	Singapore	8 135	18 363	36 924	28 714	221 513
韩　国	Republic of Korea	1 574	5 438	8 365	14 027	61 837
英　国	United Kingdom	1 554	6 245	11 469	10 949	88 289
德　国	Germany	6 735	54 020	16 840	5 198	161 492
法　国	France	733	2 531	12 546	13 760	74 647
荷　兰	the Netherlands	3 392	8 424	5 519	30 319	114 991
瑞　士	Switzerland	3 788	1 340	1 307	5 143	36 456
美　国	the United States of America	16 859	41 169	44 524	38 883	543 094
加拿大	Canada	340	1 101	1 119	961	23 120
澳大利亚	Australia	1 400	787	1 080	1 384	18 454
海外中资集团	Overseas Chinese Group Companies	-35				20 657
当年增资	**Capital Increase in Current Year**		**339 384**	**353 172**	**399 527**	**1 686 740**

注：资金负数是当年项目的投资不抵当年增资(减资)的数值。

Note: The negative figures in the table only reflect the investment in projects in this particular year. The increase or decrease of investment is not included.

表4-4 外商直接投资1000万美元以上企业按三次产业分的生产经营情况（2008）

指 标	Indicators	单 位 Unit	合 计 Total
企业单位数	**Enterprises**	**个 unit**	**931**
投资情况(历年)	**Investment (Accumulative)**		
外商实际投资	Actual Foreign Investment	亿美元 USD 100 million	245.56
#外商实际增资额	Actual Investment Increased	亿美元 USD 100 million	86.93
中方实际投资	Actual Chinese Investment	亿元 100 million yuan	789.65
#中方实际增资额	Actual Chinese Investment Increased	亿元 100 million yuan	184.25
企业境外借款投资	Foreign Loan Investment	亿美元 USD 100 million	28.21
#外方股东贷款	Number of Loans of Foreign Stockholders	亿美元 USD 100 million	15.44
生产经营和财务情况(当年)	**Operation and Finance Standing in Current Year**		
营业(销售)收入	Operating (Sales) Income	亿元 100 million yuan	6 754.89
营业(销售)税金	Operating (Sales) Tax	亿元 100 million yuan	78.24
实缴税金总额	Total Tax Paid Up	亿元 100 million yuan	248.29
利润总额	Total Profit	亿元 100 million yuan	359.41
可供所有者分配的利润	Distributable Profit	亿元 100 million yuan	283.40
年末资产总值	Total Value of Assets (Year End)	亿元 100 million yuan	9 878.67
#流动资产	Circulating Assets	亿元 100 million yuan	5 142.55
固定资产	Fixed Assets	亿元 100 million yuan	2 295.17
年末负债合计	Total Liabilities (Year End)	亿元 100 million yuan	5 890.70
#流动负债	Circulating Liability	亿元 100 million yuan	4 272.29
长期负债	Long-term Liability	亿元 100 million yuan	1 368.49
商品进出口和外汇收支情况(当年)	**Commodities Imported and Exported & Foreign Exchange in Current Year**		
外汇总收入	Total Foreign Exchange Revenue	亿美元 USD 100 million	450.35
外汇总支出	Total Foreign Exchange Expenditure	亿美元 USD 100 million	333.90
年末外汇结存	Foreign Exchange Balance (Year End)	亿美元 USD 100 million	24.00
从业人员和劳动报酬情况(当年)	**Employees and Wages in Current Year**		
年末从业人员	Employed Persons (Year End)	人 person	353 797
#中方人员	Employed Persons (Chinese)	人 person	345 456
年从业人员工资总额	Annual Wages of Employed Persons	万元 100 00 yuan	3 460 500
#中方人员	Employed Persons (Chinese)	万元 100 00 yuan	2 985 452

FIEs of Over USD 10 Million by Primary, Secondary and Tertiary Industries

第二产业 Secondary Industry	工业 Industry	建筑业 Construction	第三产业 Tertiary Industry	#交通运输、仓储和邮政业 Transportation, Warehousing and Post Service	批发、零售及餐饮业 Wholesale, Retail and Catering	房地产业 Real Estate	租赁和商务服务业 Lease and Commercial Services
355	**340**	**9**	**576**	**57**	**104**	**127**	**131**
98.47	97.88	0.59	147.09	17.56	10.80	51.98	21.31
35.64	35.49	0.15	51.29	2.57	3.58	18.86	11.36
295.22	294.14	1.08	494.43	219.23	15.41	112.70	10.90
73.54	73.54		110.71	19.74	2.12	47.77	1.12
21.72	21.72		6.49		0.99	5.43	0.03
11.07	11.07		4.37		0.54	3.75	0.03
3 280.25	3 220.73	35.94	3 474.64	987.54	1 367.96	140.13	523.73
25.91	25.05	0.84	52.33	19.70	2.49	7.09	7.07
121.43	119.6	1.23	126.86	43.32	17.70	14.32	22.03
155.06	151.32	1.44	204.35	22.52	33.76	57.11	49.02
67.86	65.45	1.12	215.54	125.21	12.17	26.21	33.15
2 741.74	2 606.09	74.43	7 136.93	2 258.18	707.59	1 349.29	1 085.28
1 511.89	1 433.33	67.12	3 630.66	683.66	456.24	975.78	453.54
810.00	758.63	2.76	1 485.17	1 050.09	73.84	169.48	94.24
1 502.29	1 419.34	57.46	4 388.41	1 365.12	492.32	722.00	469.42
1 254.37	1 180.54	54.98	3 017.92	914.73	338.80	388.96	378.79
226.36	217.74	1.97	1 142.13	444.34	11.90	277.43	76.95
330.29	330.27	0.01	120.06	28.96	65.36	0.33	11.25
189.11	189.04	0.01	144.79	56.26	66.41	0.58	9.54
9.57	9.49	0.08	14.43	1.91	2.05	0.21	2.31
161 521	157 638	1 610	192 276	58 512	36 693	9 283	23 012
157 024	153 384	1 367	188 432	58 099	36 155	9 062	21 822
1 268 108	1 228 543	27 553	2 192 392	557 363	265 026	77 024	426 353
1 138 731	1 114 664	12 166	1 846 721	532 350	227 751	66 496	316 607

表4-5 当年签约投资2000万美元以上的外商投资企业

FIEs with Current Year Contracted Investment Over USD 20 Million (2008)

单位:万美元 (USD 10 000)

序号 No.	单位名称	Enterprises	国别(地区)	Country/Region	总投资 Total Investment	外商合同投资 Contracted Foreign Investment
1	上海祥大房地产发展有限公司	Shanghai Xiangda Real Estate Development Co., Ltd.	日本	Japan	41 953	6 269
2	新开发联合创业投资企业	New Development United Business Holdings Enterprise	英属维尔京群岛	British Virgin Islands	20 838	208
3	上海嘉东仓储有限公司	Shanghai Jiadong Storage Co., Ltd.	香港	Hong Kong	9 900	4 476
4	上海万庆仓储有限公司	Shanghai Wanqing Storage Co., Ltd.	巴巴多斯	Barbados	9 472	4 330
5	上海传富网络科技有限公司	Shanghai Fortunetree Network and Science Co., Ltd.	香港	Hong Kong	6 800	3 000
6	申能集团财务有限公司	Finance Co., Ltd of Shenergy Group	比利时	Belgium	6 492	649
7	三仁投资(中国)有限公司	Sunline Investment (China) Co., Ltd.	香港	Hong Kong	6 000	6 000
8	启明创业投资企业	Qiming Venture Partners Enterprise	香港	Hong Kong	4 200	2 800
9	艾里逊变速箱(上海)有限公司	Allison Gearbox (Shanghai) Co., Ltd.	香港	Hong Kong	3 000	1 200
10	斯考根(中国)投资有限公司	Skaugen (China) Holding Co., Ltd.	新加坡	Singapore	3 000	3 000
11	罗氏(中国)投资有限公司	Roche (China) Investment Co., Ltd.	瑞士	Switzerland	3 000	3 000
12	上海普川仓储有限公司	Shanghai Puchuan Storage Co., Ltd.	巴巴多斯	Barbados	2 980	1 200
13	一兆韦德(上海)健身管理有限公司	Tera Weider (Shanghai) Wellness Management Co., Ltd.	香港	Hong Kong	2 980	2 000
14	马良(上海)管理咨询有限公司	Maliang (Shanghai) Management and Consultation Co., Ltd.	香港	Hong Kong	2 980	2 000
15	远壮信息技术(上海)有限公司	Yuanzhuang Information Technologies (Shanghai) Co., Ltd.	香港	Hong Kong	2 900	2 500
16	农银汇理基金管理有限公司	ABC-CA Fund Management Co., Ltd.	法国	France	2 745	915
17	荷皇橙派货运代理(上海)有限公司	TNT Cargo Agent (Shanghai) Co., Ltd.	荷兰	The Netherlands	2 642	1 321
18	巴克莱信息技术(上海)有限公司	Barclay Information Technologies (Shanghai) Co., Ltd.	英国	England	2 607	1 043
19	威康健身管理咨询(上海)有限公司	Will's Fitness Management and Consultation (Shanghai) Co., Ltd.	英属维尔京群岛	British Virgin Islands	2 500	1 000
20	分众(中国)信息技术有限公司	Focus Media (China) Information Technologies Co., Ltd	香港	Hong Kong	2 500	1 000
21	联合包裹物流(上海)有限公司	UPS Logistics (Shanghai) Co., Ltd.	香港	Hong Kong	2 388	1 000
22	丰合仓储(上海)有限公司	Fenghe Storage (Shanghai) Co., Ltd.	香港	Hong Kong	2 325	1 162
23	富美实(上海)设备租赁有限公司	FMC (Shanghai) Equipment Leasing Co., Ltd.	美国	The United States	2 000	800
24	欣润(上海)生物药业有限公司	Xinrun (Shanghai) Biological Medicine Co., Ltd.	英属维尔京群岛	British Virgin Islands	2 000	1 000
25	科誉高瞻融资租赁(中国)有限公司	Q-TZG Financial Leasing (China) Co., Ltd.	香港	Hong Kong	2 000	2 000

注:本表由浦东新区经济贸易委员会提供。
Note: The data in this table are provided by Pudong Economic & Trade Commission.

表4-6　外商直接投资实际到位金额
Capital in Place of Foreign Direct Investment

单位:万美元　　　　　　　　　　　　　　　　　　(USD 10 000)

指　标	Indicators	2005	2006	2007	2008
总　计	**Total**	**311 142**	**321 957**	**330 615**	**343 518**
按投资方式分	**By Way of Investment**				
#中外合资	Joint -venture	105 486	90 706	86 559	78 867
中外合作	Sino -foreign Cooperative	14 092	1 211	1 500	7 709
外商独资	Solely Foreigner Funded	191 564	230 040	242 556	256 942
按投资行业分	**By Sector**				
第二产业	Secondary Industry	87 759	88 245	38 592	73 116
#工　业	Industry	86 582	87 133	37 992	73 001
第三产业	Tertiary Industry	223 383	233 712	292 023	270 399
#批发和零售业餐饮业	Wholesale and Retail Catering	28 059	37 319	33 072	44 009
房地产业	Real Estate	50 194	64 779	125 335	65 769
租赁和商务服务业	Leasing and Business Service	57 667	83 996	88 298	66 270
按投资国别、地区分	**By Country/Region**				
#中国香港	Hong Kong,China	23 088	61 458	80 724	84 752
日　本	Japan	72 377	18 664	37 788	26 982
新加坡	Singapore	8 996	7 697	15 349	24 807
英　国	United Kingdom	1 889	3 891	10 715	6 749
德　国	Germany	21 414	49 914	7 065	5 205
法　国	France	3 095	1 301	11 602	10 664
荷　兰	the Netherlands	11 414	6 629	8 507	7 211
开曼群岛	Cayman Islands	27 761	40 733	6 895	38 470
英属维尔京群岛	British Virgin Islands	93 636	63 556	78 703	60 783
美　国	the United States of America	28 238	25 605	26 084	34 654
萨摩亚	Samoa	695	10 684	4 932	6 970

表4-7 内资企业工商注册情况
Registered Domestic Enterprises

指 标	Indicators	单 位 Unit	2007	2008
期末实有注册企业	**Actual Registered Enterprises at End of Term**	**个 unit**	**12 703**	**12 423**
第一产业	Primary Industry	个 unit	126	143
第二产业	Secondary Industry	个 unit	2 930	2 807
制造业	Manufacturing	个 unit	2 516	2 294
建筑业	Construction	个 unit	414	460
第三产业	Tertiary Industry	个 unit	9 647	9 473
#交通运输、仓储和邮政业	Transportation, Warehousing and Post Service	个 unit	485	566
批发和零售业	Wholesale and Retail	个 unit	4 569	4 326
金融业	Banking	个 unit	545	490
房地产业	Real Estate	个 unit	780	805
期末实际注册资金总额	**Actual Total Registered Capital at End of Term**	**亿元 (100 million yuan)**	**2 575.52**	**2 736.14**
第一产业	Primary Industry	亿元 (100 million yuan)	5.94	4.51
第二产业	Secondary Industry	亿元 (100 million yuan)	504.95	679.78
制造业	Manufacturing	亿元 (100 million yuan)	347.14	364.32
建筑业	Construction	亿元 (100 million yuan)	157.81	175.65
第三产业	Tertiary Industry	亿元 (100 million yuan)	2 064.63	2 051.85
#交通运输、仓储和邮政业	Transportation, Warehousing and Post Service	亿元(100 million yuan)	250.70	185.41
批发和零售业	Wholesale and Retail	亿元(100 million yuan)	457.04	329.97
金融业	Banking	亿元 (100 million yuan)	70.69	35.62
房地产业	Real Estate	亿元 (100 million yuan)	382.78	451.58

表4-8 市外在沪投资企业情况
Investment in Shanghai by Enterprises Registered in Other Provinces and Municipalities

指 标	Indicators	企业数(个) Number of Enterprises (unit)		注册资金(亿元) Registered Capital (100 million yuan)	
		2007	2008	2007	2008
总 计	**Total**	**1 573**	**1 360**	**107.83**	**108.86**
按行业分	**By Sector**				
工 业	Industry	49	26	35.63	3.96
国内商业餐饮业	Domestic Commerce and Catering	850	814	19.80	43.66
进出口贸易业	Import and Export	64	61	1.46	4.15
科技咨询业	Scientific and Technical Consultation	285	261	4.80	9.75
投资类企业	Investing Enterprises	290	182	43.25	43.80
房地产业	Real Estate	28	14	2.47	3.51
其 他	Others	7	2	0.42	0.03
按地区分	**By Province**				
#北京市	Beijing	67	66	39.82	10.81
江苏省	Jiangsu Province	268	240	8.56	11.20
浙江省	Zhejiang Province	261	201	21.06	15.77
安徽省	Anhui Province	131	128	3.21	2.73
福建省	Fujian Province	61	82	3.18	2.03
江西省	Jiangxi Province	57	52	1.10	1.29
山东省	Shandong Province	71	56	4.41	4.75
广东省	Guangdong Province	75	59	4.85	28.82
按注册资金分	**By Registered Capital**				
1 000 万元以下	< 10 million yuan	1 370	1 188	18.76	16.39
1 000 ~ 3 000 万元	10 ~ 30 million yuan	139	99	16.22	13.08
3 000 ~ 5 000 万元	30 ~ 50 million yuan	28	22	8.92	7.05
5 000 万元以上	> 50 million yuan	36	51	63.93	72.34

表4-9　私营企业基本情况
Statistics of Private Enterprises
(2008)

指　标	Indicators	户　数（户）Number of Enterprises (unit)	投资人数（人）Number of Investors (person)	雇工人数（人）Employed Persons (person)	注册资金（万元）Registered Capital (10 000 yuan)
总　计	**Total**	**35 177**	**82 024**	**409 983**	**13 317 922**
农、林、牧、渔业	Farming, Forestry, Animal Husbandry and Fishery	291	524	2 018	26 511
采掘业	Mining and Quarrying	1	2		50
制造业	Manufacturing	7 017	15 567	146 488	1 282 655
建筑业	Construction	902	2 327	25 822	428 471
交通运输业、仓储和邮政业	Transportation, Warehousing and Post Service	985	2 457	15 198	314 266
信息传输、计算机服务和软件服务	Information Transmission, Computer Service and Computer Software	1 758	4 782	19 332	513 762
批发零售贸易业	Wholesale and Retail	12 538	28 369	92 255	3 297 307
住宿和餐饮业	Catering	1 077	2 181	17 533	77 841
居民服务和其他服务业	Resident Service and Other Services	1 298	2 422	8 379	47 329
房地产	Real Estate	1 334	3 009	18 876	1 255 524
其　他	Others	7 976	20 384	64 082	6 074 206

注：本表至表4－10数据由工商局资料整理。
Note: This table to Table 4－10 are a summary of the data provided by the Administration for Industry and Commerce.

表4-10　个体工商户基本情况
Self -Employment Business
(2008)

指　标	Indicators	户　数（户）Number of Enterprises (unit)	从业人数（人）Employed persons (person)	注册资金（万元）Registered Capital (10 000 yuan)
总　计	**Total**	**35 496**	**36 734**	**41 279**
农、林、牧、渔	Farming, Forestry, Animal Husbandry and Fishery	2	2	6
制造业	Manufacuring	145	147	158
建筑业	Construction	46	48	65
交通运输业、仓储业	Transportation and Warehousing	362	368	987
批发零售贸易业、住宿和餐饮业	Wholesale, Retail and Catering Businesses	4 826	4 892	6 944
批发零售贸易业	Wholesale and Retail	4 539	4 570	6 167
住宿和餐饮业	Catering	287	322	777
居民服务和其他服务业	Resident Service and Other Services	3 954	4 336	5 449
其　他	Others	26 161	26 941	27 670

主要统计指标解释

外商直接投资

外商直接投资是指外国企业和经济组织或个人(包括华侨、港澳台胞以及我国在境外注册的企业)按我国有关政策、法规,用现汇、实物、技术等在我国境内开办外商独资企业、与我国境内的企业或经济组织共同举办中外合资经营企业、合作经营企业或合作开发资源的投资(包括外商投资收益的再投资)以及企业投资总额内直接投资者对企业的贷款,即外方股东贷款(需在报告期内将相应合同及贷款协议报商务部备案核查)。

合同投资额

是指经有关部门批准的我方与外商正式签订的合同规定的可使用的贷款额、外商投资额和中方对外发行债券、股票总值,以及"补偿贸易"外商提供的设备价款,"国际租赁"境外出租人提供的设备等价款总值。

外商实际投资额

是指按合同(章程)规定,外商以现金、实物及专有技术等工业产权计价的全部实缴资本额,包括经有关部门批准,外商用于扩大再生产、发展企业规模或补充基本建设资金不足而投入的追加资金。外商的实缴资本额一律折成美元计算。

EXPLANATORY NOTES TO MAJOR STATISTICAL INDICATORS

Foreign Direct Investment

Foreign Direct Investment refers to the investments made inside China by foreign enterprises and economic organizations or individuals (including overseas Chinese, compatriots in Hong Kong, Macao and Chinese enterprises registered abroad) , in line with the relevant policies and laws of China, for the establishment of wholly foreign-owned enterprises, and joint ventures or development projects launched in China (including re-investment of profits from foreign businesses) , and the funds that enterprises borrow from abroad in the total investment of projects which are approved by the relevant departments of the governments and the loans from the direct investors within the total investment of the projects, i. e. , foreign shareholders´ loans. (The related contracts and loans agreements in the report period should be filed with the Ministry of Commerce)

Agreed (Contracted) Investment

Agreed (Contracted) Investment includes usable loans which are approved by government departments and with contracts signed formally by Chinese units and foreign investors, investment of foreigners, total value of bonds and stocks issued in international market by Chinese units, the value of equipment provided by foreign investors for compensation trade, the value of equipment which are leased from foreign firms, etc.

Actual Investment of Foreign Investors

refers to all foreign investors paid-in capital, in cash, in kind or in special technique, based on contracts, which includes the additional funds used for extensional reproduction, expanding enterprise scale or complements to capital construction. All the foreigners paid-in capital is measured by or converted to US dollars.

第五篇

Chapter 5

农 业

AGRICULTURE

SHANGHAI PUDONG NEW AREA STATISTICAL YEARBOOK

2009 / 上海浦东新区统计年鉴

表5-1　主要年份农村户数、人口和劳动力
Rural Households, Population and Workforce in Main Years

指　标	Indicators	单　位 Unit	1990	1993	2000	2005	2007	2008
户　数	Households	万户 10 000 households	15.74	14.67	13.67	12.67	11.19	10.82
人　口	Population	万人 10 000 persons	47.00	42.37	36.82	35.57	32.45	31.36
劳动力使用	Workforce	万人 10 000 persons	27.70	23.70	19.86	19.66	16.99	14.37
#农　业	Agriculture	人 person	68 339	48 325	40 430	16 725	6 772	6 238
工　业	Industry	人 person	141 352	123 940	84 042	107 767	103 089	85 813
建筑业	Construction	人 person	7 723	6 552	5 793	7 499	6 482	5 616
运输、仓储及邮电业	Transportation, Warehousing, Post and Telecommunications	人 person	4 363	2 616	3 631	6 276	7 078	6 736
批发零售贸易、餐饮业	Wholesale/Retail/ Catering	人 person	3 633	4 715	7 748	9 542	10 989	10 068
外出劳动力	Workforce to Other Places	人 person	33 603	31 508	35 098	24 316	26 030	22 380
外省市流入劳动力	Total Non-PNA Workforce	人 person	15 262	44 418	91 268	265 223	443 912	283 239
第一产业	Primary Industry	人 person	2 828	4 190	14 743	16 453	20 233	9 688
第二产业	Secondary Industry	人 person	11 846	36 097	52 715	184 437	285 187	167 115
第三产业	Tertiary Industry	人 person	588	4 131	23 810	64 333	138 492	106 436

注：表中涉及的户数、人口和劳动力是指居住在农村地区的本市户籍人口。

Note: The number of households, population and labor force involved in this table are referred to those that live in the rural area and are registered in Shanghai.

表5-2 农业用地面积
Area of Farm Land

单位:公顷 (hectare)

指 标	Indicators	2000	2005	2007	2008
农业用地合计	**Total Area of Farm Land**	**15 151**	**14 177**	**12 726**	**12 374**
园地面积	Area of Garden	452	43	40	40
#竹园面积	Area of Bamboo Garden	103	43	40	40
林地面积	Area of Forest Land	718	4 245	3 632	3 521
#苗圃面积	Area of Nursery Garden	173	851	690	646
果园地面积	Area of Orchard	213	489	480	456
渔业养殖面积	Area of Aquatic Farm	1 315	1 040	1 025	1 019
内陆水域养殖面积	Area of Aquatic Farm in Landlocked Waters	1 315	1 040	1 025	1 019
耕地面积	Area of Cultivated Land	12 666	8 849	8 029	7 794
水 田	Paddy Field	11 239	8 022	7 374	7 182
旱 田	Dry Field	1 427	827	655	612

表5-3 主要年份耕地面积增减情况
Increase and Decrease of Cultivated Land in Main Years

单位:公顷 (hectare)

指 标	Indicators	2000	2005	2007	2008
年初耕地面积	Cultivated Area(Year Beginning)	12 799	9 483	8 287	8 029
当年增加	Increase in Current Year			14	
当年减少	Decrease in Current Year	133	634	272	235
年末耕地面积	Cultivated Area (Year End)	12 666	8 849	8 029	7 794

表5-4　各镇耕地面积
Cultivated Area by Town

单位:公顷　(hectare)

镇 Town		2007年末耕地面积 Cultivated Area (End of 2007)	2008年净减少耕地面积 Net Decrease in Cultivated Area in 2008	2008年末耕地面积 Cultivated Area (End of 2008)	水　田 Paddy Field	旱　田 Dry Field
总　计	**Total**	**8 028.9**	**234.7**	**7 794.2**	**7 181.9**	**612.3**
川沙新镇	Chuansha New Town	2 614.1	1.8	2 612.3	2 490.6	121.7
高桥镇	Gaoqiao Town	280.9	5.3	275.6	241.9	33.7
北蔡镇	Beicai Town	373.9		373.9	320.9	53.0
合庆镇	Heqing Town	929.3	36.6	892.7	815.4	77.3
唐　镇	Tangzhen Town	336.0	54.5	281.5	255.3	26.2
曹路镇	Caolu Town	808.0	101.5	706.5	677.3	29.2
金桥镇	Jinqiao Town	21.7		21.7	17.1	4.6
高行镇	Gaohang Town	324.2		324.2	253.7	70.5
高东镇	Gaodong Town	566.9		566.9	521.4	45.5
张江镇	Zhangjiang Town	797.7		797.7	720.5	77.2
三林镇	Sanlin Town	926.6	35.0	891.6	818.2	73.4
农　场	Farm	26.1		26.1	26.1	
棉种场	Cotton Farm	23.5		23.5	23.5	

表5-5 主要年份农业总产值
Gross Output Value of Agriculture in Main Years

单位:万元 (10 000 yuan)

指 标	Indicators	1990	1993	2000	2005	2007	2008
按1990年不变价格计算	**At the Constant Price of 1990**						
总 计	**Total**	**55 318**	**46 604**	**61 474**	**41 081**	**35 616**	**34 075**
种植业	Planting	24 015	21 762	29 691	24 310	21 220	20 945
林 业	Forestry	234	101	615	5 833	4 299	3 740
牧 业	Animal Husbandry	29 528	23 095	28 289	8 265	7 426	6 743
渔 业	Fishery	1 541	1 646	2 879	2 673	2 671	2 647
按当年价格计算	**At Current Year Price**						
总 计	**Total**	**55 318**	**69 277**	**125 732**	**116 248**	**116 509**	**121 850**
种植业	Planting	24 015	31 544	59 584	66 809	68 312	72 596
林 业	Forestry	234	136	1 279	25 424	20 251	19 612
牧 业	Animal Husbandry	29 528	34 608	60 837	19 488	23 711	24 863
渔 业	Fishery	1 541	2 989	4 032	4 527	4 235	4 779
构 成(%)	**Composition(%)**						
总 计	**Total**	**100.0**	**100.0**	**100.0**	**100.0**	**100.0**	**100.0**
种植业	Planting	43.4	45.5	47.4	57.5	58.6	59.6
林 业	Forestry	0.4	0.2	1.0	21.9	17.4	16.1
牧 业	Animal Husbandry	53.4	50.0	48.4	16.8	20.4	20.4
渔 业	Fishery	2.8	4.3	3.2	3.8	3.6	3.9

表5-6 各镇农业总产值
Gross Output Value of Agriculture by Town
(2008)

单位:万元 (10 000 yuan)

指 标	Indicators	农业总产值(按现行价格计算) Gross Output Value of Agriculture (at Current Price)	种植业 Planting	林 业 Forestry	牧 业 Animal Husbandry	渔 业 Fishery
总 计	**Total**	**121 850**	**72 596**	**19 612**	**24 863**	**4 779**
川沙新镇	Chuansha New Town	37 663	22 029	8 172	5 414	2 048
高桥镇	Gaoqiao Town	1 926	1 379	515		32
北蔡镇	Beicai Town	623	558			65
合庆镇	Heqing Town	5 627	3 526		1 471	630
唐 镇	Tangzhen Town	2 548	2 420	8		120
曹路镇	Caolu Town	13 102	8 392	378	4 087	245
金桥镇	Jinqiao Town	1 310	658	588		64
高行镇	Gaohang Town	717	717			
高东镇	Gaodong Town	1 808	929	823		56
张江镇	Zhangjiang Town	8 885	8 554	157		174
三林镇	Sanlin Town	2 905	2 107	610		188
其 他	Others	44 736	21 327	8 361	13 891	1 157

表5-7 各镇粮食和蔬菜作物播种面积和产量
Sown Area and Output of Grain Crops and Vegetables by Town (2008)

指 标 Indicators		粮食播种面积(公顷) Sown Area (hectare)	粮食总产量(不包括大豆)(吨) Total Output of Grain Crops (Soybean Not Included in Grain Crops) (ton)	夏 粮 Summer Harvested	秋 粮 Autumn Harvested	粮食单位面积产量(千克/公顷) Yield Per Unit (kg/hectare)	蔬菜播种面积(公顷) Sown Area of Vegetables (hectare)	蔬菜总产量(吨) Total Output of Vegetables (ton)
总 计	**Total**	**1 581**	**12 208**	**2 575**	**9 633**	**37 936**	**5 271**	**212 100**
川沙新镇	Chuansha New Town	856	6 738	1 140	5 598	7 871	1 980	65 294
高桥镇	Gaoqiao Town						338	8 068
北蔡镇	Beicai Town						54	3 718
合庆镇	Heqing Town	149	1 124	236	888	7 544	589	15 124
唐 镇	Tangzhen Town	92	674	163	511	7 326	192	4 600
曹路镇	Caolu Town	229	1 786	511	1 275	7 799	518	37 460
金桥镇	Jinqiao Town						149	2 136
高行镇	Gaohang Town						147	4 018
高东镇	Gaodong Town						78	6 940
张江镇	Zhangjiang Town	255	1 886	525	1 361	7 396	283	7 420
三林镇	Sanlin Town						239	7 273
农民自种	Farmer						704	50 049

表5-8 主要农产品产量
Output of Main Farm Products

指 标	Indicators	单 位 Unit	2005	2007	2008
粮食作物	Grain Crops	吨 ton	13 671	12 528	12 208
夏熟作物	Summer Harvested	吨 ton	1 303	1 861	2 575
#大 麦	Barley	吨 ton			
小 麦	Wheat	吨 ton	1 064	1 861	2 575
秋熟作物	Autumn Harvested	吨 ton	12 368	10 667	9 633
#单季晚稻	Single-Season Late Harvested Rice	吨 ton	10 580	10 549	9 606
油菜籽	Rapeseed	吨 ton	89	8	8
蔬 菜	Vegetables	万吨 10 000 tons	30.09	23.38	21.21
西甜瓜	Watermelons	万吨 10 000 tons	2.18	1.85	1.54
水果产量	Output of Fruits	吨 ton	4 219	4 560	4 074
#柑 桔	Mandarin Oranges	吨 ton	607	577	372
生 梨	Pears	吨 ton	274	264	245
葡 萄	Grapes	吨 ton	727	895	816
桃 子	Peaches	吨 ton		1 660	2 120
生猪饲养数	Stock of Hogs	万头 10 000 in number	16.72	13.99	13.43
生猪出栏数	Hogs on Market	万头 10 000 in number	8.80	8.28	7.38
猪肉产量	Pork Output	万吨 10 000 tons	0.77	0.72	0.65
牛奶产量	Milk Output	万吨 10 000 tons	1.27	0.85	0.90
家禽出栏数	Poultry on Market	万羽 10 000 in number	24.28	23.86	21.01
鲜蛋产量	Output of Fresh Eggs	万吨 10 000 tons	0.17	0.05	0.05
水产品产量	Output of Aquatic Products	万吨 10 000 tons	0.23	0.26	0.22
#淡水产品	Fresh Water Products	万吨 10 000 tons	0.23	0.26	0.22

表5-9 农业企业基本情况
Agricultural Enterprises

指标	Indicators	单位 Unit	2006	2007	2008
农业企业数	Number of Agricultural Enterprises	个 Unit	196	205	192
年末从业人数	Number of Employed Persons at Year End	人 person	4 263	4 438	4 211
#女性人数	Number of Female Employees	人 person	1 732	1 770	1 695
实收资本	Paid-in Capital	万元 10 000 yuan	68 265	69 064	64 892
全年营业收入	Annual Operating Income	万元 10 000 yuan	54 006	56 018	54 912
#主营业务收入	Income from Main Businesses	万元 10 000 yuan	53 121	54 568	54 085
年末资产总计	Total Assets at Year End	万元 10 000 yuan	149 620	152 185	147 634

表5-10 农业生产资料使用情况
Utilization of Agricultural Means of Production

指标	Indicators	单位 Unit	2006	2007	2008
商品有机肥施用面积	Application Area of Commodity Organic Fertilizers	公顷 hectare	1 745	1 950	2 260
商品有机肥施用量	Application Amount of Commodity Organic Fertilizers	吨 ton	3 284	3 680	4 235
化肥施用面积	Application Area of Fertilizers	公顷 hectare	6 969	6 774	6 073
化肥施用量	Application Amount of Fertilizers	吨 ton	9 925	9 518	8 958
农药施用面积	Application Area of Pesticide	公顷 hectare	7 386	7 105	6 863
农药施用量	Application Amount of Pesticide	吨 ton	129	122	114
农用塑料薄膜使用量	Utilization of Agricultural Plastic Film	吨 ton	1 178	1 150	1 197
#地膜使用量	Utilization of Plastic Film	吨 ton	210	207	226
地膜覆盖面积	Coverage of Plastic Film	公顷 hectare	1 627	1 589	1 384

表5-11 农业机械拥有量
Farm Machinery Holding

指 标	Indicators	单 位 Unit	2005	2007	2008
农业机械总动力	**Total Power of Farm Machinery**	**千瓦 kw**	**18 584**	**15 551**	**16 174**
每公顷耕地拥有动力	Power Per Hectare	千瓦 kw	2.10	1.94	2.08
每万公顷耕地拥有拖拉机	Tractors Per 10 000 Hectare	台 set	295	310	331
#耕作机械动力合计	Total Power of Farm Machinery	千瓦 kw	7 591	6 977	7 025
大、中型拖拉机	Large/Medium Tractors	台 set	285	148	150
		千瓦 kw	7 467	3 890	4 099
手扶拖拉机	Walking Tractors	台 set	97	133	108
		千瓦 kw	425	582	472
排灌机械动力合计	Total Power of Drainage and Irrigation Machinery	千瓦 kw	5 534	4 215	4 504
种植机械动力合计	Total Power of Cultivation	千瓦 kw	183	243	293
植物保护机械动力合计	Total Power of Crop Protection Machinery	千瓦 kw	432	587	706
#机动喷雾器	Motorized Sprayers	台 set	353	319	327
		千瓦 kw	432	587	652
收获机械动力合计	Total Power of Harvest Machinery	千瓦 kw	713	866	1 338
#联合收割机	Combines	台/千瓦 set/kw	85/688	42/756	30/1 243
农产品加工机械动力合计	Power of Farm Processing Machinery	千瓦 kw	1 060	458	461
运输机械动力合计	Power of Transport Machinery	千瓦 kw	1 874	424	558
#农用载重汽车	Trucks for Agricultural Use	辆 unit	30	5	1
渔用机动船	Motorized Fishing Boats	艘 in number	23		
拖拉机	Tractors	台 set	97	133	108
积肥机械动力合计	Power of Manure-Collecting Machinery	千瓦 kw	183	186	186
畜牧机械动力合计	Power of Animal Husbandry Machinery	千瓦 kw	183	124	179
渔业机械动力合计	Total Power of Fishery Machinery	千瓦 kw	782	849	465
蔬菜机械动力合计	Total Power of Vegetable Machinery	千瓦 kw	624	368	158

表5-12 农田水利建设情况
Construction of Farmland Water Conservancy

指 标	Indicators	单 位 Unit	2005	2007	2008
有效灌溉面积	Effectively Irrigated Area	公顷 hectare	5 125	4 228.4	2 139.33
本年实灌面积	Actually Irrigated Area	公顷 hectare	1 271	1 167.5	1 858.93
当年新增改善灌溉面积	Increased and Improved Irrigated Area (Current Year)	公顷 hectare	224	50	97.43
旱涝保收面积	Ensured Area from Drought and Flood	公顷 hectare	1 271	1 168	1 120
易涝面积	Area Subjected to Flood	公顷 hectare	1 447	1 447	2 117
水 闸	Dams	座 unit	28	28	12
堤 防	Dikes	公里 km	129.14	120.61	407.15
#郊区海塘	Rural/Suburban Sea Wall	公里 km	59.02	55.30	55.30
江 堤	Embankment	公里 km	70.12	65.31	62.31
围垦面积	Enclosed Tideland for Cultivation	公顷 hectare	3 755	3 755	3 755
泵站改造	Pump Houses Transformed	座/台套/千瓦 unit /set /kw	2/2/22.0	1/1/15.0	
小机口新增	Small Machinery Newly Increased	座/台套/千瓦 unit /set /kw	12/17/123.5	2/2/13.0	8/9/57.5
新增排涝泵站	Newly Built Pump Houses for Draining Water-logging Fields	座/台套/千瓦 unit /set /kw			2/4/33
新建排涝涵洞	Newly Built Culvert for Draining Water-logging Fields	座/米 unit /meter	10/717	42/1 655	121/6 509
改造地下渠道	Underground Irrigation Ditch Reformed	公里 km	6.14	5.90	4.61
改造渡槽倒虹吸	Siphon Aqueduct Transformed	条/米 unit/meter	25/426	11/283	7/157

注：本表至表5-13由浦东新区环保局提供。
Note: The data in from this table to Table 5-13 are provided by Pudong Environmental Protection Bureau.

表5-13 历年农田水利工程投资
Investment in Farmland Water Conservancy Projects in Main Years (1990~2008)

单位:万元 (10 000 yuan)

年 份 Year	合 计 Total	国家投资 State-invested	乡村自筹 Funded by Villages	乡村自筹所占比重(%) Percentage of Investment Funded by Villages(%)
1990	1 363.74	668.75	694.99	51.0
1991	906.70	354.80	551.90	60.9
1992	826.30	311.90	514.40	62.3
1993	1 517.22	357.80	1 159.42	76.4
1994	2 673.15	1 253.61	1 419.54	53.1
1995	2 426.99	1 262.82	1 164.17	48.0
1996	3 357.97	1 766.90	1 591.07	47.4
1997	4 203.64	2 154.13	2 049.51	48.8
1998	4 849.08	2 419.01	2 430.07	50.1
1999	4 907.60	2 152.70	2 754.90	56.1
2000	6 321.21	2 333.20	3 988.01	63.1
2001	5 627.80	2 787.75	2 840.05	50.5
2002	7 975.97	3 423.95	4 552.02	57.1
2003	7 259.27	3 281.75	3 977.52	54.8
2004	7 137.29	3 583.26	3 554.03	49.8
2005	10 131.48	4 403.23	5 728.25	56.5
2006	15 053.70	6 661.95	8 391.75	55.7
2007	14 859.89	7 510.40	7 349.49	49.5
2008	43 846.67	21 908.07	21 938.60	50.0

表5-14 孙桥现代农业园区主要经济指标
Major Economic Indicators of Sunqiao Modern Agricultural Park

指 标	Indicators	单 位 Unit	2005	2007	2008
园区面积	**Area of the Park**				
规划面积	Planned Area	公顷 hectare	932	932	932
已开发利用面积	Area Put to Use	公顷 hectare	346	346	346
引进项目历年累计情况	**Accumulated Introduced Projects in Consecutive Years**				
引进投资项目数	Number of Investment Projects Introduced	项 item	52	74	79
#引进外资项目数	Number of Foreign Investment Projects Introduced	项 item	10	10	10
外省市项目数	Number of Investment Projects Introduced From Other Provinces and Municipalities	项 item	8	6	8
引进投资项目金额	Number of Investment Projects Introduced	万元 10 000 yuan	60 935	61 135	61 934
#引进外资项目金额	Value of Investment Projects Introduced	万美元 USD 10 000	2 714	2 714	2 714
开发总投资累计	**Accumulated Total Investment for Development**	**万元 10 000 yuan**	**75 243**	**80 701**	**83 271**
招商引资	Business Promotion and Foreign Funds Attraction	万元 10 000 yuan	60 935	63 535	64 334
政府扶持资金	Government Grant	万元 10 000 yuan	5 192	6 946	8 217
其 它	Others	万元 10 000 yuan	9 116	10 220	10 720
企业和从业人员	**Enterprises and Employed Persons**				
年末实有企业数	Number of Enterprises (Year End)	个 unit	52	51	56
#农产品生产企业	Enterprises Producing Farm Products	个 unit	41	27	29
农产品加工企业	Enterprises Processing Farm Products	个 unit	6	6	7
农产品贸易服务企业	Enterprises Engaged in Trading and Service of Farm Products	个 unit	5	5	5
年末从业人员数	Employed Persons (Year End)	人 person	1 416	1 400	1 425
#各类专业技术人员	Technical Professionals	人 person	95	115	130

表 5－14　续表　Continued

指　标　Indicators		单　位　Unit	2005	2007	2008
品牌生产及认证	**Enterprises Producing Branded Farm Products**				
品牌农产品生产企业	Enterprises Producing Branded Farm Products	个 unit	3	3	3
品牌农产品产值	Output Value of Branded Farm Products	万元 10 000 yuan	2 950	3 804	2 093
认证品牌生产个数	Number of Authenticated Branded Products	个 in number	2	2	2
认证品牌生产面积	Production Area of Authenticated Brands	公顷 Hectare	9	9	9
认证品牌生产产值	Output Value of Authenticated Brands	万元 10 000 yuan	2 950	2 138	2 833
生产经营情况	**Operation**				
农业总产值	Output Value of Agriculture	万元 10 000 yuan	96 578	115 148	143 205
农产品出口总额	Total Value of Exported Farm Products	万元 10 000 yuan	8 675	6 933	5 360
农产品加工产值	Output Value of Farm Products Processing	万元 10 000 yuan	8 096	10 571	10 335
农产品服务贸易销售收入	Sales Revenue from Service and Trading of Farm Products	万元 10 000 yuan	1 408	1 129	2 093
利税总额	Profit Before Tax	万元 10 000 yuan	5 579	246	1 150
园区产业化生产经营（辐射）能力	**Operating Capacity of the Park**				
带动本市园区外农户户数	Number of Rural Households Outside the Park Which Have Benefited	户 household	59 882	53 500	61 271
带动外省市农户户数	Number of Rural Households in Other Provinces and Municipalities Which Have Benefited	户 household	58 148	51 300	59 188
对外省市产品及技术服务输出总额	Total Value of Products and Service Transferred to Other Provinces	万元 10 000 yuan	475	835	3 330
旅游观光	**Tourism**				
接待参观人数	Persons Received	万人次 10 000 person-times	4	8	6
旅游观光收入	Revenue From Tourism	万元 10 000 yuan	85	163	142

主要统计指标解释

农村从业人员

指乡村人口中16岁以上实际参加生产经营活动并取得实物或货币收入的人员，既包括劳动年龄内实际参加劳动人员，也包括超过劳动年龄但实际参加劳动的人员，但不包括户口在家的在外学生、现役军人和丧失劳动能力的人，也不包括待业人员和家务劳动者。劳动者年龄为16岁以上。

农业总产值

农业总产值是以货币表现的农、林、牧、渔业全部产品的总量和对农林牧渔生产活动进行的各种支持性服务活动的价值。它反映一定时期内农业生产的总规模和总成果。

农、林、牧、渔业的统计范围是：

（1）农业 包括农作物种植业和其他农业。

农作物种植业包括谷物、豆类、薯类、棉、油料、糖料、麻类、烟叶、蔬菜、药材、瓜类和其他农作物的种植，以及茶园、桑园、果园的生产经营。

其他农业包括采集野生植物的果实、纤维、树胶、树脂、油料以及柴草、野生药材、菌类等及农民家庭兼营的商品性工业。

（2）林业 包括林木的栽培（不包括茶园、桑园和果园的栽培、管理和收获等活动）、林产品的采集和村及村以下合作经济组织和农户的竹木采伐。

（3）牧业 包括除渔业养殖以外的一切动物饲养和放牧，以及野生动物的捕猎和饲养。

（4）渔业 包括水生动物和海藻类植物的养殖和捕捞。

（5）农林牧渔服务业 包括农林牧渔业生产活动进行的各种支持性服务活动。但不包括各种科学技术和专业技术服务活动。

从所有制看，包括国有经济的各种专业农（农、林、牧、渔）场以及国家各级机关团体学校、科研机构、部队经营的农业；集体所有制的乡镇村各级办农场；农村各种经济组织经营的农、林、牧、渔业以及工矿企业家属集体经营的农业；农民家庭自营的农林牧渔业及兼营商品性工业等。

农业总产值的计算方法通常是按农林牧渔业产品及其副产品的产量分别乘以各自单位产品价格求得，少数生产周期较长、当年没有产品或产品产量不易统计的，则采用间接方法匡算其产值，然后将四业产品产值和服务业产值相加即为农业总产值。

1957年以前的农业总产值中包括了厩肥和农民自给性手工业（如农民自制衣服、鞋、袜，自己从事粮食初步加工等）。1958年及以后的农业总产值，林业中增加了村及村以下竹木采伐产值；牧业中取消了厩肥产值；副业中取消了农民自给性手工业产值，增加了村及村以下办的工业产值；渔业中增加了海洋捕捞水产品产值。1980年及以后的农业总产值，在副业中增加了农民家庭兼营工业商品部分的产值。从1984年起村及村以下办工业产值划归工业。从1993年起，取消副业。将野生动物的捕猎划入牧业，野生植物采集和农民家庭兼营商品性工业划归农业。从2003年起，农业总产值中包括了农林牧渔服务业产值。

当年价格

当年价格（或现行价格）是指报告期的实际价格，如工业品的出厂价格、农产品的收购价格、商品零售价格等。用当年价格计算的一些以货币表现的物量指标或劳务总量指标，如国内生产总值、工农业总产值、社会商品零售额等，反映当年的实际情况，使国民经济各项指标互相衔接，便于考察当年社会经济效益，便于对生产和流通、生产和分配、生产和消费之间进行经济核算和综合平衡。

按当年价格计算的以货币表现的指标，在不同年份之间进行对比时，因包含各年间价格变动的因素，不能确切地反映实物量的增减变动，必须消除价格变动的因素后，才能真实反映经济发展动态。因此，在计算增长速度时都使用按可比价格计算的数字。

可比价格

可比价格指在对不同时期的价值指标对比时，扣除了价格变动的因素，以确切反映物量的变化。按可比价格计算有两种方法，一种是直接按产品产量乘其某一年的不变价格计算；另一种是用价格指数换算。

不变价格

指以同类产品某年的平均价格作为固定价格，用于计算各年的产品价值。按不变价格计算的产品价值消除了价格变动因素，不同时期对比可以反映生产的发展速度。新中国成立后，随着工农业产品价格水平的变化，国家统计局先后五次制定了全国统一的工业产品不变价格和农业产品不变价格。从1952年到1957年使用1952年工（农）业产品不变价格，从1957年到1970年使用1957年不变价格，从1971年到1980年使用1970年不变价格，从1981年到1990年使用1980年不变价格，从1991年到2000年使用1990年不变价格，从2001年开始使用2000年不变价格。

年末耕地面积

年末耕地面积指能够种植农作物，经常进行耕锄的田地。包括熟地、当年新开荒地、新开垦围垦地、连续撂荒未满三年的耕地和当年休闲地（轮歇地）。以种植农作物为主并附带种植桑树、茶树、果树和其他林木的土地，以及沿海、沿湖地区已围垦利用的“海涂”、“湖田”等也应包括在内，但不包括专业性桑园、茶园、果园、果木苗圃、林地、芦苇地、天然草原等。小于一米宽的渠、路、田埂,包括在耕地中。

农作物播种面积

农作物播种面积指报告期内收获农产品的作物的实际播种或移植有农作物的面积。凡是实际种植农作物的面积,不论种植在耕地上还是种植在非耕地上,均包括在农作物播种面积中。在播种季节基本结束后,因遭灾而重新改种和补种的农作物面积,也包括在内。

粮食产量

指全社会的产量。包括国有经济经营的、集体统一经营的和农民家庭经营的粮食产量,还包括工矿企业办的农场和其他生产单位的产量。粮食除包括稻谷、小麦、玉米、高粱、谷子及其他杂粮外,还包括薯类和豆类。其产量计算方法,豆类按去豆荚后的干豆计算;薯类(包括甘薯和马铃薯,不包括芋头和木薯)1963 年以前按每 4 公斤鲜薯折 1 公斤粮食计算,从 1964 年开始改为按 5 公斤鲜薯折 1 公斤粮食计算。城市郊区作为蔬菜的薯类(如马铃薯等)按鲜品计算,并且不作粮食统计。其他粮食一律按脱粒后的原粮计算。1989 年以前全国粮食产量数据主要靠全面报表取得,1989 年开始使用抽样调查数据。

水产品产量

指人工养殖的水产品和天然生长的水产品的捕捞量。包括海水的鱼类、虾蟹类、贝类和藻类以及内陆水域的鱼类、虾蟹类和贝类,不包括淡水生植物。水产品产量是通过各级水产和统计部门逐级上报取得数据。1995 年及以前,贝类中牡蛎按鲜肉计算;蛆、蛤、蛙按 5 斤鲜品折 1 斤计算。1996 年以后则统一按鲜品计算。

猪、牛、羊肉产量

指当年出栏并已屠宰、除去头蹄下水后带骨肉(即胴体重)的重量。包括全社会范围内的产量。1996 年前为各级逐级上报数据。1996 年第一次农业普查以后,由于畜牧业产品年报数据与普查数据之间存在一定的差距,国家统计局农调总队对畜牧业年报数据与普查数据进行衔接。1999 年以后,国家统计局开展了猪、牛、羊、禽等主要畜禽品种的抽样调查,并用抽样数据作为国家定案数据使用。未开展抽样调查的品种,仍使用各级统计部门逐级上报数据。

农业机械总动力

农业机械总动力指用于农、林、牧、渔业生产的各种动力机械的动力总和。动力机械包括耕作、排灌、种植、植物保护、收获、农产品加工、运输、畜牧、渔业、农田水利等各种机械。不包括专门用于乡办工业、基本建设、非农业运输、科学试验和教学等非农业生产方面用的动力机械与作业机械的数量。

农村经济收益分配主要指标

农村经济收益分配和效益指标,是为了全面观察农村经济收入分配情况,研究农村经济的规模、发展速度、多种经营、商品化程度,国家、集体和个人的分配关系及经济效益。其计算范围包括乡村企业、集体统一经营(含家庭承包)新经济联合体以及农民家庭经营(含家庭承包)四个部分。

(1)总收入:指本单位当年经营的收入中可用以抵偿本年开支并在国家、集体、农民之间进行分配的农、林、牧、渔业、工业、交通运输业、建筑业、商业、饮食业、服务业等各项经营收入和利息、租金等非生产收入,但不包括那些不能用来分配,属于借贷性质或暂收性质的收入,如贷款收入、预购定金、国家投资、农民投资等。

(2)总费用:是指为实现当年各项生产经营收入应由当年负担的各项费用开支,包括生产费用、管理费用和其他费用三项。

(3)净收入总额:是指当年"总收入"减去"总费用"后,当年所得的净收入部分。

(4)农村居民净收入:是指农村居民从当年的净收入中减去国家税金和集体提留以后,归个人支配的部分,包括现金和实物折款。

EXPLANATORY NOTES TO MAJOR STATISTICAL INDICATORS

Personnel Employed in Rural Areas

Personnel Employed in Rural Areas refers to people in rural areas who are older than 16 years and engaged in production and business activities that generate incomes in cash or in practicality. It includes all working laborers, no matter whether they are within the working age or not, whereas students studying outside but with their registered residence at home, active serviceman, people who lost their ability to work, unemployed people, and those engaged in housework are not included. The working age is defined as older than 16 years.

Gross Output Value of Agriculture

Gross Output Value of Agriculture refers to the total volume of products of farming, forestry, animal husbandry and fishery expressed in the monetary terms and output value of all kinds of service activities that support farming, forestry, animal husbandry and fishery production. It reflects the overall scale and achievements of agricultural production during a given period of time.

The scope of statistics on farming, forestry, animal husbandry, and fishery are as follows:

(1) Farming includes cultivation of farm crops and other agricultural activities.

Cultivation of farm crops include cultivation of grain crops, legume crops, tuber-crops, cotton, oil-bearing crops, sugar crops, bastfiber plants, tobacco, vegetables, medicinal herbs, melon crops, and cultivation and management of tea plantations, mulberry fields and orchards.

Other agricultural activities include harvesting wild fruits, fiber, tree gum, resin, oil-bearing plants, firewood, wild medicinal herbs, fungus, and rural-household commodity industries.

(2) Forestry refers to planting trees of various kinds (excluding tea plantations, mulberry fields and orchards), collection of forestry products and cutting and felling of bamboo and trees by villages and other cooperative organizations under village level.

(3) Animal husbandry refers to raising and grazing of all kinds of farm animals except fishing and aquatic cultivating, and hunting and rising of wild animals.

(4) Fishery refers to cultivation and catching of fish and other aquatic products and cultivation and collection of seaweed and other aquatic plants.

(5) Service Industry for Farming, Forestry, Animal Husbandry and Fishery refers to all kinds of service activities that support farming, forestry, animal husbandry and fishery production, whereas activities of science, technology and professional service are not included.

In terms of ownership, China's agriculture includes specialized state farms (for farming, forestry, animal husbandry, fishery), farms managed by various government agencies, organizations, schools, research institutions, and army; farms managed by rural collective organizations at levels of the township, town, and village; farming, forestry, animal husbandry, fishery run by various rural collective organizations and farming run by collective family members' organizations of mining and industrial enterprises; farming, forestry, animal husbandry and fishery and some commodity industries run by individual farmers.

Gross output value of agriculture is obtained by first multiplying the output of products or by products by their unit price. For a small number of products, annual output of which is not available or difficult to get due to the long production/growing process involved, the output value will be estimated through an indirect approach. The sum of output value of all products of farming, forestry, animal husbandry and fishery and output value of service activities will then and together to form gross output value of agriculture.

Before 1957, China's gross agricultural output value included the value of barnyard manure and handicraft products for self-consumption (clothes, shoes, stockings, and initial grain processing under-taken by peasants). After 1958, the output value of cutting and felling of bamboo and trees by villages and other cooperative organizations under villages have been included in forestry; value of barnyard manure has been excluded from animal husbandry; the value of self-consumed handicrafts has been excluded from sideline occupations, while output value of industries run by villages and cooperative organizations under village level has been included in sideline occupations and output value of fish catches by motor fishing boats has been added to fishery. Since 1980, the output value of handicraft products made for sale by farmer households has been added to sideline occupations, From 1984, industries run by villages and cooperative organizations under village level have been included in the sector of industry. After 1993, the category of sideline occupations has been canceled and hunting of wild animals has been classified into husbandry, and harvesting of wild vegetation and commodity industry run by rural households have been grouped into the category of agriculture. Since 2003, the output value of service industry for farming, forestry, animal husbandry and fishery is included in the gross output value of agriculture.

Current Prices

Current prices refer to the actual prices in the report period, for example, industrial producers prices, procurement prices of agricultural products, retail prices, and so on. Goods and services measured by the current prices, such as gross national product, gross output value of industry and agriculture, total retail sales, reflect the current-year actual activities. The various national economic indicators, such as current-year social economic efficiency, production, exchange, distribution and consumption could be understood and compared directly if they are measured by the current prices.

The indicators measured by the current prices can not exactly reflect the real change over different years, if the price level changes during the period of time. The comparable prices would be used in measuring growth rates, in order to deflate the price change.

Comparable Prices

Comparable Prices are applied when comparing indicators over time to reflect accurately the changes in real term. Two methods are used for calculating comparable prices: 1. output by constant price of certain year; 2. output in current prices divided by relevant price index.

Constant Price

Constant Price refers to the average price of a given product in certain year, which is used for comparison of output value over time. As the output value at constant prices removes the factor of price changes, it reflects the trend of production development over time. Since 1949, with the changes in general price level, National Bureau of Statistics has issued nationally unified constant prices five times: the 1952 constant prices for 1949 – 1957; the 1957 constant prices for 1957 – 1971; the 1970 constant prices for 1971 – 1981; the 1980 constant prices for 1981 – 1990; the 1990 constant prices for 1991 – 2000; and the 2000 constant prices have been used since 2001.

The Actual Area of Plowland at Year End

The Area of Plowland at Year End refers to the area of arable land and frequently-tended farm-fields at the beginning of a year. It includes cultivated land, the newly-reclaimed wasteland and inning land in the year, the farmland which has been laid idle for no more than three consecutive years, and land on fallow that year. It shall also include farmland with mulberry, tea, fruit and other trees but used mainly for growing crops as well as the reclaimed "beach-land" and "lake-land" along the sea coasts and the lake banks. However, it shall not include the land devoted especially for mulberry and the tea gardens, orchards, nurseries, woodlands, reed marches and natural grasslands. Ditches, pathways and ridges of field which are less than one meter wide are included in plowland.

Sown Area of Crops

Sown Area of Crops refers to area of land sown or transplanted with crops that have been harvested during report period, regardless of being in cultivated area or non-cultivated area. Area of land resown due to natural disasters is also included.

Grain Output

Grain Output refers to the total output in the whole country including grains produced by state farms, collective units, rural households, as well as by farms affiliated to industrial and mining enterprises and other production units. Grain includes rice, wheat, corn, sorghum, millet and other miscellaneous grains as well as tubers and bean. Output of beans refers to dry beans without pods. The output of tubers (sweet potatoes and potatoes, not including taros and cassava) was converted into that of grain at the ratio 4:1, i.e. 4 kilograms of fresh tubers was equivalent to 1 kilogram of grain up to 1963. Since 1964 the ratio for conversion has been 5:1. Tubers supplied as vegetables (such as potatoes) in cities and suburbs are calculated as fresh vegetables and their output is not included in the output of grain. Output of all other grains refers to husked grain. Data on grain production before 1989 were obtained through Comprehensive Statistical Reporting System. Since 1989, data from sample surveys are used.

Output of Aquatic Products

Output of Aquatic Products refers to catches of both artificially cultured and naturally grown aquatic products, including fish, shrimps, crabs and shellfish in sea and inland water as well as seaweed. Freshwater plants are not included. Data on output of aquatic products are reported by aquatic product and statistical agencies level by level. Before 1995, among the shellfish, the oyster was counted as fresh meat; 5 kilograms of ark shell, clams and frogs are equivalent to 1 kilogram of fresh aquatic products; they are all counted as fresh aquatic products since 1996.

Output of Pork, Beef, and Mutton

Output of Pork, Beef, and Mutton refers to the meat of slaughtered hogs, cattle, sheep and goats with head, feet, and offal taken away. Data refers to the production of the whole country. The first agriculture census of China in 1996 revealed some discrepancy between the production of animal products from the annual reports and that from the census. Efforts were made by the Rural Socio-economic Survey Organization of NBS to adjust the output value of animal husbandry to make the figures from the annual reports consistent with the census data. Since 1999, NBS conducted sample survey for the major animal husbandry products, such as hogs, cattle, sheep and goats and fowls, and the data from sample surveys are used as national finalized data. Those products, which are not covered by the sample survey, are still reported by statistical agencies level by level.

Total Power of Farm Machinery

Total Power of Farm Machinery refers to the total mechanical power of machinery used in farming, forestry animal husbandry and fishery, including machines used for ploughing, irrigation and drainage, crop growing, plant protection, harvesting, farm product processing, transport, stock breeding, fishery and water conservancy. Machinery employed for non-agricultural purposes such as township industry, capital construction, non-agricultural transport, scientific experiments and for teaching is excluded.

Major Indicators of Rural Income Distribution

Indicators of rural income distribution and efficiency are used for investigating the overall income distribution in rural area and for studying the rural economy in scale, development, multi-operation, commercialization, income distribution among state, collective units and individuals and economic efficiency. The statistical scope includes village enterprises, collective operations (collectively contracted operation), new economic unions and farmers family operations (family contracted operation).

(1) Gross income refers to current year operating revenue in farming, forestry, animal husbandry, fishery, industry, transportation, construction, commerce, catering, services and interest, rent, which can be used to compensate for current year's expenses and distributed among the state, collective units and farmers, but excludes the credit or actual revenue which can not be distributed, such as loan revenue, advance payments for purchases, state investment and farmers investment.

(2) Total expenses refers to current year expenses which realize current year's productive operating revenue, including production expenses, managerial expenses and other expenses.

(3) Total net income refers to current year's net gross revenue of total expenses.

(4) Net Income of Residents in Rural Area refers to the disposable portion of such residents after deduction of state tax and collective retention from net income, including cash and income in kind in money terms.

第六篇

Chapter 6

建筑业、工业

CONSTRUCTION AND INDUSTRY

表6-1　建筑业企业主要指标(一)
(2008)

指　标	Indicators	企业单位数(个) Number of Enterprises (unit)	年末从业人员数(人) Employed Persons (Year End) (person)	年从业人员平均数(人) Annual Average Employed Persons (person)	建筑业总产值(万元) Gross Output Value of Construction (10 000 yuan)	竣工产值(万元) Output Value of Completed Construction Projects (10 000 yuan)
合　计	**Total**	**522**	**181 687**	**203 498**	**6 607 274**	**3 507 229**
#外省市	Non-Shanghai	62	29 570	51 052	470 209	231 624
按登记注册类型分	**By Type of Registration**					
内　资	Domestic Investment	483	175 967	197 905	5 996 144	3 146 033
国　有	State-owned	33	11 002	10 552	611 393	206 948
集　体	Collective-owned	15	1 475	1 653	36 446	40 954
股份合作	Share-holding	3	61	83	1 142	1 092
联　营	Jointly Operated	3	203	203	3 698	3 041
责任有限公司	Companies with Limited Liabilities	81	83 360	97 078	2 631 286	1 279 366
股份有限公司	Companies Limited by Shares	17	18 763	20 415	963 048	635 266
私　营	Private	331	61 103	67 921	1 749 131	979 366
港澳台商投资	HK/Macao/Taiwan Invested	18	2 479	2 138	239 863	74 859
外商投资	Foreigner Invested	21	3 241	3 455	371 267	286 337
按行业分	**By Sector**					
房屋和土木工程建筑业	Housing and Civil Engineering Construction	249	148 271	168 504	5 088 670	2 359 824
建筑安装业	Installation	146	19 822	20 477	840 736	648 117
建筑装饰业	Furnishing/Decoration	109	12 100	12 829	627 421	465 119
其他建筑业	Other Construction	18	1 494	1 688	50 447	34 169
按建筑业资质等级分	**By Qualification of Construction Industry**					
#特　级	Special Grade	11	55 097	58 099	1 767 614	1 031 675
一　级	Grade A	97	55 668	66 244	2 563 210	993 117
二　级	Grade B	167	50 435	56 120	1 721 065	1 100 769
三　级	Grade C	247	20 487	23 035	555 385	381 668

注：建筑业总产值为建筑业企业自行完成的施工产值；建筑业资质等级为新标准资质。

Note: Gross Output Value of Construction refers to Output Value of Construction Completed by Construction Enterprises themselves. Qualification of Construction Industry refers to qualification under new standards.

Major Indicators of Construction Enterprises(1)

房屋建筑施工面积（万平方米）Floor Space Under Construction (10 000 sq・m)	#本年新开工 New Start in Current Year	房屋竣工面积（万平方米）Floor Space Completed (10 000 sq・m)	#住宅 Residential Housing	全员劳动生产率（元/人）Overall Labor Productivity (yuan/person)	平均每个职工竣工房屋面积（平方米/人）Floor Space Completed Per Staff Member (sq・m/person)	房屋建筑面积竣工率（%）Ratio of Floor Space Completed(%)
4 324.58	**1 569.65**	**877.13**	**477.70**	**324 685**	**43.10**	**20.3**
318.63	97.33	93.62	41.82	92 104	18.34	29.4
4 247.94	1 523.13	831.33	477.70	302 981	42.01	19.6
247.93	65.94	27.84	17.87	579 409	26.38	11.2
26.69	11.59	14.92	10.75	220 485	90.27	55.9
				137 627		
				182 167		
2 270.75	889.51	360.28	189.95	271 049	37.11	15.9
813.92	258.95	183.28	93.15	471 735	89.78	22.5
888.65	297.14	245.01	165.98	257 524	36.07	27.6
				1 121 906		
76.64	46.52	45.80		1 074 578	132.55	59.8
4 324.58	1 569.65	877.13	477.70	301 991	52.05	20.3
				410 576		
				489 064		
				298 860		
2 861.00	1 006.29	478.66	245.63	304 242	82.39	16.7
672.59	241.81	119.78	77.31	386 935	18.08	17.8
685.31	268.99	253.00	152.43	306 676	45.08	36.9
105.68	52.56	25.69	2.33	241 105	11.15	24.3

表6-2　主要年份建筑业企业主要指标(二)

指　标　Indicators		单　位　Unit	1995
施工企业单位数	Number of Construction Enterprises	个 unit	243
年末从业人员数	Employed Persons (Year End)	人 person	125 627
全年从业人员平均数	Annual Average Employed Persons	人 person	140 994
建筑业总产值	Gross Output Value of Construction	万元 10 000 yuan	1 045 601
#建筑工程	Construction Projects	万元 10 000 yuan	905 848
安装工程	Installation Projects	万元 10 000 yuan	110 763
竣工产值	Output Value of Construction Projects Completed	万元 10 000 yuan	446 202
房屋建筑面积	Floor Space of Buildings		
施工面积	Floor Space Under Construction	万平方米 10 000 sq·m	1 042.05
#本年新开工	New Start in Current Year	万平方米 10 000 sq·m	285.02
竣工面积	Floor Space Completed	万平方米 10 000 sq·m	290.25
#住　宅	Housing	万平方米 10 000 sq·m	150.63
全员劳动生产率	Overall Labor Productivity	元/人 yuan/person	74 159
房屋建筑面积竣工率	Ratio of Floor Space Completed	%	27.9
平均每个职工竣工房屋面积	Floor Space Completed Per Staff Member	平方米/人 sq. m/person	20.59

注：建筑业总产值为建筑业企业自行完成的施工产值。
Note: Gross output value of construction refers to output value of construction completed by construction enterprises themselves.

Major Indicators of Construction Industry in Main Years(2)

2000	2001	2002	2003	2004	2005	2006	2007	2008
367	365	411	406	398	398	489	469	522
93 753	92 957	95 372	104 026	104 314	159 099	176 109	123 957	181 687
116 722	130 927	150 956	198 081	173 411	208 807	237 537	273 887	203 498
935 731	1 315 185	1 747 815	2 446 016	2 568 544	3 353 790	4 168 060	5 416 041	6 607 274
886 356	1 400 354	1 475 534	1 937 758	1 842 495	2 599 981	3 555 436	4 655 203	5 421 540
115 164	155 917	218 759	399 700	297 125	643 346	487 822	611 949	1 020 528
786 808	998 899	1 197 182	1 760 501	1 551 801	2 322 347	2 716 496	3 319 285	3 507 229
1 149.25	1 303.31	1 565.60	2 321.60	2 572.04	3 009.91	3 542.14	3 798.19	4 324.58
426.18	626.78	680.00	1 049.37	1 087.98	1 291.18	1 284.94	1 430.47	1 569.65
520.61	477.18	487.10	736.35	699.35	903.45	1 042.95	1 066.82	877.13
350.65	139.01	303.81	401.72	426.64	523.94	543.25	469.87	477.70
80 167	100 452	115 783	123 486	148 119	160 617	175 470	197 747	324 685
45.3	36.6	31.1	31.7	27.2	30.0	29.4	28.1	20.3
44.60	36.45	32.27	37.17	40.33	43.27	43.91	38.95	43.10

表6-3　主要年份工业企业单位数和从业人数(镇及镇以上)
Industrial Enterprises, and Employed Persons in Main Years (Town Level and Above)

指　标	Indicators	1990	1993	2000	2005	2007	2008
企业单位数总计(个)	**Total Enterprises (unit)**	**1 272**	**1 574**	**2 406**	**4 375**	**3 851**	**3 558**
按隶属关系分	**By Subordination**						
中央工业	Central	34	39	45	69	48	44
市属工业	Municipal	235	296	285	233	192	176
非中央、市属工业	Local	1 003	1 239	2 076	4 073	3 611	3 338
按登记注册类型分	**By Type of Registration**						
国　有	State-owned	383	432	244	86	55	42
集　体	Collective-owned	729	723	396	157	88	83
港澳台及外商投资	Overseas Invested	36	287	545	961	960	910
其　他	Others	124	132	1 221	3 171	2 748	2 523
按轻、重工业分	**By Light/Heavy Industry**						
轻工业	Light Industry	708	890	1 314	1 867	1 630	1 502
重工业	Heavy Industry	564	684	1 092	2 508	2 221	2 056
按企业规模分	**By Scale of Enterprises**						
大型企业	Large	29	63	171	27	24	25
中型企业	Medium	46	77	176	227	257	252
小型企业	Small	1 197	1 434	2 059	4 121	3 570	3 281
年末从业人数总计(万人)	**Total Employed Persons (Year End) (10 000 Persons)**	**33.98**	**56.52**	**38.20**	**50.25**	**49.69**	**47.64**
按隶属关系分	**By Subordination**						
中央工业	Central	6.58	6.55	7.22	6.27	4.94	5.03
市属工业	Municipal	12.33	35.11	12.12	10.03	10.27	9.50
非中央、市属工业	Local	15.07	14.86	18.86	33.95	34.48	33.11
按登记注册类型分	**By Type of Registration**						
国　有	State-owned	18.73	31.58	7.39	3.72	3.68	3.30
集　体	Collective-owned	11.20	10.51	3.61	0.90	0.64	0.52
港澳台及外商投资	Overseas Invested	0.65	7.44	14.39	24.94	26.16	25.54
其　他	Others	3.40	6.99	12.81	20.69	19.21	18.28
按轻、重工业分	**By Light/Heavy Industry**						
轻工业	Light Industry	14.90	24.62	16.28	18.15	16.94	15.47
重工业	Heavy Industry	19.08	31.90	21.92	32.10	32.75	32.17
按企业规模分	**By Scale of Enterprises**						
大型企业	Large	11.16	27.87	18.93	11.09	10.96	10.92
中型企业	Medium	4.38	7.03	5.08	14.80	17.24	16.97
小型企业	Small	18.44	21.62	14.19	24.36	21.49	19.75

注：表中2003年后大中小型企业数据按新标准统计，后续各表口径相同;2008年人数为平均人数。
Note: In this table, data of Large and Medium or Small Enterprises are listed according to new standards after 2003. The rest tables are to be adjusted accordingly. The number of persons in 2008 is an averaged number.

表6-4 工业企业单位数和从业人员平均人数的各种分组
Classification of Industrial Enterprises and Average Number of Persons Employed

指 标	Indicators	企业单位数(个) Enterprises (unit)		从业人员平均人数(人) Average Number of Persons Employed (person)	
		2007	2008	2007	2008
总 计	**Total**	**4 214**	**3 880**	**510 702**	**497 458**
按隶属关系分	**By Subordination**				
中央工业	Central	48	44	48 290	50 275
市属工业	Municipal	192	176	100 315	94 984
非中央、市属工业	Local	3 974	3 660	362 097	352 199
按登记注册类型分	**By Type of Registration**				
内 资	Domestic Funded	3 217	2 935	250 578	237 960
国 有	State-owned	55	43	35 688	33 030
集 体	Collective-owned	250	218	13 287	11 444
股份合作	Share-holding	140	123	11 305	9 537
联 营	Jointly Operated	45	44	3 867	3 245
有限责任公司	Companies with Limited Liabilities	229	213	47 725	50 915
股份有限公司	Companies Limited by Shares	13	18	16 722	16 370
私 营	Private	2 471	2 266	121 658	113 175
其 他	Others	14	10	326	244
港澳台商投资	HK/Macao/Taiwan Invested	232	215	48 205	43 945
#港澳台商独资	HK/Macao/Taiwan Funded	106	94	23 313	21 787
外商投资	Foreigner Invested	765	730	211 919	215 553
#外商独资	Foreigner Funded	489	468	124 991	129 689
按轻、重工业分	**By Light/Heavy Industry**				
轻工业	Light Industry	1 787	1 643	180 108	165 215
重工业	Heavy Industry	2 427	2 237	330 594	332 243
按企业规模分	**By Scale of Enterprises**				
大型企业	Large	24	25	105 351	109 225
中型企业	Medium	262	259	172 264	173 247
小型企业	Small	3 928	3 596	233 087	214 986

注：表中没有注明的即为全社会统计口径，后续各表相同。
Note: The fields that have not been specified in this table have been counted with the total statistical approuch. And the tables followed are the same.

表6-5 历年工业总产值及其构成

单位:亿元

指 标	Indicators	1990	1991	1992	1993	1994	1995	1996
总 计	**Total**	**176.85**	**228.90**	**363.71**	**604.40**	**886.35**	**968.03**	**1 130.42**
按隶属关系分	**By Subordination**							
中央工业	Central	42.48	56.17	69.78	94.40	214.75	225.99	269.28
市属工业	Municipal	88.44	88.78	177.66	333.19	448.92	491.63	562.02
非中央、市属工业	Local	45.93	83.95	116.27	176.81	222.68	250.41	299.12
按登记注册类型分	**By Type of Registration**							
国 有	State-owned	110.18	136.09	208.79	315.74	441.09	449.57	494.03
集 体	Collective-owned	49.09	67.35	79.70	133.35	126.53	122.54	131.93
港澳台及外商投资	Overseas Invested	7.07	10.74	17.01	84.63	151.85	231.94	303.77
其 他	Others	10.51	14.72	58.21	70.68	166.88	163.98	200.69
按轻、重工业分	**By Light/Heavy Industry**							
轻工业	Light Industry	72.08	90.95	135.45	241.07	371.08	424.42	509.85
重工业	Heavy Industry	104.77	137.95	228.26	363.33	515.27	543.61	620.57
按企业规模分	**By Scale of Enterprises**							
大型企业	Large	81.32	104.04	192.39	341.64	582.31	632.35	746.06
中型企业	Medium	21.40	27.76	43.00	52.92	95.77	96.37	106.57
小型企业	Small	74.13	97.10	128.32	209.84	208.27	239.31	277.79
构 成(%)	**Composition (%)**							
总 计	**Total**	**100.0**	**100.0**	**100.0**	**100.0**	**100.0**	**100.0**	**100.0**
按隶属关系分	**By Subordination**							
中央工业	Central	24.0	24.5	19.2	15.6	24.2	23.3	23.8
市属工业	Municipal	50.0	38.8	48.8	55.1	50.7	50.8	49.7
非中央、市属工业	Local	26.0	36.7	32.0	29.3	25.1	25.9	26.5
按登记注册类型分	**By Type of Registration**							
国 有	State-owned	62.3	59.5	57.4	52.2	49.8	46.4	43.7
集 体	Collective-owned	27.8	29.4	21.9	22.1	14.3	12.7	11.7
港澳台及外商投资	Overseas Invested	4.0	4.7	4.7	14.0	17.1	24.0	26.9
其 他	Others	5.9	6.4	16.0	11.7	18.8	16.9	17.7
按轻、重工业分	**By Light/Heavy Industry**							
轻工业	Light Industry	40.8	39.7	37.2	39.9	41.9	43.8	45.1
重工业	Heavy Industry	59.2	60.3	62.8	60.1	58.1	56.2	54.9
按企业规模分	**By Scale of Enterprises**							
大型企业	Large	46.0	45.5	52.9	56.5	65.7	65.3	66.0
中型企业	Medium	12.1	12.1	11.8	8.8	10.8	10.0	9.4
小型企业	Small	41.9	42.4	35.3	34.7	23.5	24.7	24.6

Gross Output Value of Industry and Its Composition in Main Years

(100 million yuan)

1997	1998	1999	2000	2001	2002	2003	2004	2005	2006	2007	2008
1 349.01	**1 414.99**	**1 450.81**	**1 625.77**	**1 888.74**	**2 193.82**	**2 856.68**	**3 519.71**	**4 242.47**	**4 758.76**	**5 188.12**	**5 649.22**
302.61	331.21	323.62	381.41	386.40	431.13	549.05	677.04	1 321.05	1 538.42	1 663.26	1 999.48
728.43	640.62	610.35	599.57	779.48	805.98	1 082.55	1 254.17	1 135.29	1 249.74	1 373.81	1 289.49
317.97	443.16	516.84	644.79	722.86	956.71	1 225.08	1 588.50	1 786.13	1 970.60	2 151.05	2 360.25
483.40	396.46	309.87	275.85	344.02	241.56	290.97	358.04	550.18	573.84	662.21	679.71
156.89	105.85	90.04	70.91	57.02	49.57	46.02	49.09	38.67	36.87	34.89	31.60
520.85	695.25	851.48	1 012.34	1 242.91	1 522.31	1 985.30	2 461.66	2 632.70	2 980.46	3 001.98	3 088.54
187.87	217.43	199.42	266.67	244.79	380.38	534.39	650.92	1 020.92	1 167.59	1 489.04	1 849.37
597.73	575.55	533.52	514.58	535.06	541.28	647.92	764.94	825.40	878.66	952.26	1 070.62
751.28	839.44	917.29	1 111.19	1 353.68	1 652.54	2 208.76	2 754.77	3 417.07	3 880.10	4 235.86	4 578.60
836.48	861.03	988.53	1 138.11	1 294.24	1 564.20	1 229.85	1 426.29	1 989.45	1 976.08	2 309.39	2 731.96
162.70	163.34	163.48	187.00	239.26	209.92	862.86	1 083.29	1 173.99	1 725.62	1 841.13	1 822.86
349.83	390.62	298.80	300.66	355.24	419.70	763.97	1 010.13	1 079.03	1 057.06	1 037.60	1 094.40
100.0	**100.0**	**100.0**	**100.0**	**100.0**	**100.0**	**100.0**	**100.0**	**100.0**	**100.0**	**100.0**	**100.0**
22.4	23.4	22.3	23.5	20.4	19.7	19.2	19.3	31.1	32.3	32.0	35.4
54.0	45.3	42.1	36.9	41.3	36.7	37.9	35.6	26.8	26.3	26.5	22.8
23.6	31.3	35.6	39.6	38.3	43.6	42.9	45.1	42.1	41.4	41.5	41.8
35.8	28.0	21.4	17.0	18.2	11.0	10.2	10.2	13.0	12.1	12.8	12.0
11.6	7.5	6.2	4.3	3.0	2.3	1.6	1.4	0.9	0.8	0.7	0.6
38.6	49.1	58.7	62.3	65.8	69.4	69.5	69.9	62.0	62.6	57.8	54.7
14.0	15.4	13.7	16.4	13.0	17.3	18.7	18.5	24.1	24.5	28.7	32.7
44.3	40.7	36.8	31.7	28.3	24.7	22.7	21.7	19.5	18.5	18.4	19.0
55.7	59.3	63.2	68.3	71.7	75.3	77.3	78.3	80.5	81.5	81.6	81.0
62.0	60.9	68.1	70.0	68.5	71.3	43.1	40.5	46.9	41.5	44.5	48.3
12.1	11.5	11.3	11.5	12.7	9.6	30.2	30.8	27.7	36.3	35.5	32.3
25.9	27.6	20.6	18.5	18.8	19.1	26.7	28.7	25.4	22.2	20.0	19.4

表6-6 工业总产值、销售产值和出口交货值
(2008)

单位:亿元

指 标	Indicators	工业总产值(按现行价格计算) Gross Output Value of Industry (at Current Price)
总 计	**Total**	**5 649.22**
按隶属关系分	**By Subordination**	
中央工业	Central	1 999.48
市属工业	Municipal	1 289.49
非中央、市属工业	Local	2 360.25
按登记注册类型分	**By Type of Registration**	
内 资	Domestic Funded	2 560.68
国 有	State-owned	679.71
集 体	Collective-owned	31.60
股份合作制	Share-holding	30.74
联 营	Jointly-operated	12.52
有限责任公司	Companies with Limited Liability	554.32
股份有限公司	Companies Limited by Shares	916.10
私 营	Private	334.71
其 他	Others	0.98
港澳台商投资	Hong Kong/Macao/Taiwan Invested	338.33
#港澳台商独资	Hong Kong/Macao/Taiwan Funded	188.01
外商投资	Foreigner Invested	2 750.21
#外商独资	Foreigner Funded	1 391.05
按轻、重工业分	**By Light/Heavy Industry**	
轻工业	Light Industry	1 070.62
重工业	Heavy Industry	4 578.60
按企业规模分	**By Scale of Enterprises**	
大型企业	Large	2 731.96
中型企业	Medium	1 822.86
小型企业	Small	1 094.40

Gross Output Value, Sales Value and Export Delivery Value

(100 million yuan)

#镇及镇以上 Town and Above	工业销售产值 Sales Value of Industry	#镇及镇以上 Town and Above	出口交货值 Export Delivery Value	#镇及镇以上 Town and Above
5 588.57	**5 619.96**	**5 559.41**	**1 589.53**	**1 585.92**
1 999.48	1 991.23	1 991.23	551.60	551.60
1 289.49	1 292.24	1 292.24	265.57	265.57
2 299.60	2 336.49	2 275.94	772.36	768.75
2 511.33	2 551.90	2 502.94	523.69	522.83
679.67	680.90	680.86	7.99	7.99
12.46	31.42	12.49	0.96	0.23
18.45	30.47	18.25	0.58	0.58
9.71	12.39	9.62		
545.15	549.62	540.57	242.56	242.43
915.98	909.33	909.22	250.53	250.53
329.06	336.79	331.08	21.07	21.07
0.85	0.98	0.85		
331.57	344.92	338.20	128.28	126.97
187.99	192.77	192.75	106.18	106.18
2 745.67	2 723.14	2 718.27	937.56	936.12
1 391.05	1 359.30	1 359.30	607.05	607.05
1 047.31	1 068.85	1 045.52	303.42	301.10
4 541.26	4 551.11	4 513.89	1 286.11	1 284.82
2 731.96	2 722.08	2 722.08	803.22	803.22
1 814.74	1 804.23	1 796.28	599.98	599.75
1 041.87	1 093.65	1 041.05	186.33	182.95

表6-7 按行业分的工业总产值、销售产值和出口交货值
Gross Output Value, Sales Value and Export Delivery Value by Sector
(2008)

单位:亿元 (100 million yuan)

指 标	Indicators	工业总产值(按现行价格计算) Gross Output Value of Industry (at Current Price)	工业销售产值 Sales Value of Industry	出口交货值 Export Delivery Value
总 计	**Total**	**5 649.22**	**5 619.96**	**1 589.53**
农副食品加工业	Processing of Agricultural Side-line Food	111.36	110.07	0.03
食品制造业	Food Manufacturing	43.42	43.57	0.80
饮料制造业	Beverage Manufacturing	101.58	80.14	2.41
烟草制品业	Tobacco Products	1.85	1.85	0.02
纺织业	Textile Industry	53.03	52.89	14.53
纺织服装、鞋、帽制造业	Textile Products, Clothes, Shoes and Hats	46.95	43.47	14.22
皮革、毛皮、羽(毛)绒及其制品业	Leather, Fur, Down & Related Products	6.34	6.27	2.65
木材加工及木、竹、藤、棕、草制品业	Timber-processing, Bamboo, Cane, Palm Fiber and Straw Products	5.62	5.60	1.63
家具制造业	Furniture Manufacturing	12.58	12.60	4.14
造纸及纸制品业	Paper-making and Paper Products	28.45	28.73	1.96
印刷业和记录媒介的复制	Printing and Record Pressing	38.87	38.74	1.21
文教体育用品制造业	Stationery, Educational and Sports Goods	17.86	17.93	13.20
石油加工、炼焦及核燃料加工业	Petroleum Processing, Coke Products and Processing of Nuclear Fuel	571.52	568.17	27.30
化学原料及化学制品制造业	Raw Chemical Materials and Chemical Products	294.19	294.08	56.37
医药制造业	Medicine Manufacturing	105.49	105.66	9.67

单位:亿元　　　　表 6－7　续表　Continued　　　　(100 million yuan)

指　标	Indicators	工业总产值（按现行价格计算）Gross Output Value of Industry (at Current Price)	工业销售产　值 Sales Value of Industry	出口交货值 Export Delivery Value
化学纤维制造业	Chemical Fiber Manufacturing	49.42	53.22	15.53
橡胶制品业	Rubber Products	10.90	10.79	1.22
塑料制品业	Plastic Products	74.20	76.24	10.94
非金属矿物制品业	Nonmetal Mineral Products	55.51	53.82	3.85
黑色金属冶炼及压延加工业	Smelting and Pressing of Ferrous Metal	43.03	42.03	8.10
有色金属冶炼及压延加工业	Smelting and Pressing of Nonferrous Metal	37.30	37.67	0.21
金属制品业	Metal Products	129.48	130.97	18.94
通用设备制造业	General Purpose Equipment Manufacturing	528.21	532.66	251.78
专用设备制造业	Special Purpose Equipment Manufacturing	142.80	147.76	31.24
交通运输设备制造业	Transportation Equipment Manufacturing	929.67	936.81	276.71
电气机械及器材制造业	Electric Equipment and Machinery	253.13	251.75	113.46
通信设备、计算机及其他电子设备制造业	Manufacturing of Electronic and Telecommunications Equipment, Computers and Other Electronic Equipment	1 190.43	1 172.67	646.62
仪器仪表及文化办公用机械制造业	Instruments, Meters, Cultural and Office Equipment	117.43	116.53	60.31
工艺品及其他制造业	Handicrafts and Other Production	3.25	3.25	0.48
废弃资源和废旧材料回收加工业	Recycling of Abandoned Recources and Wastes	1.12	1.12	
电力、热力的生产和供应业	Production and Supply of Electricity and Heating Power	608.35	608.28	
燃气生产和供应业	Gas Production and Supply	29.42	29.41	
水的生产和供应业	Production and Supply of Tap Water	6.46	5.21	

表6-8　工业重点发展行业主要指标(全部口径)
(2008)

单位:万元

指　标	Indicators	企业单位数(个) Enterprises (unit)	从业人员平均人数(人) Average Number of Employed Persons(person)	工业总产值 Gross Output Value of Industry
总　计	**Total**	**1 220**	**264 070**	**38 406 701**
按登记注册类型分	**By Type of Registration**			
内　资	Domestic Funded	725	94 491	15 670 117
国　有	State-owned	17	13 087	1 041 669
集　体	Collective-owned	44	2 739	88 243
股份合作制	Share-holding	32	3 003	117 098
联　营	Jointly-operated	20	1 166	35 725
有限责任公司	Companies with Limited Liability	95	31 676	4 123 586
股份有限公司	Companies Limited by Shares	10	14 921	9 062 804
私　营	Private	504	27 818	1 195 301
其　他	Others	3	81	5 691
港澳台商投资	Hong Kong/Macao/Taiwan Invested	83	24 362	2 606 004
#港澳台商独资	Hong Kong/Macao/Taiwan Funded	52	17 421	1 748 427
外商投资	Foreigner Invested	412	145 217	20 130 580
#外商独资	Foreigner Funded	285	99 950	9 957 506
按轻、重工业分	**By Light/Heavy Industry**			
轻工业	Light Industry	215	38 927	4 488 530
重工业	Heavy Industry	1 005	225 143	33 918 171
按企业规模分	**By Scale of Enterprises**			
大型企业	Large	21	86 759	21 014 962
中型企业	Medium	150	105 231	12 221 584
小型企业	Small	1 049	72 080	5 170 155
按行业分	**By Industry**			
电子信息产品制造业	Electronic and Information Technology Products Manufacturing	442	120 539	13 193 011
汽车制造业	Auto Manufacturing	103	40 757	5 989 766
石油化工及精细化工制造业	Petrochemical and Fine Chemical Manufacturing	166	22 409	8 716 341
精品钢材制造业	High Quality Steel Products Manufacturing	35	2 447	430 336
成套设备制造业	Complete Plants and Equipment	361	56 408	8 727 651
生物医药制造业	Biological and Modern Medical Industry	113	21 510	1 349 596

Major Indicators of PNA Pillar Industries(Whole Approach)

(10 000 yuan)

工业销售产值 Sales Value of Industry	流动资产平均余额 Average Balance of Floating Assets	资产总计 Total Assets	负债总计 Total Liabilities	主营业务收入 Revenue of Primary Operations	税金 Tax	利润总额 Total Profits
38 323 642	**21 941 631**	**38 215 514**	**21 138 939**	**43 270 876**	**959 718**	**1 584 853**
15 604 385	10 139 179	18 845 579	10 510 814	15 389 754	310 080	460 900
1 064 205	539 411	1 183 650	420 133	1 142 634	31 775	78 837
88 183	64 682	77 370	48 830	83 165	3 310	1 009
113 279	78 557	125 349	43 078	113 597	5 316	12 991
35 111	25 664	38 576	18 822	35 252	1 298	929
4 068 435	4 522 911	6 233 760	4 359 482	3 552 528	76 087	385 595
8 996 683	4 247 884	10 127 064	4 960 783	9 229 365	163 231	-71 721
1 232 811	656 591	1 053 973	657 255	1 228 024	28 873	52 923
5 678	3 479	5 837	2 431	5 189	190	337
2 655 637	1 308 523	2 726 834	1 326 163	3 729 842	34 875	82 307
1 794 671	877 592	2 052 123	830 955	1 850 893	21 771	70 101
20 063 620	10 493 929	16 643 101	9 301 962	24 151 280	614 763	1 041 646
9 846 421	4 523 331	7 826 399	4 376 797	11 196 666	109 848	397 573
4 514 037	2 235 549	3 750 825	1 836 051	4 588 958	92 250	273 938
33 809 605	19 706 082	34 464 689	19 302 888	38 681 918	867 468	1 310 915
20 896 386	13 007 720	23 423 834	13 174 298	24 525 779	609 658	639 159
12 277 974	5 650 222	9 690 153	5 299 133	13 547 526	225 105	608 584
5 149 282	3 283 689	5 101 527	2 665 508	5 197 571	124 955	337 110
13 029 840	7 010 844	11 679 427	6 506 635	15 279 276	128 672	277 628
6 069 628	3 663 836	9 656 137	3 631 987	9 082 756	483 084	790 417
8 721 178	2 017 472	3 820 127	2 133 575	8 867 331	183 731	-382 054
420 311	194 418	488 124	306 197	452 526	2 527	-25 691
8 744 617	8 125 347	10 787 893	7 658 086	8 196 030	111 697	778 301
1 338 068	929 714	1 783 806	902 459	1 392 957	50 007	146 252

表6-9　高技术工业主要指标
(2008)

单位:万元

指　标	Indicators	企业单位数(个) Enterprises (unit)	从业人员平均人数(人) Average Number of Employed Persons(person)	工业总产值 Gross Output Value of Industry
总　计	**Total**	**352**	**125 059**	**14 711 826**
按登记注册类型分	**By Type of Registration**			
内　资	Donestic Funded	123	19 501	784 273
国　有	State-owned	4	1 976	68 426
集　体	Collective-owned	2	54	504
股份合作制	Share-holding Enterprises	3	241	2 766
联　营	Cooperative Enterprises	7	273	12 384
有限责任公司	Companies with Limited Liability	32	11 706	526 710
股份有限公司	Companies Limited by Shares	3	1 370	68 315
私　营	Private	71	3 873	105 125
其　他	Others	1	8	43
港澳台商投资	Hong Kong/Macao/Taiwan Invested	37	13 902	1 611 481
#港澳台商独资	Hong Kong/Macao/Taiwan Funded	25	11 835	905 307
外商投资	Foreigner Invested	192	91 656	12 316 072
#外商独资	Foreigner Funded	136	68 098	7 178 329
按轻、重工业分	**By Light/Heavy Industry**			
轻工业	Light Industry	116	27 337	3 361 732
重工业	Heavy Industry	236	97 722	11 350 094
按企业规模分	**By Scale of Enterprises**			
大型企业	Large	11	47 576	5 426 009
中型企业	Medium	73	56 618	8 057 574
小型企业	Small	268	20 865	1 228 243
按工业行业分	**By Sector**			
信息化学品制造	Information and Chemical Manufacturing	2	105	8 696
医药制造业	Pharmaceutical Manufacturing	71	16 556	1 054 898
航空航天器制造	Aviation and Spacecraft Manufacturing	2	149	11 327
电子及通信设备制造业	Electronics and Telecommunications Equipment Manufacturing	163	80 952	8 666 520
电子计算机及办公设备制造业	Computer and Office Equipment Manufacturing	23	14 341	3 864 071
医疗设备及仪器仪表制造业	Medical Equipment and Instruments Manufacturing	91	12 956	1 106 314

Major Indicators of High-Tech Enterprises

(10 000 yuan)

工业销售产值 Sales Value of Industry	流动资产平均余额 Average Balance of Floating Assets	资产总计 Total Assets	负债总计 Total Liabilities	主营业务收入 Revenue of of Floating Assets	税金 Tax	利润总额 Total Profits
14 512 769	**7 910 541**	**13 215 240**	**7 331 165**	**16 790 059**	**179 353**	**475 732**
729 838	639 107	1 439 333	799 956	762 439	25 539	46 497
69 521	65 334	143 298	46 156	72 930	3 797	13 146
504	617	669	342	478	18	5
2 413	3 910	6 777	3 885	2 444	293	-535
12 418	8 328	15 938	4 145	13 097	432	459
472 788	434 504	1 029 442	635 700	504 308	15 059	23 562
61 561	54 795	105 174	40 049	64 050	1 444	3 168
110 603	71 591	137 992	69 652	105 102	4 494	6 690
30	28	43	27	30	2	2
1 608 993	832 581	1 881 689	866 619	2 675 356	21 771	30 936
909 346	526 029	1 429 565	509 448	954 023	11 150	23 000
12 173 938	6 438 853	9 894 218	5 664 590	13 352 264	132 043	398 299
7 078 369	3 038 970	5 501 993	3 217 861	8 315 523	57 221	186 484
3 348 404	1 655 179	2 606 746	1 285 689	3 379 896	65 011	215 472
11 164 365	6 255 362	10 608 494	6 045 476	13 410 163	114 342	260 260
5 224 777	3 480 059	6 007 566	3 322 680	6 432 169	40 215	73 340
8 035 718	3 445 117	5 590 933	3 238 742	9 078 642	105 154	326 321
1 252 274	985 365	1 616 741	769 743	1 279 248	33 984	76 071
10 078	4 242	4 912	2 412	10 287	97	725
1 056 594	731 007	1 467 810	733 532	1 069 185	38 417	104 256
10 766	11 489	16 579	3 692	12 679	328	3 551
8 483 848	5 091 258	9 296 038	4 811 348	8 470 010	83 477	183 259
3 862 073	1 441 828	1 550 158	1 291 983	6 121 197	34 338	70 955
1 089 410	630 717	879 743	488 198	1 106 701	22 696	112 986

表6-10 独立核算工业企业主要财务指标(规模以上)
(2008)

单位:万元

指 标	Indicators	企业单位数(个) Enterprises (unit)	从业人员平均人数(人) Average Number of Employed Persons(person)	工业总产值 Gross Output Value of Industry
总 计	**Total**	**2 499**	**472 242**	**56 127 872**
按隶属关系分	**By Subordination**			
中央工业	Central	42	50 233	19 994 378
市属工业	Municipal	168	94 908	12 887 986
非中央、市属工业	Local	2 289	327 101	23 245 508
按登记注册类型分	**By Type of Registration**			
内 资	Domestic Funded	1 640	214 590	25 278 677
国 有	State-owned	40	32 902	6 796 332
集 体	Collective-owned	114	9 165	295 854
股份合作制	Share-holding	88	8 492	299 005
联 营	Jointly-operated	38	3 132	124 278
有限责任公司	Companies with Limited Liability	173	49 785	5 533 186
股份有限公司	Companies Limited by Shares	16	16 346	9 154 552
私 营	Private	1 167	94 587	3 066 964
其 他	Others	4	181	8 506
港澳台商投资	Hong Kong/Macao/Taiwan Invested	186	43 334	3 376 248
#港澳台商独资	Hong Kong/Macao/Taiwan Funded	82	21 453	1 877 097
外商投资	Foreigner Invested	673	214 318	27 472 947
#外商独资	Foreigner Funded	434	128 989	13 901 937
按轻、重工业分	**By Light/Heavy Industry**			
轻工业	Light Industry	971	151 736	10 546 966
重工业	Heavy Industry	1 528	320 506	45 580 906
按企业规模分	**By Scale of Entrerprises**			
大型企业	Large	25	109 225	27 319 566
中型企业	Medium	259	173 247	18 228 643
小型企业	Small	2 215	189 770	10 579 663

Major Indicators of Industrial Enterprises with Independent Accounting Systems (Above-Certain-Scaled Enterprises)

(10 000 yuan)

工业销售产值 Sales Value of Industry	流动资产平均余额 Average Balance of Floating Assets	资产总计 Total Assets	负债总计 Total Liabilities	主营业务收入 Revenue of of Floating Assets	税金 Tax	利润总额 Total Profits
55 837 769	**28 504 703**	**59 899 938**	**28 716 365**	**61 387 502**	**1 664 048**	**2 199 338**
19 911 864	9 868 512	24 635 748	11 391 869	19 422 185	560 445	133 170
12 915 541	7 063 931	16 474 002	6 729 267	16 159 281	639 869	987 234
23 010 364	11 572 260	18 790 188	10 595 229	25 806 036	463 734	1 078 934
25 193 574	12 657 359	34 147 739	14 748 409	25 168 367	768 966	616 662
6 808 101	1 009 408	12 597 946	2 613 587	6 858 783	354 318	115 031
294 131	194 346	273 965	171 938	291 654	10 112	8 919
297 094	201 769	317 747	154 964	298 680	13 122	22 289
123 131	88 264	148 084	77 413	130 007	3 997	5 534
5 485 984	5 183 992	8 076 325	5 141 109	5 031 348	143 630	426 504
9 086 909	4 280 532	10 188 204	4 995 162	9 432 255	165 147	-70 959
3 089 718	1 693 234	2 536 766	1 589 675	3 117 624	78 348	108 984
8 506	5 814	8 702	4 561	8 016	292	360
3 442 307	1 820 506	3 473 926	1 678 848	4 537 843	65 207	128 947
1 924 950	942 493	2 144 303	876 931	1 986 417	25 122	78 293
27 201 888	14 026 838	22 278 273	12 289 108	31 681 292	829 875	1 453 729
13 584 337	6 326 272	10 302 670	5 827 403	15 097 578	250 460	615 230
10 530 097	5 041 668	8 422 605	4 293 299	10 965 941	267 104	595 403
45 307 672	23 463 035	51 477 333	24 423 066	50 421 561	1 396 944	1 603 935
27 220 771	13 587 848	34 920 264	15 303 711	30 783 955	933 850	664 111
18 042 314	8 489 511	14 482 066	7 803 996	19 668 932	444 143	911 080
10 574 684	6 427 344	10 497 608	5 608 658	10 934 615	286 055	624 147

表6-11　独立核算工业企业经济效益指标(规模以上)
(2008)

指　标	Indicators	工业经济效益综合指数 Composite Index of Industry Economic Results	总资产贡献率(%) Total Assets Contribution Ratio(%)
总　计	**Total**	**230.6**	**6.9**
按隶属关系分	**By Subordination**		
中央工业	Central	501.1	3.2
市属工业	Municipal	250.6	10.3
非中央、市属工业	Local	192.5	8.8
按登记注册类型分	**By Registration Categories**		
内　资	Domestic Funded	201.9	4.6
国　有	State-owned	469.4	3.9
集　体	Collective-owned	119.4	7.8
股份合作制	Share-holding	151.0	11.6
联　营	Jointly-operated	143.7	7.0
有限责任公司	Companies with Limited Liabilities	288.3	7.9
股份有限公司	Companies Limited by Shares	115.1	1.5
私　营	Private	129.2	8.0
其　他	Others	166.8	8.6
港澳台商投资	Hong Kong/Macao/Taiwan Invested	187.5	6.0
#港澳台商独资	Hong Kong/Macao/Taiwan Funded	218.2	5.1
外商投资	Foreign Invested	269.5	10.6
#外商独资	Foreign Funded	246.9	8.9
按轻、重工业分	**By Light/Heavy Industry**		
轻工业	Light Industry	199.5	10.8
重工业	Heavy Industry	249.8	6.2
按企业规模分	**By Scale of Enterprises**		
大型企业	Large	347.2	4.9
中型企业	Medium	238.6	10.0
小型企业	Small	170.7	9.1

Economic Results Indicators of Industrial Enterprise with Independent Accounting Systems(Above-Certain-Scaled Enterprises)

资本保值增值率(%) Ratio of Capital Holding and Adding(%)	资产负债率(%) Ratio of Capital to Liabilities(%)	流动资产周转率(次) Turnover Period of Circulating Assets(time)	成本费用利润率(%) After-tax Profit/Cost(%)	工业全员劳动生产率(元/人) Overall Industrial Labor Productivity (yuan/person)	工业产品销售率(%) Sales Rate of Industrial Products(%)
103.0	**47.9**	**2.2**	**3.7**	**236 656**	**99.5**
100.1	46.2	2.0	0.7	716 634	99.6
104.6	40.8	2.3	6.3	239 682	100.2
106.2	56.4	2.2	4.3	162 068	99.0
102.7	43.2	2.0	2.5	206 748	99.7
110.1	20.7	6.8	1.7	575 056	100.2
96.6	62.8	1.5	3.1	67 552	99.4
104.1	48.8	1.5	7.8	75 625	99.4
145.4	52.3	1.5	4.3	90 586	99.1
94.9	63.7	1.0	9.1	317 592	99.1
92.6	49.0	2.2	0.7	91 455	99.3
117.5	62.7	1.8	3.6	69 466	100.7
107.9	52.4	1.4	4.7	131 149	100.0
100.0	48.3	2.5	2.9	167 707	102.0
101.1	40.9	2.1	4.1	219 453	102.5
104.1	55.2	2.3	4.8	280 543	99.0
102.3	56.6	2.4	4.2	250 589	97.7
107.3	51.0	2.2	5.7	159 417	99.8
102.4	47.4	2.1	3.2	273 223	99.4
104.5	43.8	2.3	2.2	442 224	99.6
94.7	53.9	2.3	4.8	232 346	99.0
109.9	53.4	1.7	6.0	122 273	100.0

表6－12　独立核算大中型工业企业主要指标
(2008)

单位:万元

指　标	Indicators	企业单位数（个）Enterprises (unit)	从业人员平均人数(人) Average Number of Employed Persons(person)	工业总产值 Gross Output Value of Industry
总　计	**Total**	**284**	**282 472**	**45 548 209**
按隶属关系分	**By Subordination**			
中央工业	Central	20	48 180	19 712 434
市属工业	Municipal	68	80 809	11 088 384
非中央、市属工业	Local	196	153 483	14 747 391
按登记注册类型分	**Type of Registration**			
内　资	Domstic Funded	92	99 383	20 862 355
国　有	State-owned	16	30 175	6 688 941
集　体	Collective-owned	2	930	24 417
股份合作制	Share-holding	4	1 615	46 761
联　营	Jointly-operated	1	363	9 155
有限责任公司	Companies with Limited Liability	35	34 427	4 468 012
股份有限公司	Companies Limited by Shares	10	15 829	9 089 255
私　营	Private	24	16 044	535 814
港澳台商投资	Hong Kong/Macao/Taiwan-Invested	35	26 369	2 428 743
#港澳台商独资	Hong Kong/Macao/Taiwan-Funded	17	14 776	1 457 972
外商投资	Foreigner-Invested	157	156 720	22 257 111
#外商投资	Foreigner-Funded	93	93 874	10 794 259
按轻、重工业分	**By Light/Heavy Industry**			
轻工业	Light Industry	111	71 401	7 589 776
重工业	Heavy Industry	173	211 071	37 958 433
按从业人员平均人数分	**By Average Number of Employed Persons**			
5 000 人及以上	≥5000 persons	10	69 262	19 825 086
3 000～4 999 人	3000～4999 persons	4	16 065	1 274 681
1 000～2 999 人	1000～2999 persons	56	90 371	12 702 933
999 及以下	≤ 999 persons	214	106 774	11 745 509
按工业总产值分	**By Gross Output Value of Industry**			
5 亿元及以上	≥500 million	105	180 718	42 051 323
10 000～49 999 万元	100～499.99 million yuan	135	82 381	3 197 879
5 000～9 999 万元	50～99.99 million yuan	35	15 715	261 738
5 000 万元以下	<50 million yuan	9	3 658	37 269
按利税总额分	**By Pre～Tax Profit**			
1 亿元及以上	≥100 million yuan	15	55 748	19 391 024
5 000～9 999 万元	50～99.99 milion yuan	16	19 571	5 072 275
1 000～4 999 万元	10～49.99 milion yuan	54	51 988	8 504 029
1 000 万元以下	<10 million yuan	199	155 165	12 580 881

Major Indicators of Large and Medium Industrial Enterprises with Independent Accounting Systems

(10 000 yuan)

工业销售产值 Sales Value of Industry	流动资产平均余额 Average Balance of Floating Assets	资产总计 Total Assets	负债总计 Total Liabilities	主营业务收入 Revenue of of Floating Assets	税金 Tax	利润总额 Total Profits
45 263 085	**22 077 359**	**49 402 330**	**23 107 707**	**50 452 887**	**1 377 993**	**1 575 191**
19 629 538	9 670 322	24 356 696	11 197 662	19 140 203	546 609	115 119
11 121 760	6 100 282	14 410 777	5 809 638	14 345 503	580 130	855 391
14 511 787	6 306 755	10 634 857	6 100 407	16 967 181	251 254	604 681
20 801 722	10 096 070	29 689 703	12 234 365	20 621 675	617 205	396 622
6 697 342	959 779	12 500 966	2 565 549	6 745 713	350 265	110 271
24 471	16 974	24 670	16 634	25 854	2 028	1 819
43 884	25 648	48 249	17 691	44 159	2 413	4 107
9 043	5 705	10 818	5 367	9 878	423	-518
4 426 800	4 579 523	6 520 891	4 391 602	3 946 853	86 876	323 961
9 022 085	4 257 844	10 139 567	4 972 601	9 262 054	164 176	-73 273
578 097	250 597	444 542	264 921	587 164	11 024	30 255
2 490 278	1 184 441	2 412 370	1 157 556	3 556 332	34 849	51 249
1 511 571	733 443	1 830 933	732 339	1 565 122	15 696	20 991
21 971 085	10 796 848	17 300 257	9 715 786	26 274 880	725 939	1 127 320
10 451 645	4 422 707	7 490 639	4 318 931	11 839 690	184 099	423 326
7 554 805	3 264 238	5 443 540	2 756 449	7 827 894	187 556	409 220
37 708 280	18 813 121	43 958 790	20 351 258	42 624 993	1 190 437	1 165 971
19 801 219	7 249 258	21 490 695	8 447 183	23 752 624	852 509	-277 978
1 227 006	1 001 169	5 319 995	1 305 593	1 336 002	39 776	312 245
12 633 565	8 452 158	13 854 848	8 850 205	12 206 422	187 917	930 659
11 601 295	5 374 774	8 736 792	4 504 726	13 157 839	297 791	610 265
41 781 349	19 996 987	45 283 199	21 132 122	46 794 349	1 277 114	1 357 446
3 179 846	1 827 320	3 623 501	1 751 373	3 314 925	87 604	211 682
263 448	211 655	427 419	183 171	300 178	11 263	7 668
38 442	41 397	68 211	41 041	43 435	2 012	-1 605
19 250 154	6 570 023	24 481 415	8 096 732	22 140 424	1 086 913	220 664
5 097 235	3 277 736	4 535 857	2 381 073	6 087 052	120 579	246 979
8 386 879	5 787 615	9 523 369	5 693 767	9 991 823	126 746	573 739
12 528 817	6 441 985	10 861 689	6 936 135	12 233 588	43 755	533 809

表6-13 港澳台及外商投资工业企业主要指标
(2008)

单位:万元

指标	Indicators	企业单位数(个) Enterprises (unit)	从业人员平均人数(人) Average Number of Employed Persons(person)	工业总产值 Gross Output Value of Industry
总 计	**Total**	**945**	**259 498**	**30 885 438**
按登记注册类型分	**By Type of Registration**			
与港澳台商合资经营企业	China-Hong Kong/Macao/Taiwan Joint Venture	111	21 322	1 462 355
与港澳台商合作经营企业	China-Hong Kong/Macao/Taiwan cooperative	7	260	26 250
港澳台商独资企业	Hong Kong/Macao/Taiwan Funded	94	21 787	1 880 083
港澳台商投资股份有限公司	Hong Kong/Macao/Taiwan Investment Companies Limited by Shares	3	576	14 602
中外合资经营企业	Sino-Foreign Jointly-operated	231	71 430	10 961 117
中外合作经营企业	Sino-Foreign Cooperative	25	5 350	625 459
外商独资企业	Foreigner Funded	468	129 689	13 910 515
外商投资股份有限公司	Foreign Investment Company Limited by Shares	6	9 084	2 005 057
按行业分	**By Sector**			
农副食品加工业	Processing of Agricultural Side-Line Food	8	1 024	1 081 080
食品制造业	Food Manufacturing	14	3 135	355 790
饮料制造业	Beverage Manufacturing	9	2 904	1 005 094
烟草制品业	Tobacco Products	1	341	18 517
纺织业	Textile Industry	39	5 351	144 384
纺织服装、鞋、帽制造业	Textile Products, Clothes, Shoes and Hats	51	8 911	297 776
皮革、毛皮、羽毛(绒)及其制品业	Leather, Fur, Down & Related Products	10	1 157	13 598
木材加工及木、竹、藤、棕、草制品业	Timber-Processing, Bamboo, Cane, Palm Fiber and Straw Products	3	576	19 255
家具制造业	Furniture Manufacturing	7	1 311	73 343
造纸及纸制品业	Paper-making and Paper Products	13	3 531	172 592

Major Indicators of HK/Macao/Taiwan & Overseas Invested Industrial Enterprises

(10 000 yuan)

工业销售产值 Sales Value of Industry	流动资产平均余额 Average Balance of Floating Assets	资产总计 Total Assets	负债总计 Total Liabilities	主营业务收入 Revenue of of Floating Assets	税金 Tax	利润总额 Total Profits
30 680 586	**15 871 862**	**25 817 774**	**14 015 050**	**36 234 707**	**895 787**	**1 575 010**
1 480 700	798 932	1 144 138	714 039	2 499 499	38 630	45 724
26 056	41 253	49 014	38 385	24 053	919	2 370
1 927 660	945 114	2 149 065	880 702	1 988 657	25 162	77 140
14 791	45 335	165 977	72 589	30 231	643	-1 202
11 030 390	5 195 935	8 628 553	4 407 345	13 902 201	520 698	744 025
623 484	421 043	583 754	357 119	636 438	16 462	48 450
13 593 028	6 334 482	10 324 758	5 844 161	15 104 107	250 824	612 732
1 984 477	2 089 768	2 772 515	1 700 710	2 049 521	42 449	45 771
1 067 129	282 954	410 593	252 646	1 085 194	12 895	42 847
361 901	118 348	248 768	145 201	376 887	44 075	53 238
791 043	303 975	478 629	306 564	857 528	67 663	24 404
18 517	23 541	41 250	4 877	18 249	2 759	3 173
145 747	108 036	146 660	88 359	143 146	2 080	1 897
263 887	215 727	253 715	188 141	278 589	1 975	-3 205
13 346	13 696	16 645	15 834	14 281	55	-869
19 255	15 588	19 054	15 338	17 505	162	-48
73 381	40 279	56 641	31 329	72 661	709	4 514
174 805	82 427	156 891	84 076	172 224	3 785	7 385

单位:万元

表 6－13 续表 Continued

指 标	Indicators	企业单位数(个) Enterprises (unit)	从业人员平均人数(人) Average Number of Employed Persons(person)	工业总产值 Gross Output Value of Industry
印刷业、记录媒介的复制	Printing and Record Medium Reproduction	21	3 104	90 314
文教体育用品制造业	Stationery, Educational and Sports Goods	18	5 471	114 986
石油加工、炼焦及核燃料加工业	Petroleum Processing, Coke Products and Processing of Nuclear Fuel	7	375	111 382
化学原料及化学制品制造业	Raw Chemical Materials and Chemical Products	62	9 497	2 143 372
医药制造业	Medicine Manufacturing	35	7 624	690 885
化学纤维制造业	Chemical Fiber Manufacturing	2	1 386	485 779
橡胶制品业	Rubber Products	8	890	76 491
塑料制品业	Plastic Products	61	12 886	383 511
非金属矿物制品业	Nonmetal Mineral Products	24	4 175	278 776
黑色金属冶炼及压延加工业	Smelting and Pressing of Ferrous Metal	3	772	310 764
有色金属冶炼及压延加工业	Smelting and Pressing of Nonferrous Metal	4	582	158 019
金属制品业	Metal Products	41	7 766	701 757
通用设备制造业	General Purpose Equipment Manufacturing	82	18 317	1 491 576
专用设备制造业	Specialized Equipment Manufacturing	82	10 876	882 731
交通运输设备制造业	Transportation Equipment Manufacturing	63	25 215	4 946 348
电气机械及器材制造业	Electrical Machinery and Equipment	82	25 247	2 070 706
通信设备、计算机及其他电子设备制造业	Manufacturing of Telecommunications Equipment, Computers and Other Electronic Equipment	136	84 703	11 592 656
仪器仪表及文化、办公用机械制造业	Instrument, Meter, and Office Machines	45	10 176	1 099 186
工艺品及其他制造业	Handicrafts and Other Production	11	774	9 391
电力、热力的生产和供应业	Production and Supply of Electricity and Heating Power	2	223	19 714
水的生产和供应业	Production and Supply of Tap Water	1	1 198	45 665

(10 000 yuan)

工业销售产值 Sales Value of Industry	流动资产平均余额 Average Balance of Floating Assets	资产总计 Total Assets	负债总计 Total Liabilities	主营业务收入 Revenue of of Floating Assets	税金 Tax	利润总额 Total Profits
91 536	68 782	120 520	52 913	90 164	5 840	6 509
115 326	83 914	156 992	64 284	127 261	1 047	5 878
111 840	30 919	69 269	39 622	111 340	1 708	5 158
2 129 165	998 946	1 611 535	772 505	2 153 169	56 446	163 924
695 424	358 503	721 218	343 254	678 943	24 355	83 072
523 832	194 089	386 399	236 066	534 495	4 815	-9 295
75 731	31 674	41 995	16 544	77 016	1 038	3 455
401 521	219 152	366 213	164 494	400 944	8 200	10 860
264 332	373 896	692 224	331 561	363 016	12 286	21 544
301 641	140 659	396 413	251 160	332 112	210	-30 475
161 565	66 054	78 327	36 526	166 048	604	-6 144
711 414	381 863	578 004	267 655	755 927	24 568	76 468
1 541 784	961 434	1 296 351	619 052	1 601 554	38 058	114 189
879 419	567 806	906 682	505 253	926 926	21 090	88 197
5 051 211	2 527 659	4 022 414	2 285 509	7 891 981	418 981	498 050
2 074 430	851 418	1 234 014	660 872	2 099 255	26 198	76 095
11 458 567	6 045 308	9 952 067	5 591 656	13 700 207	100 876	197 530
1 094 195	703 799	893 490	442 485	1 108 561	9 803	119 962
9 549	7 435	14 608	5 528	9 600	102	-1 343
19 714	36 717	104 599	13 531	30 419	1 043	13 286
39 379	17 264	345 594	182 215	39 505	2 361	4 754

表6-14　私营工业企业主要指标

（2008）

单位：万元

指标	Indicators	企业单位数（个）Enterprises（unit）	从业人员平均人数（人）Average Number of Employed Persons（person）	工业总产值 Gross Output Value of Industry
总　计	**Total**	**2 266**	**113 175**	**3 347 099**
按轻、重工业分	**By Light/Heavy Industry**			
轻工业	Light Industry	1 025	49 891	999 396
重工业	Heavy Industry	1 241	63 284	2 347 703
按主要工业行业分	**By Main Sector**			
#农副食品加工业	Processing of Agricultural Side-line Food	13	562	24 796
食品制造业	Food Producing	13	297	13 824
饮料制造业	Beverage Producing	2	70	476
纺织业	Textile Industry	203	13 723	304 587
纺织服装、鞋、帽制造业	Textile Products, Clothes, Shoes and Hats	162	11 926	135 494
皮革、毛皮、羽毛(绒)及其制品业	Leather, Fur, Down & Related Products	43	2 407	38 615
木材加工及木、竹、藤、棕、草制品业	Timber-processing, Bamboo, Cane, Palm Fiber and Straw Products	37	808	33 877
家具制造业	Furniture Making	48	2 479	51 705
造纸及纸制品业	Paper-making and Paper Products	74	2 075	64 383
印刷业和记录媒介的复制	Printing and Record Medium Reproduction	149	4 745	98 282
文教体育用品制造业	Education Goods and Sports Goods	36	1 690	34 065
石油加工、炼焦及核燃料加工业	Petroleum Processing, Coke Products and Processing of Nuclear Fuel	11	308	32 094
化学原料及化学制品制造业	Raw Chemical Material and Chemical Products	88	3 162	119 835
医药制造业	Medicine Manufacturing	16	1 061	33 657
化学纤维制造业	Chemical Fiber Manufacturing	3	135	7 443
橡胶制品业	Rubber Products	26	901	18 271
塑料制品业	Plastic Products	173	6 592	215 722
非金属矿物制品业	Nonmetal Mineral Products	69	3 033	136 904
黑色金属冶炼及压延加工业	Smelting and Pressing of Ferrous Metal	24	881	91 285
有色金属冶炼及压延加工业	Smelting and Pressing of Nonferrous Metal	33	1 109	107 925
金属制品业	Metal Products	325	15 670	388 976
通用设备制造业	Manufacturing of General Purpose Equipment	261	11 721	430 604
专用设备制造业	Specialized Equipment Manufacturing	103	7 010	344 007
交通运输设备制造业	Transportation Equipment Manufacturing	117	9 464	210 553
电气机械及器材制造业	Electrical Machinery and Equipment	144	7 515	310 856
通信设备、计算机及其他电子设备制造业	Manufacturing of Telecommunications Equipment, Computers and Other Electronic Equipment	30	1 628	48 421
仪器仪表及文化、办公用机械制造业	Instrument, Meter, and Office Machines	20	834	20 620
工艺品及其他制造业	Handicrafts and Other Production	36	1 142	20 580
废弃资源和废旧材料回收加工业	Recycling of Abandoned Resources and Wastes	5	201	8 534

Major Indicators of PNA Private Industrial Enterprises

(10 000 yuan)

工业销售产值 Sales Value of Industry	流动资产平均余额 Average Balance of Floating Assets	资产总计 Total Assets	负债总计 Total Liabilities	主营业务收入 Revenue of of Floating Assets	税金 Tax	利润总额 Total Profits
3 367 919	**1 862 401**	**2 778 439**	**1 730 610**	**3 317 703**	**87 030**	**110 225**
999 858	559 705	820 433	477 458	978 405	27 683	24 639
2 368 061	1 302 696	1 958 006	1 253 152	2 339 298	59 347	85 586
25 938	78 630	88 473	12 459	37 225	246	8 378
13 949	6 367	12 785	6 396	13 867	154	-294
476	1 238	1 681	1 112	469	10	3
300 629	129 715	184 576	129 996	286 643	7 369	1 744
134 536	61 280	84 235	54 707	132 999	5 104	2 653
38 144	17 401	24 329	16 815	35 156	875	193
33 826	20 062	23 993	18 867	34 276	657	153
51 888	29 954	44 374	27 195	51 438	937	315
63 933	32 170	43 731	29 090	61 555	1 728	781
97 757	52 021	84 631	54 391	92 134	2 933	655
35 156	19 146	25 693	14 210	32 490	241	379
31 136	11 633	15 879	11 298	34 139	499	674
117 938	76 533	107 315	59 599	117 916	4 223	4 291
37 565	22 531	68 144	37 756	32 788	1 895	3 730
7 443	1 275	1 890	1 331	7 443	101	32
18 266	10 911	14 290	6 985	18 517	736	1 425
215 605	111 338	161 645	90 445	218 727	6 931	10 378
134 440	166 793	251 414	194 662	135 437	5 977	-658
91 180	41 296	71 003	47 286	91 364	1 578	4 389
108 401	45 387	53 545	40 365	107 499	537	128
383 727	188 940	278 722	178 344	366 655	10 979	9 712
424 843	234 594	325 225	209 686	414 824	11 779	19 992
401 118	183 873	295 608	192 923	407 757	6 990	16 973
205 675	91 979	178 858	119 702	199 045	5 742	6 706
294 040	163 316	241 694	130 384	290 049	5 671	13 433
50 195	33 076	45 225	19 931	50 189	1 626	1 918
20 419	12 752	22 018	9 511	19 961	718	1 073
20 496	11 662	19 965	9 425	17 735	578	985
8 491	6 198	6 958	5 551	8 698	143	18

表6-15 分地区工业企业主要指标
Major Indicators of Industrial Enterprises by Location
(2008)

单位:万元 (10 000 yuan)

地 区	Subdistrict/Town	企业单位数(个) Enterprises (unit)	从业人员平均人数(人) Average Number of Employed Persons (person)	工业总产值 Gross Output Value of Industry	工业销售产值 Sales Value of Industry	利润总额 Total Profits
总 计	**Total**	**3 880**	**497 458**	**56 492 221**	**56 199 642**	**2 189 154**
街道小计	**Subdistrict Tot**	**170**	**64 657**	**17 893 615**	**17 916 449**	**-187 720**
潍坊新村街道	Weifangxincun Subdistrict	22	23 514	6 637 929	6 694 701	5 994
陆家嘴街道	Lujiazui Subdistrict	9	779	23 353	26 052	1 794
周家渡街道	Zhoujiadu Subdistrict	4	335	15 785	15 412	1 496
塘桥街道	Tangqiao Subdistrict	14	2 890	102 567	102 588	7 748
上钢新村街道	Shanggangxincun Subdistrict	12	2 998	316 477	297 982	-30 442
南码头路街道	Nanmatou Road Subdistrict	16	3 574	2 871 249	2 874 806	247 971
沪东新村街道	Hudongxincun Subdistrict	15	20 610	7 292 368	7 282 877	-437 903
金杨新村街道	Jinyangxincun Subdistrict	9	2 811	50 475	46 053	678
洋泾街道	Yangjing Subdistrict	34	4 111	344 181	334 660	11 525
浦兴路街道	Puxing Road Subdistrict	2	731	125 848	125 792	-1 210
花木街道	Huamu Subdistrict	33	2 304	113 383	115 526	4 629
镇小计	**Town Tot**	**3 100**	**230 598**	**12 861 871**	**12 823 923**	**729 614**
川沙新镇	Chuansha New Town	889	51 304	1 481 672	1 530 977	56 196
高桥镇	Gaoqiao Town	167	11 072	1 050 727	1 027 914	23 347
北蔡镇	Beicai Town	166	14 967	608 714	609 266	46 361
合庆镇	Heqing Town	438	33 180	1 480 235	1 448 892	61 686
唐 镇	Tangzhen Town	197	14 250	554 516	555 297	9 988
曹路镇	Caolu Town	326	30 602	1 275 845	1 257 195	56 470
金桥镇	Jinqiao Town	64	6 368	183 574	185 206	5 562
高行镇	Gaohang Town	187	17 807	1 426 276	1 433 807	61 678
高东镇	Gaodong Town	149	18 826	3 667 720	3 637 020	312 700
张江镇	Zhangjiang Town	256	13 232	532 328	538 372	27 991
三林镇	Sanlin Town	261	18 990	600 264	599 977	67 635
重点开发小区小计	**Key Development Zones Tot**	**610**	**202 203**	**25 736 735**	**25 459 270**	**1 647 260**
金桥出口加工区	Jinqiao Export Processing Zone	230	51 124	5 554 277	5 550 646	332 671
外高桥保税区	Waigaoqiao Free Trade Zone	252	106 595	16 082 324	15 996 936	888 042
张江高科技园区	Zhangjiang High-Tech Park	128	44 484	4 100 134	3 911 688	426 547

主要统计指标解释

建筑业总产值

建筑业总产值是以货币形式表现的建筑(安装)业企业在一定时期内生产的建筑业产品和提供的服务的总和。建筑业总产值包括:

(1)建筑工程产值:指列入建筑工程预算内的各种工程价值。

(2)(设备)安装工程产值:指设备安装工程价值,不包括被安装设备本身价值。

(3)其他产值:建筑业总产值中除建筑工程、安装工程以外的产值。包括房屋构筑物修理产值、非标准设备制造产值、总包企业向分包企业收取的管理费以及不能明确划分的施工活动所完成的产值。

a. 房屋构筑物修理产值:指房屋和构筑物修理所完成的产值,但不包括被修理房屋、构筑物本身价值和生产设备的修理产值。

b. 非标准设备制造产值:指加工制造没有定型的非标准生产设备的加工费和原材料价值(如化工厂、炼油厂用的各种罐、槽,矿井生产统一使用的各种漏斗、三角槽、阀门等)以及附属加工厂为本企业承建工程制作的非标准设备的价值。

房屋建筑施工面积

房屋建筑施工面积指在报告期内施过工的全部房屋建筑面积,包括本期新开工的房屋面积、上期施工跨入本期继续施工的房屋面积、上期停缓建在本期恢复施工的房屋面积、本期竣工的房屋面积及本期施工后又停缓建的房屋面积。

房屋建筑竣工面积

房屋建筑竣工面积指在报告期内房屋建筑按照设计要求全部完工,达到了(住人和)使用条件,经验收鉴定合格,正式移交使用单位的房屋建筑面积

房屋建筑面积竣工率

指一定时期内房屋竣工面积占同期房屋施工面积的比率。该指标从房屋建筑施工速度的角度反映投资效果。

工　业

指从事自然资源的开采,对采掘品和农产品进行加工和再加工的物质生产部门。具体包括:(1)对自然资源的开采,如采矿、晒盐等(但不包括禽兽捕猎和水产捕捞);(2)对农副产品的加工、再加工,如粮油加工、食品加工、缫丝、纺织、制革等;(3)对采掘品的加工、再加工,如炼铁、炼钢、化工生产、石油加工、机器制造、木材加工等,以及电力、自来水、煤气的生产和供应等;(4)对工业品的修理、翻新,如机器设备的修理、交通运输工具(包括小卧车)的修理等。

1984年以前农村的村及村以下办工业归属农业,1984年以后划归工业。

工业统计调查单位为独立核算法人工业企业。

独立核算法人工业企业指从事工业生产经营活动的单位。独立核算法人工业企业应同时具备以下条件:①依法成立,有自己的名称、组织机构和场所,能够承担民事责任;②独立拥有和使用资产,承担负债,有权与其他单位签订合同;③独立核算盈亏,并能够编制资产负债表。

轻工业

指主要提供生活消费品和制作手工工具的工业。按其所使用的原料不同,可分为两大类:(1)以农产品为原料的轻工业,是指直接或间接以农产品为基本原料的轻工业。主要包括食品制造、饮料制造、烟草加工、纺织、缝纫、皮革和毛皮制作、造纸以及印刷等工业;(2)以非农产品为原料的轻工业,是指以工业品为原料的轻工业。主要包括文教体育用品、化学药品制造、合成纤维制造、日用化学制品、日用玻璃制品、日用金属制品、手工工具制造、医疗器械制造、文化和办公用机械制造等工业。

重工业

指为国民经济各部门提供物质技术基础的主要生产资料的工业。按其生产性质和产品用途,可以分为下列三类:(1)采掘(伐)工业,是指对自然资源的开采,包括石油开采、煤炭开采、金属矿开采、非金属矿开采等工业;(2)原材料工业,指向国民经济各部门提供基本材料、动力和燃料的工业。包括金属冶炼及加工、炼焦及焦炭、化学、化工原料、水泥、人造板以及电力、石油和煤炭加工等工业;(3)加工工业,是指对工业原材料进行再加工制造的工业。包括装备国民经济各部门的机械设备制造工业、金属结构、水泥制品等工业,以及为农业提供的生产资料如化肥、农药等工业。

根据上述划分原则,修理业中以重工业产品为修理作业对象的划为重工业,反之划为轻工业。

工业总产值

(1)定义:工业总产值是以货币形式表现的,工业企业在一定时期内生产的工业最终产品或提供工业性劳务活动的总价值量。它反映一定时间内工业生产的总规模和总水平。

(2)计算原则:工业生产的原则,即凡是企业在报告期生产的经检验合格的产品,不管是否在报告期销售,均包括在内。

最终产品的原则,即凡是计入工业总产值的产品,必须是本企业生产的经检验合格的,不需要再进行任何加工的最终产品。如果企业有中间产品(半成品)对外销售,则对

外销售的中间产品应视为企业的最终产品。

工厂法原则，即工业总产值是以工业企业作为基本计算（核算）单位，即按企业的最终产品计算工业总产值。按这种方法计算的工业总产值，不允许同一产品价值在企业内部重复计算，不能把企业内部各个车间（分厂）生产的成果相加，但允许企业间的重复计算。

（3）内容及计算方法：1995 年全国工业普查对工业总产值（原规定）的内容及计算原则和方法做了某些修订，修订后的工业总产值（新规定）包括三项内容：即本期生产成品价值、对外加工费收入、在制品半成品期末期初差额价值三部分。

本期生产成品价值：指企业本期生产，并在报告期内不再进行加工，经检验、包装入库的全部工业成品（半产品）价值合计，包括企业生产的自制设备及提供给本企业在建工程、其他非工业部门和福利部门等单位使用的成品价值。本期生产成品价值为按自备原材料生产的产品的数量乘以本期不含增值税（销项税额）的产品实际销售平均单价计算；会计核算中按成本价格转帐的自制设备和自产自用的成品，按成本价格计算生产成品价值。生产成品价值中不包括用定货者来料加工的成品（半产品）价值。

对外加工费收入：指企业在报告期内完成的对外承接的工业品加工（包括用定货者来料加工产品）的加工费收入和对外工业修理作业所取得的加工费收入。对外加工费收入按不含增值税（销项税额）的价格计算，可根据会计“产品销售收入”科目的有关资料取得。

对于本企业对内非工业部门提供的加工修理、设备安装的劳务收入，如果企业会计核算基础较好，能取得这部分资料，而且这部分价值所占比重较大，应包括在对外加工费收入中。

自制半成品在制品期末期初差额价值：指企业报告期在制品期末减期初的差额价值，本指标一般可以从会计核算资料中取得。如果会计产品成本核算中不计算半成品、在制品的成本，则总产值中也不包括这部分价值，反之则包括。

（4）工业总产值统计范围变化和计算方法修订情况：1984 年以前工业总产值不包括村办工业，村办工业总产值划归农业。1984 年以后工业总产值包括村办工业。

1995 年工业普查对工业总产值计算方法做了修订，即从 1995 年始按新修订（新规定）方法计算工业总产值。新规定与原规定的区别如下：

全价与加工费的计算原则不同：新规定为凡自备原材料，不论其生产繁简程度如何，一律按全价计算工业总产值；凡来料加工，允许按加工费计算工业总产值。原规定则视生产加工的繁简程度不同，规定哪些行业按全价，哪些行业按加工费计算工业总产值。

自制半成品、在产品期末期初差额价值的计算原则不同：新规定要求，凡会计产品成本核算时计算了成本的差额价值，总产值中就应包括，否则可不包括；原规定则按生产周期六个月的界限区分，凡生产周期六个月以上的企业，总产值计算中应包括这部分差额价值，否则可不包括。

计算价格不同：新规定按不含增值税（销项税额）的价格计算；原规定则按含增值税（销项税额）的价格计算。

工业销售产值

是以货币表现的工业企业在一定时期内销售的、本企业生产的工业产品总量。包括已销售的成品、半成品价值，对外提供的工业性作业价值和对本单位基本建设部门、生活福利部门等提供的产品和工业性作业及自制设备的价值。工业销售产值依循的是以产品所有权转移为计算原则，因此，已销售的成品、半成品不论是本期生产的、还是上期生产的，只要是本期销售出去的均包括在内。对外提供的工业性作业是指企业按合同对外提供的工业性劳务。

工业销售产值的计算范围、计算价格和计算方法与工业总产值一致，但两者计算的基础不同，工业销售产值计算的基础是产品销售总量，工业总产值计算的基础是工业产品生产总量。

出口交货值

是指工业企业交给外贸部门或自营（委托）出口（包括销往香港、澳门地区、台湾省）的产品价值；批量销于国内或在过境批量出口等但用外汇价格结算的产品价值；外商来样、来料加工，来件装配和补偿贸易等生产，分别参照计算总产值的规定要求按全价或加工费计算的价值。

大、中、小型企业

大中小型企业划分标准：自 2003 年年报起，大中小型企业划分标准执行“统计上大中小型企业划分办法（暂行）”（国统字[2003]17 号）。即大型企业必须同时达到从业人员数 2000 人、销售收入 30000 万元、资产总额 40000 万元；中型企业必须同时达到 300 人≤从业人员数＜2000 人、3000 万元≤销售收入＜30000 万元、4000 万元≤资产总额＜40000 万元；其余的均为小型企业。

独立核算工业企业、非独立核算工业生产单位

工业企业按其行政和财务是否独立，分为独立核算工业企业和非独立核算工业生产单位。

独立核算工业企业应同时具备下列三个条件：(1)行政上有独立的组织形式；(2)经济上独立核算，自负盈亏，编制独立的资金平衡表（或资产负债表）；(3)有权与其他单位签订合同，并在银行设有独立帐户。独立核算工业企业不论是单一性生产或联合性生产的企业，均以整个企业作为一个基层单位进行统计，而不按分厂、车间统计。

非独立核算工业生产单位是指不同时具备独立核算工业企业三个条件，附设于其他企业、事业、机关、团体、学校、科研机构、部队等单位的工业生产单位。非独立核算工业

生产单位必须同时具备下列三个条件，才可列入工业统计范围，即：(1)有固定的生产场所和生产设备；(2)有固定的生产工人和学徒在10人以上；(3)一般单位常年生产，季节性生产的单位全年开工时间在三个月以上。

资产总计

资产是指企业拥有或者控制的能以货币计量的经济资源，包括各种财产、债权和其他权利。资产按其流动性(即资产的变现能力和支付能力)划分为：流动资产、长期投资、固定资产、无形资产、递延资产和其他资产。该指标根据企业会计“资产负债表”中“资产总计”项目的期末数增列。

流动资产合计

指可以在一年或者超过一年的一个营业周期内变现或者耗用的资产，包括现金及各种存款、短期投资、应收及预付货款、存款等。

流动资产平均余额

指企业在报告期内全部流动资产的平均余额。

固定资产净值年平均余额

指固定资产净值在报告期内余额的平均数。计算公式为：

固定资产净值年平均余额＝1至12月各月月初、月末固定资产净值之和/24

该指标根据“资产负债表”中“固定资产原价”、“累计折旧”指标的期初、期末数计算填列。

固定资产净值指固定资产原价减去历年已提折旧额后的净额。计算公式为：

固定资产净值＝固定资产原价－累计折旧

负债合计

负债合计是指企业所承担的能以货币计量，将以资产或劳务偿付的债务总计。负债一般按偿还期长短分为流动负债和长期负债。流动负债合计是指企业在一年内或超过一年的一个营业周期内偿还的债务；长期负债合计是指偿还期在一年以上或者超过一年的一个营业周期内偿还债务。

所有者权益

指企业投资人对企业净资产的所有权。企业净资产等于企业全部资产减去全部负债后的余额，包括企业投资人对企业的最初投入的实际到位的资产及资本公积金、盈余公积金和未分配利润。所有者权益合计数小于零，表示企业资不抵债。

利润总额

指企业生产经营活动的最终成果，是企业在一定时期内实现的盈亏相抵后的利润总额（亏损以“－”号表示），它等于营业利润加上补贴收入加上投资收益加上营业外净收入再加上以前年度损益调整。

总资产贡献率

反映企业全部资产的获利能力，是企业经营业绩和管理水平的集中体现，是评价和考核企业盈利能力的核心指标。计算公式为：

总资产贡献率(％)＝利润总额＋税金总额＋利息支出/平均资金总额×100％

公式中：税金总额为产品销售税金及附加与应缴增值税之和；平均资产总额为期初期末资产之和的算术平均值。

资产负债率

该指标既反映企业经营风险的大小，也反映企业利用债权人提供的资金从事经营活动的能力。计算公式为：

资产负债率(％)＝负债总额/资产总额×100％

资产与负债均为报告期期末数。

流动资产周转次数

指一定时期内流动资产完成的周转次数，反映投入工业企业流动资金的周转速度。计算公式为：

流动资产周转次数＝产品销售收入/全部流动资产平均余额

公式中：全部流动资产平均余额为期初和期末的流动资产之和的算术平均值。

产品销售率

该指标反映工业产品已实现销售的程度，是分析工业产销衔接情况、研究工业产品满足社会需求的指标。计算公式为：

产品销售率(％)＝工业销售产值/工业总产值(现价)×100％

资本保值增值率

该指标反映企业净资产的变动状况，是企业发展能力的集中体现。计算公式为：

资本保值增值率＝报告期期末所有者权益/上年同期期末所有者权益

所有者权益等于资产总计减负债总计。

成本费用利润率

反映企业投入的生产成本及费用的经济效益，同时也反映企业降低成本所取得的经济效益。计算公式为：

成本费用利润(％)＝利润总额/成本费用总额×100％

公式中:成本费用总额为产品销售成本、销售费用、管理费用、财务费用之和。

全员劳动生产率

该指标反映企业的生产效率和劳动投入的经济效益。计算公式为:

$$全员劳动生产率(元/人)=\frac{工业增加值}{全部从业人员平均人数}$$

EXPLANATORY NOTES TO MAJOR STATISTICAL INDICATORS

Gross Output Value of Construction

Gross Output Value of Construction refers to total of construction products and services, expressed in money terms, produced or rendered by (completed by) construction and installation enterprises during a given period of time. It includes:

(1) Output value of construction projects, that is the value of projects covered by the project budgets;

(2) Output value of installation projects, that is the value of the installation of equipment, (excluding the value of the equipment to be installed);

(3) Output value of other projects refers to other output value of gross output value of construction industry besides construction and installation projects. It includes the output value of building repairing, nonstandard equipment manufacturing, the management fees going from subcontractor to original contractor and other construction output value which can not be measure off definitely.

a. Output value of repair of buildings and structures, that is the value created through the repairs of buildings or structures, but does not include the value of buildings or structures being repaired and the value of the repair of production equipment;

b. Output value of manufactured non-standard equipment, that is the value of non-standard production equipment (including raw materials and manufacturing cost) made for the construction project, irrespective of whether the equipment is manufactured on the construction site or by subsidiary workshops.

Floor Space of Buildings Under Construction

Floor Space of Buildings Under Construction refers to floor space of buildings under construction during the reference period, including newly started buildings, buildings started earlier and continued during the reference period, and buildings suspended earlier but restarted during the reference period, buildings completed during the reference period, and buildings under construction and then suspended during the reference period.

Floor Space of Buildings Completed

Floor Space of Buildings Completed refers to the floor space of buildings that are completed in the reference period in accordance with the requirements of the design, up to the standard for putting them into use, and have been checked and accepted by concerned departments as qualified ones.

Completion Rate of Floor Space of Buildings

Completion Rate of Floor Space of Buildings refers to the ratio of the floor space of buildings completed in certain period of time to the floor space of buildings under construction in the same period. This indicator reflects the investment result from the perspective of the speed of construction.

Industry

Industry refers to the material production sector which is engaged in extraction of natural resources and processing and reprocessing of minerals and agricultural products, including (1) extraction of natural resources, such as mining, salt production (but not including hunting and fishing); (2) processing and reprocessing of farm and sideline produces, such as rice husking, flour milling, wine making, oil pressing, silk reeling, spinning and weaving, and leather making; (3) manufacture of industrial products, such as steel making, iron smelting, chemicals manufacturing, petroleum processing, machine building, timber processing; water and gas production and electricity generation and supply; (4) repairing of industrial products such as the repairing of machinery and means of transport (including cars).

Prior to 1984, the rural industry run by villages and cooperative organizations under village was classified into agriculture. Since 1984, it has been grouped into industry.

Units of industrial statistics survey corporate industrial enterprises with independent accounting system.

Corporate industrial enterprises with independent accounting system refer to enterprises engaging in industrial production activities, which meet the following requirements: ①They are established legally, having their own names, organizations, location, able to take civil liability; ②They possess and use their assets independently, assume liabilities, and are entitled to sign contracts with other units; ③They are financially independent and compile their own balance sheets.

Light Industry

refers to the industry that produces consumer goods and hand tools. It consists of two categories, depending on the materials used:

(1) Industries using farm products as raw materials. These are branches of light industry which directly or indirectly use farm products as basic raw materials, including the manufacture of food and beverages, tobacco processing, textile, clothing, fur and leather manufacturing, paper making, printing, etc.

(2) Industries using non farm products as raw materials. These are branches of light industry which use manufactured goods as raw materials, including the manufacture of cultural, educational articles and sports goods, chemicals, synthetic fiber, chemical products for daily use, glass products for daily use, metal products for daily use,

hand tools, medical apparatus and instruments, and the manufacture of cultural and clerical machinery.

Heavy Industry

refers to the industry which produces capital goods, and provides various sectors of the national economy with necessary material and technical basis. It consists of the following three branches according to the purpose of production or the use of products:

(1) Mining, quarrying and logging industry refers to the industry that extracts natural resources, including extraction of petroleum, coal, metal and non-metal ores.

(2) Raw materials industry refers to the industry that provides various sectors of the national economy with raw materials, fuels and power. It includes smelting and processing of metals, coking and coke chemistry, chemical materials and building materials such as cement, plywood, and power, petroleum refining and coal dressing.

(3) Manufacturing industry refers to the industry that processes raw materials. It includes machine building industry which equips sectors of the national economy, industries of metal structure and cement products, industries producing means of agricultural production, such as chemical fertilizers and pesticides. According to the above principle of classification, the repairing trades which are engaged primarily in repairing products of heavy industry are classified into heavy industry while these engaged in repairing products of light industry are classified into light industry.

Gross Output Value of Industry

(1) Definition: Gross industrial output value is the total volume of final industrial products produced and industrial services provided during a given period. It reflects the total achievements and overall scale of industrial production during a given period.

(2) Principles for calculation: Statistics on industrial production follow the principle that all products produced by the enterprises and accepted during the reference period are to be included no matter whether they are sold or not during the reference period

Determination of final products follow the principle that all products that are included in the calculation of grow industrial output value are the final products of the enterprise which have been accepted through quality check and require no further processing. If an enterprise has intermediate (semi-finished) products to sell, these intermediate products are considered as the final products of the enterprise.

Gross industrial output value is calculated following the principle of factory approach, i. e. industrial enterprise is used as the basic accounting unit in calculating the gross industrial output value. By this approach, value of the same product is not to be double counted, and the output value of different workshops (branch factories) should not be added. However, this approach does not exclude the possibility of double counting between enterprises.

(3) Content and calculation method: The old definition of gross industrial output value was modified duringthe national industrial census in 1995. The revised (new) definition of gross industrial output value consists of 3 components: value of the finished products during the reference period, income from external processing, and value of change in semi-finished products at the end and at the beginning of the reference period.

Value of the finished products during the reference period: refers to the value of all finished (semi-finished) industrial products that are produced during the reference period without the need for further processing, checked for acceptance, packed and put into the warehouse of the enterprise, including the value of own-produced equipment and the value of products provided to the projects under construction of the enterprise, and to other non-industrial or welfare units. Value of finished products during the reference period is calculated by the quantity of products produced using own materials multiplied by the average unit prices at which products are sold (excluding value-added tax). Own-produced equipment and products produced for own use are value at cost prices as in the case of enterprise accounting. Value of finished products does not include the value of finished products (semi-finished products) that are produced using the materials from the clients who make the orders.

Income from external processing: refers to income from contracted external processing of industrial products (including processing of industrial products using materials from the clients), and the income from industrial repairing work provided to other units. Income from external processing is calculated using information from the item "products sales income" in the enterprise accounting at the prices excluding value-added tax.

For income from services such as processing, repairing and installation of equipment provided to non-industrial units within the enterprise, if the accounting work of the enterprise is good enough to separate it from other records, and the share of such services is significant, it should also be included in the income from external processing.

Value of change in semi-finished products at the end and at the beginning of the reference period: refers to the value of change in semi-finished products at the end and at the beginning of the reference period, which generally can be obtained from accounting records of enterprises. If the enterprise accounting excludes the cost of semi-finished products, then it should not be included in the gross industrial output value, and vice versa.

(4) Changes in the coverage and method of calculation of gross industrial output value. Prior to 1984, the value of rural industry run by villages was classified into agriculture instead of industry Since 1984, it has been included in the gross industrial output value.

Method of calculation for the gross industrial output value was modified in the industrial census in 1995. The difference in the new method as compared with the old one is outlined below:

Principle in using full value vs. processing fee: The new method stipulates that all products produced using own materials are to be calculated with full value in reporting the gross industrial output value irrespective of sophistication of production, and for external processing, it allows calculation using processing fee. In the old method, however, the use of full value or processing fee was determined by the degree of sophistication of production in different branches of industries.

Principle in determining the value of change in semi-finished products: The new method requires that value of the change in semi-finished products should be included in the gross industrial output value if it is included in the accounting record of the enterprise, otherwise it should not be included. By the old method, it is determined by the type of enterprises in terms of production cycle. If the production cycle is over 6 months, the value of change in semi-finished products is included in the gross industrial output value, otherwise it is excluded.

Difference in prices: The new method uses prices excluding value-added tax in the calculation of gross industrial output value, while the old method used prices including value-added tax.

Sales Output Value of Industry

refers to total sales value of products produced by industrial enterprises during a given period, including sales of finished goods, value of semi-products, value of industrial services provided to other units, value of products provided for capital construction sector, welfare sector and value of industrial services provided and self produced equipment within enterprises. Sales of finished goods and-semi-products in current period are taken into account regardless of their production period.

The coverage, pricing, and calculation method for sales output value of industry are the same as for gross output value of industry except that the former is based on sales of products and the latter is based on the output of products.

Export Delivery Value of Industry

refers to the product value which industrial enterprises deliver to Foreign Trade Department, or value of products which are exported directly from producers (including the sales to Hong Kong, Macao and Taiwan); the product value, (at foreign exchange rate,) of domestic batch sale or transit batch export; full price or processing fee of the production with design, materials, assembling parts supplied by foreign businessmen and compensation trade.

Large, Medium and Small Enterprises

Since 2003 annual report enforcement, the criteria for classifying large, medium and small enterprises has been based on The Method for Classifying Large, Medium and Small Enterprises (Provisional) (State Statistics Bureau [2003] No. 17). That is, an enterprise could be entitled Large Enterprise only when it has more than 2000 employees, its sales revenue exceeds 300 million yuan and total property exceeds 400 million yuan , simultaneously. An enterprise could be entitled Medium Enterprise when its employee number ranges from 300 to 2000, its sales revenue ranges from 30 million to 300 million yuan and its total property ranges from 40 million to 400 million yuan, simultaneously. All other enterprises should be entitled Small Enterprises.

Industrial Enterprises with Independent Accounting

Systems and Industrial Production Units with Non-Independent Accounting Systems.

Depending on whether they have independent administration and accounting, industrial enterprises can be divided into industrial enterprises with independent accounting system and industrial production units with non-independent accounting system. An industrial enterprise with independent accounting system shall operate simultaneously under the following three conditions: (1) having an independent organization in terms of administration; (2) economically having independent accounting, taking care of its own profits and losses, and filing independent balance sheets; and (3) enjoying the right to sign contracts with other units and to open independent bank accounts. An industrial enterprise with independent accounting system, no matter under a unitary management or cooperative operation, shall be counted as single grassroots unit in statistics and its branch factories and workshops shall not be calculated separately.

An industrial production unit with non-independent accounting system is an industrial production unit which does not operate simultaneously under the above mentioned three conditions of industrial enterprises with independent accounting systems and is attached to an enterprise, institution, government department, organization, school, scientific research institution, or army unit. An industrial production with non-independent accounting system unit can be included into the industrial statistics only when it operates simultaneously under the following three conditions: (1) having fixed production sites and production equipment; (2) having more than 10 permanent workers and apprentices; and (3) operating all year round if it's a normal production unit or operating more than three months a year if it's a seasonal production unit.

Aggregate Assets

Total Assets refer to all economic resources, in monetary terms, that is owned or controlled by enterprises, including properties, creditors equity and other economic rights of all forms. Classified by the degree of equitability, total assets include circulating assets, long-term investment, fixed assets, intangible assets and deferred assets, and other assets. Data on this indicator can be obtained by the year-end figures of total assets in the Assets and Liability Table of accounting records of enterprises.

Total of Working Capitals

Total of Working Capitals refer to capitals which can be cashed in or spent or consumed in an operating cycle of one year or over one year, including cash, all kinds of deposits, short term investment, receivable and payable payment for goods or deposits.

Average Value of Working Capitals

Average Value of Working Capitals refers to the average value of all working capitals of the enterprise during the reference period.

Annual Average of Net Value of Fixed Assets

refer to average of the net value of fixed assets during the reference period, calculated with the following formula:

Annual Average of Net Value of Fixed Assets = sum of net value of fixed assets at the beginning and at the end of each month from January to December / 24.

Information on this indicator can be obtained from the beginning and ending figures of the original value of fixed assets and cumulative depreciation from the Assets and Liability Table of enterprises.

Net value of fixed assets refers to the original value of fixed assets minus depreciation over the years, i. e. :

Net value of fixed assets = original value of fixed assets-cumulative depreciation

Aggregate Liabilities

Aggregate liabilities refer to the total debts of an enterprise which can be calculated in monetary term and will be repaid in the forms of assets or service. Usually, the debts are divided into liquid liability and long-term debt according to the length of the payback period. The liquid liability is the debt that an enterprise will pay back during an operation cycle which is either shorter or longer than a year. The long-term debt refers to a debt whose payback period is longer than a year or which will be repaid during an operation cycle that is longer than a year.

Creditors' Equity

Creditors' Equity refers to investors ownership of net assets of the enterprise, which is equal to the total assets of the enterprise minus its total liabilities, including the primary input actually received at the enterprise from investors, capital accumulation fund, surplus accumulation fund and undistributed profit. When the total of creditors' equity is less than zero, that indicates the liability of the enterprise is larger that its assets.

Total Profits

Total Profits refer to the final achievements of production and operation of the enterprises, represented by the total profits after deducting losses (loss is expressed by the negative figure). It is the sum of profits from operation, income from subsidies, investment earnings, net income from activities other than operation, and adjustment of profits and losses of previous years.

Ratio of Profits, Taxes and Interests to Average Assets

Ratio of Profits, Taxes and Interests to Average Assets reflects the profit-making capability of all assets of the enterprise and is a key indicator manifesting the performance and management and evaluating the profit-making potential of the enterprise. It is calculated as follows:

Ratio of Profits, Taxes and Interests to Average Assets (%) = [(total profits + total taxes + interest payment) / average assets] × 100%

In the above formula, total taxes is the sum of tax and extra charges on the sales of products and value-added tax payable; and average assets is the arithmetic mean of the sum of beginning assets and ending assets.

Ratio of Debts to Asset

Ratio of Debts to Assets reflect both the operation risk and the capability of the enterprise in making use of the capital from the creditors. It is calculated as follows:

Ratio of Debts to Assets (%) = (total debts / total assets) × 100%

Both assets and debts are figures at the end of the reference period.

Turnover of Working Capital

Turnover of Working Capital refers to the number of times of turnover of working capital in a given period of time, which reflects the speed of the turnover of working capital of industrial enterprises, and is calculated as follows:

Turnover of Working Capital = (sales revenue of products) / (average balance of total working capital)

In the above formula, average balance of total working capital refers to the arithmetic mean of the sum of working capital at the beginning and at the end of the reference period.

Ratio of Sales to Gross Output Value

Ratio of Sales to Gross Output Value reflects the degree at which industrial products are sold. It helps to analyze the linkage between production and sales and the extent of the needs of the society that has been met by the supply of industrial products. It is calculated as follows:

Ratio of Sales to Gross Output Value = (Industrial sales / Gross industrial output value at current prices) × 100%

Capital Maintenance and Appreciation Rate

Capital Maintenance and Appreciation Rate reflects the changes of an enterprise's net assets. It epitomizes the growth capability of an enterprise. Its calculating formula is:

Capital maintenance and appreciation rate = Ownership equity at the end of the reporting period/Ownership equity at the same period of the previous year. Ownership equity is the result of total assets minus total liabilities.

Ratio of Profits to Total Industrial Costs

Ratio of Profits to Total Industrial Costs refers to the ratio of profits realized in a given period to the total costs in the same period, which reflects the economic efficiency of input cost and is calculated as follows:

Ratio of Profits to Total Industrial Cost (%) = (total profits/ total costs) × 100%

Total costs in the above formula is the sum of cost of products sold, marketing cost, management cost and financial cost.

Overall Labour Productivity

Overall Labour Productivity is an indicator reflecting the production efficiency of an enterprise and the economic efficiency of its labour input, calculated by the formula:

Overall Labour Productivity (yuan/person) = industrial value-added/average of all persons engaged.

第七篇

Chapter 7

金融业及要素市场

FINANCE AND BANKING, AND FACTOR MARKETS

表 7-1　各类金融机构数
Statistics of all Kinds of Financial Institutions

单位:个　　(unit)

指　标　Indicators		2005	2007	2008
总　计	**Total**	**369**	**493**	**544**
银行类机构合计	**Subtotal of Banks**	**141**	**166**	**178**
中资银行	Chinese Banks	19	19	21
外资银行法人行	Foreign Banks and Corporate Banks		10	14
外资银行分行	Branches of Foreign Banks	53	56	53
外资银行代表处	Representative Offices of Foreign Banks	44	43	52
银行营运中心	Bank Operation Centers	14	16	17
非银行金融机构	Non-banking Financial Institutions	11	22	21
证券类机构合计	**Subtotal of Securities Institutions**	**117**	**188**	**215**
中资证券(包括中介机构)	Chinese Securities Institutions(inclucling intermediary organs)	50	47	55
外资证券(包括代表处)	Foreign Securities Institutions(including representative offices)	36	33	42
基金公司	Fund Companies	25	40	41
期货公司	Futures Companies		62	71
非证券金融机构	Non-securities Financial Institutions	6	6	6
保险机构合计	**Subtotal of Insurance Companies**	**111**	**139**	**151**
中资保险(集团)	Chinese Insurance Companies(Groups)	30	38	40
外资保险	Foreign Insurance Companies	20	22	22
外资保险代表处	Representative Offices of Foreign Insurance Companies	20	20	21
保险中介	Agencies of Insurance Companies	39	57	65
保险营运中心	Insurance Operation Centers	2	2	3

表 7-2 主要年份中外资金融机构网点数
Number of Outlets of Chinese and Foreign Financial Institutions in Main Years

单位:个 (unit)

指 标	Indicators	1990	1995	2000	2005	2007	2008
总 计	**Total**	**131**	**387**	**463**	**859**	**1 038**	**1 135**
银行机构	Banking Institutions	116	282	310	476	526	623
#外 资	Foreign Investment				102	124	207
证券机构	Securities Institutions		30	49	123	222	223
保险机构	Insurance Institutions	1	16	37	150	194	183
#外 资	Foreign Investment				52	58	62
邮政储汇局	Postal Savings Offices	13	48	51	93	96	106
其他经营机构	Others	1	11	16	17		

注: 1. 2004 年以前银行机构网点中含信用社网点,2005 年起信用社并入银行系统。
2. 原其他机构已经拆分到各相应金融机构。
3. 2007 年期货公司纳入金融机构统计。
4. 2008 年邮政储汇局网点含邮储银行网点。

Note: 1. The establishments of the banking institutions included credit cooperatives before 2004. The credit cooperatives have been merged into the banking system since 2005.
2. The original other institutions have been split into their respective financial institutions.
3. Futures companies have been brought into the field of financial institutions since 2007.
4. In 2008, Establishments of Postal Savings and Remittances Bureau include those of Postal Savings Bank.

表 7-3 主要年份中资银行人民币存贷款年末余额
Chinese Banks' Year-end RMB Balance of Deposits and Loans in Main Years

单位:亿元 (100 million yuan)

指 标	Indicators	1990	1995	2000	2005	2007	2008
存款余额合计	**Total Deposit Balance**	**36.48**	**503.69**	**1 046.81**	**2 915.41**	**3 945.50**	**5 000.43**
#企业存款	Enterprise Deposit	9.67	286.20	644.79	1 530.99	2 271.48	2 787.36
居民储蓄存款	Resident Savings Deposit	20.62	180.94	360.99	1 105.96	1 312.80	1 766.49
其他存款	Others	1.66	13.73	10.61	166.38	261.95	304.23
贷款余额合计	**Total Loan Balance**	**28.19**	**417.05**	**891.59**	**2 674.76**	**3 413.98**	**3 805.24**
#企业贷款	Enterprise Loans				2 014.23	2 773.99	3 143.56
#短期贷款	Short Term Loans				716.01	955.02	1 088.81
中长期贷款	Medium and Long Term Loans				1 298.22	1 818.97	2 054.75
票据融资	Securities Financing				193.73	115.19	95.61
个人贷款	Individual Loans				464.40	523.77	565.70
#住房按揭贷款	Housing Mortgage Loans				431.28	465.81	513.07
汽车消费贷款	Car Loans				4.08	1.75	1.47

表 7-4 外资银行主要指标
(2008)

指 标	Indicators	单位数(个) Enterprises (unit)	从业人数(人) Employed Persons (person)	普通贷款(万美元) Ordinary Loans (USD 10 000)
总 计	**Total**	**69**	**11 397**	**2 016 626**
按各大洲分	**By Continent**			
亚洲地区	Asia	32	6 156	1 194 443
欧洲地区	Europe	26	1 807	537 069
美洲地区	America	10	3 418	284 114
大洋洲地区	Oceania region	1	16	1 000
按进驻各大厦分	**By Respective Mansion where Enterprises Handle their Businesses**			
汇丰大厦	HSBC Building	10	2 121	435 544
金茂大厦	Jin Mao Building	10	464	141 111
汇亚大厦	Azia Center	10	1 893	453 274
中银大厦	Bank of China Tower	6	555	143 274
花旗大厦	Citigroup Mansion	5	1 116	102 014
证券大厦	Shanghai Stock Exchange Building	4	239	78 090
招商局大厦	China Merchants Tower	4	2 076	195 641
船舶大厦	Marine Tower	3	121	33 711
浦项大厦	POS Plaza	3	104	76 546
其他大厦	Other Buildings	14	2 708	357 421
按普通贷款分	**By Regular Loans**			
7 亿美元以上	> USD 700 million	6	4 888	811 195
5 - 7 亿美元	USD 500 ~ 700 million	6	1 951	375 017
3 - 5 亿美元	USD 300 ~ 500 million	5	570	185 034
1 - 3 亿美元	USD 100 ~ 300 million	30	2 075	586 218
1 亿美元以下	< USD 100 million	22	1 913	59 162
按普通存款分	**By Regular Deposit**			
10 亿美元以上	> USD 1 000 million	4	2 799	425 631
3 ~ 10 亿美元	USD 300 ~ 1 000 million	4	3 322	425 699
1 ~ 3 亿美元	USD 100 ~ 300 million	9	2 031	391 503
1 千万 ~ 1 亿美元	USD 10 ~ 100 million	24	1 314	512 657
1 千万美元以下	< USD 10 million	28	1 931	261 136
按资产总额分	**By Total Assets**			
10 亿美元以上	> USD 1 000 million	17	7 654	1 143 690
5 ~ 10 亿美元	USD 500 ~ 1 000 million	12	1 706	444 851
3 ~ 5 亿美元	USD 300 ~ 500 million	12	1 066	175 328
1 ~ 3 亿美元	USD 100 ~ 300 million	21	682	220 988
1 亿美元以下	< USD 100 million	7	289	31 769
按税金分	**By Tax**			
2000 万元以上	≥20 million yuan	24	9 102	1 389 398
500 ~ 2000 万元	5 ~ 20 million yuan	17	720	295 699
100 ~ 500 万元	1 ~ 5 million yuan	18	1 055	279 869
100 万元以下	< 1 million yuan	10	520	51 660

Major Indicators of Foreign Banks

普通存款 (万美元) Ordinary Deposits (USD 10 000)	人民币贷款 (万元) RMB Loans (10 000 yuan)	人民币存款 (万元) RMB Deposits (10 000 yuan)	资产总额 (万美元) Total Assets (USD 10 000)	利润总额 (万元) Operation Profit (10 000 yuan)	拆入同业(万元) Borrowing from Correspondence Banks (10 000 yuan)	拆放同业 (万元) Banker Call Loans (10 000 yuan)
1 135 379	**19 340 073**	**17 011 933**	**6 429 643**	**857 916**	**2 099 755**	**1 339 650**
649 709	10 602 424	9 696 761	2 922 972	317 164	990 990	905 500
248 090	5 075 443	2 685 523	2 127 773	363 867	871 765	43 200
237 570	3 662 206	4 629 649	1 374 017	176 899	237 000	390 950
10			4 881	-14		
287 511	3 143 579	4 341 985	1 382 375	143 458	330 250	324 900
14 825	751 810	350 783	319 045	55 409	108 000	
342 415	4 114 188	3 144 136	1 349 781	247 137	891 740	210 000
31 931	1 589 844	844 942	201 242	43 014		
152 987	1 186 219	2 237 414	670 388	153 838		193 950
49 029	683 414	433 241	456 040	93 428	112 200	
91 138	2 663 439	2 209 947	777 823	30 332	223 655	182 000
1 693	270 070	76 758	91 388	5 406	20 000	
7 187	610 489	153 884	111 001	26 399	10 000	
156 663	4 327 021	3 218 843	1 070 560	59 495	403 910	428 800
584 305	7 165 830	8 210 432	2 438 244	311 830	955 990	809 700
234 111	4 073 189	4 101 685	1 018 145	146 291	109 000	100 150
35 335	1 554 083	1 156 613	419 728	63 891	106 155	240 500
249 154	5 487 616	3 236 728	1 667 021	310 145	721 310	35 500
32 474	759 355	306 475	886 505	25 759	207 300	153 800
628 945	4 630 529	7 033 218	1 950 461	250 525	433 990	556 650
254 370	4 835 638	4 092 602	1 218 061	136 922	483 000	345 000
180 098	5 332 996	3 736 602	1 030 739	283 912	617 155	35 000
68 172	3 908 038	1 776 573	1 136 068	171 977	274 700	229 700
3 794	632 872	372 938	1 094 314	14 580	290 910	173 300
956 767	12 057 959	12 702 012	4 647 598	729 037	1 575 145	1 231 850
117 242	4 474 159	2 973 414	858 751	139 311	180 410	47 500
13 640	733 926	335 622	436 442	-8 275	279 900	60 300
45 368	1 812 805	851 197	448 695	-10 895	64 300	
2 362	261 224	149 688	38 157	8 738		
1 066 325	16 335 554	15 824 901	4 795 022	803 264	1 650 345	1 238 850
45 712	2 487 170	839 831	631 159	98 526	301 510	21 500
17 983	517 349	347 201	783 832	-24 784	147 900	79 300
5 359			219 630	-19 090		

表7－5　外资银行存贷款年末余额
Foreign Banks' Year-end Balance of Deposits and Loans

指　标 Indicators		单　位 Unit	2005	2007	2008
外汇存贷款	**Deposits and Loans of Foreign Exchange**	**亿美元 USD 100 million**	**197.19**	**287.20**	**315.20**
客户存款	Deposits of Customers	亿美元 USD 100 million	59.43	95.14	113.54
#短　期	Short Term	亿美元 USD 100 million	22.35	38.13	48.11
同业存款	Inter-bank Deposits	亿美元 USD 100 million	4.13	17.20	13.37
拆入同业	Deposits From Other Banks	亿美元 USD 100 million	29.30	106.61	83.12
普通贷款	Ordinary Loans	亿美元 USD 100 million	137.76	192.06	201.66
#短　期	Short Term	亿美元 USD 100 million	67.05	86.06	87.41
投　资	Investment	亿美元 USD 100 million	8.21	15.34	24.62
拆放同业	Deposits to Other Banks	亿美元 USD 100 million	15.64	75.61	124.83
人民币存贷款	**RMB Deposits and Loans**	**亿元 100 million yuan**	**1 203.72**	**3 050.59**	**3 635.20**
客户存款	Deposits of Customers	亿元 100 million yuan	615.44	1 430.66	1 701.19
拆入同业	Deposits From Other Banks	亿元 100 million yuan	53.76	220.49	209.98
普通贷款	Ordinary Loans	亿元 100 million yuan	588.28	1 619.93	1 934.01
投　资	Investment	亿元 100 million yuan	115.83	895.96	1 057.68
拆放同业	Deposits to Other Banks	亿元 100 million yuan	5.63	185.68	133.97

表7-6 历年中资保险机构原保险保费收入和赔款支出

Former Premium Income and Indemnity Expenditure of Chinese Insurance Business in Main Years (1992～2008)

单位:亿元 (100 million yuan)

年 份 Year	原保险保费收入 Former Premium Income	财产险 Property Insurance	人身险 Life Insurance	原保险赔款支出 Former Indemnity Expenditure	财产险 Property Insurance	人身险 Life Insurance	赔款率(%) Rate of Indemnity(%)	财产险 Property Insurance	人身险 Life Insurance
1992	1.13	0.75	0.38	0.69	0.20	0.49	61.1	26.7	128.9
1993	2.51	1.42	1.09	0.30	0.06	0.24	12.0	4.2	25.9
1994	5.37	3.30	2.07	1.77	1.63	0.14	33.0	49.4	6.8
1995	13.63	10.42	3.21	3.12	2.97	0.15	22.9	28.5	4.7
1996	22.02	7.70	14.32	3.83	3.41	0.42	17.4	44.3	2.9
1997	38.34	9.19	29.15	4.91	4.71	0.20	12.8	51.3	0.7
1998	44.09	9.93	34.16	6.28	4.48	1.80	14.2	45.1	5.3
1999	51.42	10.84	40.58	7.76	5.71	2.05	15.1	52.7	5.1
2000	63.31	13.40	49.91	7.06	3.87	3.19	11.2	28.9	6.4
2001	99.36	13.73	85.63	9.08	4.92	4.16	9.1	35.8	4.9
2002	118.31	16.55	101.76	10.12	7.17	2.95	8.6	43.3	2.9
2003	129.83	21.88	107.95	20.73	9.04	11.69	16.0	41.3	10.8
2004	118.09	29.52	88.57	19.59	11.62	7.97	16.6	39.4	9.0
2005	140.63	40.03	100.60	23.16	20.09	3.07	16.5	50.2	3.1
2006	171.47	45.51	125.96	26.17	22.16	4.01	15.3	48.7	3.2
2007	182.33	52.47	129.86	29.29	24.54	4.75	16.1	46.8	3.7
2008	230.84	55.25	175.59	37.01	30.99	6.02	16.0	56.1	3.4

表7-7 中资保险机构主要险种的原保险保费收入和赔款支出
Former Premium Income and Indemnity Expenditure of Major Types of Chinese Funded Insurance Business
(2008)

单位:亿元 (100 million yuan)

指 标	Indicators	原保险保费收入 Former Premium Income	原保险赔款支出 Former Indemnity Expenditure	赔款率(%) Rate of Indemnity(%)
总 计	**Total**	**230.84**	**37.01**	**16.0**
财产险小计	Subtotal of Property Insurance	55.25	30.99	56.1
企业财产险	Enterprise Property Insurance	7.72	4.56	59.1
机动车辆险	Motor Vehicle Insurance	34.76	22.84	65.7
其 他	Others	12.77	3.59	28.1
人身险小计	Subtotal of Life Insurance	175.59	6.02	3.4
个 险	Individual Insurance	142.29	0.87	0.6
团 险	Team Insurance	33.30	5.15	15.5

表7-8 外资保险机构主要险种的原保险保费收入和赔款支出
Former Premium Income and Indemnity Expenditure of Major Types of Foreign Funded Insurance Business
(2008)

单位:亿元 (100 million yuan)

指 标	Indicators	原保险保费收入 Former Premium Income	原保险赔款支出 Former Premium Income	赔款率(%) Rate of Indemnity(%)
总 计	**Total**	**72.87**	**6.02**	**8.3**
财产保险小计	Subtotal of Property Insurance	13.30	4.81	36.2
#企业财产险	Enterprise Property Insurance	3.36	1.89	56.3
货运险	Cargo Transportation Insurance	5.09	1.89	37.1
家财险	Household Property Insurance	0.05	0.01	20.0
责任保险	Liability Insurance	3.45	0.64	18.6
人身险	Life Insurance	59.57	1.21	2.0

表7-9 上海证券交易所市场交易主要指标
Statistics of Shanghai Stock Exchange

指 标	Indicators	单 位 Unit	2000	2005	2007	2008
交易天数	**Trading Days**	**天 day**	**239**	**242**	**242**	**246**
上市证券数	**Number of Securities Traded**	**个 unit**	**657**	**1 073**	**1 125**	**1 184**
股 票	Stocks	个 unit	614	878	904	908
A 股	A Share	个 unit	559	824	850	854
B 股	B Share	个 unit	55	54	54	54
债 券	Bonds	个 unit	25	165	198	246
国债现货	Spots of National Debts	个 unit	7	43	62	77
企业债券	Enterprise Bonds	个 unit	8	47	70	100
可转债券	Transferable Bonds	个 unit	2	18	12	12
回 购	Repurchase	个 unit	8	57	54	57
证券投资基金	Funds of Securities Investment	个 unit	18	25	14	13
ETF	Exchange Traded Funds	个 unit		1	3	3
权 证	Warrant	个 unit		4	6	14
市价总值	**Total Capitalization**	**亿元 100 million yuan**	**27 294.80**	**38 067.81**	**288 807.83**	**115 654.56**
成交金额	**Turnover Value**	**亿元 100 million yuan**	**49 901.47**	**49 775.61**	**380 025.56**	**271 842.03**
股 票	Stocks	亿元 100 million yuan	31 373.86	19 240.21	305 434.29	180 429.95
A 股	A Share	亿元 100 million yuan	31 029.69	19 061.49	301 960.30	179 762.44
B 股	B Share	亿元 100 million yuan	344.17	178.72	3 473.99	667.51
债 券	Bonds	亿元 100 million yuan	16 895.82	28 138.41	20 399.37	28 090.64
国债现货	Spots of National Debts	亿元 100 million yuan	3 657.06	2 772.79	1 262.20	2 075.90
企业债券	Enterprise Bonds	亿元 100 million yuan	39.12	124.88	316.41	1 406.38
可转债券	Transferable Bonds	亿元 100 million yuan	52.43	321.68	211.83	301.59
回 购	Repurchase	亿元 100 million yuan	13 147.21	24 919.06	18 608.93	24 306.77
基 金	Funds	亿元 100 million yuan	1 334.18	576.78	4 298.24	3 700.23
权 证	Warrant	亿元 100 million yuan		1 763.07	49 893.66	59 621.21
其 他	Others	亿元 100 million yuan	297.61	57.14		
成交数量	**Volume Turnover**					
股 票	Stocks	亿手 100 million contracts	2 437.65	3 986.59	24 325.38	16 311.60
A 股	A Share	亿手 100 million contracts	2 310.87	3 926.89	23 931.39	16 207.24
B 股	B Share	亿手 100 million contracts	126.78	59.70	393.99	104.36
债 券	Bonds	亿手 100 million contracts	16.53	28.15	20.38	28.38
国债现货	Spots of National Debts	亿手 100 million contracts	3.31	2.81	1.27	2.08
企业债券	Enterprise Bonds	亿手 100 million contracts	0.03	0.12	0.37	1.73
可转债券	Transferable Bonds	亿手 100 million contracts	0.04	0.30	0.13	0.26
回 购	Repurchase	亿手 100 million contracts	13.15	24.92	18.61	24.31
基 金	Funds	亿手 100 million contracts	995.32	778.73	1 981.36	2 001.43
权 证	Warrant	亿手 100 million contracts		1 274.79	28 950.81	43 769.92
其 他	Others	亿手 100 million contracts	31.65	0.12		

注：本表至表7－12由上海证券交易所提供。
Note: The data in from this table to Table 7－12 are provided by Shanghai Stock Exchange.

表7-10　上海证券交易所市盈率和换手率
P/E Ratio & Turnover Rate of Shanghai Stock Exchange

指　标	Indicators	2000	2005	2007	2008
市盈率(%)	**P/E Rate**	**58.2**	**16.3**	**59.2**	**14.8**
A　股	A Share	59.1	16.4	59.2	14.9
B　股	B Share	25.2	12.4	59.3	11.7
换手率(%)	**Turnover Rate**	**449.1**	**274.4**	**927.2**	**392.5**
A　股	A Share	504.1	290.7	953.2	401.6
B　股	B Share	151.2	58.5	351.6	87.9

表7-11　上海证券交易所市场筹集资金
Capital Raising of Shanghai Stock Exchang

单位:亿元　　(100 million yuan)

指　标	Indicators	2000	2005	2006	2007	2008
A股小计	**A Share Subtotal**	**882.41**	**308.75**	**1 714.41**	**6 805.81**	**2 238.16**
A股首次发行	A Share Issuing	568.67	28.55	1 180.23	4 379.92	733.54
A股再次发行	A Share Secondary Issuing	313.74	280.20	534.18	2 425.89	1 504.62
A股增发	Additional Issuance of A Share	62.86	278.78	529.86	2 192.56	1 331.86
A股配股	A Share Rights Issuing	250.88	1.42	4.32	43.87	142.00
A股行权	A Share Righting				189.46	30.76

表7-12　浦东新区上市公司分行业汇总情况
Listed Companies in PNA by Sector
(2008)

指　标	Indicators	单　位　Unit	地产类 Real Estate	工业类 Industry	公用事业类 Public Utilities	商业类 Commerce	综合类 Comprehens-ive
发行股数	Capital Stock	亿股 100 million in number	67.32	253.09	355.82	35.75	473.85
流通股数	Floating Stock	亿股 100 million in number	37.46	136.69	155.99	22.75	333.55
成交额	Volume	亿元 100 million yuan	1 574.51	5 084.79	3 843.86	626.32	6 438.00
成交股数	Clinched Stock	亿股 100 million in number	131.50	533.92	349.15	46.01	533.59
市盈率	P/E Ratio	%	21.80	14.84	22.24	24.45	13.09
换手率	Turnover Rate	%	404.83	492.82	478.94	234.24	536.46
市价总值	Total Market Value	亿元 100 million yuan	509.25	1 355.77	1 650.48	312.30	2 995.17
流通市值	Circulating Market Value	亿元 100 million yuan	237.85	671.01	781.22	194.00	2 270.08

注：1. 浦东新区上市公司指公司注册地含"浦东"的公司。
2. 数据包含A股和B股。
3. "成交额"、"成交股数"、"换手率"为2008年整年数据。
4. "发行股数"、"流通股数"、"市盈率"、"市值总值"、"流通市值"为2008年12月28日数据。

Note：1. Newly listed companies in PNA refer to those companies that registered in Pudong.
2. The data include both A shares and B shares.
3. The items of Business Volume, Number of Transacted Stocks and Turnover Rate are data in the whole year of 2008.
4. The items of Number of Issued Stocks, Number of Circulated Stocks, P/E Ratio, Total Market Value and Circulating Market Value are data of December 28, 2008.

表7-13 上海期货交易所市场交易主要指标
Major Indicators of Shanghai Futures Exchange

指 标 Indicators		单 位 Unit	2000	2005	2007	2008
会员单位	**Membership**	**户 unit**	**216**	**215**	**210**	**207**
经纪单位	Broking	户 unit	162	175	172	167
非经纪单位	Non-Broking	户 unit	54	40	38	40
交易天数	Business Days in the Year	天 day	241	242	242	246
上市交易品种	Business Lines	个 unit	3	4	5	6
成交量	**Total Volume of Business**	**万手 10 000 contracts**	**825.27**	**6 757.95**	**17 112.77**	**28 052.64**
铜	Copper	万手 10 000 contracts	534.72	2 470.41	3 265.60	4 154.65
铝	Aluminum	万手 10 000 contracts	91.00	425.00	964.71	2 957.79
锌	Zinc	万手 10 000 contracts			2 043.09	4 707.78
黄 金	Gold	万手 10 000 contracts				778.09
天然橡胶	Natural Rubber	万手 10 000 contracts	199.53	1 900.63	8 438.35	9 292.22
燃料油	Fuel oil	万手 10 000 contracts		1 961.91	2 401.02	6 162.11
成交金额	**Total Value of Business**	**亿元 100 million yuan**	**6 663.42**	**65 402.03**	**231 304.66**	**288 719.90**
铜	Copper	亿元 100 million yuan	5 037.73	40 463.23	101 451.23	99 640.89
铝	Aluminum	亿元 100 million yuan	731.79	3 714.46	9 377.90	22 078.82
锌	Zinc	亿元 100 million yuan			24 753.79	39 074.26
黄 金	Gold	亿元 100 million yuan				14 975.49
天然橡胶	Natural Rubber	亿元 100 million yuan	893.90	15 601.79	87 225.28	92 758.34
燃料油	Fuel oil	亿元 100 million yuan		5 622.55	8 496.46	20 192.10
年末持仓量	**Year End Contracts**	**万手 10 000 contracts**	**14.85**	**30.95**	**50.15**	**107.62**
铜	Copper	万手 10 000 contracts	11.10	10.58	18.37	34.36
铝	Aluminum	万手 10 000 contracts	2.04	7.89	8.60	21.83
锌	Zinc	万手 10 000 contracts			5.87	12.76
黄 金	Gold	万手 10 000contracts				4.63
天然橡胶	Natural Rubber	万手 10 000 contracts	1.71	5.70	9.13	17.29
燃料油	Fuel oil	万手 10 000 contracts		6.78	8.18	16.75
交割量	**Volume of Transaction**	**万手 10 000 contracts**	**7.20**	**8.73**	**11.07**	**14.12**
铜	Copper	万手 10 000 contracts	5.23	3.07	3.72	2.71
铝	Aluminum	万手 10 000 contracts	1.49	2.18	2.42	5.57
锌	Zinc	万手 10 000 contracts			0.72	1.83
黄 金	Gold	万手 10 000 contracts				0.09
天然橡胶	Natural Rubber	万手 10 000 contracts	0.48	1.52	2.51	2.16
燃料油	Fuel oil	万手 10 000 contracts		1.96	1.70	1.76
交割金额	**Value of Transaction**	**亿元 100 million yuan**	**61.93**	**88.29**	**179.65**	**174.85**
铜	Copper	亿元 100 million yuan	47.69	54.54	118.05	79.07
铝	Aluminum	亿元 100 million yuan	12.09	18.07	23.37	47.76
锌	Zinc	亿元 100 million yuan			8.26	13.05
黄 金	Gold	亿元 100 million yuan				1.69
天然橡胶	Natural Rubber	亿元 100 million yuan	2.15	10.79	24.30	25.95
燃料油	Fuel oil	亿元 100 million yuan		4.89	5.67	7.33
交割率	**Rate of Transaction**					
铜	Copper	%	1.8	0.2	0.3	0.2
铝	Aluminum	%	4.1	1.0	0.4	0.8
锌	Zinc	%			0.1	0.1
黄 金	Gold	%				…
天然橡胶	Natural Rubber	%	0.8	0.3	0.1	0.1
燃料油	Fuel oil	%		0.2	0.2	0.1

注：黄金为2008年新增，本表由上海期货交易所提供。
Note: The item of gold was increased in 2008. This table is provided by Shanghai Futures Exchange.

表 7-14 上海联合产权交易所基本情况
Shanghai United Assets and Equity Exchange

指 标	Indicators	单 位 Unit	2000	2005	2007	2008
成交企业数	**Number of Enterprises Acquired /Merged**	**户 unit**	**2 794**	**3 395**	**2 610**	**2 057**
按企业产权出让分	By Property Rights Transferring Out					
# 国有企业	State-owned Enterprises	户 unit	748	1 457	1 257	1 098
集体企业	Collective-owned Enterprises	户 unit	719	488	224	173
有限责任	Limited Liability	户 unit		659	599	311
按企业产权受让分	By Property Rights Transferring In					
# 国有企业	State-owned Enterprises	户 unit	255	777	785	703
集体企业	Collective-owned Enterprises	户 unit	222	76	54	49
有限责任	Limited Liability	户 unit		567	589	326
外商独资	Solely Foreigner Funded	户 unit	29	231	194	126
私营企业	Private Enterprises	户 unit	38	385	299	297
自然人	Natural Person	户 unit		1 329	658	530
交易额合计	**Amount Concluded**	**亿元 100 million yuan**	**480.31**	**4 002.80**	**4 051.48**	**3 589.68**
按企业产权出让分	By Property Rights Transferring Out					
# 国有企业	State-owned Enterprises	亿元 100 million yuan	68.73	1 489.64	1 400.78	1 391.57
集体企业	Collective-owned Enterprises	亿元 100 million yuan	38.82	46.78	30.06	30.35
有限责任	Limited Liability	亿元 100 million yuan		225.29	329.09	213.35
按企业产权受让分	By Property Rights Transferring In					
# 国有企业	State-owned Enterprises	亿元 100 million yuan	42.58	690.52	1 366.58	1 244.24
集体企业	Collective-owned Enterprises	亿元 100 million yuan	13.85	11.95	16.55	10.35
有限责任	Limited Liability	亿元 100 million yuan		835.91	317.01	302.84
外商独资	Solely Foreigner Funded	亿元 100 million yuan	9.56	116.72	125.94	84.98
私营企业	Private Enterprises	亿元 100 million yuan	0.52	96.07	88.54	85.54
自然人	Natural Person	亿元 100 million yuan		154.86	64.77	49.85

注：本表由上海联合产权交易所提供。
Note: This table is provided by Shanghai United Assets and Equity Exchange.

表7-15 中国上海人才市场中介(交流)服务情况
Basic Statistics of Professional Resources Market of Shanghai, China

指 标	Indicators	单位 Unit	2006	2007	2008
举办人才交流大会	**Number of Exchange Activities**				
举办人才交流大会	Number of Exchange Activities	次 times	797	648	527
参加人才交流大会的求职人数	Number of Job Seekers Attending Exchange Activities	万人 10 000 persons	394.44	311.98	287.51
参加人才交流大会的招聘单位	Number of Participating Organizations	万个 10 000 unit	4.70	5.70	4.96
招聘岗位数	Number of Posts Recruited	万个 10 000 unit	42.26	51.11	44.73
达成流动意向协议的人数	Number of Job Seekers Who Have Signed Letters of Intent	万人 10 000 persons	84.06	72.02	58.85
流动人才情况	**Flow of Personnel**				
按学历分	**Grouped by Education**				
大专及以下	Below College	万人 10 000 persons	336.13		
大学本科	Bachelor Degree	万人 10 000 persons	551.89		
研究生(含硕士、博士)	Master and Ph. D Degrees	万人 10 000 persons	90.47		

注：本表由中国上海人才交流市场提供。
Note: This table is provided by China Shanghai Talents Services Market.

表7-16 区属人才交流市场基本情况
Basic Statistics of PNA Professional Resources Market (PPRM)

指 标	Indicators	单位 Unit	2000	2005	2007	2008
全年举办交流活动	Number of Exchange Activites in the Year	场 in number	54	133	119	177
参与人才招聘单位	Number of Participating Organizations	个 unit	1 890	3 859	4 477	5 352
接待咨询服务人次	Job-seeking Visitors	万人次 10 000 person-times	8.27	19.67	18.75	21.38
办理择业登记人数	Registered Job-seeking Visitors	人次 person-time	26 670	90 452	195 254	36 225
达成意向人数	Number of Job-seekers Who Have Signed Letters of Intent	人 person	68 963	37 302	52 520	64 270
#从外省市引进人数	Talents Recruited from Other Parts of the Country	人 person	1 216	180	514	
#高级人才	Senior Professionals	人 person	131	55	40	
获得上海市居住证人数	Number of Persons Who Have Obtained Shanghai Residence Permits	人 person		7 158	16 215	24 751
后续服务	**Follow-up Service**					
档案保管	File-keeping	件 file	2 727	5 691	6 075	7 316
户籍挂靠(迁入)	Domiciling(immigration)	户 unit		1 605	853	1 516

注：本表由浦东新区人才交流市场提供。
Note: This table is provided by Pudong Talents Services Market.

主要统计指标解释

存　款

是企业、机关、团体或居民等根据资金必须收回的原则，把货币资金存入银行或其他信用机构保管并取得一定利息的一种信用活动形式。根据存款对象的不同可划分为企业存款、财政存款、机关团体存款、储蓄存款等科目。它是银行信贷资金的主要来源。

贷　款

是银行或其他信用机构根据资金必须归还的原则，按一定利率，为企业、个人等提供资金的一种信用活动形式。我国银行贷款分为短期贷款、中期流动资金贷款、中长期贷款、信托贷款以及工业贷款、商业贷款等科目。

居民储蓄存款年末余额

居民和农民个人在银行、信用社等金融机构储蓄存款年末余额。不包括居民的手存现金和企事业单位、部队、机关团体等的集体存款。

保险金额

指保险人承担赔偿或者给付保险金责任的最高限额。

保险费

保险费是指投保人根据保险合同的有关规定，为保险受益人取得因保险事故发生所造成的经济损失予以补偿（或给付）权利，付给保险人的代价。包括财产险和人身险储金类支出。

保险赔款及给付

保险赔款及给付指保险事故发生后，经查证确属保险责任范围以内的保险标的损失，保险人根据保险合同的规定履行赔偿义务，给予被保险人（或投保人指定的受益人）的款项。

市价总值

市价总值即全部股份乘上市场价格。

流通市值

流通市值指在某特定时间内当时可交易的流通股股数乘以当时股价得出的流通股票总价值。

市盈率

市盈率是某种股票每股市价与每股盈利的比率。

市盈率 = 普通股每股市场价格 ÷ 普通股每年每股盈利

换手率

换手率是指在一定时间内市场中股票转手买卖的频率。

金融债券

金融债券，是指银行和非银行金融机构为筹集资金而发行的债券。其债务人为发行债券的金融机构。

企业债券

企业债券通常又称为公司债券，是企业依照法定程序发行，约定在一定期限内还本付息的债券。企业债券代表着发债企业和投资者之间的一种债权债务关系。债券持有人是企业的债权人，不是所有者，无权参与或干涉企业经营管理，但债券持有人有权按期收回本息。企业债券与股票一样，同属有价证券，可以自由转让。

可转换债券

可转换债券，又译可换股债券，是债券的一种，它可以转换为债券发行公司的股票，其转换比率一般会在发行时确定。可转换债券通常具有较低的票面利率，因为可以转换成股票的权利是对债券持有人的一种补偿。另外，将可转换债券转换为普通股时，所换得的股票价值一般远大于原债券价值。可转换债券是在发行公司债券的基础上，附加了一份期权，并允许购买人在规定的时间范围内将其购买的债券转换成指定公司的股票。

持仓量

持仓量指的是在交易所市场上未平仓的期权合约的数量，也指某一种类或系列中未平仓的期权合约的数量。

成交量

成交量指当天成交的股票数量。

交　割

交割概念来源于期货，分为：实物交割和现金交割。

实物交割，是指期货合约的买卖双方于合约到期时，根据交易所制订的规则和程序，通过期货合约标的物的所有权转移，将到期末平仓合约进行了结的行为。商品期货交易一般采用实物交割的方式。

现金交割，是指到期末平仓期货合约进行交割时，用结算价格来计算未平仓合约的盈亏，以现金支付的方式最终了结期货合约的交割方式。这种交割方式主要用于金融期货等期货标的物无法进行实物交割的期货合约。

EXPLANATORY NOTES TO MAJOR STATISTICAL INDICATORS

Deposits

Deposits are a form of credit by which enterprises, institutions, organizations or residents put money into banks and other credit institutions for safekeeping and earn interests under the principle of free withdrawal. According to different depositors, deposits are divided into enterprise deposits, treasury deposits, deposits of institutions and organizations, urban savings deposits and other deposits. Deposits constitute a major source of bank credit funds.

Loans

Loans are a form of credit by which banks and other credit institutions provide funds with a specified interest to enterprises and individuals under the principle of free repayment. Loans from Chinese banks include short term loans, medium term circulating capital loans, long term loans, trust loans, industrial loans and commercial loans.

Savings Deposit Balance of Urban and Rural Residents

refers to year-end savings deposit balance of urban residents and farmers at banks, credit unions and other financial institutions, excluding cash held by residents and collective savings of enterprises, institutions, military units and government agencies.

Amount Insured

Amount Insured refers to the maximum that the insurant will get for the claim of the case insured .

Premium

Premium is the fee paid by the insurant to the insurer to obtain the obligation of compensation from the insurance within the agreed terms. It includes saving payment for property and life insurance.

Insurance Indemnity

Insurance Indemnity is the compensation paid by the insurer to the insurant or the beneficiary, when an accident has happened to the insured property or life and the loss has been investigated and verified to be within the insurance obligation.

Total Market Value

Total Market Value means all of the stock shares multiplied by their relevant market price.

Circulation Value on the Market

Circulation Value on the Market means the tradable circulation shares multiplied by their relevant share prices during a certain period of time.

P/E Ratio

P/E Ratio refers to the ratio between the price of a certain share and its earnings per year. The P/E ratio is the price of a traded common share divided by its annual earnings.

Exchange Rate

Exchange Rate means the trading frequency of certain stock shares on the market during a certain period of time.

Financial Bonds

Financial Bonds refer to those that banks and non – banking financial institutions issue to raise funds. Their debtors are the financial institutions that issue the bonds.

Corporate Bonds

Corporate Bonds usually refer to business bonds, which will be issued in accordance with the statutory procedures of the business and repay the original investment plus agreed interest within a certain period of time. Corporate bonds represent a kind of debtor – creditor relationship between the issuing enterprises and the investors. Bondholders are creditors of the certain enterprise, not the owners, and they do not have the right to participate or interfere with the business management. However, the bondholders have the right to claim the principal and interest on time. Like the stock shares, corporate bonds belong to marketable securities and can be freely transferable.

Convertible Bonds

Convertible Bonds, also translated into convertible exchangeable bonds, can be converted into the stock shares of the enterprise that issue the bonds. The conversion rate will usually be determined at the time of distribution. Convertible bonds generally have lower nominal interest rates, because the right of being converted into stock shares is a kind of compensation to the bondholders. In addition, when the bonds are converted into ordinary shares, the prices of these shares usually are far higher than the original value of the bonds. In essence, the convertible bonds have an additional option on the basis of the business bonds, and these bondholders are allowed to convert the convertible bonds they have purchased into the stock shares of specific companies during the specific period.

Open Interest

Open Interest refers to the number of open option contracts in the exchange market, also refers to the number of one or series of open option contracts.

Turnover

Turnover refers to the transaction volume of stock shares traded on that certain day.

Delivery

Delivery, its concept comes from futures, can be divided into physical delivery and cash delivery.

Physical delivery refers to the behavior that the vendor and the purchaser finish the open contracts at the end of the term by means of the ownership transfer of the object of futures contracts in accordance with rules and procedures of the stock exchange when the contract expires. The transaction of commodity futures usually adopts the physical delivery.

Cash delivery refers to the way that the two sides finally close their futures contracts by means of cash, with the settlement price used to calculate earnings or loss of the open contracts when the open futures contracts are delivered at the end of term. This kind of delivery is mainly used for futures contracts that their objects can not be dealt with physical delivery such as the financial futures.

第八篇

Chapter 8

房地产

REAL ESTATE

表8-1 房地产开发投资

(2008)

单位:亿元

指 标 Indicators		企业个数(个) Enterprises (unit)	本年完成投资 Current Year Investment Completed	土地开发投资 Investment in Land Development
总 计	**Total**	**488**	**279.97**	**13.13**
按登记注册类型分	**By Type of Registration**			
内 资	Domestic Investment	381	195.58	12.65
国 有	Statc-owned	32	6.19	0.01
集 体	Collective-owned	5	1.75	
股份合作	Share-holding	2		
联 营	Jointly-operated	7	19.53	
有限责任公司	Companies with Limited Liability	140	77.10	3.77
股份有限公司	Companies Limited by Shares	50	15.95	
私 营	Private	145	75.06	8.87
其 他	Others			
港澳台商投资	Hong Kong/Macao/Taiwan Investment	66	33.55	0.46
#港澳台商独资	Solely Hong Kong/Macao /Taiwan Funded	25	21.43	
外商投资	FIE	41	50.84	0.02
#外商独资	Solely Foreign Funded	25	44.57	0.02
按隶属关系分	**By Subordination**			
中央属	Central Government	18	2.45	
市(局)属	Municipality/Bureau	42	11.93	
区 属	PNA	137	60.03	1.53
外省市属	Non-Shanghai	4	1.42	0.01
其他属	Others	287	204.14	11.59
按企业资质等级分	**By Qualifications of Enterprises**			
一 级	Grade 1	49	18.16	0.78
二 级	Grade 2	87	25.88	
三 级	Grade 3	72	31.35	0.02
无 级	No Grade	280	204.58	12.33

注：本表至表8-4中的数据由上海市统计局返还。
Note: Data from this table to table 8-4 have been returned from Shanghai Statistics Bureau.

Investment in Real Estate Development

(100 million yuan)

完成投资按构成分 By Composition of Completed Investment				完成投资按工程用途分 By Project Use of Completed Investment			
建筑工程 Construction Project	安装工程 Installation	设备工器具购置 Equipment Purchasing	其他费用 Other Cost	住　宅 Residential Housing	办公楼 Office Buildings	商业营业用房 Commerce/ Operation	其　他 Others
177.64	**25.12**	**12.31**	**64.90**	**142.06**	**55.05**	**45.58**	**37.28**
129.14	17.39	3.82	45.24	118.70	28.42	27.59	20.89
5.24	0.42	0.02	0.51	3.84	1.43	0.09	0.83
1.61	0.15			1.58			0.17
11.29	2.25		5.99	16.41		3.12	
52.01	10.14	1.13	13.82	39.25	14.43	12.81	10.62
13.02	0.04	0.14	2.76	10.09	2.08	2.29	1.50
45.97	4.39	2.53	22.16	47.53	10.48	9.28	7.77
25.46	3.23	0.62	4.24	6.12	14.91	7.57	4.93
16.48	2.80	0.50	1.65	1.92	9.74	5.43	4.34
23.04	4.50	7.87	15.42	17.24	11.72	10.42	11.46
19.61	3.88	7.87	13.21	16.71	10.84	5.59	11.44
2.45				0.37	1.79	0.10	0.20
8.03	1.91	0.01	1.99	5.14	3.27	1.84	1.68
48.99	2.95	0.53	7.55	30.37	8.38	17.97	3.30
0.97			0.46	0.79	0.63		
117.20	20.26	11.77	54.90	105.39	40.98	25.67	32.10
6.99	2.14	0.22	8.81	14.07	0.28	1.01	2.81
20.33	1.75	0.23	3.57	18.10	4.54	1.38	1.85
24.25	1.08	2.32	3.69	21.02	3.33	5.15	1.85
126.07	20.15	9.54	48.83	88.87	46.90	38.04	30.77

表8-2　房地产开发企业投资资金来源

（2008）

单位:亿元

指　标	Indicators	本年资金来源合计 Total Sources of Funds	上年末结余资本 Remnant Capital of Previous Year	本年资金来源小计 Subtotal of Current Year
总　计	**Total**	**554.55**	**156.55**	**398.00**
按登记注册类型分	**By Type of Registration**			
内　资	Domestic Investment	384.22	101.49	282.73
国　有	State-owned	11.79	3.63	8.16
集　体	Collective-owned	4.42	1.87	2.55
股份合作	Share-holding			
联　营	Jointly-operated	20.63	3.61	17.02
有限责任公司	Companies with Limited Liability	173.77	43.30	130.47
股份有限公司	Companies Limited by Shares	31.04	12.30	18.74
私　营	Private	142.57	36.78	105.79
其　他	Others			
港澳台商投资	Hong Kong/Macao/Taiwan Investment	81.77	25.66	56.11
#港澳台商独资	Solely Hong Kong/Macao/Taiwan Funded	29.66	3.99	25.68
外商投资	FIE	88.56	29.40	59.16
#外商独资	Solely Foreign Funded	79.80	26.51	53.28
按隶属关系分	**By Subordination**			
中央属	Central Government	5.42	1.37	4.05
市(局)属	Municipality/Bureau	34.48	10.59	23.89
区　属	PNA	91.18	16.33	74.86
外省市属	Non-Shanghai	5.06	1.12	3.93
其他属	Others	418.41	127.14	291.27
按企业资质等级分	**By Qualifications of Enterprises**			
一　级	Grade 1	37.76	6.02	31.75
二　级	Grade 2	56.90	21.72	35.17
三　级	Grade 3	49.89	14.93	34.97
无　级	No Grade	410.00	113.88	296.11

Sources of Funds of Investment in Real Estate Development

(100 million yuan)

国内贷款 Domestic Loans	利用外资 Foreign Funds	自筹资金 Self-raised Funds	#自有资金 Self-owned	其他资金来源 Other Funds	本年各项应付款合计 Current Year Total Amount Payable	#工程款 Project Funds
133.65	**4.69**	**120.45**	**78.16**	**139.20**	**73.84**	**41.65**
63.16		112.57	70.89	107.00	54.76	30.84
5.85		0.75	0.75	1.56		
0.48		0.20	0.20	1.87	2.90	2.89
1.14		15.88	9.33			
29.45		46.81	18.22	54.21	24.82	16.93
2.54		11.17	11.17	5.03	2.93	0.29
23.70		37.76	31.22	44.33	24.11	10.73
33.64	2.27	5.57	4.95	14.63	10.91	4.64
19.84	2.27	0.73	0.73	2.84	4.54	3.92
36.85	2.42	2.31	2.32	17.57	8.17	6.17
33.87	1.13	2.17	2.17	16.12	5.92	5.90
1.00		3.05	3.00		1.11	0.94
1.63		6.93	0.31	15.33	3.28	0.71
21.52	1.29	35.00	18.50	17.04	16.14	8.60
2.40		0.15	0.15	1.38		
107.10	3.40	75.32	56.20	105.45	53.31	31.40
7.70		4.72	4.66	19.32	1.91	1.64
10.94		17.12	11.48	7.12	7.78	3.02
10.89		10.64	2.85	13.44	4.40	0.53
104.12	4.69	87.97	59.17	99.32	59.75	36.46

表8-3　房地产开发企业房屋施工面积、竣工面积和销售面积(2008)

单位:万平方米

指　标	Indicators	施工面积 Floor Area Under Construction	#新开工面积 Floor Area of New Starts	竣工面积 Floor Area Completed
总　计	**Total**	**1 964.30**	**478.69**	**477.85**
按登记注册类型分	**By Type of Registration**			
内　资	Domestic Investment	1 537.56	379.08	402.78
国　有	State-owned	55.68	31.26	5.08
集　体	Collective-owned	34.93	4.04	
股份合作	Share-holding			
联　营	Jointly-operated	74.80		
有限责任公司	Companies with Limited Liability	614.53	188.48	165.45
股份有限公司	Companies Limited by Shares	126.13	7.96	38.21
私　营	Private	631.49	147.34	194.04
其　他	Others			
港澳台商投资	Hong Kong/Macao/Taiwan Invested	228.67	59.88	27.01
#港澳台商独资	Solely Hong Kong/Macao/Taiwan Funded	108.15		8.22
外商投资	FIE	198.07	39.73	48.06
#外商独资	Solely Foreign Funded	156.05	6.93	48.06
按隶属关系分	**By Subordination**			
中央属	Central Government	20.41	15.74	0.35
市(局)属	Municipality/Bureau	99.12	43.71	15.64
区　属	PNA	393.70	88.78	68.63
外省市属	Non-Shanghai	38.01	21.31	
其他属	Others	1 413.06	309.15	393.23
按企业资质等级分	**By Qualifications of Enterprises**			
一　级	Grade 1	147.47	27.82	37.52
二　级	Grade 2	203.63	24.62	38.41
三　级	Grade 3	267.14	68.81	72.41
无　级	No Grade	1 346.06	357.44	329.51

Floor Space Under Construction, Completed Floor Space and Sold Floor Space in Real Estate Development

(10 000 sq · m)

#住　宅 Housing	办公楼 Office Building	商业营业用房 Commerce/ Operation	竣工价值(亿元) Completion Value (100 million yuan)	现房销售面积 Sold Floor Space for Completed Housing	期房销售面积 Area of Forward Sale of Future Marketable Housing
255.77	**79.11**	**52.14**	**138.32**	**111.41**	**231.94**
232.69	48.23	42.11	107.22	99.71	188.41
	2.20	0.26	0.91	2.20	11.95
				0.53	
				1.14	43.27
105.17	26.63	25.68	46.17	30.39	61.04
16.31		2.68	10.75	4.28	12.19
111.21	19.40	13.49	49.39	61.17	59.96
14.60	8.22	1.63	10.04	6.97	6.63
	8.22		3.30		0.43
8.48	22.66	8.40	21.06	4.73	36.90
8.48	22.66	8.40	21.06	4.23	36.90
0.21		0.14	0.08	1.26	
9.41	5.71		3.56	3.33	9.91
35.61	14.42	2.05	19.51	10.97	59.28
210.54	58.98	49.95	115.17	95.85	162.75
25.34	2.26	0.95	9.60	9.02	39.16
13.17	5.70	3.06	11.42	14.17	12.17
52.30	10.05	3.94	17.31	9.32	47.86
164.96	61.10	44.19	99.99	78.90	132.75

表8-4　历年全社会房屋施工面积、竣工面积

Total Floor Space Under Construction and Completed in Main Years (1992～2008)

年　份 Year	施工面积 (万平方米) Floor Space Under Construction (10 000 sq·m)	#住　宅 Residential Housing	竣工面积 (万平方米) Floor Space Completed (10 000 sq·m)	#住　宅 Residential Housing	房屋建筑面积竣工率 (%) Construction Completion Rate(%)	#住　宅 Residential Housing
1992	312.15	123.00	104.70	69.27	33.5	56.3
1993	764.36	285.34	169.44	76.68	22.2	26.9
1994	1 158.24	450.03	458.33	113.92	39.6	25.3
1995	1 577.21	583.96	404.58	199.84	25.7	34.2
1996	2 226.58	904.18	674.49	355.31	30.3	39.3
1997	1 954.70	768.15	581.03	271.64	29.7	35.4
1998	2 014.17	911.68	578.31	301.41	28.7	33.1
1999	1 766.88	856.25	573.20	268.27	32.4	31.3
2000	1 549.57	711.80	544.22	255.21	35.1	35.9
2001	1 526.45	879.01	469.53	249.96	30.8	28.4
2002	2 328.47	1 737.98	611.48	512.11	26.3	29.5
2003	2 242.65	1 607.68	671.70	498.85	29.9	31.0
2004	2 250.62	1 569.76	632.76	453.83	28.1	28.9
2005	2 390.79	1 695.24	684.96	512.42	28.6	30.2
2006	2 204.65	1 589.11	779.65	597.52	35.4	37.6
2007	1 983.86	1 255.32	516.59	419.29	26.0	33.4
2008	1 964.30	1 058.98	477.85	255.77	24.3	24.2

表8-5 主要年份房地产开发企业房屋建筑面积和造价
Construction Space and Cost of Property Developed by Real Estate Companies in Main years

指 标	Indicators	1998	1999	2000	2005	2006	2007	2008
房屋施工面积（万平方米）	**Floor Space Under Construction (10 000 sq · m)**	**1 458.94**	**1 097.51**	**1 119.67**	**2 390.79**	**2 204.65**	**1 983.86**	**1 964.30**
住 宅	Residence	789.35	661.96	712.17	1 695.24	1 589.11	1 255.32	1 058.98
#别墅、高档公寓	Villas and Flats	77.46	54.65	72.64	490.51	407.30	319.62	266.01
办公楼	Office Building	404.07	250.74	199.39	196.68	235.31	297.23	324.69
商业营业用房	Commercial Building	155.58	110.28	106.63	222.13	195.47	198.54	256.81
其 他	Others	109.94	74.53	101.48	276.74	184.76	232.77	323.82
房屋竣工面积（万平方米）	**Floor Space Completed (10 000 sq · m)**	**360.36**	**313.70**	**384.03**	**684.96**	**779.65**	**516.59**	**477.85**
住 宅	Residence	231.94	235.73	264.91	512.42	597.52	419.29	255.77
#别墅、高档公寓	Villas and Flats	26.10	15.92	23.59	168.59	151.87	85.52	53.44
办公楼	Office Building	71.15	27.30	54.62	54.08	52.06	34.36	79.11
商业营业用房	Commercial Building	41.16	24.55	28.10	32.85	58.52	23.09	52.14
其 他	Others	16.11	26.12	36.40	85.61	71.55	39.85	90.83
房屋竣工价值（亿元）	**Value of Buildings Completed (100 million yuan)**	**141.19**	**104.99**	**110.16**	**204.11**	**259.83**	**168.22**	**138.32**
住 宅	Residence	61.74	44.56	55.36	147.55	172.71	120.30	62.23
#别墅、高档公寓	Villas and Flats	16.91	5.13	9.86	61.51	79.18	51.53	15.71
办公楼	Office Building	53.89	25.33	35.25	26.18	33.34	12.79	32.90
商业营业用房	Commercial Building	20.61	20.86	11.02	10.09	30.01	11.00	18.97
其 他	Others	4.95	14.24	8.53	20.29	23.77	24.13	24.22
竣工房屋平均造价（元/平方米）	**Average Construction Cost (yuan/sq · m)**	**3 918**	**3 347**	**2 869**	**2 980**	**3 333**	**3 256**	**2 895**
住 宅	Residence	2 662	1 890	2 090	2 879	2 890	2 869	2 433
#别墅、高档公寓	Villas and Flats	6 481	3 221	4 179	3 648	5 214	6 025	2 940
办公楼	Office Building	7 575	9 276	6 454	4 841	6 404	3 722	4 159
商业营业用房	Commercial Building	5 007	8 498	3 921	3 075	5 128	4 764	3 638
其 他	Others	3 078	5 452	2 345	2 371	3 322	6 055	2 667

表8-6 浦东房地产交易中心交易情况
Transactions in Pudong Real Estate Trading Center

指 标 Indicators		单 位 Unit	2006	2007	2008
商品房交易登记	**Registered Transaction of Commodity Housing**				
#商品房出售套数	Number of Commodity Housing Sold	套 set	38 764	44 943	33 896
商品房出售面积	Area of Commodity Housing Sold	平方米 sq·m	4 918 698	5 347 674	4 330 266
商品房出售金额	Value of Commodity Housing Sold	万元 10 000 yuan	4 851 531	5 137 559	3 767 573
商品房预售套数	Number of Forward Sale of Commodity Housing	套 set	52 422	52 803	10 375
商品房预售面积	Area of Forward Sale of Commodity Housing	平方米 sq·m	5 192 359	5 043 917	1 147 917
商品房预售金额	Value of Forward Sale of Commodity Housing	万元 10 000 yuan	4 144 007	4 109 148	2 179 594
存量房交易登记	**Registered Transaction of Housing Stock**				
存量房交易过户套数	Trading Amounts of Housing Stock	套 set	31 960	37 942	23 579
存量房交易过户面积	Trading Area of Housing Stock	平方米 sq·m	3 097 993	3 632 733	2 293 567
存量房交易过户金额	Trading Value of Housing Stock	万元 10 000 yuan	2 574 454	3 813 193	2 702 009

注：本表由浦东房地产交易中心提供。
Note: This table is provided by Pudong Real Estate Trading Center.

表8-7 主要年份浦东房地产景气指数
Price Indexes of Real Estate in Pudong in Main Years

指 标 Indicators		2000	2005	2006	2007	2008
房地产景气指数(点)	**Price Index of Real Estate**	**107.57**	**110.42**	**104.52**	**101.13**	**109.19**
开发投资分类指数	Classified Index Grouped by Development and Investment	112.10	112.25	108.14	98.54	113.80
资金来源分类指数	Classified Index Grouped by Source of Fund	105.41	103.94	99.75	99.67	106.90
土地购置面积分类指数	Classified Index Grouped by Land Area Purchased	111.83	98.38	108.02	87.56	132.65
土地开发面积分类指数	Classified Index Grouped by Land Area Developed	87.73	130.47	97.24	89.75	99.96
商品房新开工面积分类指数	Classified Index Grouped by Area of New Start-ups Commercial Housing	112.54	106.73	104.19	103.21	108.02
商品房竣工面积分类指数	Classified Index Grouped by Commercial Housing Floor Space Completed	105.92	102.33	103.27	97.21	103.42
空置面积分类指数	Classified Index Grouped by Idle Area	104.55	103.72	98.01	98.12	92.65
商品房销售价格分类指数	Classified Index Grouped by Sales Price of Commercial Housing	112.43	121.17	101.83	107.20	105.22

主要统计指标解释

房地产开发投资

指各种登记注册类型的房地产开发公司、商品房建设公司及其他房地产开发法人单位和附属于其他法人单位实际从事房地产开发或经营活动的单位统一开发的包括统代建、拆迁还建的住宅、厂房、仓库、饭店、宾馆、度假村、写字楼、办公楼等房屋建筑物和配套的服务设施,土地开发工程(如道路、给水、排水、供电、供热、通讯、平整场地等基础设施工程)的投资;不包括单纯的土地交易活动。

施工面积

指报告期内施工的全部房屋建筑面积。包括本期新开工的面积和上期开工跨入本期继续施工的房屋面积,以及上期已停建在本期恢复施工的房屋面积。本期竣工和本期施工后又停缓建的房屋,其建筑面积仍计入本期房屋施工面积中。

竣工面积

指在报告期内房屋建筑按照设计要求已经全部完工,达到住人和使用条件,经验收鉴定合格(或达到竣工验收标准),正式移交使用单位的各栋房屋建筑面积的总和。

房屋建筑面积竣工率

指一定时期内房屋竣工面积占同期房屋施工面积的比率。该指标从房屋建筑施工速度的角度反映投资效果的指标。

别墅、高档公寓

指建筑造价和销售价格明显高于一般商品住宅的商品住宅。别墅一般指地处郊区,独立成栋的商品住宅;高档公寓一般指地处市内高尚社区,高层或多层的商品住宅。别墅、高档公寓的确定标准:一是经有房地产投资计划审批权的主管部门审批建设的别墅、高档公寓开发项目;二是销售价格高于当地同等地段商品住宅平均销售价格一倍以上的别墅、公寓开发项目。该指标可以分析房地产投资结构,反映高收入家庭商品住宅的供求平衡情况。

房地产价格指数

房地产价格指数是反映一定时期内房地产价格变动趋势和程度的相对数,包括房屋销售价格指数、房屋租赁价格指数和土地交易价格指数。这三套指数的计算方法相似,均采用由下到上逐级汇总的方法。

EXPLANATORY NOTES TO MAJOR STATISTICAL INDICATORS

Investment in Real Estate Development

It includes the investment by the real estate development companies, commercial buildings construction companies and other real estate development units of various types of ownership in the construction of house buildings, such as residential buildings, factory buildings, warehouses, hotels, guesthouses, holiday villages, office buildings, and the complementary service facilities and land development projects, such as roads, water supply, water drainage, power supply, heating, telecommunications, land leveling and other projects of infrastructure. It excludes the activities in simple land transactions.

Floor Space under Construction

Floor Space under Construction refers to total floor space of all buildings under construction during the reference period, including floor space of newly started buildings during the reference period, floor space of construction extended from the previous period to the current period, and floor space of construction suspended during the previous period and resumed in the current period. Floor space of construction completed in the current period, and floor space of construction started and then suspended in the current period are also included in the floor space under construction of the current year.

Floor Space of Buildings Completed

Floor Space of Buildings Completed refers to the floor space of all buildings completed in the reference period, which have been appraised and accepted (or come up to the designed standards) and have been transferred to the owners for use.

Completion Rate of Floor Space of Buildings

Completion Rate of Floor Space of Buildings refers to the ratio of the floor space of buildings completed in certain period of time to the floor space of buildings under construction in the same period. This indicator reflects the investment result from the perspective of the speed of construction.

Villas, High-Grade Apartments

Villas, High-Grade Apartments refers to commercial houses whose construction costs and marketing prices are significantly higher than ordinary housing. Villas are independent structures generally located in the suburbs; high-grade apartments are multi-story buildings located in elegant urban neighborhoods. Criteria for villas and high-grade apartments include: 1) projects for the construction of villas or high-grade apartments have to be approved by competent departments in charge of real estate development and investment plans, and 2) prices for projects on villas or high-grade apartments are higher by over 100% compared with the average prices of ordinary commercial housing projects in similar location. This indicator helps to analyze the investment structure of the real estate industry and the demand and supply of housing for high-income households.

Price Indices for Real Estate

Price Indices for Real Estate reflect the trend and degree of changes in prices of real estate during a given period, including price indices for selling houses and buildings, price indices for leasing houses and buildings and price indices for land transaction. The methods for the compilation of the three sets of indices are similar in that they all use bottom-up approach under which data are reported from lower level to higher level.

第九篇
Chapter 9

国内外贸易

DOMESTIC AND FOREIGN TRADES

表9-1　连锁商业零售额
Retail Sales of Commercial Chains

	指　标　Indicators	单　位　Unit	2007	2008
连锁商业零售总额	**Total Retail Sales of Commercial Chains**	**万元 10 000 yuan**	**1 368 457**	**1 603 428**
超市及大型超市	Supermarkets and Shopping Malls	万元 10 000 yuan	660 288	764 183
便利店	Convenience Stores	万元 10 000 yuan	67 175	52 455
家居建材商店	Stores of Building Materials for House Decoration	万元 10 000 yuan	87 112	88 922
家电连锁店	House Appliance Chain Stores	万元 10 000 yuan	367 812	453 443
连锁餐饮	Chain Catering	万元 10 000 yuan	77 899	87 354
医药连锁	Chain Pharmacies	万元 10 000 yuan	13 977	13 022
成品油连锁	Chain Refined Oil	万元 10 000 yuan	78 514	123 049
其他连锁	Other Chains	万元 10 000 yuan	15 680	21 000

表9-2　历年社会消费品零售总额
Total Retail Sales of Social Consumer Goods in Main Years

单位:亿元　(100 million yuan)

年　份 Year	消费品零售总额 Total Retail Sales of Consumer Goods	#餐　饮 Catering	按商品用途分 By Use				商品销售总额 Total Sales of Retail Goods
			食　品 Food	衣　着 Clothing	用　品 Articles	燃　料 Fuel	
1993	41.92		14.04	4.74	22.80	0.34	
1994	82.74	3.18	39.58	6.47	36.08	0.61	171.46
1995	110.00	4.07	49.50	8.36	51.59	0.55	200.05
1996	140.21	4.03	53.13	12.17	74.01	0.90	242.39
1997	162.23	5.41	62.89	12.54	84.72	2.08	274.26
1998	178.97	4.78	65.06	16.61	96.27	1.03	306.12
1999	198.31	19.02	74.17	15.26	104.17	4.71	593.37
2000	215.17	25.80	81.55	13.65	117.94	2.03	752.94
2001	233.02	28.50	81.27	13.99	135.28	2.48	1 004.89
2002	284.24	25.19	75.12	14.08	190.61	4.43	1 787.51
2003	313.24	24.50	72.53	14.49	220.21	6.01	2 422.87
2004	358.21	31.49	83.73	17.84	251.42	5.22	2 932.10
2005	353.69	43.80	111.00	27.53	213.52	1.64	2 807.47
2006	400.02	51.55	125.88	32.24	240.83	1.07	2 944.96
2007	456.04	60.52	128.66	35.63	283.45	8.30	3 613.46
2008	526.89	68.16	167.23	45.39	306.53	7.74	4 646.70

表9-3 社会商业商品购、销、存总额
Total Purchase, Sales Value and Inventory of Social Products

单位:亿元 (100 million yuan)

指标	Indicators	2006	2007	2008
商品购进总额	**Total Goods Purchased**	**2 638.45**	**3 337.31**	**4 174.85**
从生产者购进	Purchased from Producers	1 084.56	1 464.87	1 679.02
农副产品	Farm and Sideline Products	8.05	62.54	54.08
工业品	Industrial Products	1 076.51	1 402.33	1 624.94
从批发零售贸易业购进	Purchased from Wholesale and Retail	767.54	1 013.06	1 401.96
从市内批发、零售业	Wholesale and Retail Industry from In-Shanghai Market	542.48	671.61	563.42
从市外批发、零售业	Wholesale and Retail Industry from Out-of-Shanghai Market	225.06	341.45	838.54
进　口	Import	647.60	671.94	854.14
其　他	Others	138.75	187.44	239.73
商品销售总额	**Total Sales**	**2 944.96**	**3 613.46**	**4 646.70**
商品零售总额	Total Sales of Retail Goods	316.87	365.04	406.40
商品批发销售总额	Total Sales of Wholesale Goods	2 628.09	3 248.42	4 240.30
售给生产经营用	Sales for Production and Operation	1 198.97	1 438.90	1 811.16
售给批发零售业	Sales for Wholesale and Retail Industry	1 073.46	1 320.36	1 842.82
出　口	Export	355.66	489.16	586.32
年末库存总额	**Total Inventory(Year End)**	**220.71**	**245.43**	**376.29**

表9-4　社会消费品零售总额
Total Retail Sales of Consumer Goods

单位:万元　　(10 000 yuan)

指　标 Indicators		2005	2007	2008
社会消费品零售总额	**Total Retail Sales of Consumer Goods**	**3 536 860**	**4 560 361**	**5 268 901**
按登记注册类型分	**By Type of Registration**			
内　资	Domestic Funded	2 665 074	3 191 028	3 621 384
国　有	State-owned	205 063	339 801	328 491
集　体	Collective-owned	140 382	196 834	220 317
股份有限公司	Companies with Limited Liability	225 844	305 943	458 504
私　营	Private	816 919	1 027 937	1 123 025
其　他	Others	1 276 866	1 320 513	1 491 047
港澳台商投资	Hong Kong/Macao/Taiwan Invested	280 623	493 609	556 605
外商投资	Foreigner Invested	591 163	875 724	1 090 912
按行业分	**By Sector**			
商业零售额	Commerce	3 097 392	3 955 184	4 587 301
餐饮业零售额	Catering	439 420	605 152	681 583
其　他	Others	48	25	17
按商品用途分	**By Use**			
食品类	Food	1 110 039	1 286 549	1 672 258
衣着类	Clothing	275 260	356 337	453 902
用品类	Articles	2 135 181	2 834 436	3 065 328
燃料类	Fuel	16 380	83 039	77 413
构　成(%)	**Composition(%)**			
总　计	**Total**	**100.0**	**100.0**	**100.0**
按登记注册类型分	**By Type of Registration**			
内　资	Domestic Funded	75.4	70.0	68.7
国　有	State-owned	5.8	7.5	6.2
集　体	Collective-owned	4.0	4.3	4.2
股份有限公司	Company with Limited Liability	6.4	6.7	8.7
私　营	Private	23.1	22.5	21.3
其　他	Others	36.1	29.0	28.3
港澳台商投资	Hong Kong/Macao/Taiwan Invested	7.9	10.8	10.6
外商投资	Foreigner Invested	16.7	19.2	20.7
按行业分	**By Sector**			
商业零售额	Commerce	87.6	86.7	87.1
餐饮业零售额	Catering	12.4	13.3	12.9
其　他	Others	…	…	…
按商品用途分	**By Use**			
食品类	Food	31.4	28.2	31.7
衣着类	Clothing	7.8	7.8	8.6
用品类	Articles	60.3	62.2	58.2
燃料类	Fuel	0.5	1.8	1.5

表9-5　主要消费品零售量
Total Retail Sales of Major Consumer Goods in Quantity

指　标	Indicators	单　位　Unit	2005	2007	2008
粮　食	Grain	吨 ton	6 492	4 664	6 027
食用植物油	Vegetable Oil	吨 ton	6 463	8 577	5 674
家　禽	Poultry	吨 ton	553	589	649
水产品	Aquatic Products	吨 ton	871	789	683
卷　烟	Cigarette	万条 10 000 units	311	443	490
各种服装	All Sorts of Clothes	万件 10 000 units	589	1 217	1 268
化妆品	Cosmetics	万元 10 000 yuan	49 658	66 504	100 255
金饰品	Gold Ornament	万元 10 000 yuan	13 242	41 971	46 271
彩色电视机	Color TV Sets	架 set	115 068	98 101	113 323
微波炉	Microwave Oven	台 set	35 094	32 407	27 825
电冰箱	Refrigerators	台 set	53 033	41 426	43 546
洗衣机	Washing Machines	台 set	64 174	53 235	45 123
家用空调器	Household Air Conditioners	架 set	109 621	94 878	83 877
照相机	Cameras	架 unit	34 312	55 517	97 999
摄像机	Video Cameras	架 pcs	13 534	14 271	19 013
热水淋浴器	Electric/Gas Showers	架 pcs	33 920	28 901	30 236
电风扇	Electric Fans	台 pcs	54 720	40 802	21 484
脱排油烟机	Kitchen Rangehoods	架 pcs	26 199	24 229	18 933
家用消毒柜	Household Disinfectors	台 pcs	6 337	6 534	2 745
汽　车	Motor Vehicles	辆 unit	26 211	58 245	50 269
#轿　车	Cars	辆 unit	19 806	30 263	28 137
移动电话	Mobile Phones	只 unit	332 082	330 878	324 461
电　脑	Personal Computers	台 unit	78 264	76 660	108 000

表9-6　限额以上商业企业主要财务指标
Major Financial Indicators of Commercial Enterprises Above Quota

单位:万元　　(10 000 yuan)

指　标	Indicators	2005	2007	2008
企业单位数(个)	**Number of Enterprises(unit)**	**569**	**665**	**794**
年末资产负债	**Assets and Liabilities(Year End)**			
资产总计	Total Assets	8 981 028	11 882 513	17 914 220
#流动资产合计	Circulating Assets	7 334 193	10 204 155	14 511 698
#存　货	Goods in Stock	2 000 913	2 512 989	3 760 165
货币资金	Monetary Capital	1 179 058	1 856 014	2 964 231
短期投资	Short-term Investment	51 242	165 272	237 567
长期投资	Long-term Investment	904 363	896 464	905 724
固定资产合计	Total Fixed Assets	586 373	603 451	617 287
固定资产原价	Original Value of Fixed Assets	774 941	839 702	956 145
累计折旧	Accumulated Depreciation	229 104	293 485	318 462
#本年提取折旧	Current Year Depreciation	49 695	51 396	59 849
无形资产	Intangible Assets	94 337	95 965	99 276
负债总计	Total Liabilities	6 153 100	8 287 403	9 158 247
所有者权益总计	Owners' Equity	2 827 928	3 595 110	8 755 973
#实收资本	Paid-up Capital	1 302 017	1 749 080	2 215 976
#国家资本	State-owned Capital Assets	77 825	352 893	447 094
港澳台商资本	Hong Kong/Macao/Taiwan Capital Assets	26 705	95 607	121 128
外商资本	Foreign Capital Assets	302 926	578 589	733 036
法人资本	Legal Person Capital Assets	642 054	470 492	596 084
损益及分配	**Profit, Loss and Distribution**			
(限批发零售贸易业填)	(Only for Wholesale and Retail)			
营业收入	Operating Revenue	22 736 239	33 967 615	40 678 912
#主营业务收入	Main Operation Revenue	22 672 300	32 882 816	39 099 657
主营业务成本	Main Operation Cost	19 722 827	30 095 568	35 025 912
营业费用	Operating Expense	790 284	1 048 626	2 936 432
业务税金及附加	Operation Tax & Surtax	12 575	22 023	51 391
主营业务利润	Profit From Main Business	1 498 530	2 386 304	3 960 094
其他业务利润	Other Earnings	107 241	134 752	318 921

表9-7 商品交易市场基本情况
Commodity Market Transactions
(2008)

指 标 Indicators		市场数（个）Number of Markets(unit)	营业面积（平方米）Business Space(sq·m)	成交额（万元）Transaction Value (10 000 yuan)
合 计	**Total**	**149**	**993 078**	**10 518 795**
综合市场	**Integrated Markets**	**20**	**151 511**	**659 046**
生产资料综合市场	Integrated Market for Productive Materials	1	6 000	2 380
农产品综合市场	Integrated Market for Agricultural Products	17	137 179	655 831
其他综合市场	Other Integrated Markets	2	8 332	835
专业市场	**Professional Markets**	**129**	**841 567**	**9859 749**
生产资料市场	Market for Productive Materials	8	89 678	9079 292
农产品市场	Market for Agricultural Products	47	145 706	299 717
食品饮料烟酒市场	Market of Food, Beverage, Tobacco and Liquor	31	63 214	50 163
纺织品服装鞋帽市场	Market of Textiles, Clothes, Shoes and Hats	15	84 994	28 592
日用品及文化用品市场	Market of Commodities and Stationers Goods	2	15 367	77 372
家俱、五金装饰材料市场	Market of Furniture, Hardware and Decorative Materials	15	400 700	313 247
汽车及零配件市场	Market of Automobiles and Spare and Accessory Parts	1	7 021	3 000
电器、通讯器材市场	Market of Electric Appliances and Communication Equipment	1	450	706
花、鸟、鱼、虫市场	Market of Flowers, Birds, Fishes and Insects	5	27 900	7 019
其他专业市场	Other Professional Markets	4	6 537	641

表9-8 商品交易市场摊位数量及成交额
Number of Stalls and Transaction Value in Commodity Market (2008)

指 标	Indicators	数 量（个）Stalls (unit)	成交额（亿元）Transaction Value (100 million)
已出租摊位总计	**Total Leased Stalls**	**21 011**	**1 051.88**
食品、饮料、烟酒类	Food, Beverage, Tobacco and Liquor	11 108	98.69
服装、鞋帽、针、纺织品类	Garments, Shoes, Hats and Knitwear	3 285	2.78
化妆品类	Cosmetics	26	0.03
金银珠宝类	Gold,Silver and Jewelry	67	0.03
日用品类	Articles for Daily Use	349	0.84
五金电料类	Hardware Materials	113	0.32
体育、娱乐用品类	Recreation and Sports Articles	9	…
书报杂志类	Books and Newspapers	9	0.01
电子出版物及音像制品	Electronic Publications and Audio-Video Products	7	0.01
家用电器和音像器材类	Household Appliances and Audio-Video Equipment	46	0.08
中西药品	Western and Traditional Chinese Medicine	2	…
文化办公用品类	Culture and Office Articles	409	7.75
通讯器材类	Telecommunications Equipment	21	0.02
家具类	Furniture	589	3.38
木材及制品类	Timber and Its Products	46	0.12
石油及制品类	Petroleum and its products	274	500.00
化工材料及制品类	Chemical Materials and Products	482	371.95
金属材料及制品类	Metal Materials and Products	479	24.62
建筑及装潢材料类	Building and Decoration Materials	1 661	26.88
机电产品及设备类	Mechanical and Electrical Products and Equipment	6	1.10
汽车类	Automobiles	79	0.30
种子饲料类	Seeds and Feeding Stuff	4	…
其他类	Others	1 940	12.97

表9-9 历年进出口货物总值
Total Value of Imports and Exports in Main Years

单位:亿美元 (USD 100 million)

年 份 Year	进出口总值 Total Value of Imports and Exports	出口总值 Total Export Value	#一般贸易 Ordinary Trade	来料加工装配贸易 Processing and Assembly for Imported Materials	进料加工贸易 Processing for Imported Materials	进口总值 Total Import Value	#一般贸易 Ordinary Trade	外商投资企业作为投资进口设备物品 Imported Equipment and Supply as Foreign Investment
1993	25.92	12.02	6.67	0.79	4.52	13.90	5.26	2.48
1994	47.35	23.21	13.73	1.17	8.24	24.14	5.60	5.09
1995	71.96	39.63	24.40	1.96	12.68	32.34	11.72	5.96
1996	80.78	38.75	21.31	3.73	12.81	42.03	14.12	8.25
1997	99.01	45.86	23.06	4.59	16.72	53.15	17.00	8.72
1998	119.82	52.80	25.14	6.38	19.41	67.02	21.74	12.11
1999	153.65	66.67	28.58	10.57	25.45	86.98	35.90	5.92
2000	254.86	95.80	44.21	11.37	37.32	159.06	71.91	10.19
2001	297.83	110.22	49.56	11.30	47.49	187.61	87.74	14.26
2002	368.98	136.02	62.96	14.53	50.59	232.96	98.94	19.36
2003	581.33	211.92	102.80	28.43	67.69	369.41	156.60	14.73
2004	808.07	323.78	145.55	46.65	101.53	484.29	185.68	21.84
2005	894.75	372.12	175.38	45.21	107.33	522.63	186.52	13.30
2006	1 073.10	444.71	212.50	32.35	146.32	628.39	198.72	11.41
2007	1 280.52	528.10	257.50	47.81	135.96	752.42	248.66	13.04
2008	1 449.59	604.23	300.42	46.97	154.20	845.36	286.70	10.07

注：本表至表9－13由上海海关提供。
Note: The data in from this table to Table 9－13 are provided by Shanghai Customs District.

表9-10 主要年份按品种大类分的出口货物总值
Total Value of Exports by Category in Main Years

单位:万美元 (USD 10 000)

指 标	Indicators	2000	2005	2007	2008
总 计	**Total**	**958 044**	**3 721 174**	**5 281 027**	**6 042 273**
主要货物构成	**Composition of main goods**				
动物产品	Animal Products	5 966	3 428	7 311	7 016
植物产品	Vegetable, Fruit and Cereal	6 956	8 906	19 886	21 991
动、植物油、脂及其分解产品等	Animal Fat/Vegetable Oil, Wax and Related Analytic Products	111	93	88	304
食品、饮料、酒和醋、烟草及烟草代用品的制品	Food, Beverage, Liquor and Vinegar, Tobacco and Tobacco Substitutes	5 427	8 909	22 822	24 470
矿产品	Mineral	11 101	119 438	168 467	286 030
化学工业及其相关工业的产品	Chemical and Related Products	58 227	170 931	295 402	404 475
塑料及橡胶制品	Plastic, Rubber and Related Products	17 029	86 936	123 256	136 861
生皮、皮革、毛皮、鞍具等制品	Raw Hide, Leather, Fur, Saddle and Related Products	16 724	56 310	70 050	71 063
木、木炭、软木、稻草、篮筐等制品	Wood, Charcoal, Cork, Straw, Basket and Related Products	5 947	30 715	46 111	37 112
木浆、纸、纸板及其制品	Paper Pulp, Paper, Paperboard and Related Products	3 227	16 370	28 202	30 348
纺织原料及其制品	Textile Yarn, Fabric and Related Products	233 169	676 658	818 692	860 425
鞋、帽、伞、羽毛加工及人造花、人发等制品	Shoes, Hats, Umbrella, Processed Feather, Artificial Flower, Wig	17 294	56 039	62 371	66 097
石料、石膏、水泥、石棉、陶瓷及玻璃制品	Gypsum, Cement, Asbestos, Mica Ceramic, Glass Products	12 170	24 656	33 301	34 314
天然或养殖珍珠、宝石、金属制品	Natural/Cultivated Pearl, Precious Stone, Metal Products	11 332	22 790	23 176	26 464
贱金属及其制品	Base Metal and Related Products	51 006	219 405	537 621	504 734
机器、电气设备及其零附件	Machinery, Electrical Equipment and Related Parts	382 042	1 763 232	2 326 698	2 570 268
车辆、航空器、船舶及有关运输设备	Vehicle, Aircraft, Ship and Related Transport Equipment	65 216	190 392	314 181	499 359
光学、照相、医疗、精密仪器及设备的零件、附件	Optical/Photographic/Medical Instruments, Precision Instruments and Equipment, Related Parts and Attachments	17 036	132 341	185 251	249 364
杂项制品	Miscellaneous Products	37 481	131 596	193 865	205 990
艺术品、收藏品及古物	Works of Art, Collection and Antique	30	67	70	85
其 他	Others	553	1 962	4 206	5 503
#机电产品	**Machinery and electrical equipment**	**485 790**	**2 269 510**	**3 117 180**	**3 635 559**
#高新技术产品	**High and new technological products**	**259 938**	**1 242 868**	**1 550 866**	**1 711 061**

注：2007年机电产品和高新技术产品统计口径有调整。
Note: The statistical approach for items of machinery and electrical equipment and high and new technological products has been readjusted in 2007.

表9-11 主要年份按品种大类分的进口货物总值
Total Value of Imports by Category in Main Years

单位:万美元 (USD 10 000)

指 标	Indicators	2000	2005	2007	2008
总 计	**Total**	**1 590 555**	**5 226 325**	**7 524 167**	**8 453 663**
主要货物构成	**Composition of main goods**				
动物产品	Animal Products	8 705	25 330	23 852	27 826
植物产品	Vegetable Fruit and Cereal	22 850	24 882	50 548	126 723
动、植物油、脂及其分解产品等	Animal Fat/Vegetable Oil, Wax and Related Analytic Products	3 438	38 421	119 172	112 048
食品、饮料、酒和醋、烟草及烟草代用品的制品	Food, Beverage, Liquor and Vinegar, Tobacco and Tobacco Substitute	9 389	50 797	95 977	129 455
矿产品	Mineral	48 829	207 315	329 349	568 377
化学工业及其相关工业的产品	Chemical and Related Products	204 754	531 055	738 760	831 931
塑料及橡胶制品	Plastic, Rubber and Related Products	85 742	323 267	479 013	571 360
生皮、皮革、毛皮、鞍具等制品	Raw Hide, Leather, Fur, Saddle and Related Products	5 025	12 147	12 597	26 790
木、木炭、软木、稻草、篮筐等制品	Wood, Charcoal, Cork, Straw, Basket and Related Products	31 523	41 531	47 760	59 384
木浆、纸、纸板及其制品	Paper Pulp, Paper, Paperboard and Related Products	36 199	37 742	36 996	44 402
纺织原料及其制品	Textile Yarn, Fabric and Related Products	65 276	125 860	119 649	149 081
鞋、帽、伞、羽毛加工及人造花、人发等制品	Shoes, Hats, Umbrella, Processed Feather, Artificial Flower, Wig	1 057	11 108	7 586	10 013
石料、石膏、水泥、石棉、陶瓷及玻璃制品	Gypsum, Cement, Asbestos, Mica Ceramic, Glass Products	10 621	26 526	35 131	39 494
天然或养殖珍珠、宝石、金属制品	Natural/Cultivated Pearl, Precious Stone, Metal Products	10 399	37 506	88 969	99 098
贱金属及其制品	Base Metal and Related Products	99 165	326 288	544 631	559 455
机器、电气设备及其零附件	Machinery, Electrical Equipment and Attachment	757 104	2 602 150	3 914 991	4 143 718
车辆、航空器、船舶及有关运输设备	Vehicle, Aircraft, Ship and Related Transport Equipment	98 349	290 830	338 512	331 177
光学、照相、医疗、精密仪器及设备的零件、附件	Optical/Photographic/Medical Instrument, Precision Instrument and Equipment, Related Part and Attachment	83 829	492 493	512 065	588 957
杂项制品	Miscellaneous Products	8 267	20 020	26 646	31 321
艺术品、收藏品及古物	Works of Art, Collection and Antique	34	38	233	411
其 他	Others		1 019	1 730	2 642
#机电产品	**Machinery and electrical equipment**	**1 002 601**	**3 471 011**	**4 874 372**	**5 193 382**
#高新技术产品	**High and new technological products**	**643 020**	**2 119 533**	**3 305 896**	**3 501 444**

注：2007年机电产品和高新技术产品统计口径有调整。
Note: The statistical approach for items of machinery and electrical equipment and high and new technological products has been readjusted in 2007.

表9-12 主要年份按国别(地区)分的出口货物总值
Total Value of Exports by Country/Region in Main Years

单位:万美元 (USD 10 000)

国别(地区)	Country/Region	2000	2005	2007	2008
总 计	**Total**	**958 044**	**3 721 174**	**5 281 027**	**6 042 273**
#亚 洲	**Asia**	**450 329**	**1 697 530**	**2 483 375**	**2 826 415**
#中国香港	Hong Kong, China	94 198	468 087	616 919	608 060
中国澳门	Macao, China	1 377	1 789	2 461	3 851
中国台湾	Taiwan, China	14 717	130 197	210 542	183 921
印 度	India	4 126	35 233	96 111	104 195
孟加拉国	Bangladesh	4 194	13 023	12 424	16 738
印度尼西亚	Indonesia	7 730	26 669	43 523	60 983
日 本	Japan	190 858	451 176	614 165	743 428
马来西亚	Malaysia	12 120	66 363	86 091	111 036
巴基斯坦	Pakistan	1 857	10 116	14 965	19 646
菲律宾	Philippines	3 855	64 628	77 539	95 120
沙特阿拉伯	Saudi Arabia	3 463	14 897	27 806	26 659
新加坡	Singapore	42 076	109 379	196 030	254 896
韩 国	Republic of Korea	30 633	136 003	210 986	257 655
斯里兰卡	Sri Lanka	1 316	4 348	5 439	7 380
泰 国	Thailand	9 777	33 224	52 669	68 067
阿拉伯联合酋长国	United Arab Emirates	8 124	46 529	62 806	95 902
欧 洲	**Europe**	**210 148**	**843 460**	**1 257 229**	**1 487 388**
#欧 盟	European Union	186 765	785 409	1 150 756	1 347 969
#比利时	Belgium	17 404	61 105	73 388	94 183
英 国	United Kingdom	27 804	114 380	174 659	172 980
德 国	Germany	42 909	187 924	267 442	282 748
法 国	France	23 646	63 802	95 372	120 196
爱尔兰	Ireland	883	15 151	21 176	39 597
意大利	Italy	20 043	51 163	87 902	110 795
荷 兰	Netherlands	35 022	108 070	142 618	145 853
西班牙	Spain	8 945	42 824	78 572	85 737
波 兰	Poland	1 882	12 284	26 954	30 842
瑞 典	Sweden	3 264	22 954	34 023	32 782
瑞 士	Switzerland	2 757	11 441	17 669	17 571
俄罗斯	Russia	1 531	25 442	56 170	80 041
拉丁美洲	**Latin America**	**34 315**	**144 120**	**220 568**	**302 175**
#阿根廷	Argentina	1 551	5 739	9 379	19 723
巴 西	Brazil	5 542	34 310	50 007	77 204
智 利	Chile	3 200	11 408	18 534	23 969
墨西哥	Mexico	12 266	28 773	54 667	73 691
巴拿马	Panama	3 137	19 659	13 027	22 385
北美洲	**North America**	**213 309**	**863 433**	**1 031 271**	**1 074 238**
#加拿大	Canada	13 468	92 621	106 439	113 823
美 国	United States of America	198 503	770 807	924 829	960 407

表9-13 主要年份按国别(地区)分的进口货物总值
Total Value of Imports by Country/Region in Main Years

单位:万美元 (USD 10 000)

国别/地区	Country/Region	2000	2005	2007	2008
总　计	**Total**	**1 590 555**	**5 226 325**	**7 524 167**	**8 453 663**
亚　洲	**Asia**	**822 675**	**3 046 147**	**4 517 258**	**4 877 930**
#中国香港	Hong Kong, China	97 992	46 910	35 396	36 809
中国台湾	Taiwan, China	65 545	379 850	509 708	528 536
印　度	India	8 089	58 457	74 510	115 619
印度尼西亚	Indonesia	31 850	76 588	97 350	86 690
日　本	Japan	325 970	919 062	1 280 971	1 462 640
马来西亚	Malaysia	43 211	220 785	372 330	340 290
新加坡	Singapore	68 694	199 594	186 393	173 342
韩　国	Repubic of Korea	105 468	511 641	720 381	768 102
泰　国	Thailand	24 166	148 120	275 557	328 834
非　洲	**Africa**	**12 083**	**39 824**	**74 464**	**95 337**
欧　洲	**Europe**	**377 161**	**1 122 993**	**1 564 146**	**1 892 157**
#欧　盟	European Union	331 542	998 473	1 378 212	1 650 234
#比利时	Belgium	19 322	52 002	70 995	84 629
英　国	United Kingdom	22 873	72 078	89 599	104 671
德　国	Germany	140 814	385 695	533 202	603 060
法　国	France	59 653	159 106	237 708	283 185
意大利	Italy	30 726	102 266	123 845	147 343
荷　兰	Netherlands	12 997	44 876	56 893	67 574
西班牙	Spain	4 792	19 596	28 826	42 406
波　兰	Poland	378	4 920	11 145	16 688
瑞　典	Sweden	35 893	34 688	43 106	63 183
瑞　士	Switzerland	13 788	68 211	108 790	132 354
俄罗斯	Russia	10 962	31 450	50 606	71 415
拉丁美洲	**Latin America**	**53 163**	**127 155**	**302 660**	**370 914**
#巴　西	Brazil	15 523	26 441	47 683	78 463
智　利	Chile	25 086	35 236	125 951	121 607
墨西哥	Mexico	1 755	26 439	34 534	47 683
北美洲	**North America**	**296 704**	**820 607**	**982 369**	**1 077 532**
#加拿大	Canada	53 818	61 936	116 460	113 271
美　国	United States of America	242 869	758 389	865 643	964 245
大洋洲及其他	**Oceania**	**28 769**	**69 599**	**83 270**	**139 793**
#澳大利亚	Australia	21 627	56 073	60 453	111 868
新西兰	New Zealand	6 058	9 197	15 194	19 642

主要统计指标解释

社会消费品零售总额

指批发和零售业、餐饮业、新闻出版业、邮政业和其他服务业等,售予城乡居民用于生活消费的商品和社会集团用于公共消费的商品之总量。社会消费品零售总额包括:

(1)批发和零售业企业(单位):

①售予城乡居民的各种生活消费品;

②售予入境旅游的外国人、华侨、港澳台同胞的各类商品;

③售予行政事业单位、社会团体、军队和武警等机构的商品,以及以零售方式售予各类企业的商品。具体包括:用于非生产和社会交往的办公用品,如通讯设备、计算器具和设备、电讯网络设备、文印设备、音像视听器材和设备、纸张、本册、文具及装订文印材料、家具、日用电器、针纺织品、清洁卫生用品、文体用品、奖品、纪念品、礼品等;供内部人员乘坐的交通工具和燃料;用于办公设施修缮的各类配件、材料、工具等;用于取暖和防暑降温的设备、燃料、材料及食品等;专用于教学的用品和设备;非营利医疗机构的中、西药品、中药材和医疗设备器材;非专用的劳动保护用品;不对外营业的内部食堂用的餐具、炊具、设备、清洁卫生工具和食品、燃料等;军队、武警用于其人员生活的衣着品和个人用品;其他各类非生产性设备和用品。

(2)餐饮业出售的主食、菜肴、烟酒饮料和其他商品。

(3)新闻出版业、邮政业售予城乡居民、企事业单位、军队和武警等机构的书报杂志、音像制品、邮品等。

(4)其他服务业出售的食品、烟酒饮料、服装鞋帽、日常生活用品、医药保健用品、艺术品、工艺美术品、玩具、殡葬用品以及其他消费品。

批发零售贸易业商品购、销、存总额

指各种登记注册类型的批发、零售贸易企业(单位)以本企业(单位)为总体的,从上海、上海以外市场购进的商品总量、销售和出口的商品总量、库存商品总量等情况。该指标对促进工农业生产发展、活跃市场、平抑物价、保障供给、满足需求具有举足轻重的作用。该指标可以反映商品流转过程中商品的购进、销售、库存之间的比例关系和存在的问题。

商品购进总额

指从本企业(单位)以外的单位和个人购进(包括从境外直接进口)作为转卖或加工后转卖的商品总额。它反映批发零售贸易业从国内、国外市场上购进商品的总量。商品购进总额包括:①从工农业生产者购进的商品;②从出版社、报社的出版发行部门购进的图书、杂志和报纸;③从各种登记注册类型的批发零售贸易企业(单位)购进的商品;④从其他单位购进的商品,如从机关、团体、企业等单位购进的剩余物资,从餐饮业、服务业购进的商品,从海关、市场管理部门购进的缉私和没收的商品,从居民手中收购的废旧商品等;⑤从国(境)外直接进口的商品。不包括企业(单位)为自身经营用和未通过买卖行为而收入的商品以及销售退回、商品升溢等。

商品销售总额

商品销售总额指对本企业以外的单位和个人出售;包括对国(境)外直接出口的商品。这个指标反映批发零售贸易业在上海市场以及上海以外市场上销售商品的总量。商品销售总额包括:①售给城乡居民和社会集团消费用的商品;②售给工业、农业、建筑业、运输邮电业、批发零售贸易业、餐饮业、服务业等作为生产、经营使用的商品;③售给批发零售贸易业作为转卖或加工后转卖的商品;④对国(境)外直接出口的商品。不包括:出售本企业自用的废旧包装用品,未通过买卖行为付出的商品,经本单位介绍,由买卖双方直接结算,本单位只收取手续费的业务,购货退出的商品以及商品损耗和损失等。

批发零售贸易业年末库存

是指年末各种经济类型的批发零售贸易企业(单位)已取得所有权的商品,它反映各地区、各批发零售贸易企业的商品库存情况和对市场商品供应的保证程度。期末库存包括;①存放在批发零售贸易业经营单位(如门市部、批发站、经营处)仓库、货场、货柜和货架中的商品;②挑选、整理、包装中的商品;③已记入购进而尚未运到本单位的商品,即发货单或银行承兑凭证已到而货未到部份;④寄放他处的商品,如因购货方拒绝承付而暂存放在购货方的商品和已办完加工成品收回手续而未提回的商品;⑤委托其他单位代销(未作销售或调出)尚未售出的商品;⑥代其他单位购进尚未交付的商品。不包括所有权不属于本单位的商品、拨付除批发零售贸易业以外的其他行业所属独立核算加工厂等加工生产尚未收回成品的商品,代国家物资储备部门保管的商品等。期末库存总额计算方法是:农副产品采购单位按购进价计算;批发单位按进货价计算;零售单位按什么价格核算就按什么价格计算。

主营业务收入

指企业在销售商品、提供劳务等日常活动中所产生的收入总额。

主营业务成本

指企业已销商品应负担的进货原价和商品进价成本。

营业费用

指批发零售贸易企业在购、销、存过程中发生的各项经营费用。包括运输费、装卸费、包装费、保险费、展览费、差旅费、广告费、商品损耗、进出口商品累计佣金、经营人员的工资及福利费等。

外贸进出口总额

外贸进出口总额是指海关统计中按经营单位即进出口企业在海关注册地的行政区域口径统计的数据,它反映的是上海浦东新区行政辖区内各类具有进出口经营权企业(外贸企业)的进出口。它不包含外省市外贸企业途经上海浦东新区口岸由上海海关结关放行及统计的进出口商品,但包含上海浦东新区外贸企业经由非上海口岸进出口结关放行及统计的商品。

EXPLANATORY NOTES TO MAJOR STATISTICAL INDICATORS

Total Retail Sales of Consumer Goods

Total Retail Sales of Consumer Goods refer to the sum of retail sales of commodities sold by wholesale, retail, catering, publishing, post and telecommunications and other service industries to urban and rural households for private consumption and to social institutions for public consumption. Retail sales of consumer goods include:

(1) Sales by wholesale and retail units:

①of consumer goods sold to urban and rural households

②of commodities sold to foreigners, overseas Chinese and Chinese compatriots from Hong Kong, Macau and Taiwan visiting in China

③of commodities sold to government agencies, institutions, social organizations, military and armed police units, and commodities sold to enterprises in the form of retail sales. More specifically, they include: office facilities and articles for non-production purposes such as communications equipment, computing equipment and instruments, TV and network equipment, printing and copying equipment, audio-visual equipment and instruments, paper, notebooks, stationeries, furniture, electric appliances, knitwear, sanitation and cleaning articles, cultural and sport articles, articles for prizes, souvenirs, etc.; transport vehicles and fuels for employees; materials, spare parts and tools for the maintenance of office facilities; equipment, fuels, materials and food for winter heating or summer cooling purposes; articles and equipment for teaching purpose; Chinese and western medicines and medical equipment and facilities purchased by non profit-making medical institutes; non-specialized work safety articles; cooking utensils, tableware, equipment, cleaning articles, food and fuels purchased by internal cafeterias; clothes and personal articles purchased by military or armed police units for their officials and soldiers; and other equipment and articles for non-production purposes.

(2) Sales of stable food, cooked dishes, beverages, tobaccos and other articles by catering units.

(3) Sales of books, newspapers, magazines, audio-visual products and post products by publishing, post and telecommunications departments to urban and rural households and to enterprises, institutions, military and armed police units.

(4) Sales of food, beverages, tobaccos, clothing, hats, footwear, articles for daily use, medicines, medical and health articles, work of art, handicrafts, toys, funeral articles and other articles by other service industries.

Purchase, Sales and Stock of Commodities by Wholesale and Retail Trades

Purchase, Sales and Stock of Commodities by Wholesale and Retail Trades refer to the total volume of commodities purchased, total volume of sales and exports, and the stock of commodities by wholesale and retail enterprises (establishments) of different status of registration from Shanghai and out-of-Shanghai markets. This indicator plays an important role in promoting industrial and agricultural production, thriving market, stabilizing prices, ensuring market supply and meeting the needs of consumers. It also reflects the relationship among purchase, sales and stock of commodities in the circulation of goods and reveals the existing problems.

Total Purchase of Commodities

Total purchase of commodities refers to purchase of commodities from other establishments or individuals (including direct import abroad) for the purpose of reselling, either with or without further processing of the commodities purchased. This indicator shows the total value of purchases of commodities by wholesale and retail establishments from domestic and overseas markets, they include: ① agricultural and industrial products purchased from producers; ② books, magazines and newspapers purchased from distribution departments of the publishers; ③commodities purchased from wholesale and retail establishments; ④commodities purchased from other units, such as surplus materials purchased from government agencies, enterprises or institutions, commodities purchased from catering and service establishments, confiscated goods purchased from customs authorities or market management agencies, second hand goods and reusable stuff purchased from residents; ⑤commodities directly imported abroad. Excluded are commodities purchased by establishments for their own business operation, commodities obtained without buying or selling procedures, rejected commodities, etc.

Total Sales of Commodities

Total Sales of Commodities refer to the selling of commodities to other establishments and individuals (including direct export). Reflecting the total value of sales of commodities at Shanghai markets and out-of-Shanghai markets, this indicator includes: ① commodities sold to urban and rural households and institutions for their consumption; ② commodities sold to establishments in industry, agriculture, construction, transportation, post and telecommunications, wholesale and retail trade, catering and service trade and public utility for their production and operation; ③ commodities sold to wholesale and retail establishments for re-selling, with or without further processing; and ④commodities for direct export to other countries. Excluded are selling of waste packaging materials used by enterprises themselves commodities transferred without buying or selling procedures, commission income from brokerage in transactions whose settlement is directly handled by buyers and sellers, rejected commodities in the purchase, loss in commodities, etc.

Commodities Stock of Wholesale and Retail Enterprises at Year-end

refers to total commodities possessed by wholesale and retail enterprises (units of various ownership, which reflects the commodity stock level of various wholesale and retail enterprises and the potential for market supply. This indicator includes; ①commodities located in storage, rooms, garages, counters, and shelves of operating units(such as sales stores, wholesale stations, and operating offices) of wholesale and retail enterprises; ② commodities in the process of selecting, sorting, and packing; ③commodities not arrived but recorded as purchase in the account, i. e. commodities have not arrived but payment receipts for the commodities from the sellers or the banks have arrived;④commodities deposited in other places rather than places mentioned above, for instance; commodities in the hold of purchasers temporarily due to the refusal of payment and commodities not taken back after going through processing procedures; ⑤ commodities entrusted to other units to sell but not sold out yet; ⑥ commodities purchased for other units but not delivered yet. Commodities not included as stock are those not owned by enterprises, those allocated to financially independent factories rather than wholesale and retail enterprises for processing but not taken back yet, and finally those put in stock by wholesale and retail enterprises on behalf of the state material reserves units. The value of commodities stock at the end of period, the value is calculated at purchasing price of agricultural goods purchasing units and wholesale units and retail units at accounting prices.

Prime Operating Revenue

Prime Operating Revenue refers to the earnings a corporation receives in daily activity such as selling goods and offering labor service.

Operating Cost

Operating Cost refers to the cost a corporation paid to buy and deliver the commodities.

Operating Expenses

Operating Expenses refer to the spendings that a wholesaler or retailer pays in buying, selling or stocking goods. It includes fees incurred in transport, loading and unloading, packaging, insurance, exhibition, business trip, advertisement, commodity wastage, commissions in import and export, salaries and bonus paid to workers involved.

The Volume of Foreign Trade

The Volume of Foreign Trade is offered by Customs authorities, covering the operation units, or the enterprises involved in import and export, that have registered in the administrative regions where the Customs operate. It reflects the import and export of all the enterprises with import and export rights (foreign trade enterprises) under the administration of Shanghai Pudong New Area Municipality. It excludes those commodities of foreign trade enterprises from out of town that underwent customs clearance at Shanghai Pudong New Area ports but includes commodities of foreign trade enterprises of Shanghai Pudong New Area that underwent customs clearance in non-Shanghai ports.

第十篇

Chapter 10

旅游和住宿业

TOURISM AND HOTELS

表 10-1 主要年份接待国内外游客情况
Foreign and Domestic Tourists Received in Main Years

单位：万人次 (10 000 person-times)

指 标	Indicators	2000	2005	2007	2008
接待游客总数	**Total Tourists**	**1 133**	**1 660**	**2 018**	**1 961**
国内游客数	Domestic	1 092	1 566	1 925	1 873
国外游客数	Foreign	41	94	93	88
按接待单位分	By Receiving Agency				
#宾馆接待游客	Hotels	153	164	182	182
旅行社接待游客	Tourist Agencies	30	111	134	120
景点接待游客	Tourist Attractions	950	1 385	1 702	1 659
平均每天接待旅游人数（人次/天）	Average Number of Tourists Received Everyday(person-time/day)	31 041	45 474	55 288	53 726

注：本表至表 10-6 根据浦东新区经济贸易委员会的资料整理而成。
Note: The data in from this table to Table 10-6 are a summary of the data provided by Pudong Economic & Trade Commission.

表 10-2 旅馆、旅行社经营情况
Operation of Hotels and Travel Agencies

指 标	Indicators	单 位 Unit	2000	2005	2007	2008
旅馆业	**Hotel Industry**					
接待能力状况	**Receiving Capacity**					
客房数	Rooms	间 room	8 766	12 692	15 683	10 787
客房床位数	Beds	张 bed	15 635	20 245	23 917	
实际住宿人次数	Actual Staying Guests	万人次 10 000 person-times	152.50	163.84	182.14	182.12
#境外来沪住宿人次数	Overseas Guests	万人次 10 000 person-times	24.10	73.03	92.60	87.19
实际住宿人天数	Actual Staying Days of Guests	万人天 10 000 person · days	235.60	371.18	382.83	345.80
#境外来沪住宿人天数	Staying Days of Overseas Guests	万人天 10 000 person · days	55.10	195.58	209.08	173.44
财务经营状况	**Financial Operation**					
固定资产原值	Original Value of Fixed Assets	亿元 100 million yuan	40.21	82.35	89.47	
营业收入	Operation Earning	亿元 100 million yuan	15.52	37.09	47.18	
#客房收入	Hotel Room Earning	亿元 100 million yuan	7.51	21.77	27.27	
餐饮收入	Catering Earning	亿元 100 million yuan	6.53	15.32	12.72	
旅行社	**Travel Agency**					
旅行社接待人次数	Persons Received by PNA Travel Agencies	万人次 10 000 person-times	29.81	110.69	134.35	119.92
国内旅行社	Domestic Travel Agencies	万人次 10 000 person-times	26.03	89.86	119.34	101.27
国际旅行社	International Travel Agencies	万人次 10 000 person-times	3.78	20.83	15.01	18.65
旅行社营业收入	Operation Earning of PNA Travel Agencies	亿元 100 million yuan	3.85	14.68	20.62	21.48
国内旅行社	Domestic Travel Agencies	亿元 100 million yuan	2.67	8.44	13.42	11.99
国际旅行社	International Travel Agencies	亿元 100 million yuan	1.18	6.24	7.20	9.49

表 10-3 旅游景点经营情况
Operation of Tourist Attractions

指 标	Indicators	单 位 Unit	2005	2006	2007	2008
主要景点营业情况	**Business in Major Tourist Attractions**					
主要景点个数	Tourist Attractions	个 in number	14	13	14	15
接待参观人次	Visitors	万人次 10 000 person-times	1 385	1 518	1 683	1 659
营业收入	Operation Earning	万元 10 000 yuan	63 036	66 680	75 165	73 460

表 10-4 会议、展览情况
Conferences and Fairs

指 标	Indicators	单 位 Unit	2005	2006	2007	2008
举办展览(博览)	**Number of Exhibitions Hosted**	**次 time**	**114**	**90**	**99**	**117**
#国际性	International	次 time	91	72	65	94
#三万平方米及以上	≥30 000 sq · m	次 time	29	37	50	47
#五万平方米及以上	≥50 000 sq · m	次 time	15	22	27	34
展览面积	Display Area	万平方米 10 000sq · m	238	301	332	392
参展客商	Exhibition-Attending Investors	个 unit	48 412	52 012	58 478	67 607
接待(参观)人数	Visitors	万人次 10 000 person-times	266.90	266.88	308.63	266.62
召开会议	Conferences Hosted	次 time	1 583	1 740	1 708	1 511
#跨省市	Trans-provincial	次 time	61	77	62	90
国际性	International	次 time	199	46	21	21
参加会议人员	Number of Participants	万人次 10 000 person-times	16.69	32.21	16.61	16.81
#海外与会人员	Overseas Participants	万人次 10 000 person-times	3.00	1.99	0.99	1.09

注：表中会议召开情况统计的范围为国际会议中心及部分高星级宾馆。
Note: The statistics of conferences come from the data of International Convention Center and part of the high Star hotels.

主要统计指标解释

接待国外游客人数

指来上海浦东新区参观、访问、旅行、探亲、访友、休养、考察、参加会议和从事经济、科技、文化、教育、体育、宗教等活动的外国人、华侨、港澳和台湾同胞的人数。不包括来上海浦东新区常住1年以上的外国专家、留学生等。上海浦东新区入境的境外旅游人数包括从上海浦东新区口岸入境的境外旅游人数和从我国其他口岸入境的境外旅游人数。

EXPLANATORY NOTES TO MAJOR STATISTICAL INDICATORS

Number of Overseas Tourists through Shanghai Customs

Number of Overseas Tourists through Shanghai Pudong New Area Customs refers to the number of foreigners, overseas Chinese, and compatriots from Hong Kong, Macao and Taiwan coming to Shanghai Pudong New Area for sightseeing, visits, tours, family reunions, meeting friends, vacations, study tours, attending meetings and other activities of an economic, scientific and technological, cultural, physical culture and religious nature. This does not include foreign experts and students residing in Shanghai Pudong New Area for over 1 year. The number of overseas tourists to Shanghai Pudong New Area includes those overseas tourists entering China through Shanghai Pudong New Area customs and through customs other than Shanghai.

第十一篇

Chapter 11

科学技术

SCIENCE AND TECHNOLOGY

表 11-1 历年科技成果
Achievements in Scientific & Technological Research in Main Years
(1995~2008)

单位:项 (item)

年 份 Year	获上海市高新技术成果转化百佳项目 Top 100 Projects Which Have Successfully Commercialized Achievements in Scientific & Technological Research	获上海市以上科技进步奖 Shanghai and Above Level Achievement Awards in Science and Technology	按奖项分 Award Grade				
			一等奖 First Prize	#国家级 National Grade	二等奖 Second Prize	#国家级 National Grade	三等奖 Third Prize
1995		2			1		1
1996							
1997		2			1		1
1998		14			3		11
1999		12	2		3		7
2000		11			5		6
2001		16			5		11
2002		37	8		13		16
2003	11	34	8		10		16
2004	11	45	10		16		19
2005	25	35	5	1	10	3	20
2006	17	48	11	1	23	5	14
2007		73	11	2	31	11	31
2008		66	10		27	6	29

注：1. 本表至表 11-5 由浦东新区科学技术委员会提供。
2. 上海市高新技术成果转化百佳项目从 2001 年起评比。

Note：1. The data in from this table to Table 11-5 are provided by Pudong Science & Technology Commission.
2. We started to appraise the above-mentioned Top 100 Projects since 2001.

表 11-2 历年各类技术合同项目
All Kinds of Technical Contracts in Main Years
(1994~2008)

单位:项 (item)

年 份 Year	各类合同项目 Item of Contracts	技术开发 Technical Development	技术转让 Technology Tranfer	技术咨询 Technical Consultation	技术服务 Technical Service
1994	595	25	43	98	429
1995	924	42	33	147	702
1996	1 525	12	16	215	1 282
1997	1 742	23	56	291	1 372
1998	1 659	57	49	282	1 271
1999	1 998	85	21	406	1 486
2000	1 940	79	24	458	1 379
2001	2 253	260	86	405	1 502
2002	2 281	372	116	465	1 328
2003	2 406	500	284	422	1 200
2004	2 362	580	148	406	1 228
2005	3 034	1 155	225	353	1 301
2006	2 636	1 448	100	204	884
2007	2 545	1 326	118	86	1 015
2008	2 294	1 448	94	262	490

表 11-3 历年各类技术合同成交金额
Business Volume of All Kinds of Technical Contracts in Main Years (1994～2008)

单位:万元 (10 000 yuan)

年 份 Year	成交金额 Business Volume	技术开发 Technical Development	技术转让 Technology Tranfer	技术咨询 Technical Consultation	技术服务 Technical Service
1994	6 225	284	404	492	5 045
1995	12 514	3 863	2 105	936	5 610
1996	21 255	599	573	1 772	18 311
1997	15 644	749	1 286	2 386	11 223
1998	21 286	3 924	2 106	2 098	13 158
1999	24 788	7 194	1 509	2 929	13 156
2000	39 707	7 969	15 893	2 524	13 321
2001	62 892	30 778	8 709	3 317	20 088
2002	86 786	51 233	12 303	4 585	18 665
2003	112 355	79 274	12 978	5 217	14 886
2004	221 295	185 897	13 881	4 030	17 487
2005	386 406	335 848	33 096	3 087	14 375
2006	641 015	525 942	96 628	2 952	15 493
2007	839 052	694 197	125 175	2 586	17 094
2008	957 346	870 937	69 244	3 512	13 653

表 11－4　历年专利申请情况
Statistics of Patent Claiming in Main Years
（1999～2008）

单位:项 (item)

年　份 Year	专利申请总量 Total Patent Claimings	发　明 Inventions	实用新型 Utility Models	外观设计 Design in Appearance
1999	386	67	216	103
2000	718	209	241	268
2001	1 103	222	453	428
2002	2 397	467	591	1 339
2003	2 580	1 064	852	664
2004	2 871	1 676	719	476
2005	3 141	1 794	863	484
2006	6 767	2 557	1 224	2 986
2007	8 435	3 054	1 386	3 995
2008	8 980	3 065	1 893	4 022

表 11－5　历年专利授权情况
Statistics of Patents Authorized in Main Years
（2001～2008）

单位:项 (item)

年　份 Year	专利授权总量 Total Patents Authorized	发　明 Inventions	实用新型 Utility Models	外观设计 Design in Appearance
2001	519			
2002	668			
2003	1 542			
2004	1 066	95	528	443
2005	1 204	329	576	299
2006	1 432	375	655	402
2007	4 086	409	1 152	2 525
2008	3 677	841	1 442	1 394

表11－6　区属企业、事业单位各类专业技术人员(至2008年末)

Professional Personnel Working in Enterprises and Institutions in PNA (Total by the End of 2008)

单位:人　　　　(person)

指　标 Indicators		合　计 Total	#女　性 Female	按学历分 By Education Level				
				研究生 Post Graduate	大　学 本　科 University	高　等 专　科 Junior University	中等专科 Specialized Secondary School	高中及以下 Senior High School and Below
总　计	**Total**	**29 829**	**20 655**	**748**	**16 148**	**8 881**	**3 271**	**781**
工程技术人员	Engineering	1 710	394	133	813	432	146	186
农业技术人员	Agricultural	162	38	8	76	39	32	7
科学研究人员	Research	87	39	22	29	26	4	6
卫生技术人员	Healthcare	6 306	4 645	169	1 732	2 200	2 002	203
教学人员	Teaching	17 961	13 663	210	12 232	4 785	665	69
经济人员	Economic	1 238	386	137	458	420	102	121
会计人员	Financial/Accounting	1 233	883	34	358	556	207	78
统计人员	Statistical	147	97	3	45	65	25	9
翻译人员	Interpreter/Translator	24	16	5	17	2		
图书档案文博人员	Librarian/Archivist/Museum Staff	477	332	6	174	219	41	37
新闻、出版人员	News-Reporting/Publishing	23	9	4	11	5		3
律师、公证人员	Lawyer/Notary	37	17	4	33			
播音人员	Radio Crew Member	9	6		5	3		1
工艺美术人员	Artisan	7			1	5		1
体育人员	PE	53	18		34	17	1	1
艺术人员	Actor	50	20	1	8	23	2	16
政工人员	Political	305	92	12	122	84	44	43

注：本表和表11－7由浦东新区组织部提供。
Note: The data in this table and Table 11－7 are provided by Pudong Organization Department.

表 11-7 区属各年龄组专业技术职务及专业技术人员(至 2008 年末)
Professional Positions and Professionals by Age Group in PNA (Total by the End of 2008)

单位:人 (person)

指 标	Indicators	合 计 Total	按年龄分 By Age 35 岁及以下 35 Years Old and Below	36 至 40 岁 36~40 Years Old	41 至 45 岁 41~45 Yeas Old	46 至 50 岁 46~50 Years Old	51 至 54 岁 51~54 Years Old	55 岁以上 55 Years Old and Above
总 计	**Total**	**29 829**	**11 846**	**6 735**	**4 187**	**2 633**	**2 909**	**1 519**
按专业技术职务分	**By Professional Position**							
高级职务	Senior	2 435	46	436	797	444	365	347
中级职务	Intermediate	14 207	3 711	4 620	2 454	1 334	1 341	747
初级职务	Junior	12 042	7 226	1 606	874	795	1 145	396
未聘职务	Laid-off	1 145	863	73	62	60	58	29
按专业技术类别分	**By Profession**							
工程技术人员	Engineering	1 710	546	288	264	266	184	162
农业技术人员	Agricultural Technician	162	36	18	39	14	20	35
科学研究人员	Scientific	87	34	16	5	6	14	12
卫生技术人员	Healthcare	6 306	2 249	1 243	734	696	1 116	268
教学人员	Teaching	17 961	7 986	4 603	2 572	1 067	1 008	725
经济人员	Economic	1 238	296	204	164	207	212	155
会计人员	Financial/Accounting	1 233	399	197	237	187	153	60
统计人员	Statistical	147	52	35	22	17	18	3
图书档案文博人员	Librarians/Archivists/Museum Staff	477	142	89	74	69	74	29
政工人员	Political	305	35	16	51	67	86	50
其他专业技术人员	Others Professionals	203	71	26	25	37	24	20

表 11-8 大中型工业企业科技活动人员情况

Scientific and Technical Personnel of Large and Medium Industrial Enterprises (2008)

指 标 Indicators		有科技活动企业数(个) Number of Enterprises with Scientific Technical Activities (unit)	从事科技活动人员(人) Total Number of Personnel Undertaking Scientific Technical Activities (person)	#科学家和工程师(人) Scientists and Engineers (person)
总 计	**Total**	**67**	**22 363**	**17 744**
按注册登记大类分组	**Grouped by Type of Registration**			
国 有	State-owned	11	3 328	3 034
集 体	Collective-owned			
股份制及其他有限公司	Share-holding	21	7 012	4 987
私 营	Private			
外商及港澳台投资	Overseas Invested Enterprises	35	12 023	9 723
其 他	Others			
按隶属关系分	**Grouped by Subordination**			
中央工业	Central	14	9 554	8 418
地方工业	Local	53	12 809	9 326
按企业规模分组	**Grouped by Size of Enterprises**			
大型企业	Large	18	16 115	13 637
中型企业	Medium	49	6 248	4 107
按工业行业大类分组	**Grouped by Sectors**			
烟草制品业	Tabacco Manufacturing	1	24	9
造纸及纸制品业	Paper-making and Paper Products Manufacturing	1	11	4
印刷业和记录媒介的复制	Printing and Record Duplicating	2	149	106
石油加工、炼焦及核燃料加工业	Oil Processing, Coking and Nuclear	1	175	161
化学原料及化学制品制造业	Raw Chemical Materials and Chemical	3	389	279
医药制造业	Medicine Manufacturing	8	1 025	650
非金属矿物制品业	Nonmetal Mineral Products	1	131	93
金属制品业	Metal Products Manufacturing	1	166	73
通用设备制造业	General Equipment Manufacturing	6	2 145	1 620
专用设备制造业	Special Purpose Equipment Manufacturing	5	854	519
交通运输设备制造业	Transportation Equipment Manufacturing	12	7 172	5 305
电气机械及器材制造业	Electric Machinery Equipment and Manufacturing	7	722	413
通信设备、计算机及其他电子设备制造业	Communications Equipment, Computer and Other Electronic Equipment Manufacturing	12	6 476	5 775
仪器仪表及文化、办公用机械制造业	Instruments, Meters, Culture and Office Equipment Manufacturing	2	378	233
电力、热力的生产和供应业	Production and Supply of Electricity and Thermal Power	2	2 441	2 425
燃气生产和供应业	Production and Supply of Gas	2	46	31
水的生产和供应业	Production and Supply of Water	1	59	48

表 11-9　大中型工业企业技术开发项目和人员情况

Technical Development Projects and Personnel of Large and Medium Industrial Enterprises (2008)

指　标	Indicators	项目数（项） Number of Projects (item)	从事技术开发人数（人） Number of Technical Development Personnel (person)	科技项目经费内部支出（千元） Internal Expenditure for Projects of Science and Technology (1 000 yuan)
总　计	**Total**	**1 818**	**16 604**	**9 639 870**
按注册登记大类分组	**Grouped by Type of Registration**			
国　有	State-owned	437	3 016	593 321
集　体	Collective-owned			
股份制及其他有限公司	Share-holding	403	5 026	3 124 346
私　营	Private			
外商及港澳台投资	Overseas Invested Enterprises	978	8 562	5 922 203
其　他	Others			
按隶属关系分	**Grouped by Subordination**			
中央工业	Central	869	6 953	2 411 049
地方工业	Local	949	9 651	7 228 821
按企业规模分组	**Grouped by Size of Enterprises**			
大型企业	Large	1 055	12 635	7 572 236
中型企业	Medium	763	3 969	2 067 634
按工业行业大类分组	**Grouped by Sectors**			
烟草制品业	Tabacco Manufacturing	6	16	1 942
造纸及纸制品业	Paper-making and Paper Products Manufacturing	1	9	350
印刷业和记录媒介的复制	Printing and Record Duplicating	23	119	33 046
石油加工、炼焦及核燃料加工业	Oil Processing, Coking and Nuclear	58	175	15 194
化学原料及化学制品制造业	Raw Chemical Materials and Chemical	61	319	125 447
医药制造业	Medicine Manufacturing	114	546	154 448
非金属矿物制品业	Nonmetal Mineral Products	13	103	24 969
金属制品业	Metal Products Manufacturing	16	53	47 289
通用设备制造业	General Equipment Manufacturing	169	1 736	1 287 994
专用设备制造业	Special Purpose Equipment Manufacturing	53	302	106 099
交通运输设备制造业	Transportation Equipment Manufacturing	413	5 671	4 000 299
电气机械及器材制造业	Electric Machinery Equipment and Manufacturing	81	556	307 888
通信设备、计算机及其他电子设备制造业	Communications Equipment, Computer and Other Electronic Equipment Manufacturing	502	4 213	3 101 104
仪器仪表及文化、办公用机械制造业	Instruments, Meters, Culture and Office Equipment Manufacturing	39	316	47 910
电力、热力的生产和供应业	Production and Supply of Electricity and Thermal Power	258	2 385	382 731
燃气生产和供应业	Production and Supply of Gas	9	42	1 510
水的生产和供应业	Production and Supply of Water	2	43	1 650

表 11 - 10 大中型工业企业技术开发机构情况

Technical Development Institutions of Large and Medium Industrial Enterprises (2008)

指 标	Indicators	企业办技术开发机构数（个）Technical Development Institutions in Enterprises (unit)	技术开发机构科技活动人数（人）Technical Development Personnel (person)	技术开发机构科技经费内部支出（千元）Expenditure of Technical Development (1 000 yuan)
总 计	**Total**	**65**	**13 363**	**7 944 596**
按注册登记大类分组	**Grouped by Type of Registration**			
国 有	State-owned	11	526	194 975
集 体	Collective-owned			
股份制及其他有限公司	Share-holding	16	3 394	2 876 902
私 营	Private			
外商及港澳台投资	Overseas Invested Enterprises	38	9 443	4 872 719
按隶属关系分	**Grouped by Subordination**			
中央工业	Central	7	5 492	2 025 261
地方工业	Local	58	7 871	5 919 335
按企业规模分组	**Grouped by Size of Enterprises**			
大型企业	Large	18	10 345	6 355 499
中型企业	Medium	47	3 018	1 589 097
按工业行业大类分组	**Grouped by Sectors**			
造纸及纸制品业	Paper-making and Paper Products Manufacturing	1	5	180
印刷业和记录媒介的复制	Printing and Record Duplicating	5	93	29 716
化学原料及化学制品制造业	Raw Chemical Materials and Chemical	2	306	91 108
医药制造业	Medicine Manufacturing	8	187	39 722
非金属矿物制品业	Nonmetal Mineral Products	1	63	24 969
金属制品业	Metal Products Manufacturing	1	26	47 289
通用设备制造业	General Equipment Manufacturing	6	1 136	1 017 048
专用设备制造业	Special Purpose Equipment Manufacturing	2	249	82 579
交通运输设备制造业	Transportation Equipment Manufacturing	10	5 147	3 346 008
电气机械及器材制造业	Electric Machinery Equipment and Manufacturing	4	139	56 250
通信设备、计算机及其他电子设备制造业	Communications Equipment, Computer and Other Electronic Equipment Manufacturing	22	5 826	3 153 402
仪器仪表及文化、办公用机械制造业	Instruments, Meters, Culture and Office Equipment Manufacturing	1	142	43 430
电力、热力的生产和供应业	Production and Supply of Electricity and Thermal Power	1	38	12 385
燃气生产和供应业	Production and Supply of Gas	1	6	510

表11－11　大中型工业科技活动经费来源及经费支出情况

（2008）

单位：千元

指　标	Indicators	科技活动经费筹集总额 Total Scientific Technical Funds Raised	#企　业资　金 Self-raised Funds	金融机构贷　款 Loans from Financial Institutions
总　计	**Total**	**11 386 095**	**10 994 276**	**12 830**
按注册登记大类分组	**Grouped by Type of Registration**			
国　有	State-owned	937 468	928 802	2 000
集　体	Collective-owned			
股份制及其他有限公司	Share-holding	3 921 518	3 705 562	
私　营	Private			
外商及港澳台投资	Overseas Invested Enterprises	6 527 109	6 359 912	10 830
其　他	Others			
按隶属关系分	**Grouped by Subordination**			
中央工业	Central	3 259 463	3 113 802	
地方工业	Local	8 126 632	7 880 474	12 830
按企业规模分组	**Grouped by Size of Enterprises**			
大型企业	Large	8 916 044	8 641 386	
中型企业	Medium	2 470 051	2 352 890	12 830
按工业行业大类分组	**Grouped by Sectors**			
烟草制品业	Tabacco Manufacturing	1 942	1 942	
造纸及纸制品业	Paper-making and Paper Products Manufacturing	450	450	
印刷业和记录媒介的复制	Printing and Record Duplicating	35 546	33 546	2 000
石油加工、炼焦及核燃料加工业	Oil Processing, Coking and Nuclear	18 572	18 572	
化学原料及化学制品制造业	Raw Chemical Materials and Chemical	153 433	149 863	
医药制造业	Medicine Manufacturing	184 782	180 692	
非金属矿物制品业	Nonmetal Mineral Products	45 054	43 514	
金属制品业	Metal Products Manufacturing	47 530	47 530	
通用设备制造业	General Equipment Manufacturing	1 341 302	1 282 712	
专用设备制造业	Special Purpose Equipment Manufacturing	157 695	156 695	
交通运输设备制造业	Transportation Equipment Manufacturing	4 763 564	4 611 489	10 830
电气机械及器材制造业	Electric Machinery Equipment and Manufacturing	390 436	390 436	
通信设备、计算机及其他电子设备制造业	Communications Equipment, Computer and Other Electronic Equipment Manufacturing	3 433 717	3 271 339	
仪器仪表及文化、办公用机械制造业	Instruments, Meters, Culture and Office Equipment Manufacturing	48 420	48 020	
电力、热力的生产和供应业	Production and Supply of Electricity and Thermal Power	758 471	752 295	
燃气生产和供应业	Production and Supply of Gas	3 531	3 531	
水的生产和供应业	Production and Supply of Water	1 650	1 650	

Funds and Expenditure of Scientific and Technical Activities of Large and Medium Industrial Enterprises

(1 000 yuan)

来自政府部门资金 Funds from Government Departments	科技活动经费支出总额 Total Scientific Technical Expenditure	#内部支出合计 Total Interual Expenditure	#研究与试验发展经费支出 R&D Expenditure	新产品开发经费支出 Expenditure on New Products	其他技术活动费用支出 Expenses of Other Technological Activities: 技术改造经费支出 Expenditure on Technical Transformation	技术引进经费支出 Expenditure on Technical Introduction	消化吸收经费支出 Expenditure on Technical Digestion and Absorption	购买国内技术经费支出 Expenditure in Buying Domestic Technology
365 139	**12 098 865**	**10 973 809**	**8 709 254**	**7 929 710**	**2 915 075**	**2 445 965**	**244 543**	**65 878**
6 666	1 003 134	617 110	425 822	225 654	461 618	2 144	5 207	342
202 106	4 358 250	3 924 310	2 886 525	2 627 256	2 230 005	783 554	33 438	64 244
156 367	6 737 481	6 432 389	5 396 907	5 076 800	223 452	1 660 267	205 898	1 292
131 811	3 686 818	3 128 490	2 278 965	1 783 033	1 198 538	479 863	32 288	57 064
233 328	8 412 047	7 845 319	6 430 289	6 146 677	1 716 537	1 966 102	212 255	8 814
260 808	9 490 936	8 544 422	6 978 665	6 306 200	2 517 647	1 777 301	163 208	58 664
104 331	2 607 929	2 429 387	1 730 589	1 623 510	397 428	668 664	81 335	7 214
	2 783	2 783	580		2 819			
	470	370	350	350				
	34 987	34 017	9 996	28 417	26 955			
	18 572	15 194		252	134 250			
3 570	178 254	162 618	89 078	114 083	192 719			
4 090	205 121	191 445	152 560	48 000	68 238	67 885	10 809	7 190
1 540	45 054	45 054	16 884	22 527				
	71 439	71 439	47 289	47 289		10 392	190	
58 590	1 390 779	1 374 829	1 173 344	1 107 537	178 823	315 249	2 053	332
1 000	166 282	163 252	111 264	105 284		2 618		
127 395	5 271 643	4 763 466	3 731 588	3 173 739	2 002 591	1 746 382	50 069	57 064
	450 884	372 120	254 822	300 650	76 076	83 486	137 444	
162 378	3 422 286	3 323 252	2 813 253	2 897 414	13 522	219 953	43 978	1 292
400	77 742	63 792	49 003	47 910	1 080			
6 176	757 221	386 851	257 533	34 608	196 482			
	3 549	1 528	60		21 200			
	1 799	1 799	1 650	1 650	320			

表 11－12 大中型工业企业获奖成果及专利情况
（2008）

单位：项

指标	Indicators	获奖科技成果数 Prized Achievements
总 计	**Total**	**49**
按注册登记大类分组	**Grouped by Type of Registration**	
国 有	State-owned	21
集 体	Collective-owned	
股份制及其他有限公司	Share-holding	15
私 营	Private	
外商及港澳台投资	Overseas Invested Enterprises	13
其 他	Others	
按隶属关系分	**Grouped by Subordination**	
中央工业	Central	30
地方工业	Local	19
按企业规模分组	**Grouped by Size of Enterprises**	
大型企业	Large	36
中型企业	Medium	13
按工业行业大类分组	**Grouped by Sectors**	
烟草制品业	Tabacco Manufacturing	
印刷业和记录媒介的复制	Printing and Record Duplicating	
石油加工、炼焦及核燃料加工业	Oil Processing, Coking and Nuclear	3
化学原料及化学制品制造业	Raw Chemical Materials and Chemical	4
医药制造业	Medicine Manufacturing	2
非金属矿物制品业	Nonmetal Mineral Products	6
金属制品业	Metal Products Manufacturing	
通用设备制造业	General Equipment Manufacturing	7
专用设备制造业	Special Purpose Equipment Manufacturing	
交通运输设备制造业	Transportation Equipment Manufacturing	7
电气机械及器材制造业	Electric Machinery Equipment and Manufacturing	
通信设备、计算机及其他电子设备制造业	Communications Equipment, Computer and Other Electronic Equipment Manufacturing	3
电力、热力的生产和供应业	Production and Supply of Electricity and Thermal Power	17
燃气生产和供应业	Production and Supply of Gas	

Prized Achievements and Patents of Large and Medium Industrial Enterprises

(item)

# 国家级 National Prizes	专利申请数 Patent Applications	# 发明专利数 Patents of Creations and Inventions	专利授权数 Patent Applications Certified	拥有发明专利数 Patents of Creations and Inventions Certified
4	**1 788**	**596**	**904**	**614**
	195	68	105	21
1	241	110	188	164
3	1 352	418	611	429
	414	233	233	221
4	1 374	363	671	393
2	1 369	303	572	253
2	419	293	332	361
	2		2	
	5	1	4	1
	19	19	10	32
	29	21	19	23
2	5	3	10	13
	2		3	
1	102	53	101	72
	42	24	15	5
1	298	71	193	67
	8	4	4	3
	1 101	345	449	396
	172	55	94	2
	3			

表 11-13 大中型工业企业新产品产出情况

Output of New Products of Large and Medium Industrial Enterprises (2008)

单位:千元 (1 000 yuan)

指 标	Indicators	新产品产 值 Output of New Products	新产品销售收入 Sales Revenue	# 出 口 Export
总 计	**Total**	**143 362 868**	**171 137 819**	**41 429 594**
按注册登记大类分组	**Grouped by Type of Registration**			
国 有	State-owned	3 428 089	7 635 517	30 132
集 体	Collective-owned			
股份制及其他有限公司	Share-holding	51 021 139	52 151 873	20 391 413
私 营	Private			
外商及港澳台投资	Overseas Invested Enterprises	88 913 640	111 350 429	21 008 049
其 他	Others			
按隶属关系分	**Grouped by Subordination**			
中央工业	Central	46 224 825	47 320 174	24 852 697
地方工业	Local	97 138 043	123 817 645	16 576 897
按企业规模分组	**Grouped by Size of Enterprises**			
大型企业	Large	108 440 330	136 369 629	30 950 816
中型企业	Medium	34 922 538	34 768 190	10 478 778
按工业行业大类分组	**Grouped by Sectors**			
印刷业和记录媒介的复制	Printing and Record Duplicating	378 285	552 760	2 877
石油加工、炼焦及核燃料加工业	Oil Processing, Coking and Nuclear	6 340 000	6 340 000	
化学原料及化学制品制造业	Raw Chemical Materials and Chemical	3 170 942	3 183 609	208 640
医药制造业	Medicine Manufacturing	2 918 615	3 413 131	8 479
非金属矿物制品业	Nonmetal Mineral Products	195 450	195 450	101 489
金属制品业	Metal Products Manufacturing	657 252	557 485	76 985
通用设备制造业	General Equipment Manufacturing	21 892 079	22 149 977	2 290 648
专用设备制造业	Special Purpose Equipment Manufacturing	1 629 215	1 566 100	53 945
交通运输设备制造业	Transportation Equipment Manufacturing	61 948 333	88 863 995	19 055 863
电气机械及器材制造业	Electric Machinery Equipment and Manufacturing	9 335 643	9 426 851	5 812 484
通信设备、计算机及其他电子设备制造业	Communications Equipment, Computer and Other Electronic Equipment Manufacturing	34 016 516	33 665 492	13 692 082
仪器仪表及文化、办公用机械制造业	Instruments, Meters, Culture and Office Equipment Manufacturing	880 538	1 222 969	126 102

表 11－14　主要年份民营科技企业主要经济指标
Major Economic Indicators of Technical Research Enterprises Run by Entrepreneurs in Main Years

指　标	Indicators	单　位　Unit	1998	2000	2005	2007	2008
企业单位数	Enterprises	个 unit	592	828	700	855	556
企业专利总数	Number of Enterprise Patents	项 item				1 777	1 304
职工人数	Employees	万人 10000 persons	2.43	3.04	5.76	14.77	8.55
从事科技活动人员	Persons employed in science and technology	万人 10 000 persons				3.95	2.33
资产总额	Total Assets	亿元 100 million yuan	69.1	122.40	575.47	1 917.96	1 190.9
技工贸销售总额	Total Sales	亿元 100 million yuan	38.99	82.01	521.45	1 773.08	1 693.4
# 技术性收入	Income for technology transfers	亿元 100 million yuan				57.32	3.32
产品销售收入	Income for selling products	亿元 100 million yuan				1 615.68	1 659.48
利润总额	Total Profit	亿元 100 million yuan	0.43	4.64	35.58	103.84	1.29
上交税收	Tax Payable	亿元 100 million yuan	1.37	2.70	18.22	72.15	69.66
创汇总额	Total Foreign Exchange	亿美元 USD 100 million	0.43	0.95	12.65	51.89	57.22
投入科研开发费	Investment in Research and Development	亿元 100 million yuan	2.35	4.18	34.72	90.10	28.82

注：本表由浦东新区科学技术委员会提供。
Note: This table is provided by Pudong Science & Technology Commission.

主要统计指标解释

专　利

是专利权的简称，是对发明人的发明创造经审查合格后，由专利局依据专利法授予发明人和设计人对该项发明创造享有的专有权。包括发明、实用新型和外观设计。反映拥有自主知识产权的科技和设计成果情况。

发　明

指对产品、方法或者其改进所提出的新的技术方案。是国际通行的反映拥有自主知识产权技术的核心指标。

实用新型

指对产品的形状、构造或者其结合所提出的适于实用的新的技术方案。反映具有一定技术含量的技术成果情况。

外观设计

指对产品的形状、图案、色彩或者其结合所作出的富有美感并适于工业上应用的新设计。反映拥有自主知识产权的外观设计成果情况。

专业技术人员

专业技术人员指事业、企业单位中已被聘任专业技术职务的从事专业技术工作和专业技术管理的人员，以及虽未被聘任专业技术职务，但现在专业技术岗位上工作的人员。

国有企业

指企业全部资产归国家所有，并按《中华人民共和国企业法人登记管理条例》规定登记注册的非公司制的经济组织。不包括有限责任公司中的国有独资公司。

集体企业

集体企业指企业资产归集体所有，并按《中华人民共和国企业法人登记管理条例》规定登记注册的经济组织。

科技活动

指在自然科学、农业科学、医药科学、工程与技术科学、人文与社会科学领域（简称科学技术领域）中，与科技知识的产生、发展、传播和应用密切相关的有组织的活动。可分为研究与试验发展（R&D）、研究与试验发展成果应用及相关的科技服务三类活动。该定义是联合国教科文组织考虑成员国特别是发展中国家开展科技统计工作的需要，而对科技活动所作的统计界定。

科技活动人员

指直接从事科技活动、以及专门从事科技活动管理和为科技活动提供直接服务，累计从事科技活动的时间占全年制度工作时间10%及以上的人员。（1）直接从事科技活动的人员，包括：在独立核算的科学研究与技术开发机构、高等学校、各类企业及其他事业单位内设的研究室、实验室、技术开发中心及中试车间（基地）等机构中从事科技活动的研究人员、工程技术人员、技术工人及其它人员；虽不在上述机构工作，但编入科技活动项目（课题）组的人员；科技信息与文献机构中的专业技术人员；从事论文设计的研究生等。（2）专门从事科技活动管理和为科技活动提供直接服务的人员包括：独立核算的科学研究与技术开发机构、科技信息与文献机构、高等学校、各类企业及其他事业单位主管科技工作的负责人，专门从事科技活动的计划、行政、人事、财务、物资供应、设备维护、图书资料管理等工作的各类人员，但不包括保卫、医疗保健人员、司机、食堂人员、茶炉工、水暖工、清洁工等为科技活动提供间接服务的人员。该指标用来反映投入科技活动人力的规模。

科学家和工程师

科学家与工程师指科技活动人员中具有高、中级技术职称（职务）的人员和不具有高、中级技术职称（职务）的大学本科及以上学历人员。

科技活动经费筹集

指从各种渠道筹集到的计划用于科技活动的经费，包括政府资金、事业资金、企业资金、银行贷款和其他收入等。反映各社会经济主体对促进科技进步所作的努力。

政府资金

指从各级政府部门获得的计划用于科技活动的经费，包括科学事业费、科技三项费、科研基建费、科学基金、教育等部门事业费中计划用于科技活动的经费以及政府部门预算外资金中计划用于科技活动的经费等。

新产品

指采用新技术原理、新设计构思研制、生产的全新产品，或在结构、材质、工艺等某一方面比原有产品有明显改进，从而显著提高了产品性能或扩大了使用功能的产品。既包括政府有关部门认定并在有效期内的新产品，也包括企业自行研制开发、在统计规定的新产品跟踪期限内的产品。跟踪期限规定如下：装备类跟踪五年，消费品类跟踪二年，其他类跟踪三年。用来反映科技产出及对经济增长的直接贡献。

R&D

是"科学研究与试验发展"(Research and Development)的英文缩写。其含义是指在科学技术领域,为增加知识总量,以及运用这些知识去创造新的应用进行的系统的创造性的活动。R&D 包括基础研究、应用研究、试验发展三类活动。

EXPLANATORY NOTES TO MAJOR STATISTICAL INDICATORS

Patent

Patent is an abbreviation for the patent right and refers to the exclusive right of ownership by the inventors or designers for the creation or inventions, given from the patent offices after due process of assessment and approval in accordance with the Patent Law. Patents are granted for inventions, utility models and designs. This indicator reflects the achievements of S&T and design with independent intellectual property.

Invention

Inventions refer to the new technical proposals to the products or methods or their modifications. This is universal core indicator reflecting the technologies with independent intellectual property.

Utility Models

Utility Models refer to the practical and new technical proposals on the shape and structure of the product or the combination of both. This indicator reflects the condition of technological results with certain technical content.

Exterior Design

Designs refer to the aesthetics and industrially applicable new designs for the shape, pattern and color of the product, or their combinations. This indicator reflects the appearance design achievements with independent intellectual property.

Professional and Technical Personnel

Professional and Technical Personnel refer to professional, technical and managerial staff members in institutions or enterprises who not only have professional and technical titles but also hold professional and technical posts. They also include those who work on professional and technical posts but do not have professional and technical titles.

State-owned Enterprises

State-owned Enterprises refer to non-corporation economic units where the entire assets are owned by the state and which have registered in accordance with the Regulation of the People's Republic of China on the Management of Registration of Corporate Enterprises. Excluded from this category are sole state-funded corporations in the limited liability corporations.

Collective-owned Enterprises

Collective-owned Enterprises refer to economic units where the assets are owned collectively and which have registered in accordance with the Regulation of the People's Republic of China on the Management of Registration of Corporate Enterprises.

Scientific and Technological Activities (S&T Activities)

Scientific and Technological Activities (S&T Activities) refer to organized activities which are closely related with the creation, development, dissemination and application of the scientific and technical knowledge in the fields of natural sciences, agricultural sciences, medical sciences, engineering and technological sciences, humanities and social sciences (referred to as scientific and technological fields). S&T activities can be classified into 3 categories: research and development (R&D) activities, application of R&D results, and related S&T services. This statistical definition is made by UNICHIEF for scientific and technological activities to meet the need of carrying out statistical work in this field for its member countries in particular those developing countries.

Personnel Engaged in S&T Activities

Personnel Engaged in S&T Activities refer to personnel directly engaged in S&T activities, in the management of S&T activities, and in providing direct service to S&T activities, who spend over 10% of the total working hours in a year in S&T activities. (1) Personnel directly engaged in S&T activities include researchers, engineers, technicians and other related personnel engaged in S&T activities in independent-accounting R&D institutions, institutions of higher learning, and in research institutes, laboratories, technology development centers and central experiment workshops under enterprises and institutions. Also included are people working in S&T information archiving institutes, and graduate students working on the design of their thesis. (2) Personnel engaged in the management of S&T activities and in providing direct service to S&T activities include senior management people responsible for S&T activities in independent-accounting R&D institutions, S&T information archiving institutes, institutions of higher learning, and in enterprises and institutions where S&T activities are undertaken. Also included are people responsible for the planning, administration, personnel management, financial management, logistics supply, equipment maintenance, information and library management that are related with S&T activities. People providing indirect services are excluded, such as security, medical service, drivers, plumbers, cleaners and those providing catering and related service. This indicator reflects the size of personnel engaged in S&T activities.

Scientists and Engineers

Scientists and Engineers refer to persons engaged in S&T activities who have obtained titles of senior and middle level professional positions, and those without such position but have completed university or higher education.

Funding for S&T Activities

Funding for S&T Activities refers to funds obtained from various sources for S&T activities, including government funds, self-raised funds by institutions, self-raised funds by enterprises, loans from banks and other funds. This indicator reflects the efforts made by various social economic entities in promoting the development of S&T.

Government Funds

Government Funds refer to funds obtained from government agencies at all levels to be used for S&T activities, including fund for scientific undertakings, 3 kinds of fund for S&T activities, fund for capital construction for scientific researches, science fund, funds from education expenditures by education departments for S&T activities, and extra-budget fund from government agencies for S&T activities.

New Products

New Products refer to new products produced with new technology and new design, or products that represent noticeable improvement in terms of structure, material, or production process so as to improve significantly the character or function of the older versions. They include new products certified by relevant government agencies within the period of certification, as well as new products designed and produced by enterprises within the new product track time limit prescribed by the statistical regulations. The new product track time limit is prescribed as following: equipment products 5 years, consumption products 2 years, other products 3 years. This indictor reflects the direct contribution of S&T output to economic growth.

R&D

R&D is an abbreviation which stands for 'Science Research and Experimental Development', which means systematic and creative endeavors aimed at expanding the overall volume of knowledge and applying the knowledge in systematic creation. R&D includes basic studies, application research and experimental development.

第十二篇

Chapter 12

人民生活

PEOPLE'S LIVELIHOOD

表 12-1　从业人员报酬
Wages of Employed Persons
(2008)

单位:亿元　　(100 million yuan)

指　标　Indicators		合　计 Total	国有单位 State-owned Enterprises	集体单位 Collective-owned Enterprises	港澳台及外商投资单位 Overseas Invested Enterprises	其他单位 Others
总　计	**Total**	**536.73**	**93.56**	**3.97**	**212.15**	**227.05**
农、林、牧、渔业	Farming, Forestry, Animal Husbandry and Fishery	0.22	0.03		0.03	0.16
采矿业	Mining	0.21	0.21			
制造业	Manufacturing	157.22	20.90	0.32	116.45	19.55
电力、燃气及水的生产和供应业	Production and Supply of Electricity, Gas and Water	8.15	5.27		2.84	0.04
建筑业	Construction	19.67	3.74	0.03	3.37	12.53
交通运输、仓储和邮政业	Transportation, Warehousing and Post Service	64.75	11.33	0.09	7.56	45.77
信息传输、计算机服务和软件业	Information Transmission, Computer Service and Computer Software	15.85	0.95		11.25	3.65
#信息传输	Information Transmission	3.74	0.77		2.44	0.53
批发和零售业	Wholesale and Retail	43.31	3.42	1.11	24.24	14.54
住宿和餐饮业	Hotel and Catering	5.09	0.55		3.57	0.97
金融业	Banking	142.51	4.25		21.37	116.89
房地产业	Real Estate	7.60	2.31	0.01	3.12	2.16
租赁和商务服务业	Leasing and Business Service	22.18	5.40	0.43	12.85	3.50
科学研究、技术服务和地质勘查业	Scientific Research, Technical Service and Geological Prospecting	11.11	2.90	0.01	5.03	3.17
水利、环境和公共设施管理业	Water Conservancy, Environment and Public Facilities Administration	1.98	1.41	0.10		0.47
#公共设施管理业	Public Facilities Administration	1.26	0.73	0.06		0.47
居民服务和其他服务业	Resident Service and Other Service	3.00	0.14		0.29	2.57
教　育	Education	16.50	15.82			0.68
卫生、社会保障和社会福利业	Healthcare, Social Security and Social Welfare	10.35	8.44	1.87		0.04
卫　生	Healthcare	10.02	8.15	1.87		
社会保障	Social Security	0.28	0.24			0.04
社会福利业	Social Welfare	0.05	0.05			
文化、体育和娱乐业	Culture, Sports and Entertainment	0.94	0.40		0.18	0.36
文　化	Culture	0.72	0.29		0.07	0.36
体　育	Sports	0.10	0.10			
娱乐业	Entertainment	0.12	0.01		0.11	
公共管理和社会组织	Public Administration and Social Organizations	6.09	6.09			

注：本表至表 12-6 数据由上海市统计局返还。
Note: Data from this table to Table 12-6 have been returned from Shanghai Statistics Bureau.

表 12-2　从业人员平均报酬
Average Wages of Employed Persons
(2008)

单位:元　　　　(yuan)

指　标	Indicators	合　计 Total	国有单位 State-owned Enterprises	集体单位 Collective-owned Enterprises	港澳台及外商投资单位 Overseas Invested Enterprises	其他单位 Others
总平均	**Annual Average Wages**	**69 241**	**55 265**	**38 538**	**68 739**	**79 132**
农、林、牧、渔业	Farming, Forestry, Animal Husbandry and Fishery	36 995	14 443		25 105	55 468
采矿业	Mining	125 179	125 179			
制造业	Manufacturing	60 445	52 028	20 117	61 557	67 043
电力、燃气及水的生产和供应业	Electric Power, Gas and Water Production	80 977	69 904		116 944	41 717
建筑业	Construction	67 334	58 387	38 013	100 109	64 709
交通运输、仓储和邮政业	Transportation, Warehousing and Post	69 614	63 519	21 648	79 267	70 191
信息传输、计算机服务和软件业	Information Transmission, Computer Service and Computer Software	103 662	66 879		105 915	112 449
#信息传输	Information Transmission	80 790	66 873		90 517	67 876
批发和零售业	Wholesale and Retail	74 011	69 725	32 945	102 933	54 452
住宿和餐饮业	Hotel and Catering	22 137	44 878	8 927	18 348	42 479
金融业	Banking	109 322	178 560		175 274	100 955
房地产业	Real Estate	47 069	65 325	26 596	44 126	39 284
租赁和商务服务业	Leasing and Business Service	69 115	27 908	29 509	170 508	93 122
科学研究、技术服务和地质勘查业	Scientific Research, Technical Service and Geological Prospecting	90 416	64 101	25 286	159 042	69 386
水利、环境和公共设施管理业	Water Conservancy, Environment and Public Facilities Administration	42 884	45 457	27 093		41 057
#公共设施管理业	Public Facilities Administration	38 396	37 251	34 302		41 057
居民服务和其他服务业	Resident Service and Other Service	35 963	42 838	13 667	54 418	34 384
教　育	Education	51 481	51 714			46 604
卫生、社会保障和社会福利业	Healthcare, Social Security and Social Welfare	64 810	64 579	65 001		146 967
卫　生	Healthcare	65 773	65 953	65 001		
社会保障	Social Security	44 940	39 898			146 967
社会福利业	Social Welfare	44 881	44 881			
文化、体育和娱乐业	Culture, Sports and Entertainment	45 572	52 042		42 565	41 259
文　化	Culture	46 798	52 174		63 784	41 259
体　育	Sports	49 779	49 779			
娱乐业	Entertainment	37 065	71 500		34 792	
公共管理和社会组织	Public Administration and Social Organizations	51 638	51 638			

表12-3　历年职工工资总额
Total Wages of Staff and Workers in Main Years
(1990～2008)

单位:亿元 (100 million yuan)

年　份 Year	总　计 Total	国有单位 State-owned Enterprises	集体单位 Collective-owned Enterprises	其他单位 Others	#港澳台及外商投资单位 Overseas Invested Enterprises
1990	11.52	9.05	2.24	0.23	
1991	13.69	10.55	2.77	0.37	
1992	23.17	19.01	3.52	0.64	
1993	47.26	35.49	4.24	7.53	
1994	60.75	44.77	5.02	10.96	
1995	80.29	58.22	5.88	16.19	
1996	83.37	55.98	6.35	21.04	
1997	84.18	52.32	6.23	25.63	
1998	89.70	47.13	4.63	37.94	
1999	106.67	53.08	4.95	48.64	
2000	120.59	54.98	4.25	61.36	
2001	140.36	53.14	3.47	83.75	
2002	160.37	54.79	3.29	102.29	
2003	170.99	56.99	2.83	111.17	49.99
2004	184.02	66.16	2.85	115.01	48.92
2005	235.03	66.55	2.70	165.78	64.67
2006	278.91	63.83	2.81	212.27	97.78
2007	354.32	94.30	3.28	256.74	124.93
2008	480.33	88.50	3.41	388.42	174.66

表 12-4 职工工资总额
Total wages of Staff and Workers
(2008)

单位:亿元 (100 million yuan)

指 标	Indicators	合 计 Total	国有单位 State-owned Enterprises	集体单位 Collective-owned Enterprises	港澳台及外商投资单位 Overseas Invested Enterprises	其他单位 Others
总 计	**Total**	**480.33**	**88.50**	**3.41**	**174.66**	**213.76**
农、林、牧、渔业	Farming, Forestry, Animal Husbandry and Fishery	0.19	0.02		0.03	0.14
采矿业	Mining	0.21	0.21			
制造业	Manufacturing	138.05	20.17	0.25	99.70	17.93
电力、燃气及水的生产和供应业	Production and Supply of Electricity, Gas and Water	8.11	5.24		2.83	0.04
建筑业	Construction	17.48	3.44	0.03	2.31	11.70
交通运输、仓储和邮政业	Transportation, Warehousing and Post service	60.54	10.78	0.09	6.56	43.11
信息传输、计算机服务和软件业	Information Transmission, Computer Service and Computer Software	14.79	0.94		10.24	3.61
#信息传输	Information Transmission	3.27	0.77		1.96	0.54
批发和零售业	Wholesale and Retail	37.16	3.71	1.07	19.10	13.28
住宿和餐饮业	Hotel and Catering	3.17	0.51	0.01	1.91	0.74
金融业	Banking	131.58	4.13		15.03	112.42
房地产业	Real Estate	5.68	2.11	0.01	2.21	1.35
租赁和商务服务业	Leasing and Business Service	19.58	5.16	0.44	10.61	3.37
科学研究、技术服务和地质勘查业	Scientific Research, Technical Services and Geological Prospecting	8.81	2.72		3.75	2.34
水利、环境和公共设施管理业	Water Conservancy, Environment and Public Facilities Administration	1.79	1.26	0.10		0.43
#公共设施管理业	Public Facilities Administration	1.12	0.63	0.06		
居民服务和其他服务业	Resident Service and Other Service	3.05	0.24		0.26	2.55
教 育	Education	15.42	15.03			0.39
卫生、社会保障和社会福利业	Healthcare, Social Security and Social Welfare	8.07	6.62	1.41		0.04
卫 生	Healthcare	7.81	6.40	1.41		
社会保障	Social Security	0.21	0.17			0.04
社会福利业	Social Welfare	0.05	0.05			
文化、体育和娱乐业	Culture, Sports and Entertainment	0.80	0.36		0.12	0.32
文 化	Culture	0.64	0.25		0.07	0.32
体 育	Sports	0.10	0.10			
娱 乐	Entertainment	0.06	0.01		0.05	
公共管理和社会组织	Public Administration and Social Organizations	5.85	5.85			

表 12-5 历年职工平均工资
Average Wages of Staff and Workers in Main Years
(1990~2008)

单位:元 (yuan)

年 份 Year	年平均工资 Annual Average Wages	国有单位 State-owned Enterprises	集体单位 Collective-owned Enterprises	其他单位 Others	#港澳台及外商投资单位 Overseas Invested Enterprises
1990	2 939	3 069	2 466	3 665	
1991	3 363	3 479	2 906	4 305	
1992	4 350	4 532	3 468	5 506	
1993	5 999	5 927	4 984	7 241	
1994	7 906	7 616	6 584	10 514	
1995	9 995	10 087	6 749	11 651	
1996	11 351	11 623	7 445	12 559	
1997	12 425	12 463	7 863	14 359	
1998	13 417	12 977	7 421	15 615	
1999	15 563	14 561	8 659	18 443	22 911
2000	17 607	15 721	9 243	21 216	24 656
2001	20 349	17 503	9 092	24 066	29 710
2002	22 740	19 410	9 863	26 255	32 342
2003	25 620	22 655	10 748	28 543	38 753
2004	29 512	26 863	11 727	32 585	41 812
2005	33 186	27 707	12 390	37 153	50 779
2006	41 725	36 065	16 953	44 698	68 658
2007	56 878	49 004	20 656	59 710	68 674
2008	69 872	49 891	24 017	78 338	71 199

表12-6 职工平均工资
Average Wages of Staff and Workers
(2008)

单位:元 (yuan)

指 标	Indicators	合 计 Total	国有单位 State-owned Enterprises	集体单位 Collective-owned Enterprises	港澳台及外商投资单位 Overseas Invested Enterprises	其他单位 Others
总平均工资	**Awnual Average wages**	**69 872**	**49 891**	**24 017**	**71 199**	**85 338**
农、林、牧、渔业	Farming, Forestry, Animal Husbandry and Fishery	35 689	12 911		25 878	55 069
采矿业	Mining	128 488	128 488			
制造业	Manufacturing	60 793	44 434	9 926	65 219	68 284
电力、燃气及水的生产和供应业	Production and Supply of Electricity, Gas and Water	81 745	70 739		116 930	41 903
建筑业	Construction	66 085	60 766	28 302	91 317	64 473
交通运输、仓储和邮政业	Transportation, Warehousing and Post service	72 754	64 271	12 587	74 854	75 694
信息传输、计算机服务和软件业	Information Transmission, Computer Service and Computer Software	103 720	67 863		106 298	111 441
#信息传输	Information Transmission	79 567	67 913		91 982	63 792
批发和零售业	Wholesale and Retail	58 637	26 137	17 057	89 000	61 893
住宿和餐饮业	Hotel and Catering	36 586	45 462	4 345	33 439	44 091
金融业	Banking	116 161	208 810		161 960	110 197
房地产业	Real Estate	53 147	71 116	24 542	39 584	64 649
租赁和商务服务业	Leasing and Business Service	57 100	26 331	20 608	151 361	60 718
科学研究、技术服务和地质勘查业	Scientific Research, Technical Services and Geological Prospecting	86 682	64 291	35 375	123 050	81 286
水利、环境和公共设施管理业	Water Conservancy, Environment and Public Facilities Administration	47 568	52 833	27 093		42 731
#公共设施管理业	Public Facilities Administration	43 380	45 091	34 302		42 731
居民服务和其他服务业	Resident Service and Other Services	22 271	4 157	15 500	48 436	34 471
教 育	Education	54 905	55 070			49 207
卫生、社会保障和社会福利业	Healthcare, Social Security and Social Welfare	69 135	67 635	75 761		154 963
卫 生	Healthcare	69 717	68 510	75 761		
社会保障	Social Security	58 079	50 408			154 963
社会福利业	Social Welfare	44 881	44 881			
文化、体育和娱乐业	Culture, Sports and Entertainment	50 205	52 077		47 960	49 077
文 化	Culture	52 144	52 418		71 469	49 077
体 育	Sports	49 322	49 322			
娱 乐	Entertainment	37 636	71 500		33 209	
公共管理和社会组织	Public Administration and Social Organizations	55 931	55 931			

表12-7 按行业分的区属单位职工工资总额

Total Wages of Staff and Workers in PNA Institutions by Sector (2008)

单位:万元 (10 000 yuan)

指标	Indicators	工资总额 Total Wages	国有经济单位 State-owned Enterprises	集体经济单位 Collective-owned Enterprises	其他经济单位 Others
总计	**Total**	**1 405 205**	**280 812**	**23 737**	**1 100 656**
农、林、牧、渔业	Farming, Forestry, Animal Husbandry and Fishery	260			260
制造业	Manufacturing	590 771	3 986	1 790	584 995
电力、燃气及水的生产和供应业	Production and Supply of Electricity, Gas and Water	21 354	331		21 023
建筑业	Construction	24 998	2 029	40	22 929
交通运输、仓储及邮政业	Transportation, Warehousing, Post and Telecommunications	51 392	2 288	154	48 950
信息传输、计算机服务和软件业	Information Transmission, Computer Service and Computer Software	93 192	31		93 161
批发和零售业	Wholesale and Retail	186 429	5 714	1 756	178 959
住宿和餐饮业	Hotel and Catering	10 609		70	10 539
金融业	Banking	568			568
房地产业	Real Estate	27 425	11 251	145	16 029
租赁和商务服务业	Leasing and Business Service	118 978	16 969	5 004	97 005
科学研究、技术服务和地质勘查业	Scientific Research, Technical Service and Geological Prospecting	25 903	5 798		20 105
水利、环境和公共设施管理业	Water Conservancy, Environment and Public Facilities Administration	14 975	11 386	649	2 940
居民服务和其他服务业	Resident Service and Other Services	3 237	1 552		1 685
教育	Education	112 500	111 513		987
卫生、社会保障和社会福利业	Healthcare, Social Security and Social Welfare	63 304	49 175	14 129	
文化、体育和娱乐业	Culture, Sports and Entertainment	4 080	3 559		521
公共管理和社会组织	Public Administration and Social Organizations	55 230	55 230		

表12-8 按行业分的区属单位职工年平均工资
Annual Average Wages of Staff and Workers in PNA Institutions by Sector (2008)

单位:元 (yuan)

指标	Indicators	年平均工资 Annual Average Wages	国有单位 State-owned Enterprises	集体单位 Collective-owned Enterprises	其他单位 Others
总平均	**Annual Average**	**56 209**	**41 317**	**26 064**	**63 650**
农、林、牧、渔业	Farming, Forestry, Animal Husbandry and Fishery	26 551			26 551
制造业	Manufacturing	52 312	26 679	10 628	53 301
电力、燃气及水的生产和供应业	Production and Supply of Electricity, Gas and Water	170 969	114 310		172 316
建筑业	Construction	92 518	80 190	30 769	94 128
交通运输、仓储及邮政业	Transportation, Warehousing, Post and Telecommunications	42 589	52 125	5 793	43 082
信息传输、计算机服务和软件业	Information Transmission, Computer Service and Computer Software	113 760	44 286		113 819
批发和零售业	Wholesale and Retail	56 880	6 083	6 312	86 865
住宿和餐饮业	Hotel and Catering	30 251		4 937	31 319
金融业	Banking	115 918			115 918
房地产业	Real Estate	53 293	70 626	24 542	45 876
租赁和商务服务业	Leasing and Business Service	60 407	19 085	23 741	111 538
科学研究、技术服务和地质勘查业	Scientific Research, Technical Service and Geological Prospecting	86 112	60 392		98 168
水利、环境和公共设施管理业	Water Conservancy, Environment and Public Facilities Administration	46 132	51 060	34 302	35 550
居民服务和其他服务业	Resident Service and Other Services	5 503	2 792		52 015
教　育	Education	53 061	53 376		31 839
卫生、社会保障和社会福利业	Healthcare, Social Security and Social Welfare	70 416	69 017	75 761	
文化、体育和娱乐业	Culture, Sports and Entertainment	57 383	63 772		34 078
公共管理和社会组织	Public Administration and Social Organizations	64 657	64 657		

表 12-9　城镇居民家庭基本情况
Background of Urban Families

指　标	Indicators	单　位 Unit	2006	2007	2008
调查户数	Households Surveyed	户 household	500	500	500
调查户总人口	Total Population of Households Surveyed	人 person	1 455	1 424	1 418
调查户就业人口	Employed Persons in Households Surveyed	人 person	735	755	724
# 国有单位就业人口	Employed by State-owned Enterprises	人 person	375	369	344
城镇集体单位就业人口	Employed by Collective-owned Enterprises	人 person	45	43	40
其他各类单位就业人口	Employed by Other Enterprises	人 person	145	193	200
平均每户常住人口	Average Number of Permanent Residents Per Household	人 person	2.91	2.85	2.84
平均每户就业人口	Average Number of Employed Persons Per Household	人 person	1.47	1.51	1.45
平均每户就业面	Average Employment Rate Per Household	%	50.5	53.0	51.1
平均每一就业者赡养人口	Number of Persons Supported by Each Employed Person	人 person	1.98	1.89	1.96
恩格尔系数	Engel's Coefficient	%	36.9	35.2	35.3
平均消费倾向	Average Propensity to Consume	%	66.9	73.3	70.4
平均每人年实际收入	Annual Actual Income Per Capita	元 yuan	23 625	26 856	30 900
平均每人年可支配收入	Annual Disposable Income Per Capita	元 yuan	21 452	24 273	27 797
平均每人年消费性支出	Annual Consumption Spending Per Capita	元 yuan	14 349	17 802	19 579
平均每人住房建筑面积	Average Floor Space Per Capita	平方米 sq · m	33.98	33.61	35.39

注：本表至表 12－18 为住户调查资料，人均住房面积由建交委提供。
Note: The contents in from this table to Table 12－18 are the survey data of households in Pudong.

表 12-10 历年城乡居民收支情况
Income and Expenditure of Urban and Suburban Residents in Main Years

单位:元 (yuan)

指标	Indicators	2003	2004	2005	2006	2007	2008
城镇居民收支状况	**Income and Expenditure of Urban Residents**						
人均总收入	Gross Income Per Capita	16 443	18 784	20 990	23 625	26 856	30 900
#可支配收入	Disposable Income Per Capita	14 817	16 980	19 089	21 452	24 273	27 797
工薪收入	Wage Income	11 717	13 176	14 149	16 320	18 690	21 728
经营性收入	Operational Income	126	227	775	590	494	400
财产性收入	Property Income	152	407	397	391	544	597
转移性收入	Transferable Income	4 448	4 974	5 669	6 324	7 128	8 175
人均总支出	Total Expenses Per Capita	16 999	17 979	18 923	21 443	26 862	29 055
#消费支出	Consumption Expenses	11 148	12 044	13 328	14 349	17 802	19 579
#食　品	Foodstuff	4 226	4 529	4 826	5 299	6 272	6 921
医疗与保健	Medical Care	731	869	895	804	831	1 064
教育文化娱乐服务	Education, Culture and Amusement Services	1 912	2 236	2 119	2 362	2 861	3 027
社会保障支出	Social Security Expenses	1 315	1 456	1 506	1 758	2 018	2 248
农村居民收入状况	**Income and Expenditure of Suburban Residents**						
人均总收入	Gross Income Per Capita	8 685	9 420	10 443	11 715	13 157	14 869
#可支配收入	Disposable Income Per Capita	8 077	8 777	9 779	10 911	12 246	13 778
工薪收入	Wage Income	6 420	6 946	7 458	8 223	9 117	10 179
经营性收入	Operational Income	432	448	460	320	298	249
财产性收入	Property Income	742	882	1 078	1 522	1 914	2 303
转移性收入	Transferable Income	1 091	1 144	1 447	1 650	1 828	2 138

表 12－11　城镇居民家庭人均收入与支出状况(按收入水平分)
Average Income and Expenses of Urban Families(by income level)
(2008)

单位:元　　(yuan)

指　标	Indicators	总平均 Overall Average	低收入户 Low-income Household	较低收入户 Lower-income Household	中等收入户 Medium-income Household	较高收入户 Medium Higher-income Household	高收入户 High-income Household
人均总收入	**Gross Income Per Capita**	**30 900**	**14 132**	**20 083**	**26 202**	**34 345**	**63 113**
#人均可支配收入	Disposable Income Per Capita	27 797	12 812	18 460	23 781	31 014	55 901
工资性收入	Wage Income	21 728	9 261	10 846	17 491	23 697	50 055
经营性收入	Operational Income	400	82	356	214	492	920
财产性收入	Property Income	597	90	181	438	762	1 622
转移性收入	Transferable Income	8 175	4 699	8 700	8 059	9 394	10 516
人均总支出	**Total Expenses Per Capita**	**29 055**	**13 871**	**16 632**	**24 908**	**26 192**	**66 852**
消费性支出	Consumption Expenses	19 579	11 690	13 420	18 054	20 416	35 889
食　品	Foodstuff	6 921	5 500	5 968	7 230	7 685	8 444
衣　着	Clothing	1 396	727	781	1 425	1 609	2 558
家庭设备用品及服务	Family Appliances and Services	1 382	511	790	1 435	1 406	2 919
医疗保健	Medical Care	1 064	522	981	989	1 263	1 655
交通和通讯	Traffic and Communications	2 909	1 269	1 382	2 112	2 817	7 347
教育文化娱乐服务	Education, Culture and Amusement Services	3 027	1 765	1 862	2 708	3 389	5 680
居　住	Habitation	1 907	1 074	1 093	1 353	1 137	5 086
其他商品及服务	Miscellaneous Commodities and Services	973	322	563	802	1 110	2 200
经营性支出	Operational Expenses	2		5			6
财产性支出	Property Expenses	170	7	19	76	68	721
转移性支出	Transferable Expenses	2 907	1 018	1 819	2 533	3 040	6 483
社会保障支出	Social Security Expenses	2 248	1 132	1 369	2 071	2 633	4 256
购、建房支出	Expenses for Purchasing/ Building Houses	4 149	24		2 174	35	19 497

注：收入水平根据居民家庭人均可支配收入由低到高排序,分别按家庭数量的20%分为5组。
Note: Income levels are sorted from the low to the high according to the dispensable income per capita of urban families. They are divided into five groups from 20% of the total number of families respectively.

表 12-12 每百户城镇居民家庭年末耐用消费品拥有量
Possession of Durable Consumer Goods Per 100 Urban Households at Year-End

指 标 Indicators		单 位 Unit	2005	2007	2008
摩托车	Mototrcycle	辆 in number	5	6	5
助力车	Scooter	辆 in number	15	16	14
家用汽车	Household Car	辆 in number	4	9	9
洗衣机	Washing Machine	台 set	97	100	99
电冰箱	Household Refrigerator	台 set	102	103	103
彩色电视机	Color TV Set	台 set	178	193	188
家用电脑	Computer	台 set	76	97	99
组合音响	Stereo System	套 set	38	54	49
摄像机	Video Camera	架 set	8	15	14
照相机	Camera	架 set	62	72	67
钢 琴	Piano	架 set	4	4	4
微波炉	Microwave Oven	台 set	93	96	94
空调器	Air Conditioner	台 set	155	195	193
淋浴热水器	Water Heater	台 set	93	100	101
健身器材	Sports Goods	套 set	8	10	9
普通电话	Fixed Telephone	部 set	105	103	101
移动电话	Mobile Phone	部 set	174	207	198

表 12-13 城镇居民家庭生活质量
Living Conditions of Urban Families

指 标	Indicators	单 位 Unit	2005	2007	2008
生活用水	**Water for Residential Use**				
独用自来水	Private Tap Water	%	97.8	100.0	100.0
公用自来水	Shared Tap Water	%	2.2		
居室卫生设备	**Sanitary Equipment**				
无卫生设备	Without Any Sanitary Equipment	%	1.8		
有厕所浴室	With Lavatory	%	94.4	96.3	96.5
有厕所无浴室	With Lavatory But No Bathroom	%	2.4	3.7	3.1
公 用	Sanitary Equipment Shared	%	1.4		0.4
居室取暖设备	**Heating Equipment**				
无取暖设备	Without Any Heating	%	14.4	4.7	3.9
冷暖空调	Air Conditioner	%	76.0	94.5	95.1
暖 气	Heating	%			
其 他	Others	%	9.6	0.8	1.0
炊用燃气	**Gas for Cooking**				
天然气	Natural Gas	%	93.8	98.2	97.3
液化石油气	Liquefied Petroleum Gas	%	4.6	1.8	2.1
煤	Coal	%	0.2		0.4
其 他	Others	%	1.4		0.2
通信设备	**Telecommunications Equipment**				
无电话	Without Telephone	%	1.0	0.8	0.4
固定电话	Fixed Telephone	部/百户 set / hundred households	104.6	102.7	101.4
移动电话	Mobile Telephone	部/百户 set / hundred households	173.6	207.0	198.4

表 12-14 城镇居民家庭人均可支配收入
Annual Disposable Income Per Capita for Urban Families

按人均年可支配收入分组	Grouped by Annual Disposable Income Per Capita	比重 Proportion	2005	2007	2008
总计	**Total**	%	**100.0**	**100.0**	**100.0**
6 000 元以下	below 6 000 yuan	%	3.6	0.7	0.8
6 000 ~ 12 000 元	6 000 ~ 12 000 yuan	%	28.3	11.8	8.2
12 000 ~ 18 000 元	12 000 ~ 18 000 yuan	%	30.0	30.8	23.6
18 000 ~ 24 000 元	18 000 ~ 24 000 yuan	%	14.8	21.3	24.4
24 000 ~ 30 000 元	24 000 ~ 30 000 yuan	%	10.0	12.2	14.7
30 000 ~ 36 000 元	30 000 ~ 36 000 yuan	%	3.5	6.9	8.3
36 000 ~ 42 000 元	36 000 ~ 42 000 yuan	%	3.5	4.9	6.5
42 000 ~ 48 000 元	42 000 ~ 48 000 yuan	%	2.4	4.1	3.7
48 000 元以上	Above 48 000 yuan	%	3.9	7.3	9.8

表 12-15 城镇居民家庭人均消费性支出
Annual Consumer Spending Per Capita for Urban Families

按人均年消费性支出分组	Grouped by Annual Nonproductive Expenditure Per Capita	比重 Proportion	2005	2007	2008
总计	**Total**	%	**100.0**	**100.0**	**100.0**
6 000 元以下	below 6 000 yuan	%	9.0	3.7	1.2
6 000 ~ 12 000 元	6 000 ~ 12 000 yuan	%	48.1	37.0	28.3
12 000 ~ 18 000 元	12 000 ~ 18 000 yuan	%	25.7	30.0	32.8
18 000 ~ 24 000 元	18 000 ~ 24 000 yuan	%	8.7	15.0	17.7
24 000 ~ 30 000 元	24 000 ~ 30 000 yuan	%	3.5	5.2	8.4
30 000 ~ 36 000 元	30 000 ~ 36 000 yuan	%	1.8	2.6	3.9
36 000 ~ 42 000 元	36 000 ~ 42 000 yuan	%	1.1	1.1	1.2
42 000 ~ 48 000 元	42 000 ~ 48 000 yuan	%	0.6	1.5	2.8
48 000 元以上	Above 48 000 yuan	%	1.5	3.9	3.7

表 12-16　城镇居民家庭人均年消费支出状况
Annual Consumption Expenditure Per Capita for Urban Families

单位:元　(yuan)

指　标	Indicators	2005	2007	2008
总　计	**Total**	**13 328**	**17 802**	**19 579**
食　品	**Food**	**4 826**	**6 272**	**6 921**
#粮油类	Cereals & Oils	447	557	656
肉禽蛋水产品	Meat, Poultry, Eggs and Aquatic Products	1 376	1 744	1 926
蔬菜类	Vegetables	404	489	537
糖烟酒饮料类	Sugar, Tobacco, Alcoholic Drinks and Other Beverages	568	702	741
干鲜瓜果类	Dry and Fresh Fruits	346	491	511
糕点、奶及奶制品	Cakes, Milk and Dairy Products	359	459	533
衣　着	**Clothing**	**945**	**1 307**	**1 396**
#服　装	Clothes	698	949	1 024
鞋　类	Shoes	191	286	297
家庭设备用品及服务	**Household Appliances and Service**	**807**	**1 130**	**1 382**
#耐用消费品	Durable Consumer Goods	404	664	754
室内装饰品	Household Ornaments	29	21	39
家具材料	Furniture and Material	1	3	8
家庭服务	Household Service	78	86	135
医疗保健	**Health Care**	**895**	**831**	**1 064**
#药品费	Medicines Expenditure	259	335	365
滋补保健品	Nutritious Health Products	232	202	278
医疗费	Medical Treatment	350	255	376
交通和通讯	**Transportation and Communications**	**1 950**	**3 232**	**2 909**
交　通	Transportation	1 157	2 265	1 917
通　讯	Communications	793	967	992
教育文化娱乐服务	**Education, Culture, Entertainment and Service**	**2 119**	**2 861**	**3 027**
文化娱乐用品	Cultural and Entertainment Products	545	888	896
文化娱乐服务	Cultural and Entertainment Service	500	921	1 050
教　育	Education	1 074	1 052	1 081
居　住	**Housing**	**1 294**	**1 310**	**1 907**
住　房	Accommodation	643	578	1 030
水电燃料及其他	Water, Electricity, Fuel and Others	533	570	624
居住服务费	Accommodation Service	118	162	253
杂项商品及服务	**Miscellancous Utensils and Service**	**492**	**859**	**973**

表 12-17 郊区居民家庭基本情况
Suburban Households

指 标	Indicators	单 位 Unit	2005	2007	2008
调查户数	Households Surveyed	户 household	1 200	1 000	1 000
调查户总人口	Total Population of Households Surveyed	人 person	3 932	3 395	3 405
调查户总劳动力	Total Number of Laborers in the Household Surveyed	人 person	2 548	2 160	2 125
调查户就业人口	Employed Persons in Households Surveyed	人 person	2 367	2 026	2 003
#纯务农	Totally Engaged in Agriculture	人 person	70	38	32
本镇内企业	Employed by Enterprises in the Town	人 person	1 006	820	804
本镇外企业	Employed by Enterprises in Other Towns	人 person	810	762	772
平均每户人口	Average Number of Residents Per Household	人 person	3.28	3.39	3.41
平均每户劳动力	Average Number of Laborers Per Household	人 person	2.12	2.16	2.13
平均每户就业人口	Average Employed Persons Per Household	人 person	1.97	2.03	2.00
平均每户就业面	Average Employed Persons Per Household	%	60.1	59.9	58.8
平均每一就业者赡养人口	Number of Persons Supported by Each Employed Person	人 person	1.66	1.67	1.71

表 12-18　郊区居民收入情况
Incomes of Suburban Citizens

单位:元　　(yuan)

指　标	Indicators	2005	2007	2008
人均总收入	Gross Income Per Capita	10 443	13 157	14 869
# 可支配收入	Disposable Income	9 779	12 246	13 778
工资性收入	Wage Income	7 458	9 117	10 179
# 非企业组织中劳动得到	Income from Other Sources	957	1 204	1 369
本镇企业中劳动得到	Income from Working in Enterprises in the Town	3 372	3 720	3 986
常住人口外出从业得到	Income from Working in Enterprises in Other Places	2 719	3 661	4 164
财产性收入	Unearned Income	1 078	1 914	2 303
# 股　息	Stock Dividend	5	8	1
租　金	Rent	762	1 232	1 518
红　利	Dividend	16	31	36
转移性收入	Transferable Income	1 447	1 828	2 138
# 农村以外亲友赠送	Gifts from Relatives and Friends in Urban Area	13	11	13
救济金、保险年金	Relief and Life Annuity	19	27	31
退休金、抚恤金	Pension and Compensation	1 293	1 664	1 959
调查补贴	Survey Subsidies	58	54	57
家庭经营所得	Income from Family-Run Operations	460	298	249
财产性支出	Property Expenditure	29	43	76
转移性支出	Transfer Expenditure	577	814	955
# 赠送农村以外亲友	Gifts to Relatives and Friends in Urban Area	85	133	190
缴纳保险金	Insurance Premium Payment	394	507	537

主要统计指标解释

从业人员报酬

从业人员报酬指各单位在一定时期内直接支付给本单位全部从业人员的劳动报酬总额。包括在岗职工工资总额和本单位其他从业人员劳动报酬两部分。

职工工资总额

工资总额指各单位在一定时期内直接支付给本单位全部职工的劳动报酬总额。工资总额的计算原则应以直接支付给职工的全部劳动报酬为根据。各单位支付给职工的劳动报酬以及其他根据有关规定支付的工资,不论是计入成本的还是不计入成本的,不论是按国家规定列入计征奖金税项目的,还是未列入计征奖金税项目的,不论是以货币形式支付的还是以实物形式支付的,均包括在工资总额内。

职工平均工资

平均工资指企业、事业、机关单位的职工在一定时期内平均每人所得的货币工资额。它表明一定时期职工工资收入的高低程度,是反映职工工资水平的主要指标。计算公式为:

平均工资＝报告期实际支付的全部职工工资总额/报告期全部职工平均人数

城市居民可支配收入

城市居民可支配收入指居民可用于最终消费支出和其他非义务性支出以及储蓄的总和,即居民家庭可以用来自由支配的收入。它是家庭总收入扣除缴纳的所得税、个人交纳的社会保障费以及调查户的记账补贴后的收入。不包括出售财物和借贷收入。

城市居民家庭消费支出

指城市居民家庭用于日常生活的全部支出,包括食品、衣着、家庭设备用品及服务、医疗保健、交通和通信、教育文化娱乐服务、居住、杂项商品和服务等八大类。

城市居民家庭人均服务性消费支出

指调查户用于本家庭支付社会提供的各种文化和生活方面的非商品性服务费用。服务性消费的特点在于其劳动过程和消费过程在时间与空间上的统一。在居民家庭八大类消费中,服务消费支出包括:⑴食品类中加工服务费和部分在外饮食费用;⑵衣着类中衣着加工服务费;⑶家庭设备用品及服务类中家庭服务(如家政服务费用);⑷医疗保健类中医疗费(如诊疗费、上门出诊费、护工费用);⑸交通和通信类中交通工具服务费(如汽车使用、维修费用)、交通费中使用飞机、轮船、火车等交通工具费用、通信服务费(如电信费、邮费);⑹教育文化娱乐服务类中文化娱乐服务费(如参观、游览费用、健身活动费、团体旅游、其他文娱活动费)、文娱用品修理服务费、教育费(如义务、非义务教育支出)、成人教育支出、家教费、培训班费用、择校费;⑺居住类中租赁费用、部分房屋装潢费用(人工费用)、居住服务费(如物业管理、维修费用);⑻杂项商品和服务(如美容、洗澡、理发费用,旅馆住宿等费用)。

农村居民可支配收入

指一定时期内农村居民总收入中,扣除家庭经营费用支出、生产性固定资产折旧、交纳税金和上交承包金、公益性及转移支付后的(包括养老、失业、合作医疗、保险基金及罚款等支付),可用于生活消费、生产投资和储蓄的收入。它与纯收入的主要区别是扣除了转移性支付,加上实际得到的公益性及转移性收入后的余额。农村居民可支配收入包括:工资性收入、家庭经营净收入、财产性收入、转移性净收入。

农村居民家庭生活消费支出

指农村住户用于物质生活和精神生活方面的支出。包括食品,衣着,居住,家庭设备用品及服务,医疗保健,交通和通信,文化教育娱乐用品及服务,其他商品和服务等消费支出。

财产性收入

指金融资产或有形非生产性资产的所有者向其他机构单位提供资金或将有形非生产性资产供其支配,作为回报而从中获得的收入。

转移性收入

指农村住户和住户成员无须付出任何对应物而获得的货物、服务、资金或资产所有权等,不包括无偿提供的用于固定资本形成的资金。一般情况下,是指农村住户在二次分配中的所有收入。

基本养老保险

(1)参加保险人数:指报告期末按照国家法律、法规和有关政策规定参加基本养老保险的职工人数。包括不能正常缴费、已中断缴费但未终止保险关系的职工人数。

(2)社会统筹基金收入:指根据国家规定,由纳入基本养老保险范围的单位,按照国家规定的缴费基数和缴费比例缴纳的社会统筹基金，以及通过其他方式取得的形成基金来源的收入，包括：单位缴纳的社会统筹基金收入、财政补贴收入、利息收入、其他收入。

（3）社会统筹基金支出：指按照国家政策规定的开支范围和开支标准从社会统筹基金中支付给参加基本养老保险的离休、退休、退职人员个人的养老金、丧葬抚恤补助，以及由于保险关系转移、上下级之间调剂资金等原因而发生的支出。包括：基础性养老金、过渡性养老金、离休金、退休金、退职金、补贴、丧葬抚恤补助、其他支出。

（4）社会统筹基金结余：指截止报告期末基本养老保险的社会统筹基金结余金额。包括银行存款、财政专户、债券投资和其他。

城镇登记失业人员

城镇登记失业人员指有非农业户口，在一定的劳动年龄内（16 岁以上及男 50 岁以下、女 45 岁以下），有劳动能力，无业而要求就业，并在当地就业服务机构进行求职登记的人员。

EXPLANATORY NOTES TO MAJOR STATISTICAL INDICATORS

Labor Compensation

Labor Compensation refers to total payment by various units to their employees during a certain period of time, including wages to permanent staff and workers and payment to other employees.

Total Wages Bill

Total Wages Bill refers to the total remuneration payment to staff and workers in various units during a certain period of time. The calculation of total wages is based on the total remuneration payment to the staff and workers. Therefore, all the wages and salaries and other payments to staff and workers are included in the total wages regardless of their sources, category, and forms (in kind or cash). (Total wages of staff and workers in this yearbook include only total wages of fully employed staff and workers, excluding the living allowances distributed to those who have left their working units while keeping their labour contract/employment relation unchanged).

Average Wage

Average Wage refers to the average wage in money terms per person during a certain period of time for staff and workers in enterprises, institutions, and government agencies, which reflects the general level of wage income during a certain period of time and is calculated as follows:

Average Wage = Total Wages of Staff and Workers at Reference Time /Average Number of Staff and Workers at Reference Time.

Disposable Income of Urban Households

Disposable Income of Urban Households refers to the actual income at the disposal of members of the households which can be used for final consumption, other non-compulsory expenditure and savings, which is part of the urban households' income that can be disposed by the urban households themselves. It is the income after deducting personal income tax, social insurance paid by individuals and investigation allowance from the total income of the households. The income from selling properties and borrowing are not included.

Consumption Expenditures of Urban Households

Consumption Expenditures of Urban Households refer to all the expenditures paid by urban households for consumption in daily life, including 8 categories as follows: food; clothing; household facilities, articles and services; medical care; traffic and telecommunication; education, culture and recreation services; housing; miscellaneous commodities and services.

Urbanities-per-capita Spending on Services

Urbanities'per-capita spending on services refers to urbanites pay for services rather than commodities. Services are offered and consumed at the same time and place. The service spending for an urban family falls into the following eight types: (1) Money paid for food processing and money spent while eating out; (2) Money paid for clothing processing; (3) Domestic services and services for home amenities; (4) Medical cost (including medical diagnosis and treatment, in-home medical services and nursing cost); (5) Transport tool service fees (such as for the use of a car and maintenance fee thereby arising), transport tools (plane, ship, train) fees, post and telecommunications fees; (6) Fees for culture and entertainment services (such as tour and fitness building), fees for repair of sports and entertainment items, education cost (spending on obligatory and non-obligatory education), adult education cost, tutor fees, training courses fees and extra money paid as sponsorship fee to a school a student outside his or her education community; (7) Housing rents, some interior decoration cost (for labor), residence service fees (such as for property management and repairs); (8) Fees for other services (such as at a beauty salon, bathhouse, hairdresser's and hotels).

Disposable Income of Rural Households

Disposable Income of Rural Households refers to the part of the rural households' income in a certain period after deducting family business expenditure, depreciation of productive fixed assets, taxes, contract expenditure, welfare funds and transferred expenditure, (including pensions, unemployment relief, cooperative medical funds, premiums and fines), which can be used for personal consumption, production investment and deposit. It differs from the net income in that it is the balance of the actual welfare and transferred income after deducting transferred expenditure. The disposable income includes: wages and salaries, net income from household business, property income, net transferred income.

Living Expenditures for Consumption of Rural Households

Living Expenditures for Consumption of Rural Households refer to expenditures of material and culture life of rural household, including expenses on food, clothing, housing, household appliances and service, medical and health care, traffic and communication items, cultural, education and recreation items and service and other commodities and service.

Income from Properties

Income from Properties refers to the income received as returns by owners of financial assets or tangible non-productive assets by providing capitals or tangible non-productive assets to other institutional units.

Income from Transfers

Income from Transfers refers to the receipt by rural households and their members of goods, services, capitals or rights of assets without giving or repaying accordingly, excluding capitals provided to them for the formation of fixed assets. In general, it refers to all income received by rural households through redistribution.

Basic Endowment Insurance

(1) Number of people participating in the insurance program: by the end of reference period, number of staff and workers participating in the insurance program in line with national laws, regulations and related policies, including those who can not make regular payment or interrupt payment but not terminate the insurance program.

(2) Revenue of social comprehensive funds: according to national provision, payments made by units covered in basic endowment insurance program, and income from other resources, including: income of social comprehensive funds paid by unites, financial subsidies, interest income and others.

(3) Expenditure of social comprehensive funds: refer to payment made to those retired and resigned people covered in endowment insurance program in terms of pension or compensation within the expenditure scope and standards according to related national policies, and the expenditure occurred due to shift of the insurance relationship or adjustment funds among agencies, including: basic pension, transitional pension, pension for resigned people, pension for retired people, pension for people quitting jobs, subsidies, funeral subsidies and other expenditure.

(4) Balance of social comprehensive funds: refer to the balance of basic endowment insurance of social comprehensive funds at the end of the reference period, including: bank savings, special fiscal account, investment in bonds and others.

Registered Urban Unemployment

Registered Urban Unemployment refers to those non-agricultural population within working age (16 – 50 years for male and 16 – 45 years for females), who are able and willing to work but unemployed and have registered for job in local employment service agencies.

第十三篇

Chapter 13

就业与社会保障

EMPLOYMENT AND SOCIAL SECURITY

表 13－1　历年从业人员数
Number of Employed Persons in Main Years
(1993～2008)

单位:人 (person)

年　份 year	从业人员 Employed Persons	国有、集体、其他经济单位从业人员 Employed Persons in State-owned, Collective-owned and Other Economic Institutions	城镇个体劳动者 Urban Self-employed	农村集体和个体劳动者 Rural Collective and Self-employed Workers	其　他 Others
1993	1 043 985	788 821	18 146	237 018	
1994	1 049 985	767 146	35 696	247 143	
1995	1 079 744	798 884	38 243	242 617	
1996	1 039 692	759 936	44 516	235 240	
1997	981 826	703 890	49 878	228 058	
1998	963 211	638 707	68 252	256 252	
1999	983 401	645 583	43 284	294 534	
2000	1 040 411	636 923	61 000	316 063	26 425
2001	1 114 514	650 633	85 608	344 027	34 246
2002	1 199 864	686 637	107 590	361 881	43 756
2003	1 268 717	674 381	135 592	404 422	54 322
2004	1 302 723	643 628	162 251	436 504	60 340
2005	1 440 763	746 714	178 173	444 433	71 443
2006	1 467 145	720 105	200 638	461 395	85 007
2007	1 490 809	708 308	194 419	498 633	89 449
2008	1 507 631	749 400	232 209	440 184	85 838

表13-2 各行业从业人员数
Number of Employed Persons by Sector
(2008)

单位:人 (person)

指 标	Indicators	从业人员 Employed Persons	国有、集体、其他经济单位从业人员 Employed Persons in State-owned, Collective-owned and Other Economic Institutions	城镇个体劳动者 Urban Self-employed	农村集体和个体劳动者 Rural Collective and Self-employed Workers	其 他 Others
总 计	**Total**	**1 507 631**	**749 400**	**232 209**	**440 184**	**85 838**
按三次产业分	**By Industry**					
第一产业	Primary Industry	9 338	556	778	8 004	
第二产业	Secondary Industry	568 293	286 316	52 143	229 834	
第三产业	Tertiary Industry	930 000	462 528	179 288	202 346	85 838
按行业分	**By Sector**					
农、林、牧、渔业	Farming, Forestry, Animal Husbandry and Fishery	9 338	556	778	8 004	
采矿业	Mining	228	165	2	61	
制造业	Manufacturing	492 330	246 593	39 418	206 319	
电力、燃气及水的生产和供应业	Production and Supply of Electricity, Gas and Water	11 462	10 098	21	1 343	
建筑业	Construction	63 273	29 460	12 702	21 111	
交通运输、仓储和邮政业	Transportation, Warehousing and Post Service	117 968	93 209	7 753	17 006	
信息传输、计算机服务和软件业	Information Transmission, Computer Service and Computer Software	41 755	15 568	4 284	21 903	
批发和零售业	Wholesale and Retail	216 151	57 385	86 636	72 130	
住宿和餐饮业	Hotel and Catering	47 693	23 275	15 412	9 006	
金融业	Banking	136 924	136 924			
房地产业	Real Estate	37 762	15 705	12 657	9 400	
租赁和商务服务业	Leasing and Business Service	104 783	32 347	32 204	40 232	
科学研究、技术服务和地质勘查业	Scientific Research, Technical Services and Geological Prospecting	28 196	12 661		15 535	
水利、环境和公共设施管理业	Water Conservancy, Environment and Public Facilities Administration	4 695	4 695			
居民服务和其他服务业	Resident Service and Other Services	128 189	8 681	16 887	16 783	85 838
教 育	Education	32 131	32 131			
卫生、社会保障和社会福利业	Healthcare, Social Security and Social Welfare	17 886	16 030	1 300	556	
文化、体育和娱乐业	Culture, Sports and Entertainment	4 999	2 049	2 155	795	
公共管理和社会组织	Public Administration and Social Organizations	11 868	11 868			

注：国有、集体、其他经济单位从业人员包括职工中的在岗职工和其他从业人员。

Note: Employed staff and workers in state-owned, collective-owned and other business enterprises include those who are actually working in those companies.

表 13-3 历年职工人数

Staff and Workers in Main Years

(1993～2008)

单位:人 (person)

年 份 Year	合 计 Total	国有经济单位 State-owned Enterprises	集体经济单位 Collective-owned Enterprises	其他经济单位 Others	#港澳台及外商投资单位 Overseas Invested Enterprises
1993	788 821	597 417	84 811	106 593	
1994	767 146	582 477	76 023	108 646	
1995	798 884	571 398	85 955	141 531	
1996	719 634	469 966	85 030	164 638	
1997	663 163	405 349	77 072	180 742	52 405
1998	661 406	354 408	60 633	246 365	111 015
1999	677 348	355 607	56 824	264 917	126 897
2000	677 544	340 605	44 654	292 285	137 332
2001	687 694	299 186	37 756	350 752	134 732
2002	701 949	276 876	33 390	391 683	160 884
2003	671 434	249 461	25 549	396 424	136 212
2004	614 014	238 073	23 217	352 724	119 658
2005	701 553	233 350	20 431	447 772	129 890
2006	665 680	173 204	16 196	476 280	145 534
2007	631 720	188 892	16 278	426 550	186 480
2008	667 882	175 428	11 823	480 631	225 566

注：本表至表 13－7 和表 13－9 数据由上海市统计局返还。
Note: Data from this table to table 13－7 and table 13－9 have been returned from Shanghai Statistics Bureau.

表 13-4 历年在岗职工人数

Working Employees in Main Years

(1999～2008)

单位:人 (person)

年 份 Year	总 计 Total	国有经济单位 State-owned Enterprises	集体经济单位 Collective-owned Enterprises	其他经济单位 Others	#港澳台及外商投资单位 Overseas Invested Enterprises
1999	571 968				
2000	557 953				
2001	554 671				
2002	570 266				
2003	559 384	197 221	10 276	351 887	127 740
2004	514 941	192 574	9 142	313 225	111 531
2005	607 881	206 246	8 605	393 030	120 065
2006	592 718	209 338	7 514	375 866	113 981
2007	567 796	165 635	6 905	395 256	179 250
2008	613 835	145 198	5 692	462 945	221 795

表 13-5 各行业职工人数
Staff and Workers by Sector
(2008)

单位:人 (person)

指 标	Indicators	职工人数 Staff and Workers	#在岗职工 Working Employees	国有经济单位 State-owned Enterprises	城镇集体经济单位 Collective-owned Enterprises	其他经济单位 Others	#港澳台及外商投资单位 Overseas Invested Enterprises
总 计	**Total**	**667 882**	**613 835**	**175 428**	**11 823**	**480 631**	**225 566**
按三次产业分	**By Industry**						
第一产业	Primary Industry	527	509	170		357	98
第二产业	Secondary Industry	256 006	236 334	56 871	2 278	196 857	152 366
第三产业	Tertiary Industry	411 349	376 992	118 387	9 545	283 417	73 102
按行业分	**By Sector**						
农、林、牧、渔业	Farming, Forestry, Animal Husbandry and Fishery	527	509	170		357	98
采矿业	Mining	162	162	162			
制造业	Manufacturing	219 302	201 129	43 538	2 160	173 604	147 359
电力、燃气及水的生产和供应业	Production and Supply of Electricity, Gas and Water	9 929	9 882	7 391		2 538	2 440
建筑业	Construction	26 613	25 161	5 780	118	20 715	2 567
交通运输、仓储和邮政业	Transportation, Warehousing and Post Sercice	83 283	77 785	16 718	678	65 887	8 913
信息传输、计算机服务和软件业	Information Transmission, Computer Service and Computer Software	14 434	13 783	1 365		13 069	9 705
#信息传输	Information Transmission	4 038	3 395	1 130		2 908	2 080
批发和零售业	Wholesale and Retail	62 307	47 798	14 985	4 336	42 986	21 885
住宿和餐饮业	Hotel and Catering	8 609	8 467	1 087	126	7 396	5 679
金融业	Banking	118 617	116 397	2 041		116 576	10 298
房地产业	Real Estate	10 193	9 807	2 902	59	7 232	5 244
租赁和商务服务业	Leasing and Business Service	34 058	29 588	18 990	2 112	12 956	7 398
科学研究、技术服务和地质勘查业	Scientific Research, Technical Services and Geological Prospecting	10 557	10 374	4 257	8	6 292	3 208
水利、环境和公共设施管理业	Water Conservancy, Environment and Publicon Facilities Administrati	3 754	3 612	2 382	375	997	
#公共设施管理业	Public Facilities Administration	2 557	2 442	1 371	189	997	
居民服务和其他服务业	Resident Service and Other Services	13 861	8 557	5 575	4	8 282	522
教 育	Education	27 992	27 333	27 199		793	
卫生、社会保障和社会福利业	Healthcare, Social Security and Social Welfare	11 585	11 419	9 711	1 847	27	
文化、体育和娱乐业	Culture, Sports and Entertainment	1 608	1 583	684		924	250
公共管理和社会组织	Public Administration and Social Organizations	10 491	10 489	10 491			

表13-6 女职工人数
Female Staff and Workers
(2008)

单位:人 (person)

指 标	Indicators	职工人数 Staff and Workers	#在岗职工 Working Employees
总 计	**Total**	**250 637**	**232 851**
按登记注册类型分	**By Type of Registration**		
国有经济单位	State-owned Enterprises	59 372	49 257
集体经济单位	Collective-owned Enterprises	4 943	2 692
其他经济单位	Others	186 322	180 902
#港澳台及外商投资单位	Overseas Invested Enterprises	94 634	90 818
按行业分	**By Sector**		
农、林、牧、渔业	Farming, Forestry, Animal Husbandry and Fishery	193	187
采矿业	Mining	35	35
制造业	Manufacturing	75 821	70 097
电力、燃气及水的生产和供应业	Production and Supply of Electricity, Gas and Water	2 464	2 456
建筑业	Construction	4 027	3 842
交通运输、仓储和邮政业	Transportation, Warehousing and Post Sercice	18 737	17 893
信息传输、计算机服务和软件业	Information Transmission, Computer Service and Computer Software	4 514	4 216
#信息传输	Information Transmission	1 161	866
批发和零售业	Wholesale and Retail	25 680	20 468
住宿和餐饮业	Hotel and Catering	3 979	3 956
金融业	Banking	60 329	59 273
房地产业	Real Estate	4 260	4 146
租赁和商务服务业	Leasing and Business Service	11 733	10 049
科学研究、技术服务和地质勘查业	Scientific Research, Technical Service and Geological Prospecting	3 458	3 419
水利、环境和公共设施管理业	Water Conservancy, Environment and Public Facilities Administration	1 081	1 027
#公共设施管理业	Public Facilities Administration	734	685
居民服务和其他服务业	Resident Service and Other Services	4 620	2 465
教 育	Education	18 380	18 114
卫生、社会保障和社会福利业	Healthcare, Social Security and Social Welfare	7 779	7 665
文化、体育和娱乐业	Culture, Sports and Entertainment	713	709
公共管理和社会组织	Public Administration and Social Organizations	2 834	2 834

表 13-7 工业企业从业人员与职工人数
Employed Staff and Workers in Industrial Enterprises (2008)

单位:人 (person)

指 标	Indicators	从业人员人数 Employed Persons	职工人数 Staff and Workers	# 在岗职工 Working Employees
总 计	**Total**	**256 836**	**229 373**	**211 153**
按登记注册类型分	**By Type of Registration**			
国有经济单位	State-owned Enterprises	46 839	51 071	40 733
集体经济单位	Collective-owned Enterprises	1 367	2 160	899
其他经济单位	Others	208 630	176 142	169 521
# 港澳台及外商投资单位	Overseas Invested Enterprises	29 054	26 343	22 417
按行业分	**By Sector**			
石油和天然气开采业	Industry of Petroleum and Natural Gas Exploration	165	162	162
农副食品加工业	Processing of Agricultural Side-line Food	1 760	1 235	1 078
食品制造业	Food Manufacturing	4 269	3 925	3 859
饮料制造业	Beverage Manufacturing	1 948	1 668	1 627
烟草加工业	Tobacco Processing	736	780	735
纺织业	Textile Industry	2 827	3 277	2 131
纺织服装、鞋、帽制造业	Textile Products, Clothes, Shoes and Hats	6 924	5 559	5 174
皮革、毛皮、羽毛(绒)及其制品业	Leather, Furs, Down and Related Products	858	539	444
木材加工及木、竹、藤、棕、草制品业	Timber Processing, Bamboo, Cane, Palm, Fiber and Straw Products	125	114	114
家具制造业	Furniture Manufacturing	871	799	636
造纸及纸制品业	Paper-making and Paper Products	1 609	1 128	1 124
印刷业和记录媒介的复制	Printing and Record Medium Reproduction	2 550	2 355	2 180
文教体育用品制造业	Stationery, Educational and Sports Good	3 044	2 556	1 620
石油加工、炼焦及核燃料加工业	Petroleum Processing and Coking Products	2 025	2 396	1 999
化学原料及化学制品制造业	Chemical Materials and Chemical Products	7 325	7 007	6 866
医药制造业	Medicine Manufacturing	12 540	11 666	11 167
化学纤维制造业	Chemical Fiber Manufacturing	17	38	4
橡胶制造业	Rubber Products	1 261	571	571
塑料制造业	Plastic Products	7 658	6 081	5 592
非金属矿物制品业	Nonmetal Mineral Products	5 613	5 825	3 944
黑色金属冶炼及压延加工业	Smelting and Pressing of Ferrous Metals	1 050	1 549	896
有色金属冶炼及压延加工业	Smelting and Pressing of Non-ferrous Metals	994	858	757
金属制品业	Metal Products	6 535	5 561	5 251
通用设备制造业	Equipment for General Use	15 695	16 670	14 551
专用设备制造业	Special Purpose Equipment Manufacturing	9 943	12 045	8 523
交通运输设备制造业	Transportation Equipment Manufacturing	51 628	45 099	42 458
电气机械及器材制造业	Electric Equipment and Machinery	16 580	10 951	10 460
通信设备、计算机及其他电子设备制造业	Telecommunications, Computer and other Electronic Equipment Manufacturing	64 303	56 325	55 345
仪器仪表及文化、办公用机械制造业	Instrument, Meter, Culture and Office Machinery	14 601	11 336	10 824
工艺品及其他制造业	Handicrafts and Other Production	655	740	550
废弃资源和废旧材料回收加工业	Recycling of Abandoned Resources and Wastes	629	629	629
电力、热力的生产和供应业	Production and Supply of Electricity and Heating Power	1 378	1 337	1 332
燃气生产和供应业	Production and Supply of Gas	5 149	4 992	4 984
水的生产和供应业	Production and Supply of Tap Water	3 571	3 600	3 566

表 13-8　区属单位各行业从业人员与职工人数

Employed Staff and Workers in PNA Enterprises by sector (2008)

单位：人　　　　(person)

指　标	Indicators	从业人员人数 Employed Persons	职工人数 Staff and Workers	#在岗职工 Working Employees
总　计	**Total**	**263 475**	**242 803**	**215 980**
按登记注册类型分	**By Type of Registration**			
国有经济单位	State-owned Enterprises	61 955	66 772	51 396
集体经济单位	Collective-owned Enterprises	6 406	8 977	4 651
其他经济单位	Others	195 114	167 054	159 933
#港澳台及外商投资单位	Overseas Invested Enterprises	173 662	147 394	146 176
按行业分	**By Sector**			
农、林、牧、渔业	Farming, Forestry, Animal Husbandry and Fishery	105	98	98
制造业	Manufacturing	126 291	106 245	101 500
电力、燃气及水的生产和供应业	Production and Supply of Electricity, Gas and Water	1 276	1 255	1 254
建筑业	Construction	3 281	2 725	2 700
交通运输、仓储和邮政业	Transportation, Warehousing and Post Service	13 068	11 914	10 714
信息传输、计算机服务和软件业	Information Transmission, Computer Service and Computer Software	8 713	8 309	8 309
批发和零售业	Wholesale and Retail	24 635	32 925	21 756
住宿和餐饮业	Hotel and Catering	3 416	3 438	3 307
金融业	Banking	56	49	49
房地产业	Real Estate	8 411	5 062	4 876
租赁和商务服务业	Leasing and Business Service	18 404	19 560	16 293
科学研究、技术服务和地质勘查业	Scientific Research, Technical Service and Geological Prospecting	4 136	3 044	2 977
水利、环境和公共设施管理业	Water Conservancy, Environment and Public Facilities Administration	4 008	3 210	3 092
居民服务和其他服务业	Resident Service and Other Services	466	5 754	455
教　育	Education	23 283	21 037	20 555
卫生、社会保障和社会福利业	Healthcare, Social Security and Social Welfare	13 059	8 908	8 786
文化、体育和娱乐业	Culture, Sports and Entertainment	928	708	699
公共管理和社会组织	Public Administration and Social Organizations	9 939	8 562	8 560

表13-9 在岗职工人数变动
Change in Number of Working Employees
(2008)

单位:人 (person)

指 标	Indicators	变动人数 Change in Number of Staff and Workers	国有经济 State-owned	#企 业 Enterprise	城镇集体经济单位 Urban Collective-owned	其他经济单位 Others
职工增加人数	**Increase in Staff and Workers**	**128 554**	**20 744**	**15 479**	**600**	**107 210**
从农村招收	From Rural Area	13 673	2 508	1 624	20	11 145
从城镇招收	From Urban Area	59 505	3 567	3 192	122	55 816
录用的退伍军人	Ex-service Persons	528	174	72	2	352
录用的大、中专、技工学校毕业生	Graduates from University/College, Technical School	21 928	3 599	2 399	102	18 227
调入人数	Local/Cross-provincial Transfer	15 721	6 856	5 413	245	8 620
#外省市调入	Non-Shanghaiese	780	207	149	8	565
离岗职工重新上岗	Re-employed Staff Members Who Have Quit Jobs	1 936	1 225	1 172	39	672
其 他	Others	15 263	2 815	1 607	70	12 378
职工减少人数	**Decrease in Staff and Workers**	**129 698**	**23 708**	**18 810**	**2 727**	**103 263**
离休、退休、退职	Old Revolutionists, Retired and Resigned	9 978	4 526	2 605	230	5 222
开除、除名、辞退	Discharged and Redundant	3 349	320	257	23	3 006
终止、解除合同	Terminated by Contract	66 301	7 582	6 492	681	58 038
调出人数	Moved-out	16 028	5 912	4 924	1 573	8 543
#调往外省市	To Other Provinces	471	179	167	1	291
在岗职工离岗	Staff Members Who Have Quit Jobs	4 580	1 288	1 232	73	3 219
其 他	Others	29 462	4 080	3 300	147	25 235

表 13-10 应届毕业生构成及就业基本情况
Composition of Fresh Graduates and Their Employment

指 标	Indicators	单 位 Unit	2004	2005	2007	2008
毕业生按性别分	**By Sex of Graduates**					
男性比重	Proportion of Male Graduates	%	48.0	48.9	48.2	50.0
女性比重	Proportion of Female Graduates	%	52.0	51.1	51.8	50.0
毕业生按学历分	**By Educational Qualifications of Graduates**					
三校毕业生比重	Proportion of Graduates from Three Kinds of Colleges	%	33.2	37.0	24.8	23.0
大专毕业生比重	Proportion of Junior College Graduates	%	41.2	38.4	42.0	41.2
本科毕业生比重	Proportion of University Graduates	%	25.1	24.1	32.2	34.2
硕士及以上毕业生比重	Proportion of Graduates with Master's or Higher Degrees	%	0.5	0.6	1.0	1.6
毕业生总体就业率	**Overall Employment Rate of Graduates**	**%**	**64.5**	**65.8**	**73.5**	**72.1**
就业率按性别分	**Employment Rate, By Sex of Graduates**					
男性就业率	Employment Rate of Male Graduates	%	61.3	62.6	70.0	70.0
女性就业率	Employment Rate of Female Graduates	%	67.5	68.7	76.8	74.3
就业率按学历分	**Employment Rate, by Educational Qualifications**					
三校生	Graduates from Three Kinds of Colleges	%	53.5	53.3	63.5	59.9
大专生	Graduates of Junior Colleges	%	64.1	69.1	68.1	70.9
本科生	Graduates of Universities	%	78.5	74.2	83.6	79.1
硕士生及以上	Graduates with Master's or Higher Degrees	%	100.0	100.0	87.1	91.9
就业率按毕业院校分	**Employment Rate, by Colleges**					
重点院校就业率	Employment Rate of Graduates from Key Universities	%	80.5	79.9	88.3	80.7
普通院校就业率	Employment Rate of Graduates from Common Universities	%	71.1	70.0	74.5	75.5
民办院校就业率	Employment Rate of Graduates from Colleges Run by Private Investment	%	49.3	64.2	65.7	66.2
首份工作薪酬收入均值	**Average Salaries of First Jobs**	**元**	**1 569**	**1 617**	**2 005**	**2 211**
#三校生	Graduates from Three Kinds of Colleges	元	1 037	1 101	1 384	1 547
大专生	Graduates of Junior Colleges	元	1 428	1 404	1 688	1 928
本科生	Graduates of Universities	元	2 081	2 218	2 589	2 666
硕士生及以上	Graduates with Master's or Higher Degrees	元	4 123	4 793	4 473	5 122

注：数据取自对新区各类应届毕业生进行的抽样调查。调查对象为常住人口口径，居住在抽中居(村)委会、应届毕业的大专院校毕业生和三校毕业生。调查时点为当年 6 月 1 日零时。

Note: These data come from sample surveys to fresh graduates of different colleges and universities in PNA. The surveyed graduates are graduated from junior colleges and three kinds of colleges who are de jure population and live in the selected urban/rural residential committees. The survey time ended on 0：00 of June 1 of that current year.

表 13-11 享受居民最低生活保障人数

Number of Residents Benefiting from Guarantee of Minimum Standard of Living (2008)

单位:人 (person)

地 区	Subdistrict /Town	保障对象 Residents to be Guaranteed	城镇低保 Guarantee of Minimum Standard of Living in Urban Area	农村贫困户 Poverty Households in Rural Area
总 计	**Total**	**64 354**	**60 248**	**4 106**
潍坊新村街道	Weifangxincun Subdistrict	1 803	1 803	
陆家嘴街道	Lujiazui Subdistrict	2 925	2 925	
周家渡街道	Zhoujiadu Subdistrict	4 074	4 074	
塘桥街道	Tangqiao Subdistrict	1 833	1 833	
上钢新村街道	Shanggangxincun Subdistrict	4 274	4 274	
南码头路街道	Nanmatou Road Subdistrict	2 769	2 769	
沪东新村街道	Hudongxincun Subdistrict	2 664	2 664	
金杨新村街道	Jinyangxincun Subdistrict	2 536	2 536	
洋泾街道	Yangjing Subdistrict	2 550	2 550	
浦兴路街道	Puxing Road Subdistrict	3 690	3 690	
东明路街道	Dongming Road Subdistrict	2 607	2 607	
花木街道	Huamu Subdistrict	2 764	2 764	
川沙新镇	Chuansha New Town	8 661	7 291	1 370
高 桥 镇	Gaoqiao Town	1 116	948	168
北 蔡 镇	Beicai Town	3 318	3 262	56
合 庆 镇	Heqing Town	2 546	1 081	1 465
唐 镇	Tangzhen Town	1 729	1 590	139
曹 路 镇	Caolu Town	3 429	3 117	312
金 桥 镇	Jinqiao Town	671	638	33
高 行 镇	Gaohang Town	1 258	1 258	
高 东 镇	Gaodong Town	1 032	911	121
张 江 镇	Zhangjiang Town	1 781	1 781	
三 林 镇	Sanlin Town	4 324	3 882	442

注：本表至表 13－14 由浦东新区劳动保障局提供。
Note： The data in from this table to Table 13－14 are provided by Pudong Labor & Social Security Bureau.

表13-12　劳动就业及社会保障
Employment and Social Security

指　标	Indicators	单　位　Unit	2007	2008
劳动就业	**Employment**			
期末城镇登记失业人数	Actual Number of Those Registered as Unemployed at Year End	人 person	39 988	39 142
招工录用总数	Total Recruitment	人 person	205 426	241 461
#招用外区县劳动力	From Other Districts and Counties	人 person	86 531	95 821
征地劳动力安置	Recruitment of Those Who Have Lost Jobs Because of Requisition of Land	人 person	10 285	3 772
新增就业岗位	Number of Newly Increased Employment	人 person	129 432	142 747
社会保险	**Social Security**			
失业保险金发放人次	Unemployment Insurance Payment Distribution	人次 person-time	320 725	274 609
失业保险金发放金额	Unemployment Insurance Payment	万元 10 000 yuan	14 205	15 404
职工互助保障投保人次	Number of Staff Members Who Joined Mutual Security Program	人次 person-time	237 808	206 680
职工互助保障投保金额	Amount Insured	万元 10 000 yuan	3 718	3 432
农村社会养老保险期末参保人数	Number of Persons Who Joined Endowment Insurance Program in Rural Area at Year End	人 person	72 870	71 141
农村社会养老保险期末享受人数	Number of Persons Who Benefit from Endowment Insurance Program in Rural Area at Year End	人 person	22 932	22 750
社会救助	**Social Relief**			
城镇居民低保人数	Urban Residents Who Benefit from Subsistence Allowances from the State	人 person	59 710	55 829
城镇居民低保金额	Subsistence Allowances to Urban Residents	万元 10 000 yuan	12 552	14 927
农村居民低保人数	Number of Rural Population Benefiting from Subsistence Allowance	人 person	6 254	5 368
农村居民低保金额	Amount of Subsistence Allowance for Rural Population	万元 10 000 yuan	813	1 159
外来人员综合保险	**Comprehensive Assurance for Mobile Population**			
外来人员综合保险参保人数	Number of Mobile Insurants with Comprehensive Assurance	万人 10 000 persons	50.0	59.7

表 13-13　收养性单位基本情况
Background of Welfare Facilities
(2008)

指　标	Indicators	单　位 Unit	合　计 Total	社会福利院 Welfare Homes	敬老院 Homes for Senior Citizens
单位数	**Total Number**	**个 unit**	**74**	**1**	**73**
年末职工人数	**Number of Staff and Workers (Year End)**	**人 person**	**2 100**	**92**	**2 008**
#医护人员	Medical Personnel and Nurses	人 person	1 415	62	1 353
年末床位数	**Number of Beds**	**张 bed**	**10 202**	**200**	**10 002**
年末在院人数	**Persons Housed (Year End)**	**人 person**	**6 463**	**200**	**6 263**
#女　性	Female	人 person	4 265	111	4 154
在院人员按性质分	Persons Housed by Category				
优抚对象	Persons Enjoying Regular Subsidies and Commiseration of the State	人 person	136		136
"三无"对象	Jobless, Homeless and Without Household Registration	人 person	175	1	174
自费人员	Those at Their Own Expenses	人 person	6 152	199	5 953
在院人员按年龄分	Persons Housed by Age				
老　人	Old People	人 person	6 463	200	6 263

表 13-14　主要年份福利企业单位基本情况
Welfare Institutions and Enterprises in Main Years

指　标	Indicators	单　位 Unit	2000	2005	2007	2008
单位数	**Total Number**	**个 Unit**	**259**	**182**	**145**	**134**
年末职工人数	**Number of Staff and Workers (Year End)**	**人 Person**	**17 302**	**10 690**	**11 303**	**11 545**
#残疾职工	Staff and Workers with Disability	人 Person	7 461	4 655	4 548	4 126
#女　性	Female	人 Person	4 012	2 086	1 676	1 570
财务状况	**Financial Position**					
资产总额	Total Assets	万元 10 000 yuan	341 867	388 714	337 984	356 160
#固定资产原值	Original Value of Fixed Assets	万元 10 000 yuan	119 446	116 433	142 004	139 218
固定资产净值	Net Value of Fixed Assets	万元 10 000 yuan	90 735	73 134	79 502	82 194
负债总额	Total Liabilities	万元 10 000 yuan	178 538	194 859	153 234	159 701
所有者权益合计	Total Equity	万元 10 000 yuan	163 329	193 855	184 750	196 459
#未分配利润	Undistributed Profit	万元 10 000 yuan	26 763	27 066	24 998	15 744
销售(营业)收入	Sales Revenue	万元 10 000 yuan	215 794	406 409	361 156	480 304
纳税总额	Total Tax Paid	万元 10 000 yuan	13 200	22 165	13 658	12 108
#应退税金总额	Total Tax Bonification	万元 10 000 yuan	13 200	18 370	13 658	12 108
#实际退税金额	Actual Tax Bonification	万元 10 000 yuan	12 513	16 073	13 658	11 007
利润总额	Total Profit	万元 10 000 yuan	17 054	47 897	33 095	16 982

表 13-15　历年残疾人事业及居家养老情况
(2000～2008)

指　标　Indicators		单　位　Unit	2000
残疾人事业	**Disabled Persons**		
白内障复明手术	Operations for Recovery from Cataract	例 in number	1 193
低视力配用助视器人数	Number of Bad Eyesighted Persons Equipped with Typoscope	人 persons	6
低听力配用助听器人数	Number of Bad Auditioned Persons Equipped with Haudiphone	人 persons	9
精神病人数	Number of Mental Patients	人 persons	8 733
监护精神病人数	Number of Mental Patients Supervised	人 persons	8 432
麻风畸残发放辅助用具	Auxiliary Appliances Dispensed for Persons Suffering from Leprosy, Malformation and Disability	件 pieces	
城镇残疾人就业人数	Employed Disabled Persons in Towns and Subdistricts	人 persons	247
居家养老	**Life of Disabled Persons Including the Aged**		
期末养老机构床位数	Number of Beds in Old-Aged Institutions at End of Term	张 bed	
居家养老护理人员数	Number of Care Workers for the Old-Aged Living at Home	人 persons	
居家养老服务总数	Number of Services for the Old-Aged Living at Home	人次 persons-times	
#补贴数	Number of the Old Disabled Persons	人次 persons-times	
新增安康通安装数	Number of New Installations for Ankangtong SIM Cards	人次 persons-times	

注：本表有新区残联和劳保局提供。
Note: This table is provided by China Disabled Persons' Federation, PNA Branch and PNA Labor and Social Security Bureau.

表 13-16　历年红十字会基本情况
(2000～2008)

指　标　Indicators		单　位　Unit	2000
救　灾	**Providing Disaster Relief**		
捐赠款物	Donation of Money and Clothes	万元 10 000 yuan	144
救　助	**Salvage**		
救助款物	Salvation of Money and Clothes	万元 10 000 yuan	138
受益人次	Number of Persons Benefited	人次 person-times	1 210
救　护	**Rescue**		
师资培训	Teachers Trained	人 persons	236
救护员培训	Rescue Workers Trained	人 persons	480
救护防病知识普及	Popularization of Rescue and Disease Protection	人次 person-times	8 841
预防艾滋病	Protection of AIDS	人次 person-times	
遗体捐献登记	Registration of Body Donations	例 in number	
基层组织	Grassroot Organizations	个 in number	230
社区公益服务站点	Community Public Service Stations	个 in number	139
志愿者	Volunteers	人 in number	75

注：本表由上海浦东新区红十字会提供。
Note: This table is provided by Shanghai Pudong New Area Red Cross.

Statistics of Disabled Persons & Life of Disabled Persons Including the Aged in Main Years

	2001	2002	2003	2004	2005	2006	2007	2008
	1 960	1 634	1 710	2 000	2 379	2 171	2 211	2 301
	26	18	26	30	44	20	44	39
	5	4	6	5	20	7	157	87
	10 252	11 610	12 387	13 003	13 518	14 016	14 440	14 732
	9 423	10 935	11 232	11 612	11 612	12 430	13 647	14 061
		1	14	14	56	56	56	28
	294	737	969	1 326	758	971	1 113	845
						7 130	8 632	10 282
						1 265	1 294	1 813
						23 943	24 275	27 792
						4 403	4 827	5 690
						2 492	1 918	6 000

Statistics of Red Cross in PNA in Main Years

	2001	2002	2003	2004	2005	2006	2007	2008
	27	175	151	131	637	842	825	8 957
	18	138	159	42	430	763	476	1 366
	593	1 203	1 138	1 944	3 319	4 800	6 080	8 093
	120	52	168	45	251	57	103	
	156	159	437	121	598	536	7 099	9 014
	61 805	16 500	16 985	15 806	14 324	32 681	71 731	119 635
	280	2 600	2 350	4 850	5 946	12 536	15 638	20 320
	224	201	118	119	132	147	192	169
	236	241	658	751	784	953	953	951
	139	140	140	176	176	216	216	218
	95	268	570	826	1 303	3 500	3 600	3 900

表 13-17　廉租住房
Low Rent Housing in Main Years

指　标	Indicators	单位　Unit	2001	2005	2007	2008
廉租住房人均居住面积认定标准	Approved Standard for Living Space Per Capita in Low-Rent Housing	平方米 sq・m	5	7	< 7	< 7
廉租住房人均月收入认定标准	Approved Standard for Monthly Income Per Capita in Low-Rent Housing	元 yuan	280	300	≦ 600	≦ 800
受理登记	Registration					
累计受理户数	Number of Households Registered	户 household	201	1 847	3 070	4 632
累计审核登记户数	Approved Number of Households Registered	户 household	163	1 730	2 863	4 425
累计实有登记户数	Actual Number of Households Registered	户 household	159	1 678	2 791	4 363
累计配租户数	Total Number of Households Assisted	户 household	159	1 670	2 791	4 352
累计配租金额	Total Rent of Assisted Households	万元 10 000 yuan	37	780	3 960	5 862

注：1. 本表由浦东新区建设和交通委员会提供。
2. 2001 年在 159 户配租户中有 6 户为实物配租。
Note：1. This table is provided by Pudong Construction and Traffic Commission.
2. Among the 159 households assisted in 2001, 6 households were assisted by the Government through providing of low-rent housing.

表 13-18　社会捐赠与帮困
Social Donations and Financial Aids

指　标	Indicators	单位　Unit	2006	2007	2008
社会捐赠	Social Donations				
捐赠款金额	Amount of Donations	万元 10 000 yuan	6 859	7 245	9 350
捐赠衣被	Clothes and Quilts for Donation	万件 10 000 unit	25	20	44
医疗救助	Medical Assistance				
医疗救助人次	Number of Medical Assistance	人次 person-time	8 545	11 432	9 990
医疗救助金额	Number of Medical Assistance	万元 10 000 yuan	1 085	1 358	2 010
帮困助学	Financial Aids for Study				
帮困助学人次	Number of Financial Aids for Study	人次 person-time	6 391	7 087	10 339
帮困助学金额	Amount of Financial Aids for Study	万元 10 000 yuan	473	521	682

注：本表至表 13－19 由浦东新区劳动保障局提供。
Note：The data in from this table to Table 13－19 are provided by Pudong Labor & Social Security Bureau.

表 13-19　社会保障标准
Standard for Social Security

指　标	Indicators	单位　Unit	2006	2007	2008
职工月最低工资标准	Standard of Minimum Monthly Salary for Employees	元 yuan	750	840	960
城镇居民月最低生活保障标准	Standard of Minimum Monthly Living Expenses for Urban Residents	元 yuan	320	350	400
农村居民月最低生活保障标准	Standard of Minimum Monthly Living Expenses for Rural Residents	元 yuan	213	234	267
浦东新区农村社会养老保险金月最低标准	Standard of Minimum Monthly Endowment Insurance for Rural Residents	元 yuan	190	255	255

主要统计指标解释

从业人员

从业人员指从事一定社会劳动并取得劳动报酬或经营收入的人员，包括在岗职工、再就业的离退休人员、私营业主、个体户主、私营和个体从业人员、乡镇企业从业人员、农村从业人员、其他从业人员（包括民办教师、宗教职业者、现役军人等）。这一指标反映了一定时期内全部劳动力资源的实际利用情况，是研究我国基本国情国力的重要指标。

各单位的从业人员指在各级国家机关、政党机关、社会团体及企业、事业单位中工作，取得工资或其他形式的劳动报酬的全部人员。包括在岗职工、再就业的离退休人员、民办教师以及在各单位中工作的外方人员和港澳台方人员、兼职人员、借用的外单位人员和第二职业者。不包括离开本单位仍保留劳动关系的职工。各单位的就业人员反映了各单位实际参加生产或工作的全部劳动力。

职　工

职工指在国有、城镇集体、联营、股份制、外商和港、澳、台投资、其他单位及其附属机构工作，并由其支付工资的各类人员。不包括下列人员：(1)乡镇企业就业人员；(2)私营企业就业人员；(3)城镇个体劳动者；(4)离休、退休、退职人员；(5)再就业的离、退休人员；(6)民办教师；(7)在城镇单位中工作的外方及港、澳、台人员；(8)其他按有关规定不列入职工统计范围的人员。（1998 年及以后的数据均为在岗职工数据，其他相关指标如职工工资总额，职工平均工资等指标也从 1998 年按此口径进行了相应调整）。

在岗职工

指在本单位工作并由单位支付工资的人员，以及有工作岗位，但由于学习、病伤产假等原因暂未工作，仍由单位支付工资的人员。

登记注册类型

登记注册类型是以工商行政管理机关登记注册的具有法人资格的各类企业为划分对象。产业活动单位和行政机关、事业单位、社会团体及其他经济组织参照执行。

国有企业指企业全部资产归国家所有，并按《中华人民共和国企业法人登记管理条例》规定登记注册的非公司制的经济组织。不包括有限责任公司中的国有独资公司。

集体企业指企业资产归集体所有，并按《中华人民共和国企业法人登记管理条例》规定登记注册的经济组织。

股份合作企业指以合作制为基础，由企业职工共同出资入股，吸收一定比例的社会资产投资组建，实行自主经营，自负盈亏，共同劳动，民主管理，按劳动分配与按股份分红相结合的一种集体经济组织。

联营企业指两个及两个以上相同或不同所有制性质的企业法人或事业单位法人，按自愿、平等、互利的原则，共同投资组成的经济组织。联营企业包括国有联营企业、集体联营企业、国有与集体联营企业和其他联营企业。

有限责任公司指根据《中华人民共和国公司登记管理条例》规定登记注册，由 2 个以上，50 个以下的股东共同出资，每个股东以其所认缴的出资额对公司承担有限责任，公司以其全部资产对其债务承担责任的经济组织。有限责任公司包括国有独资公司以及其他有限责任公司。

股份有限公司指根据《中华人民共和国公司登记管理条例》规定登记注册，其全部注册资本由等额股份构成并通过发行股票筹集资本，股东以其认购的股份对公司承担有限责任，公司以其全部资产对其债务承担责任的经济组织。

私营企业指由自然人投资设立或由自然人控股，以雇佣劳动为基础的营利性经济组织。包括按照《公司法》、《合伙企业法》、《私营企业暂行条例》规定登记注册的私营有限责任公司、私营股份有限公司、私营合伙企业和私营独资企业。

与港澳台商投资合资经营企业指港澳台地区投资者与内地企业依照《中华人民共和国中外合资经营企业法》及有关法律的规定，按合同的比例投资设立、分享利润和分担风险的企业。

港澳台商投资合作经营企业指港澳台地区投资者与内地企业依照《中华人民共和国中外合资经营企业法》及有关法律的规定，依照合同的约定进行投资或提供条件设立、分享利润和分担风险的企业。

港澳台商独资经营企业指依照《中华人民共和国外资企业法》及有关法律的规定，在内地由港澳台商地区投资者全额投资设立的企业。

港澳台商投资股份有限公司指根据国家有关规定，经外经贸部依法批准设立，其中港、澳、台商的股本占公司注册资本的比例达 25% 以上的股份有限公司。凡其中港、澳、台商的股本占公司注册资本的比例小于 25% 的，属于内资企业中股份有限公司。

中外合资经营企业指外国企业或外国人与中国内地企业依照《中华人民共和国中外合资经营企业法》及有关法律的规定，按合同规定的比例投资设立、分享利润和分担风险的企业。

中外合作经营企业指外国企业或外国人与中国内地企业依照《中华人民共和国中外合作经营企业法》及有关法律的规定，依照合作合同的约定进行投资或提供条件设立、分享利润和分担风险的企业。

外资企业指依照《中华人民共和国外资企业法》及有关法律的规定，在中国内地由外国投资者全额投资设立的企业。

外商投资股份有限公司指根据国家有关规定，经外经贸部依法批准设立,其中外资的股本占公司注册资本的比例达25%以上的股份有限公司。凡其中外资股本占公司注册资本的比例小于25%的,属于内资企业中的股份有限公司。

国民经济行业分类

《国民经济行业分类》国家标准于1984年首次发布,1994年对其进行了第一次修订,2002年为第二次修订。

本年鉴的行业分类使用2002年修订的行业分类标准。

2002年新行业分类标准按照国际通行的经济活动同质性原则划分行业,进一步打破了部门管理界限,对原标准中不符合这一原则的分类进行了调整;根据我国社会经济活动的发展状况,重点加强了第三产业的分类,新增了大量服务业方面的活动类别;对新标准的每一个行业小类,全部与国际标准产业分类的最细一层分类建立了对应关系。新修订的《国民经济行业分类》主要目的之一是与联合国的《全部经济活动的国际标准产业分类》接轨,准确反映一定时期内国民经济行业的构成状况。

失业保险

①参加保险人数:指报告期末按照国家法律、法规和有关政策规定参加了失业保险的城镇企业事业单位的职工及地方政府规定参加失业保险的其他人员的人数。

②失业保险金:指为保障失业人员的基本生活而按规定支付的失业保险金金额。

社会福利事业单位

社会福利事业单位指集中收养社会孤老、残、幼的机构。包括由民政部门管理的社会福利院、儿童福利院、精神病人福利院和城镇集体办的福利院,以及农村集体办的敬老院。

优抚对象

优抚指政府对革命烈士家庭、病故残疾工作人员以及参战负伤致残的民兵、民工的抚恤和人民群众对其的优待。优抚对象包括革命烈士家属、因公牺牲和病故军人家属、革命伤残人员、现役军属、退伍红军老战士、红军失散人员、复员军人、退伍军人、在职退役军人、在乡退役军人、带病回乡退伍军人、复退军人精神病员、孤老优抚对象等。

EXPLANATORY NOTES TO MAJOR STATISTICAL INDICATORS

Employees

Employees refer to the persons who are engaged in social working and receive remuneration payment or earn business income, including total staff and workers, re-employed retirees, employers of private enterprises, self-employ ed workers, employees in private enterprises and individual economy, employees in township enterprises, employed persons in the rural areas , and other employed persons (including teachers in the schools run by the local people, people engaged in religious profession and t he servicemen, etc.). This indicator reflects the actual utilization of total labour force during a certain period of time and is often used for the research on China's economic situation and national power.

Employees in Various Units refer to all the persons working in government agencies of various levels, political and party organizations, social organizations, enterprises and institutions, and receiving wages or other forms of payment. They include fully-employed staff and workers, re-employed retirees, teachers in schools run by the local people, foreigners and Chinese compatriots from Hong Kong, Macao, and Taiwan working in various units, part -time employees, employees of other units working temporarily at current post s, and employees holding the second job, but exclude staff and workers who have left their working units while keeping their labor contract (employment relation) unchanged. This indicator reflects the total number of laborers actually engaged in production or other operations in various units.

Staff and Workers

Staff and Workers refer to persons working in, and receive payment from units of state ownership, collective ownership, joint ownership, share holding ownership, foreign ownership, and ownership by entrepreneurs from Hong Kong, Macao, and Taiwan, and other types of ownership and their affiliated units. They do not include 1) persons employed in township enterprises, 2) persons employed in private enterprises, 3) urban self-employed persons, 4) retirees, 5) re-employed retirees, 6) teachers in the schools run by the local people, 7) foreigners and persons from Hong Kong, Macao and Taiwan who work in urban units, and 8) other persons not to be included by relevant regulations. (Data of 1998 and afterward refer to fully employed staff and workers. Other related statistics such as total wages and average wage are adjusted since 1998 accordingly).

Fully Employed Staff and Workers

Fully Employed Staff and Workers refer to persons who work in, and receive wages from their working units, as well as persons who have their work posts, but are temporarily absent from work for reasons of study or on sick, injury or maternal leave and still receive wages from their working units.

Registration Categories

Registration Categories are used to classify all kinds of enterprises that have the legal person status and have registered with the industrial and commercial administrations. The classification of business units , administrative and public institutions , social organizations and other economical bodies may refer to it.

The state-owned enterprises are economic organizations whose assets are solely owned by the state and whose registrations are made according to "Regulations of the People's Republic of China for Controlling the Registration of Enterprises as Legal Persons" excluding the state-owned liability limited companies.

The collective-owned enterprises are economic organizations whose assets are owned by collecting and whose registration are made according to "Regulations of the People's Republic of China for Controlling the Registration of Enterprises as Legal Persons."

Share-holding cooperative enterprises are a kind of collective economic organizations based on a cooperative system. In addition to the shares bought by their workers and staff, the enterprises also absorb a certain percentage of social capital. They enjoy the autonomy in operation and are responsible for their own losses and profits. The share-holders work together, conduct democratic management, and combine labor-based distribution with share-based dividents.

Joint-owned enterprises refer to economic organizations set up with joint investment from legal persons of two or more enterprises of different ownerships or institutions according to principle of voluntary participation, equality and mutual benefit. They include state-owned joint operation enterprises, collective joint operation enterprises, state-collective joint operation enterprises and other types of joint operation enterprises.

A company with limited liability is a company registered in accordance with the "Regulations of the People's Republic of China on Administration of Company Registration." Its investment comes from more than 2 and less than 50 shareholders. Each shareholder assumes limited liability for the company according to his subscription to capital stock. The company assumes liabilities for its debts according to all its assets. Such economic organizations include solely state-invested companies and other types of companies with limited liability.

A share-holding company with limited liability refers to economic organizations registered in accordance with the "Regulations of the People's Republic of China on Administration of Company Registration." All its registered capital is composed of shares of equal value and its capital is collected through share issuing. The shareholders bear limited liability for the company according to the amount of shares they have bought from the company and the company assumes liabilities for its debts according all its assets.

A private enterprise refers to profit-making economic organizations set up with investment from natural persons or with controlling interest in the hands of natural persons who employ laborers for operation. Such enterprises include private companies with limited liability private joint stock companies limited private partnership enterprises and solely individual-invested enterprises, which are registered according to the "Company Law," "Partnership Enterprises Law" and "Interim Regulations of Private Enterprises."

The joint ventures with investment from Hong Kong, Macao and Taiwan refer to those established according to the "Law of the People's Republic of China on Chinese-foreign Joint Ventures" and regulations stipulated in relevant laws, by investors from those regions and the Chinese mainland enterprises with contracted share of investment and sharing profits and ventures between the parties.

Cooperative businesses with investment from Hong Kong, Macao and Taiwan refer to enterprises jointly set up by investors from Hong Kong, Macao and Taiwan and mainland enterprises according to the "Law of the People's Republic of China on Chinese-foreign Contractural Joint Ventures" and other relevant regulations. They invest or provide conditions for establishment, decide profit distribution, and share risks according to provisions prescribed in the cooperative venture contracts.

Solely Hong Kong, Macao and Taiwan Funded enterprises refer to enterprises set up on the mainland according to the "Law of the People's Republic of China on Foreign Capital Enterprises and solely invested by investors from Hong Kong, Macao and Taiwan."

A share-holding company with limited liability with investment from Hong Kong, Macao and Taiwan refers to any joint stock company limited that is set up according relevant state regulations and is approved by the Ministry of Foreign Economic Relations and Trade. The investment from Hong Kong, Macao and Taiwan investors must account more than 25 per-cent of the company's total capital. If such investment is less than 25 percent, it shall be classified as a joint stock company limited invested by domestic investors.

A Sino-foreign joint venture refers to any enterprise that is jointly set up by foreign enterprises or foreigners with Chinese enterprises in accordance with the "Law of the People's Republic of China on Joint Ventures with Chinese and Foreign Investment." The investors shall put in investment, share profits and risks according to the contract on the joint venture.

Sino-foreign cooperative Businesses refers to the enterprises set up by foreign enterprises or foreigners with Chinese enterprises as their partners, in line with "The Sino-foreign Cooperative Ventures Law of the People's Republic of China" and other relevant laws and regulations. The partners of the cooperative ventures will invest, take profits and share risks according to the requirements of stipulated in the contract.

A Solely Foreign-Funded enterprises refers to any enterprise that is set up on the Chinese mainland according to the "Law of the People's Republic of China on Foreign-Capital Enterprises" and with all its investment coming from foreign investors.

The foreign-invested joint stock company limited refers to any joint stock company limited that is set up according to relevant state regulations and is approved by the Ministry of Foreign Economic Relations and Trade. The foreign investment must account more than 25 per-cent of the company's total capital. If such investment is less than 25 per-cent, it shall be classified as a joint stock company limited invested by Chinese investors.

Classification of the Sectors of the National Economy

Classification of the Sectors of the National Economy was first published in 1984 and revisions were made into it in 1994 and 2002 respectively.

This Yearbook follows standards in the 2002 version of the Classification of the Sectors of the National Economy.

In the 2002 version, economic sectors are classified in accordance with the international categories of the economic activities, abolishing in definition between different administrative departments. Given the development of China's social and economic activities, more detailed classification is made of the service sector. The further breakdown of each economic sector in the latest version is geared to the most specific categorization in international practice. The latest version aims at, among others, an objective and precise presentation of the composition of the national economy in a certain period.

Unemployment Insurance

①Number of people participated in unemployment insurance program: number of staff and workers in urban enterprises or institutions and other people according to local government regulations participated in unemployment insurance program in line with national law, regulations and related policies by the end of the reference period.

②Sum of Unemployment Insurance: refer to total amount of insurance paid to un-employees to guarantee their basic lives according to related regulations.

Social Welfare Institutions

Social Welfare Institutions refer to institutions taking care of old people without children, handicapped people and orphans. They include social welfare institutions run by civil affairs departments, children's welfare institutions, welfare institutions for mental patients, and collectively-run old people's homes in rural areas.

Special Care

Special Care is offered by the government to the family member of the martyrs, disabled or demobilized servicemen or laborers who were injured on duty. Entitled to the special care are family members of the revolutionary martyrs, family members of servicemen who dies on duty or died of an illness, disabled servicemen, family members of servicemen on active service, retired veteran Red Army soldiers, scattered Red Army soldiers, demobilized servicemen, ex-servicemen, servicemen who were demobilized while on duty, ex-servicemen back to their rural homes, ex-servicemen who were demobilized because of an illness and have gone back to their rural homes, ex-servicemen who suffer from mental illness and elderly persons with no family.

第十四篇

Chapter 14

教育、文化、体育、卫生

EDUCATION, CULTURE, SPORTS AND PUBLIC HEALTH

表 14－1 各级各类学校基本情况
Statistics of Schools by Education Level and Type
(2008)

单位:人 (person)

指 标 Indicators		学校(所) Schools (unit)	毕业生数 Graduates	招生数 Student Enrollment	在校学生数 Students Enrolled	教职员工数 Faculty and Staff	#专任教师 Full-time Faculty
总 计	**Total**	**232**	**74 858**	**77 978**	**291 839**	**25 997**	**18 930**
高等学校	Institutions of Higher Education	8	13 292	16 947	55 917	6 497	3 440
中等技术学校	Secondary Technical Schools	7	5 662	4 908	16 076	1 172	439
普通中学	High Schools	109	32 236	28 156	100 207	9 624	7 569
职业中学	Vocational Schools	5	5 378	5 629	17 612	904	694
小 学	Primary Schools	101	18 200	22 285	101 449	7 644	6 672
特殊教育学校	Special Education Schools	2	90	53	578	156	116

注：本表至表 14－9 由浦东新区社会发展局提供。
Note：The data in from this table to Table 14－9 are provided by Pudong Social Development Bureau.

表 14－2 各级各类学校占地面积和校舍建筑面积
Ground Space and Floor Space of School Buildings by Education Level and Type
(2008)

单位:万平方米 (10 000 sq · m)

指 标 Indicators		学校(所) Schools (unit)	占地面积 Ground Space	校舍建筑面积 Floor Space of Buildings
总 计	**Total**	**232**	**927.80**	**504.30**
高等学校	Institutions of Higher Education	8	434.06	185.39
中等技术学校	Secondary Technical Schools	7	22.76	20.71
普通中学	High Schools	109	300.16	192.91
职业中学	Vocational Schools	5	24.82	18.57
小 学	Primary Schools	101	142.33	84.16
特殊教育学校	Special Education Schools	2	3.67	2.56

表 14-3 各级各类学校女学生和女教师
Female Students and Teachers by Education Level and Type (2008)

单位:人 (person)

指 标 Indicators		女学生 Female Students		女教师 Female Faculty	
		人 数 Students	占学生总数(%) of Students(%)	人 数 Teachers	占教师总数(%) of Teachers(%)
总 计	**Total**	**141 699**	**48.6**	**12 871**	**68.0**
高等学校	Institutions of Higher Education	28 554	51.1	1 667	48.5
中等专业学校	Secondary Specialized Schools	9 305	57.9	247	56.3
普通中学	High Schools	48 730	48.6	4 960	65.5
职业中学	Vocational Schools	8 600	48.8	454	65.4
小 学	Primary Schools	46 317	45.7	5 442	81.6
特殊教育学校	Special Education Schools	193	33.4	101	87.1

表 14-4 主要年份各阶段教育实施情况
Basic Statisics of Various Phases of Education In Main Years

单位:% (%)

指 标 Indicators		2005	2006	2007	2008
小 学	**Primary School**				
小学学龄儿童净入学率	Enrollment Rate of School-age Children	100.0	100.0	100.0	100.0
初 中	**Junior School**				
初中学生净入学率	Enrollment Rate of Students In Junior Secondary Schools Phase	100.0	100.0	100.0	100.0
高 中	**Senior School**				
初中毕业生升学率	Enrollment Rate of Junior School Graduates	98.7	97.5	96.7	97.1

表 14-5　重点中学基本情况
Statistics for Key High Schools
(2008)

学校名称 Schools		班　级（个）Classes (unit)	在校学生（人）Student Enrollment (person)	教职员工（人）Faculty and Staff (person)	#专任教师 Full-time Faculty	学校占地面积（万平方米）School Ground Space (10 000 sq · m)	#运动场 Athlete Field	校舍建筑面积（万平方米）Floor Space of School Buildings (10 000 sq · m)
全区中学	**Regular Secondary Schools in PNA**	**2 662**	**100 207**	**9 624**	**7 569**	**300.16**	**94.88**	**192.91**
#重点中学合　计	**Total Key High Schools**	**362**	**14 451**	**1 603**	**1 190**	**50.75**	**14.74**	**30.02**
华师大二附中	No. 2 High School Affiliated to East China Normal University	30	1 307	167	99	10.00	2.49	5.20
建平中学	Jianping High School	38	1 481	182	144	3.92	0.71	3.11
进才中学	Jincai High School	37	1 407	195	153	12.99	3.81	7.20
洋泾中学	Yangjing High School	47	1 732	152	116	4.31	1.05	3.30
东昌中学	Dongchang High School	38	1 462	149	106	2.47	1.04	1.06
川沙中学	Chuansha High School	36	1 484	156	103	3.25	1.14	2.33
高桥中学	Gaoqiao High School	36	1 546	162	115	4.56	1.10	2.17
上南中学	Shangnan High School	34	1 389	160	128	1.82	0.80	1.61
三林中学	Sanlin High School	36	1 468	151	121	3.09	1.37	1.95
杨思高级中学	Yangsi High School	30	1 175	129	105	4.34	1.23	2.09

表 14-6　普通中学和小学专任教师学历情况
Education Level of Full-time Teachers at Regular High Schools and Primary Schools
(2008)

单位：人　　(person)

指　标 Indicators		教师数 Faculty Contracts	大学本科毕业及以上 Graduated from University or Above	大学专科毕　业 Graduated from Junior University	高中阶段毕　业 Graduated from Senior High School	高　中毕业以下 Below Senior High School or below
教师学历分布	**Education Level of Teachers**	**14 241**	**10 339**	**3 337**	**534**	**31**
高　中	Senior High Schools	2 512	2 482	30		
初　中	Junior High Schools	5 057	4 556	483	14	4
小　学	Primary Schools	6 672	3 301	2 824	520	27
教师学历构成(%)	**Education Level Composition of Teachers (%)**	**100.0**	**72.6**	**23.4**	**3.8**	**0.2**
高　中	Senior High Schools	100.0	98.8	1.2		
初　中	Junior High Schools	100.0	90.1	9.5	0.3	0.1
小　学	Primary Schools	100.0	49.5	42.3	7.8	0.4

表 14-7 幼儿园基本情况
Statistics of Kindergartens
(2008)

指 标	Indicators	幼儿园(所) Kindergartens (unit)	班级数(个) Classes (unit)	幼儿数(人) Children Enrolled (person)	教职员(人) Faculty and Staff (person)	#专任教师 Full-time Faculty
总 计	**Total**	**162**	**1 909**	**53 844**	**5 384**	**3 655**
教育部门办	Run by Government Education Department	114	1 490	44 014	3 556	2 766
集体单位办	Run by Collective Institutions					
其他部门办	Run by Other Organizations	1	5	150	25	13
民 办	Run by Entrepreneurs	47	414	9 680	1 803	876

表 14-8 民工子弟学校基本情况
Statistics of Schools for Children of Migrant Workers

指 标	Indicators	单 位 Unit	2005	2006	2007	2008
学校总计	**Total of Schools**	**所 in number**	**23**	**23**	**26**	**26**
小 学	Primary Schools	所 in number	6	6	9	18
混合型初中小学	Primary and Middle Schools with Mixed Ownership	所 in number	17	17	17	8
班级总计	**Total of Classes**	**个 in number**	**394**	**392**	**467**	**396**
小 学	Primary Schools	个 in number	339	338	359	371
初 中	Middle Schools	个 in number	55	54	108	25
教职员工数	**Number of Teaching Staff**	**人 persons**	**851**	**844**	**986**	**917**
小 学	Primary Schools	人 persons	851	820	943	825
初 中	Middle Schools	人 persons		24	43	92
学生总计	**Total of Students**	**人 persons**	**20 520**	**20 769**	**25 549**	**21 469**
小 学	Primary Schools	人 persons	18 155	18 439	20 141	20 279
初 中	Middle Schools	人 persons	2 365	2 330	5 408	1 190

表 14-9 成人教育基本情况
Statistics of Adult Education
(2008)

单位:人 (person)

指 标	Indicators	结业生数 Graduates	注册学生数 Students Contracts	教职员工数 Faculty Contracts	#专任教师 Full-time Faculty	兼任教师 Part-time Faculty
高中文化学习	**High School Education**	**1 111**	**1 616**	**347**	**54**	**30**
职工教育	Education for Staff and Workers	1 111	1 616	347	54	30
农民教育	Education for Farmers					
技术学习	**Technical Training**	**200 925**	**123 192**	**62**	**31**	**428**
教育部门和集体办教育	Education run by educational departments and the collective	200 925	123 192	62	31	428
其他部门办教育	Education run by other organizations					
民办教育	Educaton run by the local people					

表 14-10 文化馆基本情况
Statistics of Cultural Centers
(2008)

指 标	Indicators	单 位 Unit	合 计 Total	浦东文化馆 Pudong Cultural Center	浦南文化馆 Punan Cultural Center	川沙文化馆 Chuansha Cultural Center	文化艺术指导中心 Art Consulting Center
机构数	Number of Centers	个 unit	7	1	4	1	1
职工人数	Staff and Workers	人 person	158	49	32	38	39
公用房屋建筑面积	Floor Space of Building for Public Use	平方米 sq · m	18 457	6 200		5 540	6 717
组织文艺活动次数	Performances Organized	次 time	4 295	39	43	70	4 143
举办业余文艺训练班班次	Training Course for Amateurs	班次 class-time	152	50	75	6	21
结业人数	Persons Graduated	人次 person-time	1 931	500	90	85	1 256

注：1. 本表至表 14-12 由浦东新区宣传部提供。
2. 因地铁施工,浦南文化馆从 2005 年 4 月起搬迁至临时地址办公,故未计面积。

Note：1. The data in from this table to Table 14-12 are provided by Pudong Public Affaires Department.
2. Punan Cultural Center was moved to a temporary office building in April 2005 because of the construction of Rail Transport, so its floor space is excluded.

表 14－11　公共图书馆基本情况
Statistics of Public Libraries

指　标　Indicators		单　位　Unit	2000	2005	2006	2007	2008
机构数	Number of Institutions	个 unit	5	1	3	3	1
职工人数	Staff and Workers	人 person	108	110	110	102	86
公用房屋建筑面积	Floor Space of Building for Public Use	平方米 sq · m	7 443	18 343	18 343	17 915	10 337
#书　库	Stack Rooms	平方米 sq · m	2 237	6 040	6 040	3 819	2 268
阅览室面积	Floor Space of Reading Rooms	平方米 sq · m	1 354	7 550	7 550	4 360	1 576
阅览室座席	Seats in Reading Rooms	个 unit	800	1 366	1 466	1 488	566
总藏书量	Total Book Volume	万册 10 000 volumes	80	126	136	147	87
#本年新购藏书	New Books Purchased in Current Year	万册 10 000 volumes	3	12	10	11	27
发放借书证	Library Cards Distributed	张 in number	14 579	10 524	15 993	12 747	12 033
图书流通人次	Books Circulation Persons Time	万人次 10 000 person-times	67	150	169	180	126
图书外借册次	Borrowed Books-time	万册次 10 000 volume-times	80	99	83	143	91

注：从 2008 年起统计口径改变，故数据不具可比性。
Note: Since the statistical approaches have been readjusted since 2008.

表14-12 广播电视事业基本情况
Statistics of Broadcasting and Television

指标	Indicators	单位 Unit	2005	2006	2007	2008
区广播电台	PNA Radio Station	座 unit	1	1	1	1
区有线电视中心	PNA CATV Center	座 unit	1	1	1	1
市属有线电视管理站	Municipal CATV Management Station	个 unit	10	10	10	10
区属有线电视管理站	PNA CATV Management Station	个 unit	3	3	3	3
镇广播电视站	Town Radio & TV Stations	个 unit	13	12	12	12
广电工作从业人员	Persons Employed in Sectors of Broadcasting and Television	人 person	342	342	336	336
区台无线广播发射塔	Radio Broadcasting Towers of PNA TV	座 unit	1	1	1	1
区台使用频率	Frequency Occupied by PNA TV	兆赫 MHz	106.5	106.5	106.5	106.5
区台无线广播覆盖率	Radio Broadcasting Coverage of PNA TV	%	100.0	100.0	100.0	100.0
有线广播电视专线	Cabled Broadcasting and Television Private Line	杆公里 pole km	1 858	1 486	1 486	1 486
有线电视管道干线	CATV Trunk Line	公里 km	223	436	438	452
区有线电视中心播出自办节目时间	Airing Hours of Self-Produced Programs by PNA CATV Center	分钟/日 munit/day	30	30	30	30
有线电视用户	CATV Subscribers	万户 10 000 households	73	75	76	78
村通播率	Rate of Villages Access to Broadcasting	%	100.0	100.0	100.0	100.0
共缆广播喇叭	Total Broadcasting Loudspeakers	万只 10 000 units	8.0	8.0	8.0	8.0
喇叭入户率	Rate of Household Loudspeakers	%	64.0	64.0	64.0	64.0
区台平均日播音时间	Average Broadcasting Hours of PNA Radio Station	小时 hour	14.5	18.7	18.7	20.0
镇广播电视站日播放时间	Airing/Broadcasting Hours of Town Radio & TV Station	小时 hour	14.5	19.0	19.0	19.0

表 14－13 文化事业
Cultural Establishments

指 标	Indicators	单 位 Unit	2007	2008
街道、镇社区文化活动中心	Culture and Activity Center for Sub-district and Town	个 unit	24	24
行政村(居委)综合文化活动室	Comprehensive Culture and Activity Room for Administrative Village (Neighborhood Committee)	个 unit	833	944
每万人拥有公共文化设施面积	Floor Space of Public Culture Facilities per 10 000 Persons	平方米 sq · m	1 229	1 161
每万人拥有图书馆藏书量	Number of Books Collected in Libraries per 10 000 Persons	册 Book	5 121	6 098
街镇图书馆藏书量	Number of Books Collected in Sub-district and Town Libraries	万册 10 000 Books	63.23	61.07
文化资源	**Cultural Resources**			
区属文化基层单位	PNA Cultural Grassroot Unit	个 unit	5	5
公共文化设施数	Number of Public Cultural Facilities	个 unit	966	1 079
各类群众文化活动场次	Number of All Kinds of Mass Cultural Activities	场次 in number	57 522	58 425
各类群众文化活动参与人数	Number of Participants in All Kinds of Mass Cultural Activities	万人 10 000 persons	431.33	437.66
公益电影放映次数	Number of Welfare Film Screened	场次 in number	2 072	3 627
#外来务工人员公益电影放映	Number of Welfare Film Screened for Migrant Workers	场次 in number	132	107
业余文艺团队个数	Number of Amateur Literary and Artistic Teams	个 unit	2 963	2 963
文化交流	**Cultural Exchanges**			
赴境外演出、展览次数	Number of Performances and Exhibitions in Foreign Countries	次 time	3	5
境外艺术团来访个数	Number of Visiting Overseas Artist Teams	个 unit	85	67
境外艺术团演出场次	Number of Overseas Artist Teams Performances	场次 in number	179	195
文艺创作演出情况	**Literary and Artistic Creations and Performances**			
群众文艺创作数	Number of Literary and Artistic Creations	个 unit	204	241
获奖个数	Number of Prizes	个 unit	70	71
获奖人次	Number of Person-times Who Get the Prizes	人次 person-time	30	29
获奖单位	Number of Units Who Get the Prizes	个 unit	19	18
外来务工人员公益文化服务情况	**Services for Welfare Cultural Activities by Migrant Workers**			
举办文艺演出	Number of Literary and Artistic Performances Held	场次 in number	112	156
开设图书流通服务点	Circulating Establishments for Books	个 unit	3	12

表 14-14 参加市级以上体育竞赛成绩情况
PNA in State-level and International-level Competitions
(2008)

单位:次 (time)

指 标	Indicators	第1名 First Place Winners	第2名 Second Place Winners	第3名 Third Place Winners	第4名 Fourth Place Winners	第5名 Fifth Place Winners	第6名 Sixth Place Winners	第7名 Seventh Place Winners
合 计	**Total**	**408.5**	**316**	**300**	**70**	**46**	**45**	**31**
国 际	International	2		1				
市 级	Municipal Level	343.5	272	269	59	40	42	27
全 国	State Level	63	44	30	11	6	3	4
团 体	**Team**	**68**	**67**	**36**	**14**	**8**	**4**	**1**
市 级	Municipal Level	65	65	34	13	7	4	
全 国	State Level	3	2	2	1	1		1
个 人	**Individual**	**338.5**	**249**	**263**	**56**	**38**	**41**	**30**
市 级	Municipal Level	278.5	207	235	46	33	38	27
全 国	State Level	60	42	28	10	5	3	3

表 14-15 举(承)办各级体育比赛情况
Sports Games of All Levels Held or Undertaken
(2008)

比赛级别	Levels	项目(项) Items (in number)	次数(次) Times (in number)	参加人次数(人次) Athletes (person-times)
总 计	**Total**	**48**	**159**	**170 754**
区级比赛	PNA Games	25	81	58 994
市级比赛	Shanghai Games	16	59	108 440
全国比赛	National Games	7	19	3 320

表 14-16 等级运动员和裁判员情况
Graded Athletes and Referees
(2008)

单位:人 (person)

项 目	Item	二级运动员 Grade-Ⅱ Athletes	裁判员 Referees	
			二级 Grade-Ⅱ	三级 Grade-Ⅲ
合 计	**Total**	**131**	**57**	
田 径	Track and Field	9		
排 球	Volleyball	24		
武 术	Martial Art	15		
篮 球	Basketball	5	9	
射 击	Shooting	12		
散 打	Sanda	1		
足 球	Football	29		
游 泳	Swimming	17		
棒 球	Baseball	8		
柔 道	Judo	2		
围 棋	Go	3		
乒乓球	Table Tennis		8	
车辆模型	Vehicle model		9	
羽毛球	Badminton		30	
射 箭	Archery	6		
信 鸽	Homing Pigeons		1	

表 14-17 全民健身活动设施情况
Facilities for Fitness Activities

指 标	Indicators	单 位 Unit	2006	2007	2008
农民健身家园	**Fitness Garden for Farmers**				
篮球场	Basketball Court	片 in number	14	24	51
羽毛球场	Badminton Court	片 in number	2	2	3
门球场	Goal Court	片 in number			40
社区公共运动场	**Community Public Sports Ground**				
篮球场	Basketball Court	片 in number	16	22	30
门球场	Goal Court	片 in number	6	7	12
网球场	Tennis Court	片 in number	4	6	7
羽毛球场	Badminton Court	片 in number			2
健身苑(点)数量	**Number of Fitness Court (Center)**	**片 in number**	**759**	**764**	**764**
健身苑	Fitness Court	个 in number	25	25	25
街道、镇	Subdistrict or Town	个 in number	21	21	21
体育系统	Sports System	个 in number	2	2	2
学 校	School	个 in number	2	2	2
健身点	Fitness Center	个 in number	734	739	739
街道、镇	Subdistrict or Town	个 in number	734	739	739
健身苑(点)面积	**Floor Space for Fitting Courts (Center)**	**万平方米 10 000 sq·m**	**88.32**	**88.32**	**88.32**
健身苑	Fitness Court	万平方米 10 000 sq·m	11.90	11.90	11.90
街道、镇	Subdistrict or Town	万平方米 10 000 sq·m	10.75	10.75	10.75
体育系统	Sports System	万平方米 10 000 sq·m	0.60	0.60	0.60
学 校	School	万平方米 10 000 sq·m	0.55	0.55	0.55
健身点	Fitness Center	万平方米 10 000 sq·m	76.42	76.42	76.42
街道、镇	Subdistrict or Town	万平方米 10 000 sq·m	76.42	76.42	76.42
健身器材配置数	**Number of Body Fitness Apparatus**	**件 set**	**9 005**	**9 005**	**9 005**
街 道	Subdistrict	件 set	4 310	4 310	4 310
镇	Town	件 set	4 599	4 599	4 599
专业体育场馆	Professional Stadium and Gymnasium	件 set	60	60	60
学 校	School	件 set	36	36	36

表 14-18　各类卫生机构、床位及人员数

Healthcare Institutions, Hospital Beds and Professionals by Institution Type (2008)

指　标	Indicators	机构数(个) Institution (unit)	床位数(张) Beds (bed)	人员数(人) Staff (person)	#卫生技术人员 Healthcare Professional	管理人员 Administrator
总　计	**Total**	**707**	**8 297**	**17 380**	**13 778**	**906**
新区卫生部门所属合计	**Those Run by PNA Government Healthcare Department**	**131**	**6 202**	**11 691**	**9 350**	**500**
医院合计	Total Hospitals	10	4 300	7 068	5 738	376
区级医院	District Hospitals	10	4 300	7 068	5 738	376
综合医院	Comprehensive Hospitals	5	3 150	6 185	5 013	362
专科医院	Specialized Hospitals	5	1 150	883	725	14
社区卫生服务中心	Community Health Service Center	30	1 902	4 058	3 277	96
社区卫生服务站	Community Health Service Stations	85				
专科防治所、站	Specialized Clinics and Stations	5		520	295	23
中学医学教育	Medical Education in Middle Schools	1		45	40	5
工业及其他部门合计	**Those of Industry and Other Organizations**	**576**	**2 095**	**5 689**	**4 428**	**406**
综合医院	Comprehensive Hospitals	2	313	516	360	41
专科防治站、所	Specialized Clinics and Stations	1		47	31	6
民办医疗机构	Clinics Run by Local People	91	1 366	3 086	2 257	293
个体诊所、工厂保健站	Individual Clinics, Factory Health Posts	305		668	656	
村卫生室	Village Clinics	167		278	278	
市三级医院	Municipal grade Ⅲ Hospitals	8	416	930	750	49
临床检测中心	Clinical Testing Center	2		164	96	17

表14-19 各类卫生技术人员数
Number of Healthcare Professionals
(2008)

单位:人 (person)

指标 Indicators		合计 Total	执业医师 Medical Practitioners	执业助理医师 Assistant Medical Practitioners	注册护士 Registered Nurses	药剂人员 Pharmaceutical Personnel	检验人员 Laboratorians	其他卫生技术人员 Other Healthcare Professionals
总计	**Total**	**13 778**	**5 773**	**336**	**5 120**	**709**	**608**	**1 232**
新区卫生部门所属合计	**Those Run by PNA Government hcare Department**	**9 350**	**3 749**	**254**	**3 521**	**523**	**416**	**887**
医院合计	Total Hospitals	5 738	2 117	23	2 539	247	206	606
区级医院	District Hospitals	5 738	2 117	23	2 539	247	206	606
综合医院	Comprehensive Hospitals	5 013	1 857	10	2 178	204	173	591
专科医院	Specialized Hospitals	725	260	13	361	43	33	15
社区卫生服务中心	Community Health Service Center	3 277	1 464	216	970	274	165	188
专科防治所、站	Specialized Clinics and Stations	295	168	15	12	2	45	53
卫生学校	Health Schools	40						40
工业及其他部门合计	**Those of Industry and Other Organizations**	**4 428**	**2 024**	**82**	**1 599**	**186**	**192**	**345**
综合医院	Comprehensive Hospitals	360	129	1	136	19	21	54
专科防治所、站	Specialized Clinics and Stations	31	20	4	3	1	3	
民办机构	Private Establishments	2 257	923	44	953	127	101	109
个体门诊部、工厂保健站	Individual Clinics, Factory Health Posts	656	459	33	144	8	5	7
村卫生室	Village Clinic	278	278					
上海儿童医学中心	Shanghai Children's Medical Center	750	212		363	31	24	120
检验中心	Inspection Center	96	3				38	55

表 14-20　区级医院基本情况
Statistics of PNA-level Hospitals
(2008)

指　标	Indicators	人员数（人） Staff (person)	#卫生技术人员 Healthcare Professionals	建筑面积（平方米） Floor Space (sq·m)	#业务用房 Floor Space for Treatment	床位数（张） Beds (bed)	全年诊疗人次（万人次） Annual Patients Treated (10 000 person-times)
总　计	**Total**	**7 068**	**5 738**	**277 677**	**219 699**	**4 300**	**613.13**
综合医院	**Comprehensive Hospitals**	**6 185**	**5 013**	**212 540**	**168 683**	**3 150**	**520.31**
东方医院	Oriental Hospital	1 670	1 412	62 608	49 577	817	140.72
浦东新区人民医院	PNA People's Hospital	1 101	898	40 690	27 106	598	105.62
浦东新区公利医院	PNA Gongli Hospital	1 197	954	29 587	22 816	482	117.34
第七人民医院	No,7 People's Hospital	1 230	945	46 655	36 184	642	88.04
浦南医院	Punan Hospital	987	804	33 000	33 000	611	68.59
专科医院	**Specialized Hospitals**	**883**	**725**	**65 137**	**51 016**	**1 150**	**92.82**
传染病院	Infectious Disease Control Hospital	85	63	4 619	2 799	100	2.27
精神卫生中心	Mental Health Centre	163	130	22 396	17 634	475	5.09
肺科医院	Pulmonary Disease Hospital	85	67	7 176	3 928	173	0.50
妇幼保健院	Maternity and Pediatric Hospital	282	249	17 031	14 455	200	33.46
中医医院	Chinese Medicine Hospital	268	216	13 915	12 200	202	51.50

表 14-21 综合医院工作质量情况
Workload in Comprehensive Hospitals

指 标 Indicators		手术人数(人次) Operations (person-time)		入院病人数(人次) Inpatients(person-time)		出院病人数(人次) Inpatients Leaving for Home(person-time)	
		2007	2008	2007	2008	2007	2008
总 计	**Total**	**30 397**	**30 985**	**93 150**	**94 323**	**93 317**	**94 144**
东方医院	Oriental Hospital	9 213	9 711	22 428	23 276	22 439	23 272
浦东新区人民医院	PNA People's Hospital	6 677	6 288	22 264	21 595	22 349	21 561
浦东新区公利医院	PNA Gongli Hospital	5 943	5 783	17 301	17 144	17 418	17 046
第七人民医院	No. 7 People's Hospital	4 273	4 694	14 803	15 476	14 778	15 441
浦南医院	Punan Hospital	4 291	4 509	16 354	16 832	16 333	16 824

表 14-21 续表 Continued

指 标 Indicators		出院者平均住院日数(日) Average Days of Inpatients at Hospital(day)		平均病床工作日(日) Average Beds Exploitation(day)		病床使用率(%) Rate of Beds Exploitation(%)	
		2007	2008	2007	2008	2007	2008
总 计	**Total**	**11.97**	**11.92**	**374.02**	**353.94**	**102.47**	**96.97**
东方医院	Oriental Hospital	133.16	12.64	372.96	364.65	102.18	99.90
浦东新区人民医院	PNA People's Hospital	10.12	10.02	359.19	359.38	98.41	98.46
浦东新区公利医院	PNA Gongli Hospital	10.09	9.78	341.00	352.08	93.42	96.46
第七人民医院	No. 7 People's Hospital	13.37	13.94	320.35	326.44	87.77	89.43
浦南医院	Punan Hospital	13.62	13.66	517.51	364.83	141.78	99.95

表 14-22　医院诊疗人次和入院人数
Outpatients and Inpatients Treated
(2008)

指　标 Indicators		诊疗人次（万人次）Total Patients Treated (10 000 person-times)	#门、急诊 Outpatients or Emergency Treatment	入院人数（万人次）Inpatients (10 000 person-times)	每百诊次的入院人数（人）Inpatients Per 100 Total Patient/time (person)	出院人数（万人次）Inpatients Leaving for Home (10 000 person-times)
总　计	**Total**	**1 918.83**	**1 870.07**	**16.60**	**0.87**	**16.56**
区级及以上医院	District Hospitals	613.13	588.54	11.49	1.87	11.46
综合医院	Comprehensive Hospitals	520.31	499.60	9.43	1.81	9.41
专科医院	Specialized Hospitals	92.82	88.94	2.06	2.22	2.05
街道、镇医院	Subdistrict/Town Hospitals	916.90	900.84	1.49	0.16	1.49
其　他	Others	388.80	380.69	3.62	0.93	3.61

表 14-23　医疗业务效益指标
Indicators of Medical Results

指　标	Indicators	单　位 Unit	2005	2006	2007	2008
综合医院、专科医院	**Comprehensive and Specialized Hospitals**					
手术人数	Operations	人次 person-time	32 404	39 742	43 952	39 314
病床周转率	Turnover of Beds	次/床 time/bed	26.77	28.42	28.75	26.96
病床平均工作日	Average Bed in Service	日/床 day/bed	374.72	373.38	380.68	365.08
病床使用率	Rate of Bed Exploitation	%	102.66	102.30	104.30	100.02
出院者平均住院日	Average Days of Inpatient at Hospital	日 day	13.37	12.77	12.44	13.29
平均每张处方费用	**Average Fee for Each Prescription**	**元 yuan**	**93.66**	**92.20**	**97.63**	**103.54**
#综合医院	Comprehensive Hospitals	元 yuan	106.56	103.47	107.93	119.59
专科医院	Specialized Hospitals	元 yuan	101.84	79.05	109.29	121.23
街道、镇医院	Subdistrict/Town Hospitals	元 yuan	85.77	87.87	90.60	93.63
其他部门医院	Other Hospitals	元 yuan	110.23	95.16	111.02	115.23
综合医院出院病人平均医疗费	**Average Medical Fee of Inpatients at Comprehensive Hospitals**	**元/人 yuan/person**	**7 499.06**	**7 473.32**	**7 312.29**	**8 327.00**

表 14-24 家庭病床情况
Patients Staying in Family Ward Beds

指 标	Indicators	单 位 Unit	2000	2005	2007	2008
中西医师(士)赴家庭病床诊疗总人次	Total Number of Doctors of Traditional Chinese Medicine and of Western Medicine Treating Patients in Family Ward Beds	人次 person-times	102 539	109 579	129 852	138 054
期初原有家庭病床数	Number of Family Ward Beds at Beginning of Term	张 bed	1 817	2 097	2 383	2 341
期内新建家庭病床数	Number of New Established Family Ward Beds During the Term	张 bed	3 779	4 340	4 116	4 742
期内撤床病人数	Number of Patients Leaving Family Ward Beds During the Term	人 person	3 861	4 260	4 158	4 610
治 愈	Patients Cured	人 person	34	1	2	1
好 转	Patients Getting Better	人 person	484	149	292	193
稳 定	Patients Turning Stablized	人 person	2 798	3 452	3 096	3 581
转 院	Patients Turning to Another Hospital	人 person	293	419	465	562
要求撤床	Patients Asking to Cancel the Ward Beds	人 person	152	204	233	205
死 亡	Dead Patients	人 person	100	35	70	68
期末实有家庭病床数	Acutual Number of Family Ward Beds at End of Term	张 bed	1 735	2 177	2 341	2 473
期内家庭病床病人住床总床日数	Total Bed-days of Patients Staying in Familiy Ward Beds During the Term	天 day	663 099	777 590	821 876	947 880
期内撤床病人住床总床日数	Total Bed-days of Patients Who Have Stayed in Ward Beds Asking to Cancel Ward Beds During the Term	天 day	48 716	610 522	458 379	621 215
期内撤床病人诊疗总床日数	Total Bed-days of Patients Who Have Taken Medical Care Asking to Cancel Ward Beds During the Term	人次 person-times	61 482	90 942	70 410	80 626

表 14-25　公民义务献血、用血情况
Voluntary Blood Donation and Blood Transfusion

指　标	Indicators	单　位 Unit	2006	2007	2008
献血人次	Number of Person-times Who Voluntarily Donate Their Blood	人份 in number	31 094	31 926	33 191
无偿献血占献血人次比重	Ratio of Person-times Who Voluntarily Donate Their Blood in Total Number of Blood Donations	%	100.0	100.0	100.0
用血人次	Number of Person-times for Blood Transfusion				
#全　血	Whole Blood	人次 person-time	156	162	154
红细胞	Red Blood Cell	人次 person-time	27 033	28 752	31 143
血　浆	Blood Plasma	人次 person-time	33 370	29 229	32 598

表 14-26　主要年份前十五位疾病死亡原因及构成
Death Causes of 15 Major Diseases and Their Composition in Main Years

单位:%　　(%)

疾病死亡原因	Cause of Death	构成比 Composition Rate					
		1997	2000	2005	2006	2007	2008
循环系统病	Circulatory System Disease	35.85	32.40	34.55	34.08	34.93	35.21
肿　瘤	Tumor	26.87	30.40	31.04	32.03	31.09	30.68
呼吸系病	Respiratory Disease	16.11	13.80	11.00	10.12	10.25	10.57
损伤和中毒	Trauma & Toxicosis	5.86	6.30	5.48	5.66	5.39	4.95
消化系病	Digestive Disease	2.57	2.90	2.70	2.84	2.82	2.65
内分泌代谢免疫病	Internal Secretion, Metabolic & Immunity Diseases	2.64	2.70	4.10	4.30	4.13	3.76
传染病寄生虫病	Infectious Disease, Pardsitic Disease	1.94	2.10	1.52	1.78	1.77	1.43
精神病	Mental Disease	1.66	1.90	0.97	0.76	0.76	0.86
泌尿生殖系病	Genitourinary Disease	1.10	1.11	0.93	0.86	0.94	0.97
神经系病	Neuro Disease	0.66	0.62	0.78	0.92	0.90	1.00
先天异常	Congenital Anomaly	0.48	0.35	0.27	0.27	0.23	0.22
血液造血器官疾病	Haematopoietic Tissue Disease	0.24	0.29	0.34	0.27	0.31	0.30
新生儿病	Disease of the New-born	0.22	0.11	0.10	0.11	0.13	0.19
妊娠分娩产褥症	Pregnancy/Childbirth/Puerperium Disease	0.01			0.01	0.01	0.02
肌肉骨骼和结缔组织疾病	Diseases of Muscle, Bones and Connective Tissues						0.44
其他疾病	Others Diseases	3.79	5.02	6.22	4.66	4.94	5.74
诊断不明	Acatalepsia						1.03

主要统计指标解释

学　校

指按国家规定的设置标准和审批程序批准设立的，招收适龄人口实施各级各类教育活动的教育机构。

普通高等学校

指按照国家规定的设置标准和审批程序批准举办的，通过全国普通高等学校统一招生考试，招收高中毕业生为主要培养对象，实施高等教育的全日制大学、独立设置的学院和高等专科学校、高等职业学校和其他机构。

大学、独立设置的学院主要实施本科层次以上教育，高等专科学校、高等职业学校实施专科层次教育，其他机构是承担国家普通招生计划任务不计校数的机构。包括普通高等学校分校和批准筹建的普通高等学校等。

成人高等学校

指按国家规定的设置标准和审批程序举办的，通过全国成人高等教育统一招生考试，招收高中毕业或同等学历的人员为主要培养对象，利用函授、业余、脱产的多种形式对其实施高等学历教育的学校。包括：职工高等学校、农民高等学校、管理干部学院、教育学院、独立函授学院、广播电视大学、其他机构等。

民办的其他高等教育机构

指经省、自治区、直辖市教育行政部门审批并颁发办学许可证，但不具有颁发学历文凭资格的实施高等教育的单位。学历文凭考试机构是指民办的经教育行政部门专门批准，进行全日制高等教育的其他高等教育机构。

中等专业学校

指经县或县以上教育行政部门批准设立，招收初中毕业生实施中等专业课程教育的教学机构。

职业中学（职业高中、职业初中）

指经县或县以上教育行政部门批准设立，招收小学或初中毕业生实施中等职业技术教育的教学机构。按学校性质类别可分为：独立设置的职业中学（包括：职业初中、职业高中、职业初高中合设学校）；附设有普通中学班的职业中学。

普通中学（普通高中、普通初中）

普通中学分为普通高级中学和普通初级中学两个阶段。普通初级中学是指独立设置的招收小学毕业的适龄人口进行初级中等基础教育的机构；普通高级中学是指独立设置的招收初中毕业的适龄人口进行高级中等基础教育的机构；完全中学是指普通初、高中合设的教育机构；一贯制学校是指在一所学校连续实施中小学教育的机构。其中包括实施九年义务教育的九年一贯制学校和实施高中教育的十二年一贯制学校。（说明：一贯制学校的办学条件如能划分为小学、初中、高中，则分开填报；如不能划分清楚，可按就高不就低的方法填入初中、高中报表中，不能重复填写。）

普通小学

指由区或区以上教育行政部门批准，招收学龄儿童实施初等教育的教学机构。

幼儿园

指招收三周岁以上（含三周岁）学龄前幼儿，对其进行保育和教育的单位。

特殊教育学校

指本市独立设置的招收盲聋哑和智残儿童，以及其他特殊需要的儿童、青少年进行普通或职业初、中等教育的教学机构。

文化机构

是指专门从事文化工作具有法人资格，独立核算的事业，企业单位，以及单独核算，附属于事业单位的经营性专业文化活动单位。包括从事艺术、图书馆、档案馆、群众文化、文物保护、艺术教育、艺术研究、文化娱乐、新闻出版等机构，以及其他文化机构。

等级运动员人数

指经考核正式批准授予等级运动员称号的人数。运动员等级分为国际级运动健将、运动健将、一级运动员、二级运动员、三级运动员、少年级运动员。该指标主要反映运动员队伍的技术质量水平。

等级裁判员人数

指经考核正式批准授予等级裁判员称号的人数。裁判员等级分为国际裁判、国家级裁判、一级裁判、二级裁判、三级裁判。该指标主要反映裁判员队伍的技术质量水平。

卫生机构

卫生机构是指从卫生行政部门取得《医疗机构执业许可证》，或从民政、工商行政、机构编制管理部门取得法人单位登记证书，为社会提供医疗保健、疾病控制、卫生监督服务或从事医学研究、医学教育等卫生单位和卫生社会团体。

医疗机构

医疗机构是指根据《医疗机构管理条例》的规定，经登记取得《医疗机构执业许可证》的机构。包括医院、社区卫生服务中心（站）、卫生院、门诊部、诊疗所、医务室、村卫生室、妇幼保健院（所、站）、专科疾病防治院（所、站）、急救中心、临床检验中心。

医　院

医院指设有固定床位，能收容病人住院并能为病人提供医疗、护理服务的医疗机构，包括县及县以上医院、农村乡卫生院和其他医院三部分。县及县以上医院按业务性质不同分为综合医院和专科医院。

卫生技术人员

卫生技术人员指从事卫生技术工作并在卫生事业机构领取劳动报酬的专业人员。包括中医师、西医师、中西医结合高级医师、护师、中药师、西药师、检验师、其他技师、中医士、西医士、护士、助产士、中药剂士、西药剂士、检验士、其他技士、其他中医、护理员、中药剂员、西药剂员、检验员、其他初级卫生技术人员。

医　生

医生指在医疗、预防保健机构工作且取得《执业医师证书》的执业医师和执业助理医师。

EXPLANATORY NOTES TO MAJOR STATISTICAL INDICATORS

School Institutions

School Institutions refer to education establishment set up according to the government evaluation and approval procedures, enrolling population of the right age, providing various phase education activity.

Regular Institutions of Higher Education

Regular Institutions of Higher Learning refer to educational establishments set up according to the government evaluation and approval procedures, enrolling graduates from senior secondary schools and providing higher education courses and training for senior professionals. They include full-time universities, colleges, high professional schools, high professional vocational schools and others.

Universities and colleges are mainly providing undergraduate courses; those high professional schools and high professional vocational schools are mainly providing professional trainings; and others refer to educational establishments, which are responsible for enrolling students but not covered in the total number of schools, including: branch schools of universities and colleges, and universities and colleges that have been proved and prepared to construct.

Institutions of Higher Education for Adults

Institution of Higher Learning for Adults refer to educational establishments, set up in line with relevant rules approved by the government, enrolling personnel with senior secondary schools or equivalent education, and providing higher education courses in many forms of correspondence, spare time, or full time for adults. Institutions of higher schools for adults include schools of higher educations for staff and workers, schools of higher education for peasants, colleges for management cadres, pedagogical colleges, independent correspondence colleges, Radio and TV universities and other educational establishment, etc.

Civil Other Institution of Higher Education

Civil Other Institution of Higher Education refer to educational establishment set up according to rules approved and permitted by educational administration department of municipal government and not be provided with qualification to awarding diploma.

Specialized Secondary schools

Specialized Secondary schools refer to educational establishment set up according to approval and permission by educational administration department of district and above government, enrolling graduates from junior secondary schools and providing secondary professional education courses.

Vocational Secondary Schools (senior secondary schools and junior secondary schools)

Vocational Secondary Schools (senior secondary schools and junior secondary schools) refer to educational establishment set up according to approval and permission by educational administration department of district and above government, enrolling graduates from primary schools and junior secondary schools and providing secondary vocational education courses.

Regular Secondary Schools (senior secondary schools and junior secondary schools)

Regular Secondary Schools (senior secondary schools and junior secondary schools) are classified as senior secondary schools and junior secondary schools. Junior Secondary Schools refer to educational establishment enrolling graduates from primary schools and providing junior secondary educational courses. Senior Secondary Schools refer to educational establishment enrolling graduates from junior secondary schools and providing higher secondary educational courses.

Regular Primary Schools

Regular Primary Schools refer to educational establishment set up according to approval and permission by educational administration department of district and above government, enrolling graduates from children of school age and providing primary educational courses.

Kindergartens

Kindergartens refer to nursery and education establishment, enrolling children in 3 years old and above.

Special Education Schools

Special Education Schools refer to educational establishments set up independently, enrolling blind, deaf, dumb, amentia or other special children, and educational establishment, providing regular or vocational junior and senior secondary education for hobbledehoy.

Cultural Institutions

Cultural Institution refers to undertaking and business institutions which specialize in cultural work and have legal personality and independent accounting system, and those professional cultural institutions attached to undertaking institutions and have independent accounting system. It includes institutions specialize in art, library, archives, mass culture, historical relic protection, art education, art research, entertainment, news and publication and other cultural institutions.

Number of Athletes in Grades

Number of Athletes in Grades refers to the number of athletes who have been given titles through examination. The titles of athletes include international masters of sports, masters of sports, first-grade, second-grade and third-grade sportsmen and young athletes. This indicator reflects skill of the athletes.

Number of Referees in Grades

Number of Referees in Grades refers to the number of referees who have been given titles after examination. They are classified as international referees, national referees and referees of the first, second and third grades. This indicator reflects the skill of referees.

Health Care Institutions

Health Care Institution refers to medical institutions and corporations providing health care, disease control and medical supervision service or engaged in medical research and medical education, which obtain Medical Institution Practice License from Medical Administration or Corporative Registration Certificate from Civil Administration, Commercial Administration or Organizational Management Administration.

Medical Organizations

Medical Institution refers to institutions which register Medical Institution Practice License according to Medical Institution Management Regulation, including hospitals, community medical service centers, medical house, clinics, dispensaries, medicine rooms, village medicine rooms, hospitals for maternity and kids care, special disease cure hospitals, first-aid center, clinical inspection centers.

Hospitals

Hospitals refer to medical institutions with permanent hospital beds, which are able to take in patients and provide them with medical and nursing services. Hospitals are classified into three categories: hospitals at or above the county level, hospitals of rural townships, and other hospitals. Hospitals at or above county level are divided into comprehensive and specialized hospitals.

Medical Professionals

Medical Professionals refers to those professionals engaged in medical work and receive salaries from medical institutions, including doctors of Chinese and Western medicine, senior doctors of integrated Chinese-Western medicine, head nurses, pharmacists of Chinese and Western medicine, laboratory specialists , other specialists, junior doctors of Chinese and Western medicine, nurses, midwives, druggists of Chinese and Western medicine, laboratory technicians, other technicians, other practitioners of Chinese medicine, nursing attendants, pharmacological workers of Chinese and Western medicine, laboratory workers and other primary medical personnel.

Doctors

Doctors refer to certified physicians and certified assistant physicians with certifications working in medical and health care and prevention agencies.

第十五篇

Chapter 15

法律、社会治安及其他

LAWS, PUBLIC ORDER AND OTHERS

SHANGHAI PUDONG NEW AREA STATISTICAL YEARBOOK

2009/上海浦东新区统计年鉴

表 15-1 律师、公证及调解工作基本情况
Lawyers, Notaries and Mediation

指 标	Indicators	单 位 Unit	2006	2007	2008
法律律师事务所	**Law Offices**	**个 unit**	**165**	**170**	**174**
合作制所	Cooperative Offices	个 unit	67	66	23
合伙所	Partner Offices	个 unit	84	89	135
个人所	Individual Offices	个 unit	14	15	16
律师工作人员	**Lawyer Staff**	**人 person**	**1 842**	**1 915**	**2 155**
# 专职律师	Full-time Lawyers	人 person	1 714	1 792	1 927
兼职律师	Part-time Lawyers	人 person	128	123	112
律师办理各类法律事务	**All Kinds of Legal Affairs Handled by Lawyers**				
担任法律顾问	Legal Advisers	家 unit	3 877	4 131	8 604
刑事诉讼辩护及代理	Litigation Defense and Legal Representation in Criminal Cases	件 piece	2 305	2 519	2 618
民事案件诉讼代理	Legal Representation in Civil Cases	件 piece	10 099	8 320	5 443
行政案件诉讼代理	Legal Representation in Administrative Cases	件 piece	215	115	105
非诉讼法律事务	Non-Litigation Legal Affairs	件 piece	7 842	11 018	5 226
公证工作	**Notarization**				
公证处	Notary Offices	个 unit	1	1	1
公证人员	Notarization	人 person	26	25	24
# 公证员	Notaries	人 person	24	23	20
办理各类公证文件	All Kinds of Notarial Documents Conducted	件 piece	19 499	18 234	19 930
国内公证	Notarization for Domestic Affairs	件 piece	8 387	8 032	8 027
涉外公证	Notarization Concerning Foreign Affairs	件 piece	9 613	9 175	10 853
涉港澳台公证	Notarization Concerning Affairs in Macao, Hong Kong and Tai Wan	件 piece	1 499	1 027	1 050
人民调解工作	**Mediation Work**				
专职司法助理员	Full-time Judicial Assistants	人 person	81	73	61
人民调解委员会	People's Mediation Commission	个 person	900	907	901
调解员	Mediators	人 person	5 445	4 118	4 562
调解民间纠纷	Mediation for Disputes among the People	件 piece	12 632	16 526	27 203

表 15-2　道路交通事故
Road Traffic Accidents

指　标	Indicators	单　位 Unit	2006	2007	2008
次　数	Number of Traffic Accidents	起 in number	1 737	965	869
死亡人数	Death Toll	人 person	203	185	182
伤残人数	Number of Wounded and Disabled	人 person	1 710	930	826
损失折款	Amount Converted from the Loss	万元 10 000 yuan	600	217	295

注：2007 年起"道路交通事故数"因统计方法改变,故不具可比性。
Note: The field of "Road Traffic Accidents" will not be comparable since we changed the statistic method for that field since 2007.

表 15-3　火灾事故
Fire Accidents

指　标	Indicators	单　位 Unit	2006	2007	2008
次　数	Number of Traffic Accidents	起 in number	755	503	406
#纵　火	Arson	起 in number	15	13	4
电　气	Electric	起 in number	244	192	194
违章操作	False Operations	起 in number	73	53	36
吸　烟	Cigarette Smoking	起 in number	122	37	19
生活用火不慎	Careless Use of Fire in Daily Life	起 in number	175	107	47
玩　火	Playing with Fire	起 in number	25	12	10
自　燃	Spontaneous Ignition	起 in number	8	12	8
死亡人数	Death Toll	人 person	9	6	7
伤残人数	Number of Wounded and Disabled	人 person	8	6	14
损失折款	Amount Converted from the Loss	万元 10 000 yuan	484.3	432.7	384.1

表 15-4　社会治安
Public Order

指　标	Indicators	单　位 Unit	2006	2007	2008
刑事案件立案数	Number of Registered Criminal Cases	件 piece	18 844	18 809	18 302
行政(治安)案件查处	Investigation and Prosecution of Administrative (Public Order) Cases	件 piece	1 044 575	1 224 983	1 265 116
治安案件查处数	Number of Investigation and Prosecution of Public Order Cases	件 piece	122 142	118 163	99 081

表 15-5 档案管理
Archives Management

指 标	Indicators	单 位 Unit	2006	2007	2008
机构数	**Number of Institutions**	**个 Unit**	**1**	**1**	**1**
档案局(馆)	Archives Bureaus (Chanceries)	个 unit	1	1	1
从业人员	**Employees**	**人 person**	**68**	**67**	**68**
专 职	Full-time Employees	人 person	68	67	68
馆藏档案	**Collected Files**				
全 宗	Whole File	个 unit	237	243	249
案 卷	Rolls	万卷 10 000 rolls	150	156	177
录音、录象、影片档案	Archives of Records, Videos and Films	万盘 10 000 discs	0.14	0.14	0.14
照片档案	Photo Archives	万张 10 000 Pieces	6.77	7.80	9.63
底 图	Base Maps	万张 10 000 Pieces	0.21	0.21	0.21
电子档案	**Electric Archives**				
磁 盘	Discs	万盘 10 000 discs	0.03	0.03	0.03
光 盘	Compact Discs	万盘 10 000 discs	0.18	0.27	0.27
微缩胶片	**Microfiches**				
平 片	Plain Films	万张 10 000 Pieces	0.20	0.20	0.20
卷 片	Coiled Films	万米 10 000 meters	12.45	12.70	12.81
档案利用情况	**Utilization of Archives**				
利用卷次	Number of Roll-times Utilized	万卷次 10 000 roll-times	33.07	4.41	4.68
利用人次	Number of Person-times Utilized	万人次 10 000 Person-times	2.29	4.91	5.39
综合档案开放利用情况	**Open and Utilization of Comprehensive Archives**				
建国前案卷	Rolls Archived before Liberation	卷 roll	137	121	173
建国后案卷	Rolls Archived After Liberation	万卷 10 000 rolls	33.05	4.40	4.67
建筑面积	**Floor Space**	**平方米 sq·m**	**17 924**	**17 524**	**17 524**
#库 房	Storeroom	平方米 sq·m	8 200	8 200	8 200

注：2007 年起"利用卷次"统计口径作调整。
Note: The statistical approach for the field of "Number of Roll-times Utilized" was readjusted in 2007.

表 15-6 信访情况
Complaint Letters and Visits

指 标 Indicators		单 位 Unit	2006	2007	2008
信访办受理人民来信、来访数	**People's Letters and Visits Handled by Offices of Complaint Letters and Visits**	**件(批) piece (batch)**	**17 628**	**20 331**	**22 265**
来信数	Number of People's Letters	件(批) piece (batch)	14 298	15 454	15 759
#电子邮件	E-mails	件(批) piece (batch)	2 684	2 632	6 260
来访数	Number of Visits	件(批) piece (batch)	3 328	4 877	6 506
#来电数	Number of Calls	件(批) piece (batch)	2 792	2 192	2 995
按类型分	By Type				
#动迁问题	Resettlcment	件(批) piece (batch)	4 258	3 780	4 123
物业管理问题	Real Estate Management	件(批) piece (batch)	708	597	624
各类纠纷	All Kinds of Disputes	件(批) piece (batch)	1 272	1 190	1 411
环保问题	Environmental Protection	件(批) piece (batch)	707	1 014	989
规划问题	Urban Planning	件(批) piece (batch)	381	445	448
生活困难	Hard Life	件(批) piece (batch)	1 514	1 334	1 256
进京上访人次数	Number of Person-times Visiting Beijing	人次 person-times	757	911	1 243
到市政府集体上访批次	Number of Patch-times Visiting Municipal Government	批次 batch-times	106	96	165
到市政府集体上访人次	Number of Person-times Visiting Municipal Government	人次 person-times	2 515	2 445	3 674
信访办结率	Rate of Finish for Complaint Letters and Visits	%	100.0	100.0	100.0

表 15-7　法院收、结案情况
Cases Accepted and Ended by Courts

指　标	Indicators	单　位 Unit	2006	2007	2008
法院收案数	Number of Cases Accepted by Courts	件 piece	40 010	38 302	42 136
#刑　事	Criminal	件 piece	2 306	2 268	2 499
民　事	Civil	件 piece	22 048	21 401	23 572
#经　济	Economic	件 piece	5 129	4 975	5 494
婚姻家庭类	Marriage and Family	件 piece	5 629	4 491	5 234
行　政	Administrative	件 piece	183	226	278
法院结案数	Number of Cases Ended by Courts	件 piece	38 865	38 405	41 183
法院未结案数	Number of Cases Not Ended by Courts	件 piece	5 164	5 061	6 014
法院结案率	Rate of Cases Ended by Courts	%	88.3	88.4	87.3
法院上诉率	Rate of Appeals by Courts	%	24.2	27.7	26.3
法院实际执行率	Rate of Actual Executions by Courts	%	53.2	59.0	59.5
法院审限内结案率	Rate of Actual Executions by Courts	%	97.1	98.0	97.8

表 15-8　食品抽检合格率、集体性食物中毒
Acceptance Rate of Foods by Spot Checking, Collective Food Poisoning

指　标	Indicators	单　位 Unit	2006	2007	2008
食品抽检总体合格率	General Acceptance Rate of Foods by Spot Checking	%	82.3	90.8	90.2
集体性食物中毒发生次数	Number of Occurrences for Collective Food Poisoning	次 time	6		6
集体性食物中毒人数	Number of Persons Suffering from Collective Food Poisoning	人 person	120		186
集体性食物中毒发生率	Rate of Occurrences for Collective Food Poisoning	10/100 000	4.21		6.53

表 15-9　外事活动情况
Activities in Foreign Affairs

指　标 Indicators		2007		2008	
		批　数（批）Delegations (in number)	人　数（人）Visitors (person)	批　数（批）Delegations (in number)	人　数（人）Visitors (person)
接待外国人来访总计	**Foreigners Received**	**562**	**8 915**	**428**	**7 133**
#副总理以上国宾团	Deputy Prime Ministers and Above	3	80	5	37
部长级（含副部长）团	Ministers (Including Deputy Ministers)	18	185	8	63
其他政界人士团	Persons of Political/Government Circles	92	922	33	324
经贸界团	Businessmen	88	497	75	388
新闻界团	Newsreporters	23	182	24	201
其他团	Others	21	344	18	230
邀请外国人来访总计	Foreigners Invited	12 211	16 528	43 287	51 012
按签证性质分	By Type of Visa				
多次签证	Multi-Entry	1 224	1 400	1 545	1 667
一次性签证	One-Entry	10 987	15 128	41 742	49 345
按国别（地区）分	By Country/Region				
#美　国	United States of America		1 639		9 396
德　国	Germany		821		6 625
日　本	Japan		1 227		1 771
审批因公出国访问总计	Approved Overseas Visits on State Missions	928	3 562	758	3 154
按出国性质分	By Purpose				
经　贸	Business	862	3 185	720	2 934
非经贸	Non-Business	66	377	38	220
按出访国家（地区）分	By Country/Region				
#美　国	United States of America	108		70	
日　本	Japan	79		42	
中国香港	Hong Kong, China	60		51	

注：本表由浦东新区外事办公室提供。
Note: This table is provided by Pudong Foreign Affaires Office.

表 15-10　主要年份人大情况
Statistics of Deputies to the People's Congress in Main Years

指　标	Indicators	单　位　Unit	2000	2005	2007	2008
全国人大代表人数	Number of deputies to the National People's Congress	人 person	2	1	1	1
全国人大代表提出议案	Proposals suggested by deputies to NPC	件 piece	4	5		
市人大代表人数	Number of deputies to the Municipal People's Congress	人 person	70	80	81	81
#女　性	Female	人 person	13	19	26	26
市人大常委人数	Number of standing committee members in MPC	人 person	4	4	4	4
市人大代表提出议案	Proposals suggested by deputies to MPC	件 piece	5	4	6	3
新区人大代表人数	Number of deputies to PNA People's Congress	人 person	380	436	440	448
#女　性	Female	人 person	109	158	146	146
新区人大常委人数	Number of standing committee members in PPC	人 person	27	28	32	31
#女　性	Female	人 person	4	4	7	7
新区人大代表提出议案	Proposals suggested by deputies to PPC	件 piece		9	14	1

注：1. 本表由浦东新区人大提供。
　　2. 2000 年新区人大常委会成立之初，未设议案组。
Note: 1. This table is provided by Pudong People's Congress.
　　2. Since the standing committee of PNA People's Congress was established in 2000, the proposal group was not formed yet.

表 15-11　主要年份政协情况
Statistics of Political Consultative Conference Affairs in Main Years

指　标	Indicators	单　位　Unit	2000	2005	2007	2008
全国政协委员人数	National Political Consultative Conference Commissioners	人 person		7	11	12
市政协委员人数	Municipal Political Consultative Conference Commissioners	人 person		58	56	61
#女　性	Female	人 person		6	7	8
新区政协委员人数	PNA Political Consultative Conference Commissioners	人 person	270	379	400	414
#女　性	Female	人 person	47	84	103	115
新区政协常委人数	Standing Commissioners of PNA Political Consultative Conference	人 person	38	55	58	56
#女　性	Female	人 person	7	8	11	8
新区政协委员提案	Proposals Submitted by PNA Political Consultative Conference Commissioners	件 piece	82	205	232	212
#被采纳提案	Proposals Accepted	件 piece	53	165	179	198

注：1. 本表由浦东新区政协提供。
　　2. "全国政协委员人数"和"市政协委员人数"均指在浦东工作的政协委员人数。
Note: 1. This table is provided by Pudong People's Political Consultative Conference.
　　2. Both the item of "National Political Consultative Conference Commissioners" and that of "Municipal Political Consultative Conference Commissioners" refer to those who work in Pudong New Area.

表15-12　主要年份精神文明建设情况
Role Models in Main Years

单位:个　　(unit)

指　标	Indicators	2000	2005	2007	2008
市级文明社区	Model Community at Municipal Level	6	6	11	
市级文明镇	Model Town at Municipal Level	4	6	7	
文明小区	Model Quarters	298	393	393	634
#市　级	Municipal-level	119	208	208	264
文明村	Model Villages	102	101	101	122
#市　级	Municipal-level	27	53	53	49
文明开发园区	Model Development Parks	27	6	6	7
文明单位	PNA Model Institutions	469	484	484	553
#市　级	Municipal-level	52	113	113	137
军民共建先进集体(对)	Model Collective of Army-civilian (pair)	56	76	76	78
#市　级	Municipal-level	20	24	24	18
五好文明家庭(户)	Model Families (household)	199	203	211	241
"三八"红旗手(人)	Female Models (person)	252	306	283	290
#市　级	Municipal-level	33	32	30	28
"三八"红旗集体	Female Model Groups	83	99	93	97
#市　级	Municipal-level	8	11	8	8
文明班组	Model Crew	136	338	426	423
#市　级	Municipal-level	12	12	26	
区文明岗位	Model Post	66	202	138	141

注：1. 本表由浦东新区精神文明办公室、新区总工会和新区妇女联合会等单位提供。
2. 除"文明班组"和"红旗文明岗"外,表列各项均为每两年评选一次。

Note: 1. This table is jointly provided by Pudong Spiritual Civilization Office, Pudong Federation of Trade Unions, the Women's Federation, etc.
2. Except "Model Grew" and "Model Post", all the items in the listed table are choosen through public appraisal every two years.

主要统计指标解释

律　师

指依法取得律师执业证书,担任法律顾问,民事(刑事、行政)案件代理人、刑事案件辩护人、办理非诉讼业务,解答法律询问,代写法律事务文书等,为社会提供法律服务的人员。

公证人员

指在国家机关依法办理公证事务的司法人员。包括公证员、助理公证员和在公证处工作的其他人员。

公证文书

指公证处根据当事人申请,依照事实和法律,按照法定程序制作的,具有法律效力的司法证明文书。根据公证书用途和使用地,公证书分为国内公证书、国内经济公证书、涉外民事公证书、涉外经济公证书四类。

调解民间纠纷

指调解委员会按照法律规定,根据自愿原则,用说服教育的方法调解民间发生的有关民事权利和义务争执的件数,包括调解成功数和调解未成功数。该指标主要反映人民调解委员会的工作量。

立　案

指人民检察院对受理的报案、控告、举报或自首及自行发现的犯罪线索、犯罪嫌疑人进行初步调查后,认为存在职务犯罪事实和应追究刑事责任,并决定作为刑事案件进行侦查的诉讼活动,是追究犯罪的开始。该指标主要反映人民检察院依法将职务犯罪线索作为刑事案件进行侦查的诉讼活动。

EXPLANATORY NOTES TO MAJOR STATISTICAL INDICATORS

Lawyers

Lawyers are certified legal workers according to law, and who are employed by legal counseling firms to act as legal advisers, agents in criminal or civil lawsuits, or defenders in criminal lawsuits, or to handle non-litigious legal affairs, to advise on matters of law or to write legal papers for others, and provide service to the public.

Notary Personnel

Notary Personnel are judicial workers of the state notary organs handling notarization work according to law. They include notaries, assistant notaries, and other people working in notary firms.

Notary Documents

Notary Documents refer to the judicatory notary documents drawn up by the request of the party and are in accordance with facts and laws and following certain legal proceedings. According to usage and locality, the notary documents are divided into following 4 types: domestic notary documents, domestic economic notary documents, foreign-related civil notary documents and foreign-related economic notary documents.

Mediation of Civil Disputes

Mediation of Civil Disputes refers to number of cases made by mediation committees in mediating in civil disputes concerning civil rights and duties through persuasion and education in accordance with the provisions of law on a voluntary basis, so as to solve disputes by helping the parties involved come to an agreement and understanding, including those unsuccessful ones. This indicator reflects the workload of the mediation committees.

Acceptance of Case

Acceptance of Case refers to the decision made by the people's procuratorate office on reported cases, prosecution, impeachment, surrender, self-found criminal clues or suspects after initial investigation to confirm the act of crime and to start legal proceedings of the case as criminal case.

第十六篇

Chapter 16

城市建设

URBAN CONSTRUCTION

SHANGHAI PUDONG NEW AREA STATISTICAL YEARBOOK

2009 / 上海浦东新区统计年鉴

表 16－1 历年各类房屋构成情况

Composition of all Kinds of Buildings in Main Years (2003～2008)

单位:万平方米 (10 000 sq · m)

指 标	Indicators	2003	2004	2005	2006	2007	2008
总 计	**Total**	**8 438.64**	**9 634.22**	**10 430.29**	**11 150.90**	**11 504.03**	**12 567.85**
居住房屋	**Residential Buildings**	**5 725.13**	**6 000.71**	**6 430.87**	**6 883.96**	**7 147.99**	**7 835.57**
花园住宅	Garden Residence	178.22	280.66	297.66	306.66	333.67	357.77
公 寓	Apartments	19.62	19.62	19.62	19.62	19.62	19.62
新公房	Public Housing	5 143.34	5 639.23	6 063.46	6 516.55	6 747.57	7 411.05
新式里弄	New-styled Lanes	…	2.25	2.25	2.25	2.25	2.25
旧式里弄	Old-styled Lanes	350.38	50.52	39.45	37.45	37.45	37.45
简 屋	Simple Housings	33.51	8.37	8.37	1.37	7.37	7.37
其 他	Others	0.06	0.06	0.06	0.06	0.06	0.06
非居住房屋	**Non-Residential Buildings**	**2 713.50**	**3 633.51**	**3 999.42**	**4 266.94**	**4 356.04**	**4 732.28**
工 厂	Factories	416.46	624.14	684.14	695.14	724.14	786.25
学 校	Schools	193.85	213.93	256.35	272.35	278.94	297.94
仓库堆栈	Warehouses	67.93	80.93	83.88	92.78	92.78	108.58
办公建筑	Office Buildings	910.28	1 298.74	1 405.68	1 486.68	1 517.69	1 599.39
商场店铺	Emporiums and Shops	741.96	991.96	1 070.25	1 201.25	1 212.75	1 379.53
医 院	Hospitals	52.06	62.27	62.27	73.27	73.27	86.68
旅 馆	Hotels	95.74	95.74	131.02	141.02	141.02	151.22
影剧院	Theatres and Cinemas	12.80	12.80	12.80	12.80	12.80	12.80
其 他	Others	222.42	253.00	293.03	291.65	302.65	309.89

表16-2 八层以上房屋分布(至2008年累计)
Distribution of 8-storey and Above Buildings (Total by the End of 2008)

单位:万平方米 (10 000 sq·m)

类 别 Items		2007		2008		至2008年累计 Total by the End of 2008	
		幢 In Number	面 积 Area	幢 In Number	面 积 Area	幢 In Number	面 积 Area
总 计	**Total**	**202**	**167**	**870**	**828**	**3 151**	**3 719**
8~10层	8~10 Storeys	12	6	144	77	388	228
11~15层	11~15 Storeys	120	85	494	264	1 505	1 018
16~19层	16~19 Storeys	52	45	135	126	630	704
20~29层	20~29 Storeys	17	27	77	219	496	1 063
30层以上	30 Storeys and Above	1	4	20	141	132	705

表16-3 市政工程设施
Public Utilities

指 标 Indicators		单 位 Unit	2000	2005	2007	2008
城市道路长度	Length of Urban Roads	公里 km	835	960	619	619
城市道路面积	Area of Urban Roads	万平方米 10 000 sq·m	1 180	1 704	1 356	1 356
城市桥梁	Urban Bridges	座 unit	121	169	201	201
雨水、污水泵站	Pump Station for Rain/Sewage	座 unit	102	148	175	175
雨水、污水管长度	Length of Rain/Sewage Pipe	公里 km	1 196	1 858	2 121	2 720
公路里程	Length of Rural Highways	公里 km	511	905	1 079	1 060
公路面积	Area of Rural Highways	万平方米 10 000 sq·m	849	1 360	1 653	1 680
公路桥梁	Highway Bridges	座 unit	355	635	737	731

注:本表至表16-8由浦东新区环保局提供;2007年起道路长度和道路面积统计口径改变。

Note: The data in from this table to Table 16-8 are provided by Pudong Environmental Protection Bureau. The statistical approach has changed for the length and coverage of roads since 2007.

表 16-4 环境保护
Environmental Protection

指 标	Indicators	单 位 Unit	2000	2005	2007	2008
工业固体废物产生量	Amount of Industrial Solid Waste	万吨/年 10 000 tons/year	144	250	219	254
工业固体废物综合利用量	Comprehensive Utilization of Industrial Solid Waste	万吨/年 10 000 tons/year	137	242	212	229
工业废水排放量	Discharge of Industrial Waste Water	万吨/年 10 000 tons/year	12 520	7 103	6 842	6 755
#符合排放标准	Up to the Standards	万吨/年 10 000 tons/year	11 826	6 900	6 686	6 626
工业废气排放总量	Industrial Waste Gas Emission	万标立方米/年 10 000 standard cu · m/year	734	1 112	1 461	1 561
二氧化硫日平均值	Daily Average Amount of Sulphur Dioxide	毫克/立方米 milligram / cu · m	0.010	0.056	0.048	0.047
二氧化氮日平均值	Daily Average Amount of Nitrogen Dioxide	毫克/立方米 milligram / cu · m	0.018	0.046	0.046	0.043
可吸入颗粒物日平均值	Daily Average Amount of Energetic Particles	毫克/立方米 milligram / cu · m	0.116	0.081	0.078	0.075
区域环境噪声平均值	Average Value of Regional Ambient Noise	分贝 decibel	55.8	57.4	55.1	55.0
综合空气污染指数值	Comprehensive Air Pollution Indexes	年平均 year average	53.0	66.0	65.0	63.0
空气质量优良率	Rate of Fine Air Quality	%		89.3	91.2	93.1
污水纳管率	Rate of Sewage Piping	%		70.4	74.0	76.0

表16-5 城市环境卫生
Urban Environmental Sanitation

指 标	Indicators	单 位 Unit	2000	2005	2007	2008
清运垃圾	**Garbage Disposal**	**万吨 10 000 tons**	**101.50**	**104.22**	**124.14**	**117.16**
生活垃圾	Domestic Waste	万吨 10 000 tons	69.85	103.10	123.02	116.18
建筑垃圾	Construction Refuse	万吨 10 000 tons	31.65	1.12	1.12	0.98
清运粪便	**Night Soil Disposal**	**万吨 10 000 tons**	**27.69**	**31.45**	**31.61**	**31.64**
环境卫生设施	**Facilities of Environmental Sanitation**					
公共厕所	Public Restrooms	所 unit	123	219	331	342
垃圾箱桶	Garbage Bins/Cans	只 unit	8 516	9 216	10 423	10 831
废物箱	Litterbins	只 unit	3 989	8 317	9 369	13 373
倒粪站	Manure-Dumping Stations	个 unit	130	89	121	100
化粪池	Septic Tanks	个 unit	3 987	4 711	4 415	4 413
垃圾处理	**Trash Disposal**					
垃圾焚烧	Trash Burning	万吨 10 000 tons		44.49	48.12	46.03
焚烧垃圾发电量	Power Output by Trash Burning	万千瓦·时 10 000 kw·h		10 841	11 946	12 537
环卫机械总数	**Machineries Used in Environmental Sanitation**	**辆 vehicle**		**598**	**795**	**773**

表 16-6　园林绿化
Parks, Gardens and Green Space

指　标	Indicators	单　位 Unit	2000	2005	2007	2008
园林绿地面积	Total Area of Parks, Gardens and Green Space	万平方米 10 000 sq·m	3 830.15	8 439.52	8 300.37	8 923.84
#公共绿地	Public Green Space	万平方米 10 000 sq·m	1 465.08	4 154.71	4 369.94	4 452.15
单位附属绿地	Green Space of Organizations	万平方米 10 000 sq·m	1 332.11	1 508.15	1 546.82	1 772.06
居住区绿地	Residential Green Space	万平方米 10 000 sq·m	891.26	1 139.81	1 741.99	2 058.01
绿化覆盖面积	Coverage of Green Space	万平方米 10 000 sq·m	4 075.25	8 697.81	8 500.46	9 138.43
#建成区绿化覆盖面积	Green Coverage of Built Areas(%) in PNA	万平方米 10 000 sq·m	3 074.47	6 426.88	8 500.46	9 138.43
建成区绿化覆盖率	Coverage Rate of Urban Green Areas(%) in PNA	%	30.18	37.80	37.28	37.30
新辟、扩大各类绿地	New and Extended Green Space	万平方米 10 000 sq·m		199.50	399.54	709.27
#公共绿地	Public Green Space	万平方米 10 000 sq·m		78.97	111.24	101.10
公园个数	Park	个 unit	12	17	18	18
#免费公园	Ticket-free Parks	个 unit		15	15	15
公园面积	Area of Parks	万平方米 10 000 sq·m	162.62	214.25	328.98	328.98
#免费公园	Ticket-free Parks	万平方米 10 000 sq·m		68.88	68.88	68.88
人均公共绿地	Public Green Space Per Capita	平方米/人 sq·m/person	11.00	24.42	24.29	24.25
行道树年末累计数	Accumulated Trees on Streets	万株 10 000 pcs	30.40	36.79	18.33	20.07

注：因全市绿化管理部门对部分统计指标统计口径作调整，故 2007 年部分数据与 2006 年不具有可比性。
Note: Since departments of green management in Shanghai have already adjusted statistical approaches for some indicators, some data in 2007 are not comparable to those in 2006.

表16-7 水、电、煤气供应
Supply of Tap Water, Electricity and Gas

指 标 Indicators		单 位 Unit	2000	2005	2007	2008
自来水	**Tap Water**					
水厂生产能力	Capacity of Tap Water Plants	万立方米/日 10 000 cu·m/day	171.98	171.20	183.20	181.80
供水管道总长度	Length of Water Supply Pipes	公里 km	2 635	3 100	4 090	4 900
全年售水总量	Total Annual Volume of Water Sold	万立方米 10 000 cu·m	33 014	41 926	46 882	49 817
#工业用水	Industrial Water	万立方米 10 000 cu·m	14 678	10 526	11 623	11 369
生活用水	Domestic Water	万立方米 10 000 cu·m	17 655	21 749	25 690	26 891
每日平均售水量	Daily Average Tap Water Consumption	万立方米 10 000 cu·m	90	115	128	136
电 力	**Electricity**					
用电最高日负荷	Daily Maximum Load of Electricity	万千瓦 10 000 kw	146.70	285.70	349.60	380.57
全年售电量	Annual Electricity Sold	亿千瓦·时 100 million kwh	69.75	128.19	144.42	156.74
各类用电户数	Various Electricity Users	万户 10 000 households	82.14	117.91	130.08	130.81
天然气	**Natural Gas**					
管线长度	Length of Gas Pipes	公里 km	1 927	3 574	4 157	4 371
全年销售量	Annual Volume of Gas Sold	万立方米 10 000 cu·m	11 107	44 300	47 500	51 100
#生活用气	Domestic Use	万立方米 10 000 cu·m	4 540	18 700	15 907	18 467
家庭用天然气户数	Natural Gas-Using Household	万户 10 000 households	38.00	75.50	88.40	93.27
液化石油气	**Liquified Petroleum Gas (LPG)**					
全年销售量	Annual Volume of Gas Sold	吨 ton	35 790	52 000	41 000	40 848
#生活用气	Domestic Use	吨 ton	28 043	50 000	29 700	30 552
家庭用液化气户数	LPG-Using Households	万户 10 000 households	45.55	45.90	38.85	41.57

表 16-8 供电能力和用电量
Electricity Production, Capacity and Consumption

指 标	Indicators	单 位 Unit	2000	2005	2007	2008
电力架空线路	**Overhead Power Lines**					
110 千伏	110 kv	公里 km	78.49	69.66	57.18	57.18
35 千伏	35 kv	公里 km	375.60	342.71	331.51	294.88
10 千伏	10 kv	公里 km	1 883.71	1 739.54	1 673.27	1 635.31
电力电缆	**Electricity Cables**					
35 千伏	35 kv	公里 km	632	890	1 077	1 258
10 千伏	10 kv	公里 km	1 411	3 396	4 947	5 144
输电变压器	**Transformers for Transmitting Electricity**					
220 千伏	220 kv	台/万千伏安 set/10 000 kva	2/24	3/36	3/36	3/36
110 千伏	110 kv	台/万千伏安 set/10 000 kva	2/12.6	4/14.6	2/12.6	2/12.6
35 千伏	35 kv	台/万千伏安 set/10 000 kva	139/257.7	200/414.4	217/474.6	236/504.4
各类用电用户	Various Electricity Users	万户 10 000 households	82.14	117.91	130.08	130.81
用电量	Electricity Consumption	亿千瓦·时 100 million kwh	69.75	128.19	144.42	156.73
工业用电及普非动力	Industrial Power Consumption and Ordinary Non-Household Power Consumption	亿千瓦·时 100 million kwh	44.49	96.71	81.73	92.35
商业用电	Commerce	亿千瓦·时 100 million kwh	8.09	13.76	35.17	36.56
居民用电	Household	亿千瓦·时 100 million kwh	7.87	17.42	21.60	23.63
其他用电	Others	亿千瓦·时 100 million kwh	9.30	0.30	5.92	4.02
供电最高负荷	Maximum Load	万千瓦 10 000 kw	146.70	285.70	349.60	380.57
路灯盏数	Street Lamps	盏 in number	32 142	44 891	51 580	53 719
路灯功率	Power of Street Lamps	千瓦 kw	9 024	13 927	16 006	17 045

注：1. 从 2003 年起原“工业用电”和“乡办工业用电”两指标合并为“工业用电及普非动力”；
2. “城市照明用电”和“农村照明用电”合并为“居民用电”；2003 年以前资料的引用可按此口径调整；

Note：1. Since 2003, the two indicators “Industrial Power Consumption” and “Town Industrial Power Consumption” are mersed into “Industrial Power Consumption and Ordinary Non-Household Power Consumption”；
2. “Urban Illumiantion” and “Rural Illumination” are listed as “Residential Consumption of Electricity”. Data before 2003 are to be adjusted accordingly.

表 16-9 交通运输
Transportation

指 标	Indicators	单 位 Unit	2000	2005	2007	2008
公共交通	**Public Transport**					
年末实有公交线路条数	Routes of Public Transport(Year End)	条 route	97	108	128	153
年末运营线路长度	Length of Public Transport Routes (Year End)	公里 km	1 783	2 125	2 600	2 964
年末运营公共车辆	Public Transport in Operation (Year End)	辆 vehicle	1 817	2 041	2 019	2 578
全年运客量	Annual Passengers Carried	万人次 10 000 person-times	29 802	34 894	37 521	44 683
专线客运	**Public Feeder Bus System**					
专线客运线路条数	Routes of Public Feeder Buses	条 route	72	68	58	90
年末营运线路长度	Length of Routes in Operation	公里 km	2 191	2 069	1 880	2 922
运营专线车辆	Public Feeder Bus in Operation	辆 vehicle	1 136	1 575	1 370	1 877
全年运客量	Annual Passengers Carried	万人次 10 000 person-times	20 094	28 293	25 328	34 061
隧道大桥	**Tunnels and Bridges**					
越江隧道条数	Tunnel Across the Huangpu River	条 route	2	6	6	6
越江大桥座数	Bridge Across the Huangpu River	座 in number	3	4	4	4
越江桥隧道车道数	Number of Lanes on Tunnels and Bridges Across the Huangpu River	条 route	26	54	54	56
隧道、大桥过江车辆数	Vehicle Across the Huangpu River through Tunnels and Bridges	万车次 10 000 vehicle-times	12 800	19 354	30 264	30 408
# 外环隧道过江车辆数	Transport Through the Outer Ring Tunnel	万车次 10 000 vehicle-times		1 477	2 393	2 344
民用航空	**Civil Aviation**					
浦东机场旅客吞吐量	Passenger Capacity in Pudong International Airport	万人次 10 000 person-times		2 358	2 895	2 815
浦东机场货邮吞吐量	Volume of Cargo and Post Handled at Pudong International Airport	万吨 10 000 tons		185	251	263

注：本表由浦东新区建设和交通委员会提供。
Note: This table is provided by Pudong Construction and Traffic Commission.

表16-10 邮电通信设施和邮电业务量
Post and Telecommunications Facilities and the Volume of Business

指 标	Indicators	单 位 Unit	2000	2005	2007	2008
邮政设施	**Postal Facilities**					
邮电局、所	Post Office	个 unit	74	93	96	106
信筒、信箱	Mailbox	处 unit	591	624	539	609
报刊发行站	Newpaper and Magazine Distributors	个 unit	1 224	728	738	1 394
邮路单程长度	Length of Single-Way Post	公里 km	3 577	3 282	4 663	4 869
农村投递路线总长度	Total Length of Postal Routes	公里 km	3 514	3 691	3 892	4 270
邮运汽车	Postal Vehicle	辆 vehicle	132	108	203	219
邮政业务总量	**Business Value of Postal Service**					
邮政业务收入	Postal Service Income	万元 10 000 yuan		35 300	44 949	57 507
函 件	Mails	万件 10 000 pieces	4 514	5 409	13 167	17 847
包 件	Parcels	万件 10 000 pieces	37	94	142	96
汇 票	Drafts	万张 10 000 pieces	107	98	111	125
订销报刊累计数	Accumulated Circulation of Newspapers and Magazines	万份 10 000 pieces	12 493	11 750	13 116	15 118
特快专递	Special Express	万份 10 000 pieces	86	281	458	602
集邮业务	Stamp-Collecting Business	万枚 10 000 pieces	1 549	354	169	178
邮政储蓄年末收储余额	Postal Savings Balance (Year End)	万元 10 000 yuan	129 865	235 230	595 921	706 081
电讯设施、用户及业务收入	**Telecommunication Facilities, Subscribers and Operating Income**					
本地电话局用交换机容量	Urban Switchboard Capacity	万门 10 000 units	110	146	156	160
本地电话用户数	Local Telephone Users	万户 10 000 households	77	118	126	128
电信宽带用户数	Subscribers of Telecommunication Broad-Band	门 unit		281 408	458 657	547 198
电信业务收入	Telecommunication Income	万元 10 000 yuan		119 250	215 184	243 805
网络互动电视(IPTV)	Internet Interactive TV Network	线 Line			31 504	118 842
"我的 e 家"用户	"My e-Home" Subscribers	户 Household			155 537	314 957

注：1. 本表由浦东邮政局和电信局提供。
2. 电信业务收入，不包括移动通信和中国联通以及与其结算的业务量。

Note: 1. This table is jointly provided by Pudong Post Office and Telecommunication Office.
2. The business value of China Mobile and China Unicom as well as the related business is not included in the Telecommunication Income.

表16-11 房屋拆迁情况
Housing Resettlement

指 标 Indicators		单 位 Unit	2000	2005	2007	2008
房屋完成拆迁总户数	**Total Resettlement**	**户 household**	**13 311**	**23 294**	**30 173**	**1 570**
重大项目拆迁	Resettlement Because of Key Investment Projects	户 household		18 288	14 797	978
企事业单位	Resettlement of Enterprises and Institutions	户 household		351	827	146
公 房	Resettlement of Public Housing Residents	户 household		4 487	1 607	
私 房	Resettlement of Private Housing Residents	户 household		13 361	12 194	832
个体工商	Resettlement of Individuals Engaged in Industry and Commerce	户 household		89	169	
旧城改造拆迁	Resettlement Because of Renovation of Old Towns	户 household	5 720	211	1 621	446
其 他	Others	户 household	7 591	4 795	13 755	146
完成拆迁总面积	**Tota Area of Resettlement**	**万平方米 10 000 sq・m**	**184.34**	**474.63**	**721.56**	**53.84**
重大项目拆迁	Resettlement Because of Key Investment Projects	万平方米 10 000 sq・m		363.14	376.96	33.90
企事业单位	Resettlement of Enterprises and Institutions	万平方米 10 000 sq・m		59.67	153.14	17.05
公 房	Resettlement of Public Housing Residents	万平方米 10 000 sq・m		22.34	8.34	
私 房	Resettlement of Private Housing Residents	万平方米 10 000 sq・m		277.46	214.09	16.85
个体工商	Resettlement of Individuals Engaged in Industry and Commerce	万平方米 10 000 sq・m		3.67	1.39	
旧城改造拆迁	Resettlement Because of Renovation of Old Towns	万平方米 10 000 sq・m	31.85	5.83	7.74	12.86
#企事业单位	Resettlement of Enterprises and Institutions	万平方米 10 000 sq・m	7.61	3.81	0.55	4.79
其 他	Others	万平方米 10 000 sq・m	152.49	105.66	336.86	7.08

注：本表由浦东新区建设和交通委员会提供。
Note: This table is provided by Pudong Construction and Traffic Commission.

主要统计指标解释

城市基础设施

城市基础设施包括电力建设、交通运输、邮电通信、市内公共交通、自来水、煤气、市政建设、园林绿化、环境卫生等。

道路长度

道路长度指除土路外,路面经过铺装宽度在3.5米以上的道路,包括高级、次高级道路和普通道路。

城市园林绿地面积

指报告期末用作园林和绿化的各种绿地面积。包括公共绿地、居住区绿地、单位附属绿地、防护绿地、生产绿地、道路绿地和风景林地面积。

不包括:

(1) 屋顶绿化、垂直绿化、阳台绿化和室内绿化。

(2) 以物质生产为主的林地、耕地、牧草地、果园和竹园等。

(3) 城市总体规划中不列入绿地的水域。

公共绿地

公共绿地指向公众开放的市级、区级、居住区级各类公园、街旁游园,包括其范围内的水域。其中居住区级公园应不小于1万平方米,街旁游园的宽度不小于8米,面积不小于400平方米。

供水管道长度

指从送水泵至用户水表之间所有管道的长度。不包括新安装尚未使用的管道。

生活用水

生活用水包括公共服务用水和居民家庭用水。公共服务用水指为城市社会公共生活服务的用水。包括行政事业单位、部队营区和公共设施服务、社会服务业、批发零售贸易业、旅馆饮食业以及其他公共服务业等单位的用水。居民家庭用水指城市范围内所有居民家庭的日常生活用水。包括城市居民、农民家庭、公共供水站用水。

工业固体废弃物产生量

指报告期内企业在生产过程中产生的固体状、半固体状和高浓度液体状废弃物的总量,包括危险废物、冶炼废渣、粉煤灰、炉渣、煤矸石、尾矿、放射性废物和其他废物等;不包括矿山开采的剥离废石和掘进废石(煤矸石和呈酸性或碱性的废石除外)。酸性或碱性废石指采掘的废石其流经水、雨淋水的pH值小于4或pH值大于10.5者。

工业固体废物综合利用量

指通过回收、加工、循环、交换等方式,从固体废物中提取或者使其转化为可以利用的资源、能源和其他原材料的固体废物量(包括当年利用往年的工业固体废物累计贮存量),如用作农业肥料、生产建筑材料、筑路等。综合利用量由原产生固体废物的单位统计。

工业废水排放量

工业废水排放量指经过企业厂区所有排放口排到企业外部的工业废水量。包括生产废水、外排的直接冷却水、超标排放的矿井地下水和与工业废水混排的厂区生活污水,不包括外排的间接冷却水(清污不分流的间接冷却水应计算在内)。

工业废水排放达标量

指报告期内废水中各项污染物指标都达到国家或地方排放标准的外排工业废水量,包括未经处理外排达标的,经废水处理设施处理后达标排放的,以及经污水处理厂处理后达标排放的。

工业废气排放量

工业废气排放量指企业厂区内燃料燃烧和生产工艺过程中产生的各种排入空气的含有污染物的气体总量,按标准状态〔273K,101 325Pa〕计算。测算公式为:

工业废气排放量 = 燃料燃烧过程中废气排放量 + 生产工艺过程中废气排放量

生活垃圾清运量

指报告期内收集和运送到垃圾处理厂(场)的生活垃圾数量。生活垃圾指城市日常生活或为城市日常生活提供服务的活动中产生的固体废物以及法律行政规定的视为城市生活垃圾的固体废物。包括:居民生活垃圾、商业垃圾、集市贸易市场垃圾、街道清扫垃圾、公共场所垃圾和机关、学校、厂矿等单位的生活垃圾。

运营公交车辆数

指年末公交企业(单位)用于运营业务的全部车辆数。以企业(单位)固定资产台帐中已投入运营的车辆数为准。

邮政业务总量

指以货币表现的邮政部门用于邮政服务的总数量。它综合反映了一定时期邮政工作的总成果，是研究邮政业务量构成和发展趋势的重要指标。它用各种邮政分类业务量，如函件件数、电报份数、订销报刊累计份数等，分别乘以相应的平均单位(不变价)，加总后再加上其他业务收入求得。

局用交换机容量

指安装在电信企业用于接续本地固定电话的电话交换机容量。

住宅电话用户

指安装在居民住宅或农民家里并按照住宅电话用户登记注册和收费的电话用户。包括私人付费、单位付费和按规定免费安装的住宅电话用户。

EXPLANATORY NOTES TO MAJOR STATISTICAL INDICATORS

Urban Infrastructure Facilities

Urban Infrastructure Facilities include facilities for power generating, transportation, post and telecommunication, urban public transportation, supply of tap water and gas, development of municipal engineering, city landscaping and sanitation.

Length of Roads

Length of Roads refers to the roads with a paved surface, and with a width of more than 3 – 5 meters, including high quality, medium quality and ordinary roads.

Area of Urban Gardens and Green Areas

Area of Urban Gardens and Green Areas refers to the total area occupied for green projects at the end of the reference period, including public green land, green land in residential quarters, green land attached to institutions, protection green land, production green land, roadside green land and forest in scenic spots. It does not include the following:

(1) Greenery and plants on roofs, balconies, indoors and vertical green areas;

(2) Forest, cultivated land grassland, orchards and bamboo grooves that are for production purpose and etc.;

(3) Water areas that are not included in urban master plan as green land.

Public Green Area

Public Green Area refers to green areas open to the public such as municipal, community and neighborhood parks and roadside parks, including waters within parks. Neighborhood parks should occupy an area larger than 10,000 square meters, and the width of roadside parks should occupy an area larger than 400 square meters, with a width of more that 8 meters.

Length of Water Supply Pipelines

Length of Water Supply Pipelines refers to the total length of all the pipelines between the water pumps and the user's water meters, excluding pipelines newly installed but not used yet.

Consumption of Water for Residential Use

Consumption of Water for Residential Use refers to the water consumption of households for daily life and the water consumption of public service facilities. The latter refers to water consumption for urban public services, including the consumption of government agencies and public institutions, military barracks, public facilities, wholesale and retail outlets, restaurants, hotels, and other units providing public services. Household water consumption refers to consumption of water for daily life of all households in the boundary of cities, including households of urban residents and farmers, and public water supply stations.

Industrial Solid Wastes Produced

Industrial Solid Wastes Produced refers to total volume of solid, semi-solid and high concentration liquid residues produced by industrial enterprises from production process in a given period of time, including hazardous wastes, slag, coal ash, gangue, tailings, radioactive residues and other wastes, but excluding stones stripped or dug out in mining (gangue and acid or alkaline stones not included). A stone is acid or alkaline depending on the pH value of the water below 4 or above 10.5 when the stone is in, or soaked by, the water.

Volume of Industrial Solid Wastes Utilized in a Comprehensive Way

Volume of Industrial Solid Wastes Utilized in a Comprehensive Way refers to the volume of solid wastes from which useful materials can be extracted or which can be changed into utilizable resources, energy or other materials, including the volume of industrial solid wastes stored up in previous years and utilized in the current year, such as the solid wastes utilized as fertilizers, building materials, for making roads or for other purposes. Statistical data on utilization of industrial solid wastes are collected by solid wastes producing units.

Volume of Industrial Waste Water Discharged

Volume of Industrial Waste Water Discharged refers to the volume of industrial waste water discharged, through all outlets, to the outside of industrial enterprises, including waste water produced, direct-cooling water, underground water from mines that does not meet the standard of discharge, and the domestic sewage mixed up with industrial waste water when discharged, but excluding discharged indirect-cooling water.

Industrial Waste Water Meeting Discharge Standards

Industrial Waste Water Meeting Discharge Standards refers to volume of industrial waste water discharge which, with or without treatment, reaches national or local standards with regard to all pollutants.

Volume of Waste Industrial Gas Emission

Industrial Waste Air Emission refers to discharge into atmosphere of waste air containing pollutants generated from fuel burning and production process in enterprises within a given period of time. It is calculated at standard status (273K, 101325Pa) as:

Industrial waste air emission = emission through fuel burning + emission through production process

Consumption Wastes Transported

Consumption Wastes Transported refers to volume of consumption wastes collected and transported to disposal factories or sites. Consumption Wastes are solid wastes produced from urban households or from seryice activities for urban households , and solid wastes regarded by laws and regulations as urban consumption wastes, including those from households, commercial activities, markets cleaning of streets, public sites, offices, schools, factories, mining units and other sources.

Number of Vehicles under Operation

Number of Vehicles under Operation refers to the total number of vehicles under operation by public transport enterprises (units) at the end of the year, based on the records of operational vehicles by the enterprises (units).

Volume of Post Business

Volume of Post Business refers to the total amount of post services provided by the post department, which reflects the total achievements by the post departments during a given period of time in a comprehensive way, and is an important indicator to study the composition and development of the post business. It is arrived by first multiplying the business volume of different types, such as number of letters, telegrams and accumulated number of newspaper and journals subscribed and sold, etc. by their respective average unit price (fixed price) and then adding these products together, plus the income from other business revenues.

Capacity of Office Telephone Exchanges

Capacity of Office Telephone Exchanges refers to the capacity of telephone exchanges installed in the office of telecommunication service providers for communication between fixed telephones.

Household Telephone Subscribers

Household Telephone Subscribers refer to telephone sets installed in the dwelling units of urban or rural residents, and registered as residence subscribers for payment, including 3 types of payment for the service: private payment, public payment and free service.

第十七篇

Chapter 17

功能区域和重点开发小区

FUNCTIONAL ZONES AND KEY DEVELOPMENT ZONES

表 17－1　浦东新区功能区域基本情况
Statistics of Functional Zones in PNA
(2008)

区域名称	Name	土地面积（平方公里） Land Area (sq · km)	年末户籍人口（人） Year-end Registered Population (person)	人口密度（人/平方公里） Density of Population (person/sq · km)
总　计	**Total**	**569.57**	**1 942 889**	**3 411**
陆家嘴功能区域	**Lujiazui Functional Zone**	**42.77**	**474 620**	**11 097**
陆家嘴街道	Lujiazui Subdistrict	6.89	119 577	17 355
潍坊新村街道	Weifangxincun Subdistrict	3.74	93 423	24 979
塘桥街道	Tangqiao Subdistrict	3.86	59 536	15 424
洋泾街道	Yangjing Subdistrict	7.38	105 064	14 236
花木街道	Huamu Subdistrict	20.90	97 020	4 642
金桥功能区域	**Jinqiao Functional Zone**	**90.52**	**387 416**	**4 280**
金杨新村街道	Jinyangxincun Subdistrict	8.02	129 604	16 160
沪东新村街道	Hudongxincun Subdistrict	5.39	70 685	13 114
浦兴路街道	Puxing Road Subdistrict	6.25	92 528	14 804
金桥镇	Jinqiao Town	25.28	28 868	1 142
曹路镇	Caolu Town	45.58	65 731	1 442
张江功能区域	**Zhangjiang Functional Zone**	**119.31**	**160 621**	**1 346**
张江镇	Zhangjiang Town	45.02	67 735	1 505
唐　镇	Tangzhen Town	32.32	38 579	1 194
合庆镇	Heqing Town	41.97	54 307	1 294

注：功能区域土地面积按行政区划面积计算。
Note: The land area of a certain functional zone is counted as that of its administrative division.

表 17－1 续表　Continued

区域名称 Name		土地面积（平方公里）Land Area (sq. km)	年末户籍人口（人）Year-end Registered Population (person)	人口密度（人/平方公里）Density of Population (person/sq. km)
外高桥功能区域	**Waigaoqiao Functional Zone**	**97.13**	**165 501**	**1 704**
高桥镇	Gaoqiao Town	39.07	84 203	2 155
高行镇	Gaohang Town	22.85	45 331	1 984
高东镇	Gaodong Town	35.21	35 967	1 021
三林世博功能区域	**Sanlin Expo Functional Zone**	**80.11**	**587 312**	**7 331**
周家渡街道	Zhoujiadu Subdistrict	5.52	116 049	21 023
上钢新村街道	Shanggangxincun Subdistrict	7.54	106 234	14 089
南码头路街道	Nanmatou Road Subdistrict	4.25	81 785	19 244
东明路街道	Dongming Road Subdistrict	4.90	57 878	11 812
北蔡镇	Beicai Town	23.71	116 625	4 919
三林镇	Sanlin Town	34.19	108 741	3 180
川沙功能区域	**Chuansha Functional Zone**	**139.73**	**167 419**	**1 198**
川沙新镇	Chuansha New Town	139.73	167 419	1 198

表 17－2　陆家嘴功能区域主要指标
Major Indicators in Lujiazui Functional Zone

指　标	Indicators	单　位　Unit	2007	2008
居民委员会	Neighborhood Committee	个 in number	148	156
村民委员会	Villages´Committee	个 in number	3	3
居民小区	Residential Quarter	个 in number	162	162
社区服务中心	Community Service Center	个 in number	5	5
地方财政收入	Local Fiscal Revenue	亿元 100 million yuan	88.78	102.85
工业总产值	Gross Industrial Output value	亿元 100 million yuan	716.90	722.14
工业出口交货值	Amount of Delivered Industrial Exports	亿元 100 million yuan	24.69	25.76
全社会固定资产投资总额	Total Amount of Investment in Social Fixed Capital	亿元 100 million yuan	182.41	219.64
商品销售总额(限额以上)	Aggregate Sales of Commodities (Above Quota)	亿元 100 million yuan	2 102.32	2 904.04
社会消费品零售总额(限额以上)	Total Volume of Retail Sales for Social Consumer Goods (Above Quota)	亿元 100 million yuan	168.78	170.88
外商直接投资合同项目	Projects of Foreign Direct Investment	个 in number	453	261
外商直接投资合同金额	Contracted Amount of Foreign Direct Investment	亿美元 USD 100 million	18.59	18.77
市外在沪投资企业项目	Enterprises Invested from Other Provinces	个 in number	540	394
市外在沪投资企业注册资本	Registered Capital of Enterprises Invested from Other Provinces	亿元 100 million yuan	69.31	52.81
跨国公司地区总部	Regional Headquarters of Multi-national Corporations	家 in number	50	59
中外资金融机构	Financial Institutions of Domestic and Foreign Capitals	家 in number	455	504
主要商务楼宇幢数	Major Business Buildings	幢 in number	148	159
主要商务楼宇平均入驻率	Major Business Buildings Average Occupancy	%	93.3	87.7
学　校	Schools	所 in number	59	58
医　院	Hospitals	所 in number	18	16
期末登记流动人口	Registered Migrant Population at End of Term	万人 10 000 persons	11.05	11.52

注:“街道财政收入”2008 年起不作统计,下同。
Note: The data of “Sub-district financial revenue” will not be counted since 2008.

表 17-3　金桥功能区域主要指标
Major Indicators in Jinqiao Functional Zone

指　标　Indicators		单　位　Unit	2007	2008
居民委员会	Neighborhood Committee	个 in number	134	134
村民委员会	Villages´Committee	个 in number	41	40
社区服务中心	Community Service Center	个 in number	5	5
地方财政收入	Local Fiscal Revenue	亿元 100 million yuan	26.09	29.64
各镇财政收入	Town of Fiscal Revenue	亿元 100 million yuan	35.79	34.10
工业总产值	Gross Industrial Output Value	亿元 100 million yuan	2 302.72	2 501.04
#电子信息产品制造业	Electronic and Information Products Manufacturing	亿元 100 million yuan	729.02	713.62
汽车制造业	Auto Industry	亿元 100 million yuan	509.19	398.52
工业出口交货值	Amount of Delivered Industrial Exports	亿元 100 million yuan	445.12	543.72
全社会固定资产投资总额	Total Amount of Investment in Social Fixed Capital	亿元 100 million yuan	128.41	95.24
商品销售总额(限额以上)	Aggregate Sales of Commodities (Above Quota)	亿元 100 million yuan	86.58	159.48
社会消费品零售总额(限额以上)	Total Volume of Retail Sales for Social Consumer Goods (Above Quota)	亿元 100 million yuan	19.21	32.15
外商直接投资合同项目	Projects of Foreign Direct Investment	个 in number	123	76
外商直接投资合同金额	Contracted Amount of Foreign Direct Investment	亿美元 USD 100 million	7.30	3.86
市外在沪投资企业项目	Enterprises Invested from Other Provinces	个 in number	175	188
市外在沪投资企业注册资本	Registered Capital of Enterprises Invested from Other Provinces	亿元 100 million yuan	8.95	11.87
学　校	Schools	所 in number	48	46
医　院	Hospitals	所 in number	12	12
期末登记流动人口	Registered Migrant Population at End of Term	万人 10 000 persons	24.13	22.94

表 17-4　外高桥功能区域主要指标
Major Indicators in Waigaoqiao Functional Zone

指　标	Indicators	单　位 Unit	2007	2008
居民委员会	Neighborhood Committee	个 in number	52	54
村民委员会	Villages´Committee	个 in number	41	37
社区服务中心	Community Service Center	个 in number	3	3
地方财政收入	Local Fiscal Revenue	亿元 100 million yuan	51.79	65.99
各镇财政收入	Fiscal Revenue of Towns	亿元 100 million yuan	33.63	45.05
工业总产值	Gross Industrial Output Value	亿元 100 million yuan	980.19	1 169.90
工业出口交货值	Amount of Delivered Industrial Exports	亿元 100 million yuan	371.39	495.08
全社会固定资产投资总额	Total Amount of Investment in Social Fixed Capital	亿元 100 million yuan	132.84	131.62
港口货物吞吐量	Volume of Cargo Handled at Ports	万吨 10 000 tons	13 076.70	13 122.80
#外贸货物	Cargo for Foreign Trade	万吨 10 000 tons	12 642.20	12 547.10
集装箱吞吐量	Volume of Container Handled	万标箱 10 000 TEUs	1 556.80	1 538.70
商品销售总额(限额以上)	Aggregate Sales of Commodities (Above Quota)	亿元 100 million yuan	576.12	604.71
社会消费品零售总额(限额以上)	Total Volume of Retail Sales for Social Consumer Goods (Above Quota)	亿元 100 million yuan	11.75	8.43
外商直接投资合同项目	Projects of Foreign Direct Investment	个 in number	359	230
外商直接投资合同金额	Contracted Amount of Foreign Direct Investment	亿美元 USD 100 million	9.21	9.69
市外在沪投资企业项目	Enterprises Invested from Other Provinces	个 in number	303	194
市外在沪投资企业注册资本	Registered Capital of Enterprises Invested from Other Provinces	亿元 100 million yuan	10.45	13.84
学　校	Schools	所 in number	23	23
医　院	Hospitals	所 in number	5	7
期末登记流动人口	Registered Migrant Population at End of Term	万人 10 000 persons	17.61	18.77

表 17-5 张江功能区域主要指标
Major Indicators in Zhangjiang Functional Zone

指 标	Indicators	单 位 Unit	2007	2008
居民委员会	Neighborhood Committee	个 in number	35	35
村民委员会	Villages' Committee	个 in number	57	57
社区服务中心	Community Service Center	个 in number	3	7
从业人员	The Employed	万人 10 000 persons	20.44	20.74
地方财政收入	Local Fiscal Revenue	亿元 100 million yuan	27.94	35.40
各镇财政收入	Fiscal Revenue of Towns	亿元 100 million yuan	24.96	30.57
工业总产值	Gross Industrial Output Value	亿元 100 million yuan	622.11	666.87
#电子信息产品制造业	Electronic and Information Products Manufacturing	亿元 100 million yuan	236.49	258.30
生物医药制造业	Bio-pharmaceutical Products Manufacturing	亿元 100 million yuan	65.87	78.06
工业出口交货值	Amount of Delivered Industrial Exports	亿元 100 million yuan	232.19	244.03
全社会固定资产投资总额	Total Amount of Investment in Social Fixed Capital	亿元 100 million yuan	149.16	128.88
商品销售总额(限额以上)	Aggregate Sales of Commodities (Above Quota)	亿元 100 million yuan	169.53	238.06
社会消费品零售总额(限额以上)	Total Volume of Retail Sales for Social Consumer Goods (Above Quota)	亿元 100 million yuan	47.15	24.75
外商直接投资合同项目	Projects of Foreign Direct Investment	个 in number	231	149
外商直接投资合同金额	Contracted Amount of Foreign Direct Investment	亿美元 USD 100 million	11.90	12.95
市外在沪投资企业项目	Enterprises Invested from Other Provinces	个 in number	257	284
市外在沪投资企业注册资本	Registered Capital of Enterprises Invested from Other Provinces	亿元 100 million yuan	8.01	17.12
授权专利(张江园区历年累计)	Patents Authorized (Accumulative Total of Main Years in Zhangjiang Hi-tech Park)	个 in number	2 205	3 218
申请专利(张江园区历年累计)	Patents Chaimed (Accumulative Total of Main Years in Zhangjiang Hi-tech Park)	个 in number	9 142	14 233
智能化温室面积	Area of Intellectualized Greenhouses	万平方米 10 000 sq·m	14.30	14.30
学 校	Schools	所 in number	20	21
医 院	Hospitals	所 in number	7	7
期末登记流动人口	Registered Migrant Population at End of Term	万人 10 000 persons	17.81	19.10

表 17-6　三林世博功能区域主要指标
Major Indicators in Sanlin Expo Functional Zone

指　标 Indicators		单　位 Unit	2007	2008
居民委员会	Neighborhood Committee	个 in number	190	191
村民委员会	Village Committee	个 in number	31	30
居民小区	Residential Quarter	个 in number	369	369
社区服务中心	Community Service Center	个 in number	6	6
地方财政收入	Local Fiscal Revenue	亿元 100 million yuan	14.31	15.61
各镇财政收入	Subdistricts Town Fiscal Revenue	亿元 100 million yuan	31.49	26.67
工业总产值	Gross Industrial Output Value	亿元 100 million yuan	431.42	441.10
工业出口交货值	Delivery Value of Industrial Exports	亿元 100 million yuan	234.55	258.94
全社会固定资产投资总额	Total Investment in Fixed Assets	亿元 100 million yuan	62.50	147.86
商品销售总额(限额以上)	Aggregate Sales of Commodities (above quotas)	亿元 100 million yuan	49.25	60.55
社会消费品零售总额(限额以上)	Total Volume of Retail Sales for Social Consumer Goods (above quotas)	亿元 100 million yuan	27.67	36.90
外商直接投资合同项目	Projects of Foreign Direct Investment	个 in number	68	74
外商直接投资合同金额	Contracted Amount of Foreign Direct Investment	亿美元 USD 100 million	1.98	3.13
市外在沪投资企业项目	Enterprises Invested from Other Provinces	个 in number	211	230
市外在沪投资企业注册资本	Registered Capital of Enterprises Invested from Other Provinces	亿元 100 million yuan	7.91	8.18
学　校	Schools	所 in number	56	57
医　院	Hospitals	所 in number	11	15
期末登记流动人口	Registered Migrant Population at End of Term	万人 10 000 persons	43.96	39.31

表 17-7 川沙功能区域主要指标
Major Indicators in Chuansha Functional Zone

指 标 Indicators		单 位 Unit	2007	2008
居民委员会	Neighborhood Committee	个 in number	42	48
村民委员会	Village Committee	个 in number	60	59
社区服务中心	Community Service Center	个 in number	1	1
地方财政收入	Local Fiscal Revenue	亿元 100 million yuan	4.82	5.43
镇财政收入	Town Fiscal Revenue	亿元 100 million yuan	12.68	13.90
工业总产值	Gross Industrial Output Value	亿元 100 million yuan	134.78	148.17
工业出口交货值	Delivery Value of Industrial Exports	亿元 100 million yuan	22.23	22.00
全社会固定资产投资总额	Total Investment in Fixed Assets	亿元 100 million yuan	82.65	114.74
# 新市镇建设投资额	Amount of Investment for Construction of New Town	亿元 100 million yuan	19.91	18.61
商品销售总额(限额以上)	Aggregate Sales of Commodities (above quotas)	亿元 100 million yuan	159.76	240.95
社会消费品零售总额(限额以上)	Total Volume of Retail Sales for Social Consumer Goods (above quotas)	亿元 100 million yuan	15.00	17.34
外商直接投资合同项目	Projects of Foreign Direct Investment	个 in number	20	13
外商直接投资合同金额	Contracted Amount of Foreign Direct Investment	亿美元 USD 100 million	0.51	1.52
市外在沪投资企业项目	Enterprises Invested from Other Provinces	个 in number	87	70
市外在沪投资企业注册资本	Registered Capital of Enterprises Invested from Other Provinces	亿元 100 million yuan	3.20	5.04
国际机场货邮吞吐量	Throughput of Goods and Mails at Pudong International Airport	万吨 10 000 tons	251.15	263.00
国际机场旅客吞吐量	Number of Passengers at Pudong International Airport	万人次 10 000 person-Times	2 895.15	2 815.48
临空现代农业园区接待旅游人次	Number of Visitors Accepted by Linkong Modern Agricultural Park	万人次 10 000 person-Times	25.10	18.50
学 校	Schools	所 in number	26	26
医 院	Hospitals	所 in number	7	7
期末登记流动人口	Registered Migrant Population at End of Term	万人 10 000 persons	16.19	15.05

表 17-8　街道社区发展
Subdistricts and Communities

指　标	Indicators	单　位 Unit	2007	2008
文明小区建成数	Completed Model Residential Areas	个 in number	216	346
市　级	of Municipal Level	个 in number	137	164
区　级	of PNA Level	个 in number	79	182
实事建设投入	Investment on Practical Constructions	万元 10 000 yuan	53 904	80 596
失业人员再就业人次	Reemployment of the Unemployed	人次 person-times	61 969	59 528
街道安置上岗人次	Posts Arranged by Subdistricts	人次 person-times	26 767	26 918
非正规就业安置人数	Arranged Nonofficial Employments	人 persons	41 562	70 357
医疗救助人次数	Medical Assistance	人次 person-times	6 606	9 990
医疗救助金额	Amount of Medical Assistance	万元 10 000 yuan	524	2 010
家庭病床数	Family Sickbeds	张 bed	2 766	3 128
体育活动健身点	Sports Fitness Centers	个 in number	405	405
健身苑占地面积	Flooring Area of Fitness Courts	平方米 sq・m	40 300	40 300
敬老院数	Homes for the Aged	个 in number	23	35
敬老院床位数	Sickbeds in Homes for the Aged	张 bed	2 119	3 022
居家养老人数	the Aged Living in their Own Houses	人 persons	10 494	17 615
居家养老护理员人数	Nursing Staff for the Aged Living in their Own Houses	人 persons	1 334	1 132
信访结办数	Number of Handled Complaint Letters and Visits	件 piece		11 614
纠纷结办数	Number of Handled Disputes	件 piece		7 177
街道图书馆藏书数	Number of Books Collected in Libraries in Sub-districts	万册 10 000 volumes		38
志愿者人数	Number of Volunteers	人 persons		82 139
刑事案件发生数	Criminal Cases	件/万人 in number/10 000 persons	51	50
事故总数	Total Accidents	起 in number	17	18

表 17-9 各镇财政收入及工业总产值
Financial Revenue and Gross Value of Industrial Output in Towns

单位:亿元 (100 million yuan)

镇 Town		财政收入 Financial Revenue			工业总产值 Gross Value of Industrial Output		
		2006	2007	2008	2006	2007	2008
总 计	**Total**	**109.90**	**121.40**	**150.28**	**973.41**	**1 108.43**	**1 274.81**
川沙新镇	Chuansha New Town	10.51	12.68	13.90	112.23	133.40	148.17
高 桥 镇	Gaoqiao Town	8.03	13.35	16.59	77.60	85.24	105.07
北 蔡 镇	Beicai Town	8.74	11.07	12.53	58.21	60.42	60.72
合 庆 镇	Heqing Town	4.42	6.22	7.49	96.47	113.15	136.80
唐 镇	Tangzhen Town	5.93	6.37	9.63	56.02	56.88	55.45
曹 路 镇	Caolu Town	8.12	13.28	16.97	109.42	119.66	127.58
金 桥 镇	Jinqiao Town	12.73	13.69	17.13	18.37	17.93	18.36
高 行 镇	Gaohang Town	9.02	12.10	16.74	114.60	122.96	142.63
高 东 镇	Gaodong Town	6.06	8.18	11.72	213.32	277.30	366.77
张 江 镇	Zhangjiang Town	7.15	12.37	13.44	54.59	53.06	53.23
三 林 镇	Sanlin Town	9.33	12.09	14.14	62.58	68.43	60.03
花 木 镇	Huamu Town	19.86					

注：2007 年始花木撤镇建街道。
Note: Huamu Town has been replaced with Huamu Sub-district since 2007.

表 17-10　陆家嘴金融贸易区主要经济指标

Major Economic Indicators in Lujiazui Finance and Trade Zone

指　标　Indicators		单　位　Unit	2007	2008
税收总额(税务部门口径)	Total Amount of Tax Revenues (from the Tax Departments)	亿元 100 million yuan	249.86	306.02
#地方税收	Local Tax Revenues	亿元 100 million yuan	88.78	102.85
固定资产投资额	Investment in Fixed Assets	亿元 100 million yuan	182.41	219.64
#房地产投资额	Investment in Real Estate	亿元 100 million yuan	120.37	127.00
#办公楼及商业营业用房	Office and Commercial Buildings	亿元 100 million yuan	66.69	79.49
房地产新开工面积	Floor Space of New Buildings	万平方米 10 000 sq·m	65.79	177.37
房地产竣工面积	Floor Space of Completed Buildings	万平方米 10 000 sq·m	84.16	149.38
房地产预售面积	Floor Space of Forward Sold Buildings	万平方米 10 000 sq·m	13.29	21.66
外商直接投资合同项目	Projects of Foreign Direct Investment	个 unit	453	261
外商直接投资合同金额	Contracted Amount of Foreign Direct Investment	亿美元 USD 100 million	18.59	18.77
外商直接投资实际到位金额	Actual Paid Amount of Foreign Direct Investment	亿美元 USD 100 million	18.88	15.84
期末实有内资企业注册户数	Number of Actual Registered Domestic Enterprises at End of Term	个 unit		11 730
期末实有内资企业注册资本	Registered Capital of Actual Domestic Enterprises at End of Term	亿元 100 million yuan		3 367.67
金融业增加值	Added Value of Finance Industry	亿元 100 million yuan	391.29	471.55
期末金融机构数	Number of Financial Institutions at End of Term	个 unit	455	504
#外资银行法人行	Foreign Banks and Corporate Banks	个 unit	10	14
基金总公司	Head Office of Funds	个 unit	23	24
期末认定跨国公司地区总部个数	Head Office of Funds	个 unit	50	59
举办展览(博览)次数	Head Office of Funds	次 time	99	117
商品销售总额(限额以上)	Gross Sales of Commodities (Above Quota)	亿元 100 million yuan	2 102.32	2 904.04
社会消费品零售总额(限额以上)	Total Volume of Retail Sales for Social Consumer Goods (Above Quota)	亿元 100 million yuan	168.78	170.88
期末星级宾馆个数	Number of Star Hotels at End of Term	个 unit	23	25
主要景点接待人次	Person-times Accepted by Main Sight Spots	万人次 10 000 persom-times	1 682.11	1 658.56
商办楼宇数	Number of Commercial Buildings	幢 in number	148	159
商办楼宇建筑面积	Floor Space of Commercial Buildings	万平方米 10 000 sq·m	942.35	1 106.56
商办楼宇平均入驻率	Average Occupancy Rate of Commercial Buildings	%	93.3	87.7

表 17-11 金桥出口加工区主要经济指标
Major Economic Indicators in Jinqiao Export Processing Zone

指 标 Indicators		单 位 Unit	2007	2008
税收总额(税务部门口径)	Total Amount of Tax Revenues (from the Tax Departments)	亿元 100 million yuan	52.28	55.53
#地方税收	Local Tax Revenues	亿元 100 million yuan	12.51	13.99
固定资产投资额	Investment in Fixed Assets	亿元 100 million yuan	59.71	35.43
#房地产投资额	Investment in Real Estate	亿元 100 million yuan	8.91	4.32
工业投资额	Investment in Industries	亿元 100 million yuan	46.00	27.41
房地产新开工面积	Floor Space of New Buildings	万平方米 10 000 sq·m	9.00	27.39
房地产竣工面积	Floor Space of Completed Buildings	万平方米 10 000 sq·m	14.03	9.27
房地产预售面积	Floor Space of Forward Sold Buildings	万平方米 10 000 sq·m	3.96	5.12
外商直接投资合同项目	Projects of Foreign Direct Investment	个 unit	55	57
外商直接投资合同金额	Contracted Amount of Foreign Direct Investment	亿美元 USD 100 million	4.96	2.93
外商直接投资实际到位金额	Actual Paid Amount of Foreign Direct Investment	亿美元 USD 100 million	2.55	2.48
期末实有内资企业注册户数	Number of Actual Registered Domestic Enterprises at End of Term	个 unit		306
期末实有内资企业注册资本	Registered Capital of Actual Domestic Enterprises at End of Term	亿元 100 million yuan		64.80
工业总产值	Gross Value of Industrial Output	亿元 100 million yuan	1 594.56	1 608.23
#高技术产业产值	Output Value of High-tech Industries	亿元 100 million yuan	725.32	732.46
#新产品产值	Output Value of New Products	亿元 100 million yuan	828.21	778.34
工业四大重点发展行业产值	Output Value of Four Key Industrial Sectors for Development	亿元 100 million yuan	1 426.29	1 418.32
电子信息整机及配套件	Complete Machines and Supporting Parts in Electronic Information Industry	亿元 100 million yuan	614.08	572.68
汽车及零部件	Automobiles and Spare and Accessory Parts	亿元 100 million yuan	536.94	443.40
家用电器及配套件	Household Appliances and Supporting Parts	亿元 100 million yuan	200.02	241.30
生物医药及食品	Biological Medicine and Foods	亿元 100 million yuan	75.25	160.94
工业出口交货值	Delivery Value of Industrial Exports	亿元 100 million yuan	327.60	404.00
新产品产值率	Production Value Rate of New Products	%	51.9	48.4
经认定高新技术企业数	Number of Approved High-tech Enterprises	个 unit	88	97
生产性服务业经营收入	Operating Income of Productive Services	亿元 100 million yuan	158.27	148.19
期末从业人员数	Number of Employed Persons at End of Term	万人 10 000 persoms	10.62	9.78

表 17-12 外高桥保税区主要经济指标
Major Economic Indicators in Waigaoqiao Free Trade Zone

指 标 Indicators		单 位 Unit	2007	2008
税收总额(税务部门口径)	Total Amount of Tax Revenues (from the Tax Departments)	亿元 100 million yuan	176.18	216.64
#地方税收	Local Tax Revenues	亿元 100 million yuan	40.81	50.01
海关部门税收	Tax Revenues by Customs Departments	亿元 100 million yuan	270.14	300.35
固定资产投资额	Investment in Fixed Assets	亿元 100 million yuan	21.69	20.53
外商直接投资合同项目	Projects of Foreign Direct Investment	个 unit	245	149
外商直接投资合同金额	Contracted Amount of Foreign Direct Investment	亿美元 USD 100 million	8.35	7.71
外商直接投资实际到位金额	Actual Paid Amount of Foreign Direct Investment	亿美元 USD 100 million	3.26	5.34
期末实有内资企业注册户数	Number of Actual Registered Domestic Enterprises at End of Term	个 unit		1 298
期末实有内资企业注册资本	Registered Capital of Actual Domestic Enterprises at End of Term	亿元 100 million yuan		215.57
商品销售总额(限额以上)	Gross Sales of Commodities (Above Quota)	亿元 100 million yuan	450.21	573.93
商品销售总额(注册地口径)	Gross Sales of Commodities (Approach of Registered Place)	亿元 100 million yuan	4 901.95	5 508.04
保税市场交易额	Volume of Transactions in Free Trade Markets	亿美元 USD 100 million	584.08	627.07
物流企业经营收入(注册地口径)	Operating Income of Logistics Enterprises (Approach of Registered Place)	亿元 100 million yuan	2 073.59	2 237.24
货物流量	Goods Flow	万吨 10 000 tons	4 015.50	4 237.80
工业总产值	Gross Value of Industrial Output	亿元 100 million yuan	488.22	555.43
#高技术产业产值	Output Value of High-tech Industries	亿元 100 million yuan	256.73	324.57
电子信息业产值	Output Value of Electronic Information Industry	亿元 100 million yuan	261.38	324.86
进出口总额	Total Volume of Foreign Trade	亿美元 USD 100 million	570.09	626.37
出口额	Amount of Exports	亿美元 USD 100 million	154.26	158.10
进口额	Amount of Imports	亿美元 USD 100 million	415.83	468.27
期末世界 500 强入驻数量	Number of World'ms Top 500 Enterprises Occupied at End of Term	个 unit	127	111
期末从业人员数(注册地口径)	Number of Employed Persons at End of Term (Approach of Registered Place)	万人 10 000 persoms	18.83	19.49
期末历年累计竣工房屋面积	Floor Space of Accumulated Completed Buildings in Main Years at End of Term	万平方米 10 000 sq・m	740.84	755.86

表17-13 张江高科技园区主要经济指标
Major Economic Indicators in Zhangjiang High-tech Park

指 标 Indicators		单 位 Unit	2007	2008
税收总额(税务部门口径)	Total Amount of Tax Revenues (from the Tax Departments)	亿元 100 million yuan	59.29	78.77
#地方税收	Local Tax Revenues	亿元 100 million yuan	19.42	25.32
固定资产投资额	Investment in Fixed Assets	亿元 100 million yuan	107.80	98.30
#房地产投资额	Investment in Real Estate	亿元 100 million yuan	9.69	4.15
工业投资额	Investment in Industries	亿元 100 million yuan	48.62	49.58
房地产新开工面积	Floor Space of New Buildings	万平方米 10 000 sq·m	4.55	15.02
房地产竣工面积	Floor Space of Completed Buildings	万平方米 10 000 sq·m	63.10	12.01
房地产预售面积	Floor Space of Forward Sold Buildings	万平方米 10 000 sq·m	0.40	0.66
外商直接投资合同项目	Projects of Foreign Direct Investment	个 unit	176	121
外商直接投资合同金额	Contracted Amount of Foreign Direct Investment	亿美元 USD 100 million	10.38	11.52
外商直接投资实际到位金额	Actual Paid Amount of Foreign Direct Investment	亿美元 USD 100 million	5.19	7.64
期末实有内资企业注册户数	Number of Actual Registered Domestic Enterprises at End of Term	个 unit		3 502
期末实有内资企业注册资本	Registered Capital of Actual Domestic Enterprises at End of Term	亿元 100 million yuan		268.64
工业总产值	Gross Value of Industrial Output	亿元 100 million yuan	397.83	421.39
#高技术产业产值	Output Value of High-tech Industries	亿元 100 million yuan	278.36	322.68
主导产业销售收入	Sales Revenue of Leading Industries	亿元 100 million yuan	423.41	471.26
#生物医药产业销售收入	Sales Revenue of Bio-logical Medicine Industry	亿元 100 million yuan	85.00	109.13
集成电路产业销售收入	Sales Revenue of Integrated Circuits Industry	亿元 100 million yuan	144.75	145.21
软件业产业销售收入	Sales Revenue of Software Industry	亿元 100 million yuan	74.84	83.51
知识产权授权数	Number of Authorizations for Intellectual Property	件 ietm	1 009	1 454
#专利授权数	Number of Patent Authorizations	件 ietm	634	1 013
技术交易数量	Number of Technology Transfers	件 ietm	801	899
技术合同金额	Contracted Value of Technologies	亿元 100 million yuan	23.01	37.63
经认定高新技术企业数	Number of Approved High-tech Enterprises	个 unit	307	226
在孵企业数	Number of Enterprises Being Incubated	个 unit	240	447
经认定研发机构数	Number of Approved Research and Development Institutions	个 unit	93	127
公共服务平台服务企业次数	Number of Enterprises Served by Public Service Platforms	次 time	33 016	105 514
期末从业人员数	Number of Employed Persons at End of Term	万人 10 000 persoms	11.71	12.56

主要统计指标解释

非正规就业

是指失业人员以个人或组织起来的方式参与社区的便民利民服务、城市管理服务、家政服务，为机关和企事业单位提供各种临时性、突击性劳务，以及以家庭手工业、工艺作坊等个人自谋职业、合作就业方式进行生产自救，但又无法建立或暂无条件建立稳定劳动关系的一种就业形式。

港口货物吞吐量

指经水运进出港区范围，并经过装卸的货物数量，包括邮件及办理托运手续的行李、包裹以及补给运输船舶的燃、物料和淡水。货物吞吐量按货物流向分为进口、出口吞吐量，按货物交流性质分为外贸货物吞吐量和国内贸易货物吞吐量。货物吞吐量的货类构成及其流向，是衡量港口生产能力大小的重要指标。

国际标准集装箱吞吐量

凡经过水运进、出港区范围，并经过装卸的集装箱箱数和重量（含集装箱自重），通常是按进港和出港分别统计。

TEU是"折合20英尺标准箱"的英文缩写。它是指各种尺寸的国际标准集装箱的自然箱数，按各自的换算比例，折算为20英尺标准箱的换算箱数。其换算比例为：40英尺箱1：2；35英尺箱1：1.75；20英尺箱1：1；10英尺箱1：0.5。

EXPLANATORY NOTES TO MAJOR STATISTICAL INDICATORS

Informal Employment

Informal Employment refers to a form of employment that unemployed individuals, in a manner of an individual or an organization of some individuals, participate in the services for their communities to facilitate the residents, help with the city management and housekeeping, provide all kinds of temporary and pressing labor for government offices and institutions, as well as other forms of employment of individual occupation and cooperation such as cottage industries and crafts workshops that help themselves for living and can not or currently can not establish a stable labor relation.

Volume of Freight Handled in Ports

Volume of Freight Handled in Ports refers to the volume of cargo passing in and out the harbor area of the ports and having been loaded and unloaded. The volume includes that of the postal matters, registered luggage and fuels, materials and fresh water as supplies of the ships. The volume of freight handled may be classified by direction of flow as freight for import and freight for export, or by nature of cargo as freight for domestic trade and freight for foreign trade. As an important indicator, the volume of freight handled by type of cargo and by main flow direction reflects the production capacity of ports.

International Container Throughput Capacity

International Container Throughput Capacity refers to number and weight of containers which are loaded or unloaded within port area via water carriage. It is often calculated by entering and leaving port, respectively. TEU was the abbreviation of twenty foot equivalent unit, which refers to converted number of all kinds of containers. The conversion method is based on respective conversion ratio and the number of all kinds of container is converted to the standard number of twenty foot equivalent unit. The conversion ratio is: 40 feet container 1 : 2, 35 feet container 1 : 1.75, 20 feet container 1 : 1, 10 feet container 1 : 0.5.

第十八篇

Chapter 18

上海市统计资料

STATISTICS OF SHANGHAI MUNICIPALITY

表 18-1　主要年份人口、从业人员、工资和婚姻情况
Population, Employment, Wages and Marriage in Main Years

指　标	Indicators	1990	2000	2005	2007	2008
年末总人口(万人)	**Year-end Population(10 000 persons)**	**1 283.35**	**1 321.63**	**1 360.26**	**1 378.86**	**1 391.04**
按性别分	Grouped by Sex					
男	Male	647.13	665.51	683.51	691.08	695.57
女	Female	636.22	656.12	676.75	687.78	695.47
按农业、非农业分	Grouped by Agriculture and Non-agriculture					
农业人口	Agriculture	418.89	335.47	211.32	181.92	174.48
非农业人口	Non-agriculture	864.46	986.16	1 148.94	1 196.94	1 216.56
人口密度(人/平方公里)	Density of Population(person/sq·km)	2 024	2 084	2 145	2 175	2 194
总户数(万户)	Total Households(10 000 household)	415.28	475.73	496.69	503.29	506.64
每户平均人口(人)	Average Persons Per Household(person)	3.1	2.8	2.7	2.7	2.7
人口自然变动	**Natural Change**					
出生人口(万人)	Number of Birth(10 000 persons)	13.12	6.95	8.25	10.08	9.67
出生率(‰)	Birth Rate(‰)	10.2	5.3	6.1	7.3	7.0
死亡人口(万人)	Number of Death(10 000 persons)	8.63	9.45	10.23	10.22	10.70
死亡率(‰)	Death Rate(‰)	6.7	7.2	7.5	7.4	7.7
自然增长率(‰)	Natural Growth Rate(‰)	3.51	-2.50	-1.46	-0.10	-0.75
人口迁徙变动	**Migration Change**					
迁入人口(万人)	Inflows(10 000 persons)	12.18	15.16	12.96	14.69	17.28
迁入率(‰)	Rate of Inflows(‰)	9.52	11.51	9.55	10.70	12.48
迁出人口(万人)	Outflows(10 000 persons)	10.72	5.32	3.46	3.95	4.29
迁出率(‰)	Rate of Outflows(‰)	8.38	4.04	2.55	2.88	3.10
从业人员(万人)	**Employment(10 000 persons)**	**787.72**	**828.35**	**863.32**	**909.08**	**1 053.24**
职工人数(万人)	Staff and Workers(10 000 persons)	508.10	390.14	420.12	522.67	554.39
职工工资总额(亿元)	Wages of Staff and Workers(100 million yuan)	146.78	614.53	1 146.95	1 802.17	2 184.20
职工年平均工资(元)	Average Annual Wages of Staff and Workers(yuan)	2 917	15 420	26 823	34 707	39 502
婚姻登记	**Registered Marriage**					
准予登记结婚(万对)	Marriage Registration Permitted (10 000 couples)	10.77	9.31	10.27	12.01	14.16
初婚(万人)	First Marriage(10 000 persons)	19.49	15.08	16.44	18.10	22.04
再婚(万人)	Remarriage(10 000 persons)	2.04	2.89	4.09	5.93	6.28
离婚登记(万人)	Divorce(10 000 persons)	3.27	6.36	7.86	9.38	9.35

表 18-2 主要年份上海市生产总值和指数
Value Added And Indices in Main Years

指　标	Indicators	1990	2000	2005	2007	2008
上海市生产总值(亿元)	**Gross Domestic Product (100 million yuan)**	**781.66**	**4 771.17**	**9 161.10**	**12 188.85**	**13 698.15**
第一产业	Primary Industry	34.24	76.68	90.26	101.84	111.80
第二产业	Secondary Industry	505.60	2 207.63	4 452.92	5 678.50	6 235.92
工　业	Industry	469.83	1 998.96	4 129.52	5 298.08	5 784.99
建筑业	Construction	35.77	208.67	323.40	380.43	450.93
第三产业	Tertiary Industry	241.82	2 486.86	4 620.92	6 408.50	7 350.43
构成(%)	**Composition(%)**					
第一产业	Primary Industry	4.3	1.8	1.0	0.8	0.8
第二产业	Secondary Industry	63.8	47.6	48.6	46.6	45.5
工　业	Industry	59.1	43.0	45.1	43.5	42.2
建筑业	Construction	4.7	4.6	3.5	3.1	3.3
第三产业	Tertiary Industry	31.9	50.6	50.4	52.6	53.7
人均生产总值(元)	**Average GDP Per Capita(yuan)**	**6 107**	**36 217**	**67 565**	**66 367**	**73 124**
上海市生产总值指数(以1990年为100)	**Indices of GDP (1990 = 100)**	**100.0**	**319.1**	**559.5**	**716.5**	**786.0**
第一产业	Primary Industry	100.0	126.9	119.2	122.4	123.3
第二产业	Secondary Industry	100.0	305.2	570.0	713.2	771.7
第三产业	Tertiary Industry	100.0	375.4	629.3	134.6	919.8
上海市生产总值指数(以上年为100)	**Indices of GDP (preceding year = 100)**	**103.5**	**111.0**	**111.1**	**114.3**	**109.7**
第一产业	Primary Industry	104.3	103.4	91.1	102.0	100.7
第二产业	Secondary Industry	102.8	109.8	111.5	111.5	108.2
第三产业	Tertiary Industry	105.3	113.5	111.1	117.1	111.3

表 18－3　主要年份全社会固定资产投资主要指标
Major Indicators Of Total Investment In Fixed Assets in Main Years

指　标	Indicators	1990	2000	2005	2007	2008
投资总额(亿元)	**Total Investment(100 million yuan)**	**227.08**	**1 869.67**	**3 542.55**	**4 458.61**	**4 829.45**
#房地产	Real Estate	8.16	566.17	1 246.86	1 307.53	1 366.87
在投资总额中按构成分	In Total Investment Grouped by Use of Funds					
#建筑安装工程	Construction and Installation	127.63	882.91	2 079.04	2 418.61	2 588.98
设备、工具、器具购置	Purchase of Equipment and Instruments	79.51	482.47	610.38	941.22	892.87
按建设性质分	Grouped by Type of Construction					
#新　建	New Construction	78.01	730.76	1 604.58	2 005.41	2 339.64
改　建	Reconstruction	70.48	216.40	231.15	326.09	393.08
扩　建	Expansion	47.50	216.71	306.00	510.84	474.31
按三次产业分	Grouped by Type of Industry					
第一产业	Primary Industry	3.20	7.87	5.58	8.37	8.40
第二产业	Secondary Industry	133.00	615.94	1 082.10	1 397.57	1 420.82
第三产业	Tertiary Industry	90.88	1 245.86	2 454.87	3 052.67	3 400.23
按经济类型分	Grouped by Economic Types					
#国有经济	State-owned	192.24	829.98	1 240.27	1 779.43	2 295.74
集体经济	Collective-owned	18.29	156.34	131.07	121.51	104.86
联营经济	Joint Owned		41.20	21.53	15.67	31.86
股份制经济	Shareholding		421.53	916.27	1 169.49	1 026.67
外商投资经济	Foreign Funded		222.86	504.16	522.15	541.06
港澳台投资经济	Hong Kong, Macao and Taiwan Funded		96.19	136.15	189.21	207.08
房屋建筑面积(万平方米)	**Floor Space of Buildings(10 000 sq·m)**					
施工面积	Floor Space Under Construction	3 801.46	8 636.31	14 477.85	14 979.37	14 083.52
#住　宅	Residential Housing	2 269.06	4 804.12	8 267.24	7 789.91	7 060.19
竣工面积	Floor Space Completed	2 138.44	3 266.52	4 873.82	5 068.46	3 828.79
#住　宅	Residential Housing	1 339.02	1 724.02	2 819.35	2 843.62	1 899.40
房屋建筑面积竣工率(%)	Rate of Floor Space Completed of Buildings(%)	56.3	37.8	33.7	33.8	27.2
资金来源合计(亿元)	**Total Capital Source(100 million yuan)**	**261.46**	**2 061.66**	**5 108.34**	**6 281.70**	**6 556.12**
上年末结余资金	A Balance at End of Previous Year	28.85	241.05	860.75	764.26	946.20
当年资金来源小计	Sub-total Capital Source of the Year	232.61	1 820.61	4 247.59	5 517.44	5 609.92
国家预算内资金	Capital Within the State Budget	14.39	48.30	46.42	98.03	83.68
国内贷款	Domestic Loans	62.52	379.21	955.29	1 296.92	1 469.43
债　券	State Treasury Bond		4.85	2.00	18.79	26.02
利用外资	Foreign Capital Absorbed	35.46	161.83	235.61	262.41	264.67
自筹资金	Self-raised Capital	94.13	905.46	1 976.72	2 364.93	2 774.73
其他资金	Other Capital	26.11	320.96	1 031.55	1 476.36	991.39

表 18-4 主要年份城市基础设施投资额和公用事业
Investment In Urban Infrastructure And Public Utilities in Main Years

指 标	Indicators	1990	2000	2005	2007	2008
城市基础设施投资额(亿元)	**Investment in Urban Infrastructure (100 million yuan)**	**47.22**	**449.90**	**885.74**	**1 466.33**	**1 733.18**
电力建设	Electric Construction	17.53	64.61	124.22	163.30	129.53
交通邮电	Traffic and Post	10.06	117.52	443.90	942.03	947.49
公用设施	Public Facilities	19.63	267.77	317.62	361.01	656.15
公用事业	Public Utilities	10.83	104.43	41.33	60.90	112.81
#自来水	Tap Water	1.06	5.35	29.66	50.12	93.24
燃 气	Gas	1.81	6.88	11.67	10.78	19.57
市政建设	Municipal Construction	8.80	163.34	276.28	300.11	543.34
#园林建设	Parks Gardens and Green Areas	0.11	38.76	13.88	34.66	29.01
环境卫生	Environment Sanitation	0.37	19.34	15.36	11.26	20.04
市政工程	Urban Municipal Engineering	8.31	102.36	246.58	254.19	494.29
自来水	**Tap Water**					
自来水管道长度(公里)	Length of Tap Water Pipelines(km)	3483	15 943	23 718	27 659	27 858
自来水供应能力(万立方米/日)	Tap Water Supply (10 000 cu · m/day)	462	1 048	1 096	1 080	1 069
售水量(亿立方米)	Sales of Tap Water(100 milion cu · m)	12.25	19.75	22.81	23.90	24.28
#生产用水	Industrial Use	5.90	5.49	6.42	6.78	6.30
生活用水	Residential Use	6.11	11.88	16.39	17.12	17.98
燃气、液化气	**Gas and Liquefied Gas**					
管道燃气	Pipeline Gas					
管线长度(公里)	Length of Gas Pipelines(km)	2 700	6 606	8 468	8 097	7 086
燃气销售量(万立方米)	Sales of Coal Gas(10 000 cu · m)	12.15	20.56	37.47	45.10	46.03
#家庭用	Family Use	7.63	16.22	18.88	14.90	15.36
家庭用液化气户数(万户)	Household of Family Use Petroleum Gas (10 000 household)	113.19	255.89	236.54	230.22	291.58
道 路	**Road**					
铺装道路长度(公里)	Length of Road Paved(km)	1 631	6 641	12 227	15 458	15 844
铺装道路面积(万平方米)	Area of Road Paved(10 000 sq · m)	1 787	8 147	20 942	22 579	14 405
交 通	**Traffic**					
年末实有公交线路条数(条)	Lines of Public Traffic(year-end)(route)	390	978	940	991	1 058
年末实有公交线路长度(公里)	Lines of Public Traffic Routes (year-end)(km)	18 593	23 260	21 794	22 375	22 919
年末运营公交车辆(辆)	Public Transportation Vehicles(year-end) (vehicle)	6 264	17 939	17 985	16 944	16 573
客运总量(亿人次)	Passengers Carried(100 million person-times)	54.37	26.49	27.81	26.50	26.60
出租汽车运营车辆数(辆)	Passenger Volume Using Ferry Route(vehicle)	11 298	42 943	47 794	48 614	48 059
隧 道	**Tunnels**					
越江隧道条数(条)	Routes of Tunnels Across the Huangpu River(route)	2	2	6	6	6
越江大桥座数(座)	Number of Bridges Across the Huangpu River(unit)	1	5	6	6	7
城市绿化	**Urban Greenbelt**					
园林绿地面积(公顷)	Area of Parks Garden and Green Areas(hectare)	3 570	12 601	28 865	31 795	34 256
人均公共绿地面积(平方米/人)	Public Green Area Per Capita (sq · m/person)	1.02	4.60	11.01	12.01	12.51
绿化覆盖率(%)	Green Area Coverage(%)	12.4	22.2	37.0	37.6	38.0
公园数(个)	Number of Parks(unit)	83	122	144	146	147

表18-5　主要年份农业主要指标
Major Indicators of Agriculture in Main Years

指　标 Indicators		1990	2000	2005	2007	2008
农业总产值(亿元)	**Gross Output Value of Agriculture (100 million yuan)**	**68.16**	**216.50**	**233.39**	**255.98**	**280.70**
#种植业	Planting	29.09	89.82	111.25	126.74	135.52
林　业	Forestry	0.37	1.41	11.11	10.05	9.12
牧　业	Animal Husbandry	30.25	87.35	54.34	58.00	68.40
渔　业	Fishery	8.04	37.92	51.64	54.19	57.11
主要农副产品产量	**Output of Major Farm and Sideline Products**					
粮　食(万吨)	Grain(10 000 tons)	244.36	174.00	105.36	109.20	115.67
油菜籽(万吨)	Rapeseed(10 000 tons)	18.17	15.71	6.51	3.28	3.29
蔬　菜(万吨)	Vegetables(10 000 tons)	186.79	377.00	409.03	413.49	409.99
水　果(万吨)	Fruit(10 000 tons)	9.42	22.54	33.63	43.93	46.12
年末圈存量(万头)	Hogs(year-end)(10 000 in number)	237.53	241.60	153.16	122.93	162.52
猪肉产量(万吨)	Pork(10 000 tons)	23.32	25.96	18.02	15.15	16.93
牛奶产量(万吨)	Cow Milk(10 000 tons)	22.68	25.95	23.76	22.04	23.29
鲜蛋上市量(万吨)	Poulty Eggs(10 000 tons)	15.07	16.64	8.40	5.54	6.20
水产品(万吨)	Aquatic Products(10 000 tons)	27.36	28.87	35.35	37.02	32.34
淡水产品	Freshwater Aquatic Products	10.32	16.64	20.32	19.02	14.62
海水产品	Seawater Aquatic Products	17.04	12.23	15.03	18.00	17.72
农业机械总动力(万千瓦)	**Total Power of Agricultural Machinery (10 000 kw)**	**276.50**	**142.50**	**96.46**	**97.68**	**44.51**

表 18-6 规模以上工业企业主要指标

Major Indicators of the City's Above-Certain-Scale Industrial Enterprises (2008)

指标	Indicators	单位数（个）Number of Enterprises (unit)	从业人员（万人）Employees (10 000 persons)	工业总产值（亿元）Gross Output Value of Industry (100 million yuan)	年末资产总计（亿元）Total Assets (year-end) (100 million yuan)	利润总额（亿元）Total After-tax Profits (100 million yuan)	税金总额（亿元）Total Tax and Duties (100 million yuan)
总 计	**Total**	**18 792**	**295.63**	**25 121.19**	**22 751.05**	**967.20**	**865.75**
按隶属关系分	**Grouped by Subordination**						
# 中央工业	Central Government	189	14.92	5 295.86	6 105.52	126.52	363.59
市(局)属工业	Municipality	954	37.46	4 665.33	5 515.76	294.19	191.86
区属工业	District	701	10.73	704.52	696.94	8.48	17.45
县属工业	County	16	0.13	5.12	6.60	0.03	0.18
街道属工业	Subdistrict	99	1.23	71.38	53.34	3.93	2.29
镇属工业	Town	1 309	23.60	974.29	819.85	44.51	24.32
乡属工业	Township	112	3.51	125.22	76.60	3.62	4.82
村属工业	Village	845	8.43	326.12	245.68	12.18	8.71
按登记注册类型分	**Grouped by Registration Categories**						
内 资	Domestic	12 055	135.84	10 129.00	11 714.97	495.22	525.44
国 有	State-owned	364	12.40	1 888.77	2 825.81	156.37	259.70
集 体	Collective-owned	760	8.66	253.11	191.64	9.96	10.72
股份合作	Share-holding Coorperation	425	3.91	152.29	117.61	6.29	5.06
联 营	Joint Owned	136	1.86	73.08	59.71	2.10	2.79
有限责任公司	Companies with Limited Liabilities	1 183	24.54	2 111.26	2 717.25	108.11	63.44
股份有限公司	Share-holding Companies with Limited Liabilities	167	8.93	2 614.91	3 443.42	92.64	100.60
私 营	Private	8 975	75.01	2 995.75	2 330.37	118.54	82.35
其 他	Others	45	0.53	39.84	29.16	1.21	0.78
港澳台商投资	Hong Kong, Macao and Taiwan Funded	1 964	44.23	4 236.51	2 655.86	12.18	58.93
外商投资	Foreign Funded	4 773	115.57	10 755.68	8 380.22	459.80	281.38
按轻、重工业分	**Grouped by Light and Heavy Industry**						
轻工业	Light Industry	7 342	112.23	5 455.87	5 030.99	349.25	370.76
重工业	Heavy Industry	11 450	183.40	19 665.32	17 720.06	617.94	494.99
按企业规模分	**Grouped by Size of Enterprises**						
大型企业	Large	111	47.86	9 841.55	8 927.75	325.40	438.44
中型企业	Medium	1 572	98.55	7 550.66	6 749.80	294.94	202.77
小型企业	Small	17 109	149.21	7 728.99	7 073.49	346.86	224.55

注：本表为国有企业及销售收入在500万元以上的非国有企业。
Note: Data in this table is collected from state-owned enterprises and non-state-owned enterprises with revenue of sales more than 5 million yuan.

表 18－7　主要年份国内外贸易主要指标
Major Indicators of Domestic and Foreign Trade in Main Years

指　标	Indicators	1990	2000	2005	2007	2008
商业、餐饮业、服务业网点(个)	Outlets of Commerce, Catering and Services(unit)	129 054	227 549	335 600		
商业、餐饮业、服务业从业人员(万人)	Employment of Commerce, Catering and Services(10 000 persons)	75	154	196	204	203
社会消费品零售总额(亿元)	**Total Retail Sales Value of Consumer Goods(100 million yuan)**	**333.86**	**1 865.28**	**2 972.97**	**3 847.79**	**4 537.14**
按用途分	Grouped by Type of Goods					
吃的商品	Food	142.15	743.31	1 172.05	1 524.23	1 800.16
穿的商品	Clothing	52.33	248.94	381.31	476.65	556.17
用的商品	Articles	137.23	858.33	1 388.32	1 796.05	2 114.16
烧的商品	Fuels	2.15	14.70	31.29	50.86	66.65
按行业分	Grouped by Sector					
#批发零售贸易业	Wholesale and Retail Trade	265.67	1 493.13	2 340.57	3 058.25	3 605.32
餐饮业	Catering Trade	17.08	134.12	350.32	556.48	669.54
其他行业	Others	35.96	238.03	282.08	233.06	262.28
外贸出口商品总额(亿美元)	**Total Value of Exports(USD 100 million)**	**53.21**	**253.54**	**907.42**	**1 439.28**	**1 693.50**
外贸进口商品总额(亿美元)	Total Value of Imports(USD 100 million)	21.10	293.56	956.23	1 390.45	1 527.88
外商直接投资签约项目数(个)	Contracted Projects of Direct Foreign Investment(unit)	203	1 814	4 091	4 206	3 748
#中外合资	Joint Venture	161	441	601	511	360
中外合作	Cooperative Operation	12	226	44	24	23
外商独资	Foreign Enterprise	30	1 146	3 442	3 668	3 364
外商直接投资合同金额(亿美元)	Contracted Foreign Capital of Direct Foreign Investment(USD 100 million)	3.75	63.90	138.33	148.69	171.12
#中外合资	Joint Venture	1.98	13.86	19.62	21.69	24.11
中外合作	Cooperative Operation	0.40	5.86	2.66	4.31	3.25
外商独资	Foreign Enterprise	1.36	44.14	109.47	117.84	142.89

表 18-8 主要年份口岸进出口商品总额
Total Export and Import at Port in Main Years

单位:亿美元 (USD 100 million)

指 标	Indicators	1990	2000	2005	2007	2008
口岸进出口总额	**Total Value of Import and Export**	**172.89**	**1 093.11**	**3 506.78**	**5 209.09**	**6 065.57**
出口总额	**Total Value of Export**	**86.62**	**615.72**	**2 124.30**	**3 284.80**	**3 936.50**
#一般贸易	Original Trade	51.39	341.02	1 057.68	1 659.44	2 050.49
来料加工装配贸易	Processing and Assembly Trade	3.20	64.21	195.83	228.77	240.91
进料加工贸易	Processing Trade of Imported Material	30.67	205.13	813.26	1 273.71	1 467.78
对外承包工程货物	Constracted Projects in Foreign Countries	0.41	1.25	6.37	20.55	53.92
进口总额	**Total Value of Import**	**86.27**	**477.39**	**1 382.48**	**1 924.29**	**2 129.07**
#一般贸易	Original Trade	51.79	212.65	502.49	719.30	848.23
来料加工装配贸易	Processing and Assembly Trade of Income	2.40	44.87	133.69	154.88	174.86
进料加工贸易	Processing Trade of Imported Material	19.70	125.13	409.30	528.03	525.68
租赁贸易	International Leasing		2.47	7.85	24.46	22.21
外商投资企业进口设备	Imported Equipment of Foreign Funded Enterprise	6.11	40.26	74.76	75.22	76.91

表 18-9　主要年份财政、现金收支和保险
Major Indicators of Finance, Cash Balance and Insurance in Main Years

单位:亿元　　(100 million yuan)

指　标	Indicators	1990	2000	2005	2007	2008
全市财政收入	**Financial Revenue**	**284.36**	**1 752.70**	**4 095.81**	**7 310.26**	**7 532.91**
#中央财政收入	Central Financial Revenue	114.33	1 246.47	2 661.91	5 207.63	4 400.26
地方财政收入	Local Government Revenue	170.03	497.96	1 433.90	2 102.63	2 382.34
#增值税	Value-added Tax		93.55	226.12	313.42	334.89
营业税	Sales Tax		153.81	512.93	714.60	763.38
企业所得税	Enterprise Income Tax		103.03	249.15	425.63	547.99
个人所得税	Individual Income Tax		60.24	111.92	169.44	204.89
#市级财政收入	Financial Revenue at Prefectural Level		215.81	553.33	1 083.05	1 220.57
区县级财政收入	Financial Revenue at District (Country) Level		282.15	880.57	1 019.58	1 161.77
地方财政支出	**Local Government Expenditure**	**75.56**	**622.84**	**1 660.32**	**2 201.92**	**2 617.68**
现金收入	**Cash Income**	**554.62**	**7 946.79**	**21 195.88**	**30 070.03**	**27 410.94**
#商品销售收入	Commodity Sales	267.02	1 827.34	3 152.31	3 637.62	3 162.20
服务事业收入	Service Industry	45.30	552.84	745.68	1 271.51	1 394.36
储蓄存款收入	Savings Deposit	166.78	4 042.11	14 838.14	22 071.51	19 961.38
现金支出	**Cash Expenditure**	**523.97**	**8 041.05**	**21 701.53**	**30 721.55**	**28 079.20**
#国家工资及对个人其他支出	Wages and Other Payments to Individuals	213.50	897.47	1 919.32	2 488.74	2 493.72
行政管理费支出	Government Administration	52.04	1 085.23	2 615.49	3 162.89	2 861.19
储蓄存款支出	Saving Deposit	126.17	4 738.28	14 417.49	21 724.99	19 492.31
保险费收入	**Premium Income**	**8.99**	**127.23**	**333.62**	**482.64**	**600.06**
赔款及给付	Indemnite Expenditure and Payment	2.23	36.20	87.46	139.82	184.09
赔款率(%)	Indemnity and Premium Ratio(%)	24.7	28.5	26.2	29.0	30.7

表 18-10 主要年份交通运输
Transportaion in Main Years

指 标	Indicators	1990	2000	2005	2007	2008
铁路运输	**By Railway**					
运营里程(公里)	Operations in Length(km)	259	257	269	281	307
正线延展里程(公里)	Extension of Main Tracks in Length(km)	356	397	406	415	451
旅客发送量(万人次)	Volume of Passengers Carried (10 000 person-times)	2 476	2 980	4 313	4 795	5 339
旅客周转量(亿人·公里)	Volume of Passengers Circulated (100 million persons · km)	26.85	35.40	48.86	51.34	53.18
货物运输量(万吨)	Volume of Goods Transported(10 000 tons)	1 257	1 055	1 278	1 143	985
货物周转量(亿吨·公里)	Volume of Goods Circulated (100 million tons · km)	111	122	47	35	29
公路运输	**By Road**					
通车里程(公里)	Available for Traffic in Length(km)	3 050	6 078	8 110	15 458	15 844
#高速公路	Expressway	36	98	560	635	637
货运汽车每车吨年产量(万吨·公里)	Yearly Output per Truck · Ton (10 000 tons · km)	1.72	1.50	1.64	0.79	2.24
汽油车耗油(升/百吨·公里)	Oil Consumption of Gasoline Vehicles (L/100 tons · km)	6.50	6.87	8.85	8.30	4.20
柴油车耗油(升/百吨·公里)	Oil Consumption of Diesel Vehicles (L/100 tons · km)	4.00	4.77	4.51	7.53	5.48
旅客发送量(万人次)	Volume of Passengers Carried (10 000 person-times)	605	2 482	2 468	2 872	2 934
旅客周转量(亿人·公里)	Volume of Passengers Circulated (100 million persons · km)	8.42	16.44	75.06	94.02	94.07
货物运输量(万吨)	Volume of Goods Transported(10 000 tons)	605	2 482	2 468	2 872	40 328
货物周转量(亿吨·公里)	Volume of Goods Circulated (100 million tons · km)	11	56	73	85	253
水路运输	**By Water**					
旅客周转量(亿人·公里)	Volume of Passengers Circulated (100 million persons · km)	40.84	6.77	4.52	6.10	6.73
货物运输量(万吨)	Volume of Goods Transported(10 000 tons)	12 864	18 442	34 557	41 041	42 729
#远洋运输	Ocean Transportation	2 246	7 022	10 091	12 575	12 197
货物周转量(亿吨·公里)	Volume of Goods Circulated (100 million tons · km)	3 236	6 430	11 986	15 789	15 712
#远洋运输	Ocean Transportation	1 957	5 285	9 285	12 039	11 529
港 口	**Ports**					
港口旅客发送量(万人次)	Volume of Passengers Carried at Ports (10 000 person-times)	555	539	626	95	89
民用航空	**Civil Aviation**					
旅客发送量(万人次)	Volume of Passengers Carried (10 000 person-times)	199	892	2 080	2 609	2 565
旅客周转量(亿人·公里)	Volume of Passengers Circulated (100 million persons · km)	37.84	176.11	535.48	731.79	715.09
货物运输量(万吨)	Volume of Goods Transported(10 000 tons)	13	88	222	290	305
货物周转量(亿吨·公里)	Volume of Goods Circulated (100 million tons · km)	1	12	27	40	37

注：港口旅客发送量从 2006 年起不包含海港到内河部分。
Note: The volume of Passenger Departures excludes those from seaports to freshwater since 2006.

表 18-11 主要年份教育、卫生事业情况
Statistics of Education and Healthcare in Main Years

指标	Indicators	1990	2000	2005	2007	2008
学校(所)	**School(unit)**					
高等学校	Institutions of Higher Education	50	37	60	60	61
中等专业学校	Special Secondary Schools	110	84	81	76	73
职业中学	Vocational Middle Schools	80	60	37	32	28
普通中学	Regular Secondary Schools	712	861	807	786	774
小 学	Primary Schools	2 630	1 021	640	615	672
特殊教育学校	Special Schools	29	34	28	28	29
在校学生数(万人)	**Student Enrollment(10 000 persons)**					
高等学校	Institutions of Higher Education	12.13	22.68	44.26	48.49	50.29
中等专业学校	Special Secondary Schools	6.17	11.89	13.67	12.81	12.08
职业中学	Vocational Middle Schools	3.66	8.48	5.76	5.20	4.80
普通中学	Regular Secondary Schools	48.31	79.54	77.02	65.60	61.77
小 学	Primary Schools	110.19	78.86	53.50	53.33	59.06
特殊教育学校	Special Schools	0.33	0.54	0.52	0.50	0.51
教职员工(万人)	**Staff and Workers(10 000 persons)**					
高等学校	Institutions of Higher Education	7.06	6.08	7.09	7.18	7.31
中等专业学校	Special Secondary Schools	1.49	1.27	1.09	1.00	0.97
职业中学	Vocational Middle Schools	0.53	0.66	0.51	0.48	0.45
普通中学	Regular Secondary Schools	6.62	7.66	7.46	7.11	6.89
小 学	Primary Schools	7.48	6.13	4.94	4.84	5.10
特殊教育学校	Special Schools	0.11	0.16	0.16	0.16	0.16
卫生机构数(个)	**Health Care Institutions(unit)**	**7 690**	**4 400**	**2 527**	**2 646**	**2 809**
#医 院	Hospital	462	459	487	288	301
医院床位数(张)	**Hospital Beds(bed)**	**69 636**	**75 334**	**90 800**	**95 900**	**97 780**
卫生技术人员(万人)	**Medical Technical Personnel(10 000 persons)**	**15.85**	**10.71**	**10.35**	**12.24**	**12.77**
#医 生	Doctors	5.82	4.99	4.40	4.88	5.12
护师、护士	Senior and Junior Nurses	3.27	3.68	3.94	4.67	4.88
医院治疗人次(万人次)	**Total Patients Treated(10 000 person-times)**	**8 395.00**	**8 631.67**	**9 455.71**	**13 217.93**	**15 238.39**
#门、急诊	Out-patients and Emergency Patients		8 432.29	9 277.79	13 026.38	15 035.14
医院入院人数(万人次)	**In Patients(10 000 person-times)**	**95.28**	**122.79**	**147.91**	**194.81**	**209.71**
医院每百诊次的入院人数(人)	**In Patients Per 100 Patient-times (person)**	**1.10**	**1.40**	**1.56**	**1.50**	**1.40**

表 18－12 居民消费价格指数(2008 年,以上年价格为 100)
Classified Residents Consumer Price Indices(Preceding Year＝100)

指 标	Indicators	2008
居民消费价格指数	**Overall Residents Consumer Price Index**	**105.8**
食 品	**Food**	**115.3**
粮 食	Grain	107.3
淀粉及薯类	Starch and Ptatoes	107.9
干豆类及豆制品	Dry Beans and Bean Products	132.5
油 脂	Oil and Fat	124.7
肉禽及其制品	Meat Poultry and Their Products	122.9
蛋	Eggs	106.4
水产品	Aquatic Products	111.2
菜	Vegetables	120.6
#鲜 菜	Fresh Vegetables	121.3
调味品	Flavoring	109.5
糖	Sugar	107.4
茶及饮料	Tea and Beverages	106.9
干鲜瓜果	Dried and Fresh Fruits	112.3
#鲜 果	Fresh Fruits	113.0
糕点饼干面包	Cakes,Biscuits and Bread	112.5
奶及奶制品	Milk and Its Products	119.4
在外用膳食品	Out-of-home food	114.3
其他食品及食品加工服务	Other Food and Food Processing Service	104.3
烟酒及用品	**Tobacco, Alcohol and Related Products**	**101.7**
烟 草	Tobacco	100.1
酒	Liquor	103.4
吸烟饮酒用品	Related Products for Smoking and Driking	110.1
衣 着	**Clothing**	**101.6**
服 装	Garments	101.7
男式服装	Men's Wear	101.2
女式服装	Women's Wear	102.2
儿童服装	Children's Wear	99.7
衣着材料	Clothing Materials	103.8
鞋袜帽	Shoes,Socks and Hats	100.6
#鞋	Shoes	101.0
衣着加工服务	Garment Processing Service	106.6

指 标	Indicators	2008
家庭设备用品及维修服务	**Home Appliances and Required Service**	**108.3**
耐用消费品	Durable Consumer Goods	107.2
室内装饰品	Interior Decorations	100.9
床上用品	Bed Articles	101.7
家庭日用杂志	Daily Use Household Articles	110.4
家庭服务及加工维修服务	Other Daily Use Articles	116.5
医疗保健和个人用品	**Medicine,Medical Services and Personal Articles**	**103.1**
医疗保健	Medicine and Medical Services	100.5
#中药材及中成药	Chinese Medicinal Crop And Patent Medicine	102.9
西 药	Western Medicine	100.2
保健器具及用品	Healthcare and Equipment	100.5
医疗保健服务	Medical and Healthcare Service	100.0
个人用品及服务	Personal Articles and Service	106.2
交通和通信	**Means of Transportation and Communication**	**97.5**
交 通	Transport	99.2
#交通工具	Transport Tools	96.7
通 信	Communications	95.1
通信工具	Communications tools	67.9
通信服务	Communications Service	101.3
娱乐教育文化用品及服务	**Recreation,Education and Culture Articles**	**98.2**
文娱用耐用消费品及服务	Durable Consumer Goods for Recreational Use	85.0
教 育	Education	101.2
文化娱乐用品	Recreation and Culture Articles	100.7
旅游及外出	Tourism	101.7
居 住	**Residence**	**102.5**
建房及装修材料	Housing Construction And Finishing Materials	104.5
租 房	House Leasing	110.8
自有住房	Self-owned House	101.3
水电燃料	Water,Electricity and Fuels	100.5
#水	Water	100.0
电	Electricity	100.0
液化石油气	LPG	109.5
管道燃气	Gas	101.6

表 18-13 主要年份商品零售价格指数(以上年价格为 100)
Classified Retail Price Index in Main Years(Preceding Year = 100)

指标	Indicators	2001	2003	2004	2005	2007	2008
商品零售价格指数	**Overall Retail Price Index**	**98.6**	**99.0**	**100.9**	**99.4**	**102.4**	**105.3**
食品类	Food	98.4	101.5	108.6	104.7	109.6	115.3
粮　食	Grain	100.1	100.5	128.8	102.1	101.4	107.3
淀粉及薯类	Starch and Potatoes	100.4	109.2	107.2	105.2	101.8	107.9
干豆类及豆制品	Dry Beans and Bean Products	111.3	102.7	124.8	103.6	108.6	132.5
油　脂	Oil or Fat	81.4	106.8	114.4	91.2	129.8	124.7
肉禽及其制品	Meat Poultry and Their Products	100.4	101.7	117.6	105.5	123.0	122.9
蛋	Eggs	110.7	101.0	118.6	105.8	121.8	106.4
水产品	Aquatic Products	90.1	103.9	107.7	114.4	101.4	110.8
菜	Vegetables	107.1	101.5	95.5	103.4	113.5	120.6
调味品	Flavoring	99.5	98.4	103.0	102.1	104.6	109.5
糖	Sugar	104.4	98.9	103.1	103.8	99.1	107.4
干鲜瓜果	Dried and Fresh Fruits	107.3	97.6	118.3	99.4	111.8	112.3
糕点饼干面包	Cakes,Biscuits and Bread	99.8	101.4	100.9	98.4	101.5	112.5
奶及奶制品	Milk and Its Products	99.8	101.4	99.6	100.8	106.2	119.4
在外用膳食品	Out-of-home Food	100.7	100.7	103.1	104.4	107.6	114.3
其它食品	Other Food	99.5	101.5	96.9	101.1	100.9	104.3
饮料、烟酒	Beverages, Tobacco and Liquor	98.4	99.5	98.8	99.6	100.9	102.7
服装、鞋帽类	Garments, Shoes and Hats	107.7	96.7	93.9	92.6	101.2	101.5
纺织品类	Textiles	98.8	99.8	102.2	99.4	102.6	102.1
家用电器及音像器材	Household Appliances and Audio-video Appliances	95.0	95.8	93.4	93.1	92.2	94.7
文化办公用品	Cultural Office Articies	98.7	93.7	91.9	91.6	93.9	94.9
日用品	Daily Use Articles	99.0	99.1	98.4	100.5	101.8	105.8
体育娱乐用品	Sports and Recreation Goods	99.1	97.4	96.8	94.7	92.9	92.2
交通、通信用品	Transportation and Communication Goods	97.4	91.2	90.2	88.5	90.8	89.5
家　具	Furniture	90.4	99.5	98.2	100.1	101.8	108.2
化妆品类	Cosmetics	100.7	100.4	99.0	96.1	101.2	101.8
金银珠宝类	Jewelry	87.2	106.5	107.9	107.3	106.2	110.3
中西药品及医疗保健用品类	Traditional Chinese and Western Medicines	98.7	98.3	95.6	97.7	98.0	100.7
书报杂志及电子出版物类	Newspapers and Magazines and Electronic Publications	99.5	98.3	99.6	98.0	103.6	101.8
燃料类	Fuels	111.4	108.6	107.0	109.1	103.0	112.0
建筑材料及五金电料类	Building Materials and Hardwares	101.8	100.8	104.7	104.0	107.6	106.6

主要统计指标解释

居民消费价格指数

居民消费价格指数是度量一组代表性消费商品及服务项目价格水平随着时间而变动的相对数,反映居民家庭购买的消费品及服务价格水平的变动情况。它是宏观经济分析和决策、价格总水平监测和调控以及国民经济核算的重要指标。其按年度计算的变动率通常被用来作为反映通货膨胀或紧缩程度的指标。

现行的居民消费价格指数按用途分为八个大类,包括食品、烟酒及用品、衣着、家庭设备用品及维修服务、医疗保健和个人用品、交通和通信、娱乐教育文化用品及服务、居住。

商品零售价格指数

商品零售价格指数是反映一定时期内城乡商品零售价格变动趋势和程度的相对数。商品零售价格的变动直接影响城乡居民的生活支出和国家的财政收入,影响居民购买力和市场供需的平衡,影响消费与积累的比例关系。因此,该指数可以从一个侧面对上述经济活动进行观察和分析。

EXPLANATORY NOTES ON MAJOR STATISTICAL INDICATORS

Consumer Price Index

The Consumer Price Index is an index that reflects the time-based change of prices of a group of representative consumption commodities and services. It is an important reference factor for macro-economic analysis and strategy, monitoring and adjustment of overall price level and the national economic budgeting. The year-on-year change of the index is often a norm reflecting the inflation or deflation.

The current CPI covers eight categories of goods and services: food; tobacco, liquor and related articles; garments; household facilities, articles and repair services; medical and health care and personal items; traffic and telecommunications; education, culture and recreation articles and services and residence.

Retail Price Indices

Retail Price Indices reflect the trend and degree of change in retail prices of commodities during a given period. The change in retail prices of commodities directly affect the living expenditure of urban and rural residents, government revenue, purchasing power of residents and the equilibrium of market supply and demand, and the ratio of consumption to accumulation. Therefore, the retail price indices are useful to analyze the changes of the above economic activities.

中国统计出版社最新资料书简目

（仅供参考，以最后出书为准）

统计资料

中国统计年鉴－2009　中国统计摘要－2009　国际统计年鉴－2009

2009中国发展报告　中国第三产业统计年鉴－2009　中国区域经济统计年鉴－2009

长江和珠江三角洲及港澳特别行政区统计年鉴－2009　中国社会统计年鉴－2009　中国城市统计年鉴－2008

中国劳动统计年鉴－2009　中国人口和就业统计年鉴－2009　中国工业经济统计年鉴－2009

中国建筑业统计年鉴－2009　中国房地产统计年鉴－2009　中国能源统计年鉴－2009

中国商品交易市场统计年鉴－2009　中国贸易外经统计年鉴－2009　中国基本单位统计年鉴－2009

中国民政统计年鉴－2009　中国农村统计年鉴－2009　中国农产品价格调查年鉴－2009

中国建制镇统计资料－2009　中国教育经费统计年鉴－2008　中国农村贫困监测报告－2009

中国高技术产业统计年鉴－2009　中国科学技术协会统计年鉴－2009　工业企业科技活动资料－2009

全国农产品成本收益资料汇编－2009　中国棉花年鉴－2007/2008　中国城市(镇)生活与价格年鉴－2009

中国县（市）社会经济调查年鉴－2009　中国农村住户调查年鉴－2009（中、英文）　中国农村全面建设小康监测报告－2009

中国国内生产总值核算历史资料(1952－2004)　中国季度国内生产总值核算历史资料(1992－2005)　中国零售和餐饮业连锁企业统计年鉴－2009

大中型批发零售和住宿餐饮企业统计年鉴－2009　2005年中国1%人口抽样调查系列资料　第二次全国残疾人抽样调查资料系列

2009年省级综合统计年鉴系列

北京　天津　河北　山西　内蒙古　辽宁　吉林　黑龙江　上海　江苏　浙江　安徽　福建　江西　山东

河南　湖北　湖南　广东　广西　海南　重庆　四川　贵州　云南　西藏　陕西　甘肃　青海　宁夏

新疆　新疆生产建设兵团

2009年市(县)级综合统计年鉴系列

石家庄　唐山　邯郸　太原　大同　长治　阳泉　晋城　朔州　晋中　运城　忻州　临汾　呼和浩特

包头　沈阳　大连　长春　吉林市　四平　延吉　哈尔滨　齐齐哈尔　黑龙江垦区　上海浦东新区

苏州　无锡　常州　徐州　南通　盐城　镇江　江阴　丹阳　杭州　宁波　绍兴　台州　舟山　温州

金华　嘉兴　衢州　安庆　福州　福州经济技术开发区　厦门经济特区　南昌　上饶

济南　青岛　潍坊　东营　郑州　洛阳　三门峡　南阳　武汉　宜昌　十堰　荆州　黄冈　长沙　广州

东莞　惠州　深圳　桂林　南宁　柳州　来宾　河池　海口　成都　贵阳　昆明　西安　庆阳　银川

乌鲁木齐　吐鲁番

“十一五”规划教材

非参数统计　医学统计学　概率论与数理统计　统计学　现代金融投资统计分析

多元统计分析　经济计量学教程　应用时间序列分析　统计指数理论及应用

统计数据处理概论　质量管理统计方法　社会统计学　多元统计分析实验

企业经营管理统计　市场调查与预测　统计学原理（非统计专业使用）

统计学：从数据到结论　国民经济核算教程(国民经济统计学)　概率论与数理统计(经济、管理类专业使用)

重点图书

新中国六十年　挑大学选专业2010—高考志愿填报指南　挑大学选专业2010—考研择校指南

欲购以上图书请与中国统计出版社发行部联系

电话：（010）63376907,63376908　同椈行书店电话：68783171,68783172

通讯地址：北京市西城区三里河月坛南街57号　邮政编码：100826

(京)新登字041号

图书在版编目(CIP)数据

上海浦东新区统计年鉴.2009/上海市浦东新区统计局编.
——北京：中国统计出版社，2009.8
ISBN 978-7-5037-5732-7

Ⅰ.上…
Ⅱ.上…
Ⅲ.统计资料-浦东新区-2009-年鉴
Ⅳ.C832.513-54

中国版本图书馆CIP数据核字(2009)第127788号

上海浦东新区统计年鉴—2009

作　　者/上海市浦东新区统计局
责任编辑/郑淼淼　张　洁
E-mail/yearbook@stats.gov.cn
执行编辑/张瑾华　张德华
封面设计/蔡旭洲
出版发行/中国统计出版社
通信地址/北京市西城区三里河月坛南街75号　中国统计出版社
邮　　编/100826
电　　话/(010) 63376907
印　　刷/上海万卷印刷有限公司
经　　销/新华书店
开　　本/889×1240毫米1/16
字　　数/92万字
印　　张/22
印　　数/1～1300册
版　　别/2009年8月第1版
版　　次/2009年8月第1次印刷
书　　号/ISBN 978-7-5037-5732-7/C·2236
定　　价/320.00元